❧ Anne Bradstreet ❦

Frontispiece: Anne Bradstreet. Detail from a window
in St. Botolph's Church, Boston, Lincolnshire.

❧ *Anne Bradstreet* ❧
"THE TENTH MUSE"

by
ELIZABETH WADE WHITE

"Primus ego in patriam mecum
. . . deducam Musas."
(Virgil, *Georgics*, BOOK III)

New York
OXFORD UNIVERSITY PRESS
1971

For
Evelyn Virginia Holahan

❧ Preface and Acknowledgments ❧

Anne Bradstreet was the first resident poet of English-speaking North America, and also the first significant woman poet of England. Her writing has been the object of increasing interest during this century, but her life and background have been dealt with only in two unpretentious and now hardly obtainable studies, Helen Campbell's semi-fictional *Anne Bradstreet and Her Time* (Boston, 1891) and Luther Caldwell's *An Account of Anne Bradstreet the Puritan Poetess* (Boston, 1898), in the introduction to John Harvard Ellis's 1867 edition of her complete works, and in two sympathetic essays: Chapter XI of Samuel Eliot Morison's *Builders of the Bay Colony* (Boston, 1930) and George Frisbie Whicher's *Alas, All's Vanity, or a Leaf from . . . Several Poems by Anne Bradstreet* (New York, 1942). For a number of years I have been engaged in assembling the material, some of it tantalizingly elusive, for a full-length biography of this remarkable woman. The known facts of Anne Bradstreet's life are adequate but spare; there are gaps that I have not been able to fill, such as the actual

dates and places of her birth and her marriage, and I have not
been lucky enough to locate more than a few small pieces of new
evidence to add to the general picture. In her writings themselves,
however, a careful observer may find the key to an understanding
of her complex personality. Both her poetry and her prose tell us
a great deal about herself, within the boundaries of the literary
proprieties of her time, and she is occasionally more self-revealing
than she can have intended to be.

Along with this direct analysis I have felt that it was necessary,
in order to see Anne Bradstreet as a person and a writer of her
time, to examine in some detail the historic and human events
that contributed to the various episodes of her eventful life.
Many excellent books have been written about the experience of
the English Puritan colonists in creating, as they intended, a new
Jerusalem in the wilderness of North America. But only a few
serious works, such as Professor Wallace Notestein's *The English
People on the Eve of Colonization, 1603–1630* (New York, 1954),
have dealt with the conditions in the mother country that led to
the mass exodus of courageous men and women determined to
free themselves, at whatever risk and cost, from what they felt
were intolerable religious and economic pressures at home. Consequently I have given, in the earlier chapters of this book, as
complete an account as space would allow of how things stood for
a Puritan family in the England of Anne Bradstreet's childhood
and adolescence.

I have also discussed at considerable length, more than is usual
in an individual biography, the controversial question of ancestry:
that on the paternal side of Anne Bradstreet and her father
Thomas Dudley. Many genealogists and historians have en-
deavored to clarify this obscure matter, but none has succeeded
in doing so. My own contribution to the debate, in Chapter I, is
conjectural, yet I believe that the suggestion there offered is of

some value in the light that it may shed on the psychological attitudes of a founder and governor of the Massachusetts Bay colony and of his daughter who was the founder of American literature.

The first acknowledgment that I owe goes back a great many years to my grandmother, Martha Chase Starkweather Wade, a keen student of New England history, who first aroused my admiration for the colonizers of Massachusetts in general, and for Anne Bradstreet in particular. When I decided to undertake the writing of this study, I received valuable advice on how to proceed from Professors Charles M. Andrews and Alexander M. Witherspoon of Yale University, the eminent bibliographer Henrietta C. Bartlett, and the Massachusetts antiquarian Amos E. Jewett.

I am greatly indebted to the following libraries and institutions, and to their staff-members from whom I invariably have had generous help: the Sterling Memorial and Beinecke Libraries at Yale and Miss Majorie Wynne of the latter, the New York Public Library, Harvard's Widener and Houghton Libraries, the Boston Public Library and its Curator of Rare Books John Eliot Alden, the Massachusetts Historical Society, the New England Historic Genealogical Society, the Society for the Preservation of New England Antiquities and its Director Abbott Lowell Cummings, the Suffolk County Probate Court, and in other parts of Massachusetts the Ipswich Historical Society, the Essex Institute in Salem, the Andover Town Hall, and in North Andover the Stevens Memorial Library and the Historical Society. In England and elsewhere the same courteous assistance was always forthcoming, from the British Museum and its then Director Sir Frank Francis, the Public Record Office and, in its National Archives section, Miss Winifred Doris Coates and Stephen Freer, the Guildhall Library, Somerset House, Drapers' Hall, St. John's Gate, headquarters of the Knights of St. John in the British Realm, the

College of Arms and Rouge Dragon Pursuivant, Captain de La Lanne-Mirrlees, the Lincolnshire Archives Committee and Mrs. Joan Varley, and in the same county the Lincoln Borough Library, St. Botolph's Church, where Canon A. M. Cook, the vicar, was particularly helpful, and the Town Hall in Boston, the Northamptonshire Record Society and Miss Joan Wake, C.B.E., and her colleague P. I. King, the Northampton City Library and its Librarian Reginald Brown, and, on the island of Malta, the Royal Malta Library in Valletta and the Keeper of the Archives of the Order of St. John, Professor Joseph Galea.

My gratitude is unlimited for the help and encouragement that came to me, while I was preparing at Oxford University the B. Litt. thesis on which this book is founded, from Professors F. P. Wilson and Herbert J. Davis and from Hugh Macdonald, and I owe a special debt of thanks, for continuing guidance and advice, to Professor Dame Helen Gardner. I wish to express my appreciation for permission to examine family papers or other manuscripts, and privately printed material, kindly granted by the Most Hon. the Marquess of Bath, the Most Hon. the Marquess of Northampton, the Right Hon. Lord Saye and Sele, and Hugh Dudley Waddell Dudley, Esquire. Valuable information of various kinds, for which I am most grateful, has been supplied to me by Professor Lionel Butler, Buchanan Charles and Forbes Rockwell of North Andover, Massachusetts, Mrs. Hugh Bullock of New York, and my brother Henry Wade White, then Archivist of the Fogg Art Museum in Cambridge, Massachusetts. Professor Jeannine Hensley, while she was engaged in preparing her recent edition of *The Works of Anne Bradstreet*, sent me some important bibliographical data and gave me the pleasure and benefit of many stimulating conversations.

Finally I must thank those friends and encouragers, most particularly among them Professor Norman Holmes Pearson of Yale, who have read all or parts of the typescript of this book, and whose knowledgeable criticisms and wise suggestions have brought about many improvements. To them, to all the others whose interest and faith helped me to pursue my project, and to the readers of the book, I confess with humility that any errors, inconsistencies or obscurities that "here be found" are entirely my own.

The dedication bespeaks the debt of gratitude that I owe, for long-suffering patience, moral support, and shared endeavor, to my friend and companion of many years.

E. W. W.

Middlebury, Connecticut,
   1970.

≫ *A Note on the Texts Used* ≪

The Tenth Muse, the first edition of Anne Bradstreet's poems, was printed without the author's knowledge, from manuscript copies taken to England by her brother-in-law the Reverend John Woodbridge, and published in London in 1650. Anne Bradstreet therefore made many corrections, deletions, and additions in preparing the texts of these poems for their second printing, which occurred six years after her death, in *Several Poems* (Boston, 1678); this edition also contained important material that had not been printed before. Consequently, in quoting excerpts from Anne Bradstreet's verse I have generally used the second edition, which has been accepted as presenting her poems more nearly as she wished them to appear. There are occasions, however, when for historical or other reasons I have quoted passages from *The Tenth Muse*, (using the photo-reproduction, published by the Scholars' Facsimiles & Reprints, of the Indiana University Library's copy); in these instances I have indicated the differences between the first and second printings of the poem under discussion. As copy-text for *Several Poems* I have used my own fragmentary example, which lacks about one-third of its contents, supplemented by photostats of the missing pages taken from the British Museum's copy (C.39 b.48).

Excerpts from Anne Bradstreet's prose "Meditations Divine and morall," and her autobiographical legacy to her children that is in both prose and verse, come from the little manuscript book, partly in her own hand and partly in that of her son Simon, that is now in the Bradstreet collection of the Stevens Memorial Library in North Andover, Massachusetts. My friend Buchanan Charles, a trustee of the library and the prime mover in securing the manuscript for the community where Anne Bradstreet spent the later years of her life, kindly presented me with a photostatic reproduction from which the excerpts I have used are taken.[1]

In quoting from the printed texts I have corrected a few obvious typographical errors and, in the manuscript material, expanded some abbreviations and made slight changes in punctuation when it seemed proper to do so to clarify the sense of a passage. One or two textual alterations will be found that, in my opinion, restore the reading originally intended by the author; these are identified and explained in footnotes. I have also incorporated in the text of my quotations, and have so indicated, the corrected readings shown on the unique surviving *errata* leaf in the "Prince" copy, at the Boston Public Library, of *Several Poems*. Illustrative passages taken from early sources, other than the works of Anne Bradstreet, are reproduced so far as possible from the manuscript or printed documents in which they first appeared, or from later transcripts or editions in which the original spelling, punctuation, and typography are preserved. When the place of publication of any book referred to in this study is not indicated, it is to be understood that it was published in London.

1. The contents of this MS. book were first printed entirely in J.H. Ellis's edtion of *The Works of Anne Bradstreet, Charlestown* (Mass.), 1867.

❧ Contents ❧

❧ List of Illustrations ❧

Frontispiece: Anne Bradstreet. Detail from a window
in St. Botolph's Church, Boston, Lincolnshire.
Reproduced by permission of the Vicar and Churchwardens.

Tattershall Castle, Tattershall, Lincolnshire.

St. Andrew's Church, Sempringham, Lincolnshire.

John Winthrop. Reproduced by permission of the
American Antiquarian Society, Worcester, Massachusetts.

Title-page of *The Tenth Muse*, 1650.

Title-page of *Several Poems*, 1678. Both reproduced by
permission from the collection of American Literature
in the Beinecke Library of Yale University.

Simon Bradstreet in old age. Nineteenth-century copy,
by Hannah Crowninshield, of an earlier, probably lost,
portrait. Reproduced by permission of the Society
for the Preservation of New England Antiquities, Boston.

Pages 30 and 31 of Anne Bradstreet's autograph manuscript
of "Meditations Divine and morall." Reproduced by permission of the Trustees of the Stevens Memorial Library,
North Andover, Massachusetts.

The first burial-ground in old Andover, now North Andover,
Massachusetts.

❧ Anne Bradstreet ❧

CHAPTER ONE

Ancestry, Parentage, and Birth

"Which have the self-same blood yet in my veines."
(ANNE BRADSTREET—*Elegy upon Sir Philip Sidney*)

In the church of St. Botolph, in Boston, Lincolnshire, there is a large stained-glass window, completed soon after the Second World War as one of a series illustrating the continuity of the Church of Christ in that community. The central section of this window displays four stately female figures, those of the most memorable women associated with Boston's history. They are: Anne of Bohemia, the wife of King Richard II; Lady Margaret Beaufort, the mother of King Henry VII; Anne Bradstreet, the seventeenth-century poet, and Jean Ingelow, the Victorian poet.

Anne Bradstreet is shown as a young matron in the Puritan dress of her time: turned-back white cap, full skirt of purple wool and long cloak of the same material, black velvet bodice with deep collar and cuffs of white linen, and sturdy shoes with square silver buckles. Her imagined face, of which no contemporary like-ness has survived, is grave and gentle, and she holds in her hands neither a book, nor its antithesis a needle, but a green basket-like nest containing eight yellow fledgling birds. This pleasant if somewhat sentimental emblem may be taken to represent both her literary and her domestic accomplishments, for in New England, to which she emigrated from Lincolnshire in 1630, with her parents and her husband, she became a writer of verse and prose, and bore and reared eight children.

The designer of the window in St. Botolph's, Harry Grylls, was apparently familiar with Anne Bradstreet's lines to her four sons and four daughters, written about 1658 when most of them had grown beyond childhood, and beginning:

> I had eight birds hatcht in one nest,
> Four Cocks there were, and Hens the rest,
> I nurst them up with pain and care,
> Nor cost, nor labour did I spare,
> Till at the last they felt their wing,
> Mounted the Trees, and learn'd to sing.

The poems that Anne Bradstreet wrote during the first twenty years of her life in New England were published in London in 1650, as *The Tenth Muse Lately sprung up in America, or Severall Poems, compiled with great variety of Wit and Learning, full of delight . . . By a Gentlewoman in those parts.* A second edition of this collection, to which Anne's later poems were added, appeared in Boston in the Massachusetts Bay Colony, in 1678, six years after their author's death. These two small but substantial volumes are not only the fruit of an adult lifetime of continued study and of devotion to the craft of letters, but there is every indication that they were based on the excellent education, an unusually generous one for a middle-class girl of her time, that Anne Bradstreet received in her native country.

The strongest influence in her life was the man who watched over her upbringing and education, provided her with an admirable husband, and encouraged her to develop her literary inclinations into a serious vocation. This was her father, Thomas Dudley, who is known to have been a verse-writer himself although only one short metrical piece by him has survived, and to whom his daughter indicated, in several dedicatory poems and an elegy, how important his sympathetic interest was to her. During his long life Dudley was in succession a courtier's page, an Elizabethan soldier and citizen, a Puritan partisan, and finally a governor of the colony that he helped to establish in New England. He was predominantly a man of action, with a capable and courageous, if somewhat inflexible, mind, and his stern adherence to principle made him a pillar of strength to the young colony, as well as a symbol of bigoted intolerance to those who disagreed with him. To his daughter Anne he was always "Most truly honoured, and as truly dear," and she repeatedly expressed her indebtedness to him, as in these lines from the elegiac tribute she wrote in 1653:

> My mournful mind, sore prest, in trembling verse
> Presents my Lamentations at his Herse,
> Who was my Father, Guide, Instructer too,
> To whom I ought whatever I could doe.

We have an almost contemporary account of Thomas Dudley's life in *Magnalia Christi Americana*, the compendious civil and religious history of New England from 1620 to 1697, by the Reverend Cotton Mather, which is a fascinating, though not always accurate, source-book for the lives of the colonial leaders. Mather was born in 1663, only ten years after Dudley's death, so he was able as a young man to learn much about the old governor from some of those who had been closely associated with him. But he apparently also learned that the Dudleys were a proud and reticent family, unwilling to have any detailed biographical material appear in print without their prior approval. Mather was not on friendly terms with the then head of the family, the ambitious politician Joseph Dudley, Thomas's eldest son by his second marriage, so he made this apology for the brevity of the sketch of Thomas Dudley's life in the *Magnalia:*

> I had prepared and intended a more *particular Account* of this Gentleman; but not having any opportunity to commit it unto the *Perusal* of any Descended from him, (unto whom I am told it will be unacceptable for me to Publish any thing of this kind, by *them* not *Perused*) I have laid it aside, and summed all up in this more *General Account*.[1]

The fate of Mather's "more particular Account" was unknown until 1858, when the American genealogist George Adlard came upon a late seventeenth-century manuscript, entitled "The Life of Mr. Thomas Dudley," among the papers of Mr. H. A. S. D. Dudley of Roxbury, Massachusetts. There appeared to be so much similarity between this and the shorter *Magnalia* biography, in style, presentation of facts, and numerous identical passages, that Adlard concluded that it must be the longer one originally prepared by Cotton Mather, even though the document was not in Mather's own hand. He therefore published his transcription of it as a part of his genealogical study, *The Sutton-Dudleys of England and the Dudleys of Massachusetts in New England*. This account of Thomas Dudley, which I shall refer to as the *MS. Life* to distinguish it from the one included in the *Magnalia*, begins:

> Mr. Dudley was born in the town of Northampton, in the year 1574. His father was Capt. Roger Dudley, who was slain in the wars, when this, his son, and one only daughter were very young, but he might say in his experience that when he was

1. *Magnalia*, 1702, Book II, p. 16. All quotations are from this edition, the first printing of the *Magnalia*. The second (and first American) edition appeared in Hartford (Conn.) in 1820.

forsaken of father and mother, then God took him up and stirred up some friends that took special charge of him even in his childhood. 'Twas said that there was five hundred pounds left for him in an unknown hand, which was not so long concealed but that it . . . was seasonably delivered into his own hands after he came to man's estate. . . .

In his minority and childhood it pleased God to move the heart of one Mrs. *Puefroy*, a gentlewoman famed in the parts about Northampton for wisdom, piety and works of charity; by her care he was trained up in some Latin school, wherein he learned the rudiments of his grammar, which he improved afterwards by his own industry to considerable advantage.[2]

There is a mystery about the identity of "Capt. Roger Dudley," his parentage, and his ancestry, that has puzzled genealogists in both England and America for more than a century, and that has not yet been solved and perhaps never will be. But before going further into this matter, we can look at the known facts about Thomas Dudley's birth and early childhood.

He was born in the village of Yardley Hastings, eight miles from Northampton on the edge of the ancient forest of Yardley Chase, where St. Andrew's Church has the entry in its parish register: "1576—Thomas Dudley *bapt 12° Octobris.*" Four years later the same register records the baptism of "Mary Dudley daughter of Mr. Dudley" on the 16th October, 1580. The mother of these children was Susanna, daughter of Thomas Dorne (or Thorne), called "Gent." in his will, who was a landowner in Yardley Hastings and elsewhere. His wife, Susanna's mother, was Mary, daughter of Edward Purefoy, Lord of the manor of Shalston in Buckinghamshire, and through her mother a descendant of the

2. *Sutton-Dudleys of England and Dudleys of Massachusetts*, New York, 1862, pp. 24–25. All quotations that follow are taken from Adlard's transcript, pp. 24–38 of *Sutton-Dudleys and Dudleys*; the MS. *Life* was also printed in the *Proceedings of the Massachusetts Historical Society*, Vol. XI, Boston, 1869–70, pp. 207–22.

eminent families of Fettiplace, Harcourt, and de la Zouche, whose lineage has been traced from such historic figures as Charlemagne, Alfred the Great, and William the Conqueror.[3]

Susanna Dorne was baptized in St. Andrew's Church on the 5th March, 1559/60, but there is no entry in the register for her marriage. It must have taken place, however, when she was very young, as her son was born seven months after her sixteenth birthday (assuming, that is, that as was customary only a few days elapsed between her birth and her baptism). When her father made his will, on the 28th October, 1588, he bequeathed: "To the children of Susan Dudley my daughter widow x^1 [£10] to be equally devided." [4] So sometime between 1580, when Mary Dudley was born, and the autumn of 1588, the sparsely documented life of Thomas Dudley's father came to its end.

His Christian name is recorded in the pedigree of Purefoy that appears in the *Herald's Visitation* of the county of Leicester, made in 1619 by William Camden, Clarencieux King of Arms. The original manuscript of this visitation, one of the long series that periodically registered the families throughout the country that were entitled to bear arms, is in the British Museum.[5] It was apparently written hurriedly and gives no dates, but it notes, of the children of Mary Purefoy and Thomas Thorne of Yardley Hastings in Northamptonshire, that "Susanna md Roger," with the husband's surname, curiously enough, omitted.

3. Pedigree prepared for the Governor Thomas Dudley Family Association; examined and found correct at the College of Arms by Windsor Herald, 28th January, 1937; re-examined and attested by Rouge Dragon Pursuivant, October 1954.

4. *Calendar of Northampton and Rutland Wills, 1510–1652*, ed. W. P. W. Phillimore (Index Library), 1888; *Northampton Registry of Wills*, Series I, Book V, p. 328.

5. B. M.: Harleian MS. 1189, folios 18^v and 32. See also M. K. Talcott, "The Maternal Ancestry of Gov. Thomas Dudley," *New England Historical and Genealogical Register*, Vol. 60, Boston, 1912, p. 340.

Roger clearly had the status of a gentleman, as he was called "Mr. Dudley" in the baptismal record of his daughter Mary. No evidence has been found to support Mather's statement that he held the rank of Captain and was "slain in the wars," but it is not unlikely that he became bored with village life and joined one of the many musters to provide troops for the increasing hostilities between England and Spain. Young men of position were needed to officer the ragged ranks that Queen Elizabeth's parsimony kept ill-fed, ill-equipped, and underpaid, the counterparts of the "pitiful rascals" of *Henry IV, Part I* that Falstaff, with the brutal cynicism of all war-makers, pronounced "good enough to toss; food for powder, food for powder; . . . mortal men."

In May of 1579 John Purefoy, Esquire, of Shalston, Buckinghamshire, left "tenne sheepe" to his great-nephew Thomas Dudley, who was then less than three years old.[6] When Thomas Dorne made his bequest of £10 "to the children of Susan Dudley my daughter widow," in October 1588, his grandson Thomas had just passed his twelfth birthday. It may be concluded, since no further contemporary mention has been found of Susanna or her daughter Mary, that neither of them long survived Roger Dudley and that young Thomas was, as Mather wrote, "foresaken of father and mother," and of sister too, and left dependent on the kindness and generosity of his maternal relatives.

The "Mrs. Puefroy" by whom he was fortunate enough to be taken up, and apparently adopted, was his great-aunt by marriage and a woman of strong and admirable character. She was born Anne Pell, the daughter of John Pell of Eltington, Northamptonshire, and was first married to the Honorable Thomas Nicolls, of Ecton in the same county, sergeant-at-law of the Middle Temple in London, who died in 1568 at the age of thirty-eight. Their son

6. Will of John Purefoy, Somerset House, Prerogative Court of Canterbury: 22 Bakon.

was Sir Augustine Nicolls (1559–1616), a distinguished judge under Elizabeth I and James I. After her first husband's death Mrs. Nicolls married Richard Purefoy, owner of the manor of Faxton in Northamptonshire and the brother of Mary Purefoy, wife of Thomas Dorne of Yardley Hastings and the maternal grandmother of Thomas Dudley. Mrs. Purefoy bore no children to her second husband, so her son Augustine Nicolls inherited Faxton, and there his mother continued to live until her death, in 1614, in her eighty-third year. To this home of the Purefoys, only about twenty miles from Yardley Hastings, Thomas Dudley came when he was orphaned, to pursue the education that had begun while his parents were still alive. There we shall temporarily leave him, in order to discuss the vexed question of his paternal ancestry, which is of significance to this study because of the influence that it may have had on the mind and character of his daughter Anne Bradstreet.

To go back to the beginning of the matter, about the year 1262 a powerful landowner named Roger de Somery began to rebuild and enlarge the ancient castle of Dudley in Staffordshire. He died in 1273 and his daughter Margaret, the wife of John de Sutton of Nottinghamshire, as co-heiress of her father's estate, inherited Dudley Castle and its surrounding manors. Thus was established the baronial line of the Suttons, Lords of Dudley, who bore as their arms the old Sutton device, described in a Herald's Roll of the time of King Edward II as *"de or, a un lyon rampaund de vert."* [7] This green lion on a field of gold had originally a forked or double tail, but in the sixteenth century a dispute among the heralds caused the lion to be displayed with a single tail; however, it was restored to its former glory in the next century. [8]

7. H. S. Grazebrook, "The Barons of Dudley," in *Collections for a History of Staffordshire*, ed. William Salt Archaeological Society, Vol. IX, 1888, Part II, pp. 19, 42, 71.

8. Dean Dudley, *History of the Dudley Family* (3 volumes & supplement, privately printed), Wakefield (Mass.), 1886–98, Supp. p. 6 (note).

When Thomas Dudley, as an old man in Massachusetts, wrote his will in 1653, he affixed to it a seal bearing a lion rampant with single tail and with a crescent for difference, that is, to show descent from a younger son of the baronial house.[9] Although the use of such an armorial seal by a New England colonist does not, by the standards of the College of Arms in London, constitute proof of descent from the family designated by the device, there is reason to believe that Dudley had a right to own and use this seal. He apparently knew more about his father's background than he ever recorded for posterity, or seemingly wished to have publicly known, though his own children and descendants left some indications that they shared this knowledge.

Thomas's eldest son by his second marriage, Joseph Dudley, who achieved political prominence in both old and New England, possessed an elaborate seal showing the lion with double tail, the crest of a lion's head erased, and the motto: "*Nec gladio nec arcu.*"[10] And several pieces of American colonial silver, notably a salver of *circa* 1710, in the Minneapolis Institute of Art, and a handsome teapot of the mid-eighteenth century, in the Boston Museum of Fine Arts, have the Dudley lion engraved on them.

In addition to these heraldic suggestions there are two written statements that bear directly on the question. Cotton Mather, in his summing up of Thomas Dudley's qualities at the end of the *MS. Life*, wrote "He was a man of great spirit, as well as of great understanding; suitable to the family he was, by his father, descended from." And Anne Bradstreet herself gave a clear indication of ancestral consciousness in two lines from her "Elegie upon Sir Philip Sidney," as it was first printed in 1650:

> Let then, none dis-allow of these my straines,
> Which have the self-same blood yet in my veines.

9. Probate Court of Suffolk County, Massachusetts, Case 129.
10. Adlard, *Sutton-Dudleys and Dudleys*, title-page and Introduction, p. xiii.

Sidney, whose mother was the Lady Mary, daughter of John Dudley, Duke of Northumberland, expressed his own family pride in his "Defence of the Earl of Leicester," written in answer to *Leycester's Commonwealth,* a scurrilous attack on the Earl, Sidney's uncle, published anonymously in 1584 and attributed to the Jesuit Robert Parsons.

> I am a *Dudley* in blood . . . and do acknowledge, though, in all truth, I may justly affirm that I am, by my father's side, of ancient, and well-esteemed and well-matched gentry, yet I do acknowledge, I say, that my chiefest honour is to be a *Dudley,* and truly am glad to have cause to set forth the nobility of that blood whereof I am descended, which, but upon so just cause, without vainglory, could not have been uttered.[11]

Apparently Anne Bradstreet also felt some anxiety about vainglory, for she altered the couplet, for a later edition of her poems, to:

> Then let none disallow of these my strains,
> Whilst English blood yet runs within my veins.

This would seem like a change in the interest of literary decorum rather than a denial of kinship with Sidney. The whole poem, an early and obviously experimental one, was severely edited and emended by its author; a biographer of Thomas Dudley commented that Anne "may not have liked the personal, possibly boastful, allusion. . . . It was not in good taste to exalt her own strains, for the reason that she was related to Sidney. . . . She had failed in these lines of her first edition to carry out her poetic conception to completion, and, like a sensible woman, when her next edition appeared she had corrected them." [12]

11. Arthur Collins, ed., *Letters and Memorials of State, written and collected by Sir Henry, Sir Philip and Sir Robert Sydney,* 1746, Vol. I, Part 1, pp. 64–65.

12. Augustine Jones, *Thomas Dudley, Second Governor of Massachusetts,* Boston, 1899, p. 5.

An officer of the College of Arms has expressed his opinion that this circumstantial evidence provides "reasonable, *though inferential* proof" of Thomas Dudley's descent from the Suttons, Lords Dudley.[13] The missing link in Thomas's lineage is his paternal grandfather, who remains anonymous since all that we know of his son, the shadowy Roger Dudley, is that he appeared in Yardley Hastings by marrying Susanna Thorne, in 1575 or thereabouts, and disappeared by dying before the 29th October, 1588. It seems unlikely, however, that Thomas did not know who his grandfather was, and his failure to record this information in exact form makes it appear that, for some reason, he wished to suppress it. The English genealogist, H. S. Grazebrook, commenting on this suppression in a review of Adlard's *Sutton-Dudleys of England and Dudleys of Massachusetts*, wrote:

> Mr. Adlard says: "From Cotton Mather we learn that there was a *repugnance* on the part of the first Governor Dudley to make known any particulars of his ancestry."
> Whence this repugnance? If he were in truth a scion of so illustrious a stock, what motive could he have had in concealing it? I do not find that ancestry was considered any disgrace by the Puritans. . . . This repugnance then is strange and unaccountable.[14]

The efforts that have been made to identify the father of Roger Dudley have so far failed both to provide a credible connection with the noble Dudleys and to explain the reluctance of the gov-

13. Captain de La Lanne-Mirrlees, then Rouge Dragon Pursuivant, in a letter to me dated 9th February, 1953, wrote that the aristocratic background of Susanna Thorne "indicates that Roger Dudley himself came of gentle stock." And in referring to the old governor's use of the Sutton-Dudley seal, and Anne Bradstreet's mention of her relationship to Sir Philip Sidney, he made the point that "among early New England Puritans . . . no advantage was to be gained from claiming noble blood or a coat of arms, unless they were indeed theirs by right."
14. In *The Herald and Genealogist*, ed. J. G. Nichols, Vol. II, 1865, p. 498.

ernor to describe his ancestry in any detail. Two typical examples of these unsuccessful efforts are the pedigrees suggested by George Adlard and in a recent edition of *Burke's Landed Gentry*. During the course of his searches in London, Adlard found three interesting wills at Somerset House; they are those of Thomas Dudley, "citizen and draper," of 1549, his son John, who predeceased him in 1545, and John's daughter Katherine who, dying unmarried in 1563, left a bequest from her modest estate to "Roger Dudley, my brother." Adlard advanced the theory that this Thomas was a younger son of Edward Sutton, the seventh Baron Dudley, whose eldest son John, born about 1495, succeeded to the title on his father's death in 1532, and that Thomas's grandson Roger might be accepted as the father of Thomas the New England pioneer. But the records of the Company of Drapers at Drapers' Hall in London, which Adlard did not consult, show that their member Thomas Dudley was born in 1472 or 1473, more than twenty years before John Sutton, eighth Baron Dudley, whose younger brother he was supposed to be, and that Thomas's grandson Roger, listed as a draper, aged thirty-seven, in 1578, was buried as an "almes man" (or receiver of charity), aged seventy-three, at the church of St. Olave in London in 1614.[15] So he could not have been the same Roger Dudley who was living in Yardley Hastings between 1575 and 1580, and whose death had occurred before the autumn of 1588.

The same discrepancy as to the death-date, as well as other inaccuracies, makes it impossible to accept the pedigree of Governor Thomas Dudley as presented in *Burke's Landed Gentry*. Here Thomas's descent is traced from John Sutton, sixth Baron Dudley, whose younger son John was the grandfather of the Duke

15. Adlard, *Sutton-Dudleys and Dudleys*, pp. xiv, 47–50, 136–40, and Pedigrees A and D. I am indebted to N. E. M. Davies, Archivist of the Drapers' Company in March 1956, for helpful assistance in obtaining the membership records of Thomas and Roger Dudley.

of Northumberland. This John has also an illegitimate son named Simon, who died in 1555 and left a son John, of Hackney in London, who held the office of Sergeant of the Pastry to Queen Elizabeth I. In 1588 he was granted arms described as: "Or, two lions passant, azure, within a bordure engrailed, azure." The blue lions on a golden shield came to the Dudleys from the Somerys, and were used by some branches of the family instead of the green lion rampant of the Suttons.[16] The bordure engrailed, or scalloped edging of the shield, was added to John Dudley's coat of arms to show his descent from a natural, or bastard, son.

The Sergeant of the Pastry, according to *Burke*, had a son who was "Captain Roger Dudley, born 1552, married Dorothy, daughter of William Purefoy of Caldicote, Leicestershire . . . attended the Earl of Leicester in Essex and Kent, 1588, died 1627," and his son was "Colonel Thomas Dudley of Roxbury, Massachusetts." [17] Dorothy Purefoy is shown in John Nichols's *History of Leicestershire* to have married Robert Gregory of Baroden, Rutland.[18] I have not been able to corroborate the other statements made by *Burke* about "Captain Roger Dudley," or to find any clear evidence that the Sergeant John Dudley ever had a son of that name. Even if he did exist he could not be identified with the Roger Dudley who is known to have lived, however briefly, at Yardley Hastings in Northamptonshire, and who was dead by the autumn of 1588.

Also, there is the matter of the coat of arms. Thomas Dudley was a man of inflexible probity, and if he knew himself to be entitled only to the use of the two lions passant with bordure engrailed, he would hardly have sealed his will with the somewhat prouder

16. Grazebrook, "The Barons of Dudley," *op. cit.* Vol. IX, Part II, pp. 70–71.

17. *Burke's Landed Gentry*, 1952, p. 700.

18. Nichols, *History of Leicestershire*, Vol. IV, Part II, 1811, Pedigree of Purefoy, pp. 599–601.

lion rampant of the Sutton-Dudleys, and handed down this device for his descendants to display.

There were, to say the least, hundreds of persons of the name of Dudley living in England in the later sixteenth century, members of families of commoners as well as of those of rank and title. They crop up all over the country, in wills and *Inquisitiones post-mortem*, legal actions, land transactions, parish registers, and so on. Yet the fact that no man among all of these Dudleys has ever been positively identified as the paternal great-grandfather of Anne Bradstreet, coupled with Thomas Dudley's curious reluctance to publicize his ancestry, makes it appear that there *was* something "strange and unaccountable," as Grazebrook put it, about the ancestor in question as well as the family attitude towards him.

I wish to put forward, conjecturally, as a candidate for the paternity of Roger Dudley, a man who was strange enough in his life to satisfy Grazebrook's curiosity, and noble enough in his blood to justify the governor's use of the Sutton-Dudley arms. He was George Sutton-Dudley, a younger son of John Sutton, eighth Baron Dudley; he was born in 1528 or thereabouts, and the date and place of his death are, so far, unknown. The insecurity and restlessness that marked his whole career were awaiting him when he was born. His family was already in financial difficulties at the beginning of the century, and when his father succeeded to the title, in 1532, he immediately began to sell his properties and within a few years had disposed of all his possessions. The historian Dugdale wrote that he,

. . . being a weak man of understanding, . . . so became entangled in the Usurer's Bonds [that] *John Dudley*, . . . Earl of *Warwick*, (afterwards Duke of *Northumberland*) thirsting after DUDLEY-Castle (the chief seat of this Family) made those Money-Merchants his Instruments, to work him out of it; which by some Mortgage, being at length effected; this poor Lord became exposed to the Charity of his Friends for a subsistence; and spending the remainder of his life in Visits amongst them, was commonly called the Lord *Quondam*.[19]

The wife of this unfortunate nobleman was Cicely Grey, daughter of Thomas, Marquess of Dorset. In the will of her mother, dated 1527, mention is made of three Dudley grandsons, Edward, Thomas, and Henry, but the name of George does not appear, therefore he was not born until 1528 or slightly later. The Marchioness's will also records that her daughter had a modest stipend of her own, of £25 a year, the income of a legacy from her father. In 1538 the Lady Dudley wrote a pathetic letter to the Lord Privy Seal, asking for help from King Henry VIII. She was, she said, living in a convent at Nuneaton, with

little above twenty pound a year to find me and one of my daughters with a woman and a man to wait upon me; and surely, unless the good prioress did give me meat and drink of free cost, to me and all mine that here remains with me, I could not tell what shift to make. . . .

Whensoever any of my children comes hither to see me, they be welcome unto the prioress as long as they list to tarry, horse-meat and man's meat, and cost them nothing, with a piece of gold or two in their purses at their departure.[20]

George Dudley was about ten years old when this letter was written. It would seem that his parents were living in separation, and George was perhaps domiciled with some other relative, or more probably being carried about by his father on the succession of visits that he was making to sympathetic and generous kinsmen. The Sutton-Dudleys were loyal members, at this time, of the

19. Sir William Dugdale, *The Baronage of England*, 1675, Vol. II, p. 216.
20. *Letters and Papers Foreign and Domestic—Henry VIII—1538*, Vol. 13, Part 2, 1893, p. 541.

Roman Church, so it is not surprising that "Lord Quondam,"
and his eldest son Edward as well, apparently became involved in
the widespread plot to overthrow the king and restore the papal
power in England. What is rather surprising, but is shown by
clear evidence, is that George, at the age of thirteen or fourteen,
was also drawn into the plotting, and appears to have been used
as a go-between by his elders until he was either discovered or in
so precarious a position that it was thought advisable to get him
out of the country, although, as will be seen, he still had work to
do on the Continent.

From 1538 to 1542 George's second cousin, Sir John Dudley, the
future Duke of Northumberland, who had acquired Dudley Castle
and its lands from his father, was the deputy governor of the
English-held city of Calais. Perhaps through his influence George
joined the garrison there, as a foot-soldier of the lowest rank whose
pay was sixpence a day. But he did not long remain in that obscure position, as he apparently had instructions, and money, to
proceed on a secret mission to Italy.

On the 4th February, 1543, Sir William Paget, Henry VIII's
special ambassador to France, wrote to the king that "one Dudley,
one of the sonnes of the late Lord Dudley . . . who hath been
lately in six pens a day at Calais," had arrived in Paris. Paget had
secured a warrant for his arrest, and would take him into custody.
Two days later he wrote again to the king, "As touching the miserable foole George Dudley," who had confessed his treasonable
activities with many tears and appeals for mercy, a safe conduct
had been obtained and he would shortly be sent to England. "I
knowe not his lyving, nor his conditions, but he was driven to
work at Calais with a mattock and shovel." Paget's reference to
the "late" Lord Dudley was probably a sarcastic substitute for the
sad nickname "Lord Quondam," and George's complaint that, as
a common soldier, he was forced to dig with a mattock and shovel,

was undoubtedly an attempt to gain leniency from the king's official. When this did not succeed he had another solution; on the 15th February Paget wrote to his sovereign that the "false traiterous boy Dudley" had escaped and gone "clene out of sight." [21]

He is next heard of from Milan, where two English agents, Edward Raligh and John Brende, sent word to the Privy Council, on the 5th May, 1543, that "one George Dudley, the sonne of the Lord Dudley that sold his landes," had arrived in that city in the company of four Frenchmen, and made a point of avoiding the Englishmen. On making judicious inquiries, they learned that he had fled from England and escaped from Paget's custody in France, "that the King had written letters for his taking," and that he was carrying papers and messages to Cardinal Pole in Rome. He claimed to be a kinsman of the Cardinal and also of King Henry VIII; in this he was more or less correct, as his mother and the king were both grandchildren of Elizabeth Woodville, the wife of King Edward IV, and Pole's mother was a niece of Edward IV, therefore a cousin by marriage, once removed, of George's mother.

At the time of his appearance in Milan, George Dudley could not have been more than fifteen years old, yet he was already a seasoned intriguer and as elusive as a character of much greater age and experience. Raligh and Brende, aware that he was up to no good, continued their report: "In the consideracion of which matter was founde but two thinges, either to *kylle hym*, or cause hym to be detayned." They applied to the governor of Milan for a warrant for his arrest, but before they obtained it George had slipped away, with his retinue, "towards the Pope's lands." The busy Englishmen then rode to Pavia, where they secured the war-

21. *Letters and Papers Foreign and Domestic—Henry VIII—1543*, Vol. 18, Part 1, 1901, pp. 77, 81, 98.

rant and, posting thirty miles further on the road to Rome, inter-
cepted the Dudley party and brought them back to Milan, where
the governor committed George to Milan Castle as a prisoner, to
await the coming of Edmund Bonner, the Bishop of London, and
directed that the letters that young Dudley was carrying should be
sent to King Henry in England.[22]

Shortly after this Bishop Bonner, whom Henry had sent to the
Continent as a special ambassador to the Holy Roman Emperor
Charles V, wrote two letters to the king. In the first, dated the
19th June, 1543, he reported that, since there was to be some
delay in his meeting with the Emperor, he had decided to go to
Milan in order "to question Dudley about his coming out of
England." There he was told that George had once more managed
to break out of his prison and had fled; this story, he wrote, seemed
very unlikely to him, and he planned to speak of it not only to the
governor of Milan but to the Emperor himself. In his second letter,
written in Cologne on the 24th August, the Bishop introduces an
Englishman named Brant, who will deliver letters about various
matters to the king, will "report all things, and can also tell of
that naughty person, Dudley, who was suffered to escape out of
Milan Castle." [23] So the agile conspirator had apparently found a
way, by bribery or eloquence, to elude his captors, and no doubt
there were some Italians in high places who were secretly delighted
that the young Catholic aristocrat had foiled the efforts of King
Henry's emissaries to send him back to face judgment in his own
country.

After his escape from Milan, George probably remained in
hiding for a while, but further developments indicate that he did

---

22. *Letters and Papers Foreign and Domestic—Henry VIII—1543*, Vol.
18, Part 1, p. 301.
23. *Ibid.*, Vol. 18, Part 1, pp. 417–18, and Vol. 18, Part 2, 1902, p. 37.

make his way to Rome, and there delivered his seditious messages
to the man who was the prime hope of the Catholic conspirators
in England, Reginald Pole. This distinguished English churchman
had been a close adviser and friend of Henry VIII, but had refused to countenance the king's divorce from Catherine of Aragon
and so took refuge in Italy, where he was made a cardinal in 1536.
He remained abroad until he was summoned back to England by
Queen Mary in 1554 and chosen to succeed Cranmer as Archbishop of Canterbury. While he was an exile in Rome he heard
of the arrests for treason, and executions, of his brother in 1538
and his mother, then aged sixty-eight, in 1541, and during these
years he took a leading part in the plans to send an army into
England by way of Scotland, to support the English Catholics in
their long-projected rebellion against King Henry VIII.

Cardinal Pole had young George Dudley on his hands from the
time of the boy's arrival in Rome, and must have wondered what
to do with him and how best to make use of his abilities as a
secret agent. He could not safely be sent back to England as he
was wanted for treason there, and, as a known fugitive in both
France and northern Italy, he would risk recapture or assassination
if he went on a mission to those parts. What was needed was an
effective disguise or *alter ego*, and the solution to this problem that
the Cardinal hit upon was an ingenious and, it would seem, successful one. George should become a member of the ancient, aristocratic, and semi-monastic order of chivalry, the Knights Hospital-
ers of St. John of Jerusalem.

This brotherhood, originally founded to succor Christian pilgrims to the Holy Land who had been overtaken by illness, played
a vigorous part in the Crusades, and later harassed Saracen and
Turkish shipping in the Mediterranean with its powerful fleet
of galleys. In 1530 the Knights established their headquarters on

the island of Malta, eight years after being driven from their stronghold at Rhodes by the Turks, and they were generally known thereafter as the Knights of Malta.

A young man of the age of sixteen or over who wished to join the Order as a full officer-member, or knight of justice, was required to present himself, with his application, before the Grand Master and Council in Malta. Then, if he was tentatively accepted, a commission of two knights was sent by the council to his native country, to investigate and corroborate his claims of noble blood and untarnished lineage. If the commission's report was satisfactory, the applicant was admitted to membership and, after paying his "passage" or initiation fee of £100—a very large sum in the sixteenth century—and taking the vows of poverty, chastity, and obedience, he was assigned to a priory of the Order, in his own or another country, for his monastic training. When this was completed and the young knight had become of age, he returned to the convent, or headquarters of the Order, in Malta, there to prepare himself by "making Caravans," that is, serving for five years with the armed forces in the galleys, to take charge of one of the smaller chapters, known as commanderies, in the country of his origin.

The case of George Dudley, in relation to this long and complicated procedure, was an exceptional one. When he presented himself as a candidate in Malta, the Council could not send a commission to England to examine his ancestry, not only because George himself was a wanted man there, but also because Henry VIII had suppressed the English arm of the Order and confiscated all of its properties, and five of the knights had been martyred when they refused to renounce allegiance to the Pope. So the records of the Order show that on the 3rd July, 1545, when he was seventeen years old or perhaps a little younger, "the Noble George DODLA referred to as Sotton" having been recommended for membership and the fact being recognized that it was impossible for him to produce "authenticated instruments of his nobility,"

> We the Lord Great Master and the Venerable Council attending . . . because we consider the Lord Cardinal of England, as well as his own declaration, has proved and asserted his nobility, we have received the said George DODLA as a brother, and have desired that he be received in the English tongue, with food and emolument such as are usual to Knights of Justice.[24]

George was duly accepted, on the same day, into the Tongue of England, which was one of the eight national groups into which those knights who were resident in Malta were divided. He was domiciled at the English Auberge, a building that still stands in a narrow lane in the many times war-battered little town of Birgu, the Order's residence until after the Great Siege of 1565, when the city of Valletta was constructed across the Grand Harbor.

Less than a month after his election it is recorded that "The furst day of August 1545 toke apan hym to make Carvant in the galls Giorg Dodla for the tong off ingland." [25] But, having been excused from the initial training period in one of the Order's priories, he was also not required to complete his years of military service. On the 1st April, 1547, license was given to Brother George Dudley, "with all powers and faculty, to go into Germany through Italy on his private business, which could not be fulfilled without his presence." [26]

This unusual exception to the established discipline of a newly elected knight shows clearly that Dudley's function was still that

24. *Archives of the Order of St. John in Malta*, Vol. 2192, f° 20ᵛ, in the Royal Library, Valletta, Malta; English translation in *The Book of Deliberations of the Venerable Tongue of England, 1523–1567*, ed. Chevalier H. P. Scicluna, Malta, 1949, pp. 29–30.

25. *Arch. Ord. Malta*, Vol. 2192, f° 32.

26. *Ibid.* Vol. 420, f° 162 (translation from Latin).

of an operative in the conspiracy to restore the authority of Rome in England. When King Henry VIII died in January 1546/47 and was succeeded by his nine-year-old son Edward VI, it was hoped that this could be speedily brought about. Cardinal Pole was one of those most active in the effort to persuade the little king's chief advisers, the Protector Somerset and John Dudley, Earl of Warwick (later Duke of Northumberland), to reverse the anti-papal policies of Henry VIII. Pole could not yet safely return to England, but among the envoys that he sent to Edward's court may very possibly have been George Dudley, cousin to the Earl of Warwick and now dignified by his habit as a Knight of St. John and the official nature of his mission.

At any rate George did, in some capacity or another, return to England at some time during the seven years that followed his departure from Malta. There is no record of his activities until his name appears on another license, of an entirely different kind: on the 28th November, 1554, the Bishop of London granted permission to "George Sutton, *alias* Dudley, and Ellen Barnyshe, of St. Augustine's at the Gate; to marry there." [27]

This was not so strange an act, on the part of one who had taken the knightly vows of poverty, chastity, and obedience, as it might seem. George had quite apparently been admitted to the Order at the express desire of Cardinal Pole, and with the understanding that his services as a courier, for the sake of the Roman Catholic Church, might be needed at any time. Soon after the accession of Edward VI, and in spite of all the efforts to reconcile England to Rome, it became clear that that country would continue on its independent course. All of the English properties of the Knights of Malta remained confiscated, members of the Order were for-

27. *Allegations for Marriage Licences issued by the Bishop of London, 1520–1610*, ed. J. L. Chester and G. J. Armytage, Harleian Society, 1887, Vol. I, p. 15.

bidden to wear their habits or insignia, and moreover, Parliament decreed that it was legal for the clergy, and others under religious discipline, to marry if they chose to do so.

So George Dudley, whenever he arrived in England, must have found himself adrift there. He may have attempted to rejoin his family, but they were still in an unsettled and divided state and could not offer him any security. His father, the impecunious "Lord Quondam," was probably living in dependence on some generous friend or relative; he died in 1553 and was buried at St. Margaret's, Westminister, with Roman Catholic rites and the full pomp of his rank as Baron Dudley. George's eldest brother, Edward, was governor of Hume Castle in Scotland, and Henry had turned Protestant, so ardently that he was later involved in a plot to depose Queen Mary and had to flee the country and take refuge in France.

George apparently also became a Protestant, found some means of livelihood in London, and met and wooed the lady who consented to be his wife in 1554. Nothing more than this is so far known about Ellen Barnyshe; the registers of the church of St. Augustine at Paul's Gate, Watling Street, only begin in 1559 and neither her name nor that of George Dudley appears in them. That George did marry at about this time is shown in another document to which we shall shortly come, and it may be supposed that his wife was of good family and estate and that there were children of the marriage. While these changes were occurring in George Dudley's life much more momentous ones were taking place in his country. The ailing young king died in 1553 and was succeeded by his half-sister, the sombre zealot Mary Tudor, following the Duke of Northumberland's abortive attempt to place his daughter-in-law, the Lady Jane Grey, on the throne. Queen Mary was determined to restore Roman Catholicism to England; she forced Parliament to abolish the laws affecting religion passed during the reigns of her father and half-brother, executed the Duke of Northumberland, and restored all the properties that he had obtained from "Lord Quondam" to Edward, George's brother, when he inherited the title of Baron Dudley. She married her cousin the fanatical Catholic, Philip of Spain, recalled Cardinal Pole and made him Archbishop of Canterbury, gave back to the Church as much as she could of the confiscated lands and treasure, and energetically persecuted all prominent Protestants.

In the spring of 1557 the Queen authorized Archbishop Pole, by letters patent, to reinstate the Order of St. John in England and to restore all of its holdings that were still controlled by the Crown.[28] Accordingly, after a number of priors and commanders had been placed in charge of the recovered properties, it was decided that a small group of knights should return to Malta to prepare the almost-deserted English Auberge for the reception of the new recruits who were confidently expected to join the English Tongue. The Bailiff of Egle, which was an important commandery in Lincolnshire, headed the group, and with him went two other commanders, Oliver Starkey and James Shelley, and also, strangely enough, the thoroughly lapsed knight George Dudley.[29]

It is hard to understand why, at this point in his chequered career, George Dudley chose to turn again to the Order which he had deserted with apparent finality. Perhaps he was summoned into the presence of his patron, Archbishop Pole, and there told that he must go to Malta as he was still needed in the difficult and complex procedure of returning England to the Catholic fold. Or it may have been that his marriage was unsuccessful, or that his financial position had become so precarious that flight from his

28. *Six Documents relating to Queen Mary's Restoration of the Grand Priories of England and Ireland*, ed. Col. E. J. King, Order of St. John Historical Pamphlets No. 7, 1935, Introduction, p. 4.

29. Sir Edwin King, *The Knights of St. John in the British Realm*, revised by Sir Harry Luke, 1967, pp. 110–12.

country, back to the shelter of the convent at Malta, was his last
resort. No doubt it occurred to him to wonder what his reception
there would be, but he must have had both the agile wit and the
persuasive charm that the situation required, for it was chronicled
on the 12th October, 1557, that the "English knight" George
Dudley, who had formerly been received as a military brother in
the venerable Tongue of England, having become involved in

> . . . the schism and separation raised up by King Henry VIII
> of England against the Catholic Church, thereafter compounded
> the error by taking a wife and abandoning his habit and the
> fraternity. He has now returned to the Convent, has performed
> penitential service in the hospital and infirmary, and comes to
> petition the Grand Master and the venerable Council for read-
> mission to our Order.
>
> It having been established that Brother George Dudley is
> now reconciled and restored to the bosom of the Holy Mother
> Church, and through humiliation and prayers is absolved of his
> apostasy and the other crimes he has committed, it is granted to
> him to be admitted to the fellowship of our Order as a Religious
> Brother.[30]

Probably the powerful influence of the Archbishop of Canterbury had as much to do with George's reinstatement as did his
own somewhat opportunistic "humiliation and prayers." He continued to be favorably treated; at the beginning of 1558 he was
listed as the "Venerable Lieutenant Turcopilier," or presiding
officer, of the Tongue of England, and in May of that year, being
temporarily the only resident member of the Tongue and in a
state of poverty, he was given permission to collect, for his own
use, the rents of all the houses in Birgu that were owned by the

30. *Arch. Ord. Malta,* Vol. 89, f° 127. This record also appears, translated
from the Latin, in Whitworth Porter, *History of the Knights of Malta,* 1858,
Vol. II, p. 330.

English community. In the late autumn some other English knights were in residence, and these challenged Dudley's claim of seniority, on the grounds that he "had left the Convent and become a schismatic in England"; however, the Grand Master and Council decreed that his seniority must be counted from the time that he had entered the Order, that is 1545, and in December he was listed as "President of the Tongue." [31]

Meanwhile the fortunes of the knights were again deteriorating in England. In November of 1558 Queen Mary's melancholy rule ended and her half-sister Elizabeth ascended the throne. The new monarch at once reversed Mary's tyrannical religious policies and separated her country anew from the domination of Rome. For the English Knights of Malta her accession was the beginning of the end. Their remaining estates were once more confiscated, and without the financial support that they yielded, the Tongue of England in Malta could not continue to exist as a self-sustaining entity. The valuable commandery of Torphichen in Scotland still remained, however, in the control of the Order; in the late summer of 1560 it was decreed that three English knights, Henry Gerard, George Dudley, and James Shelley should go there to arrange for the installation of a new commander, John James Sandilands.[32] Gerard and Dudley, it is said, never returned to Malta,[33] and in George's case this assignment may have been yet another cloak for a secret mission to the Continent.

For it appears that he went to Spain, to visit Sir Francis Englefield, a prominent member of Queen Mary's court who was living in exile in Valladolid, and then carried a letter from Sir Francis to Sir Nicholas Throckmorton, Queen Elizabeth's ambassador to

31. *Arch. Ord. Malta*, Vol. 90, f°ˢ 7, 14ᵛ, 33ᵛ; Vol. 288, f° 59ᵛ; Vol. 2192, f° 34.
32. *Arch. Ord. Malta*, Vol. 420, f° 198ᵛ.
33. Sir Edwin King, *op. cit.* p. 116.

France. On the 5th November, 1560, Throckmorton wrote from Orleans to the Privy Council, enclosing Englefield's letter and saying that he was entrusting the delivery of these documents to George Dudley, "brother of Henry Dudley" (then living at the court of King Henry II of France), who had come to him in a poor and ragged state and "prefers being in this country (as he says) before his devotion to the cross." [34]

With this equivocal statement the chronicle of George Dudley ends; he was about thirty-two years old in 1560, and what happened to him for the rest of his life is, so far, unknown. What concerns us here is the possibility that he was the father of the elusive Roger Dudley. Certainly I have found no record of any other scion of the Sutton-Dudleys whose approximate dates of birth and marriage make it logical to suppose that he had a son born in 1555 or 1556; if this son were Roger, abandoned by his father soon after birth, the resulting insecurity of his childhood and early youth, along with the adventurous restlessness that he may have inherited from that father, could explain, in part at any rate, why we know so little about his short life. And if Thomas, Roger's son, was descended from the soldier of fortune George Dudley, conspirator against at least two of his country's monarchs, expedient Knight of Malta, turncoat in religion and deserter of his wife, it would surely account for the reluctance of the righteous old governor of Massachusetts to make public the facts of his grandfather's life.

One more romantic detail may be added to this conjectural proposition. George Dudley was apparently proud of his noble birth; certainly he traded on it whenever it suited his purpose. He may have owned the seal with the sixteenth-century single-tailed lion of the Sutton-Dudleys, and crescent to denote that he was a younger son, and this may have descended through Roger to

34. *Calendar of State Papers, Foreign*—Elizabeth—1560–61, p. 382.

Thomas and thus have been the reason why the governor's mid-seventeenth-century will was sealed with the earlier arms of his family.

There is no explanation for Cotton Mather's statement that " 'Twas said that there was five hundred pounds left for him in an unknown hand," which legacy was delivered to him after he came to man's estate. The sum was a small fortune in those days, and certainly not one of Thomas Dudley's known immediate relatives was rich enough to remember him so handsomely. But the responsibilities of kinship were taken very seriously in Elizabethan England, and it is not impossible that some powerful and generous member of his mother's or father's family arranged for an anonymous gift to be received by young Thomas on his majority.

What he did receive for certain was an excellent basic education which, although he did not go to a university, "he improved afterwards," as Mather wrote, "by his own industry to considerable advantage." There was a "Free School" for the teaching of Latin in Northampton, to which there came as Master, about 1585, an able young Oxford graduate named Simon Wastell, whom Anthony Wood called "a great proficient in classical learning and Poetry." [35] Thomas Dudley was probably sent to this school when he was about nine years old, to study for five or six years.

Two books, among the fifty-odd in the old governor's possession at the time of his death, corroborate Mather's statement, in the *MS. Life,* that he continued to study by himself until he was able "to understand any Latin author as well as the best clerk in the country." These were listed, in "An Inventory of ye goods chattells & all other estate of Thomas Dudley Esquire taken the eight day of the Sixth moneth Anno Dom. 1653," [36] as "Mantuani Buiclica"

35. *Athenae Oxonienses,* Vol. I, 1691, p. 414.
36. *Suffolk County, Massachusetts, Probate Court Records,* Vol. 2, p. 131. See Appendix: Thomas Dudley's Books.

and "Corderius." The first, which has been wrongly identified as Virgil's *Bucolics,* was the popular book of eclogues B. *Mantuani adolescentia seu bucolica,* by a fifteenth-century monk of Mantua, Johannes Baptista Spagnolo.[37] The first line of the *Bucolica,* with a tribute to the "good old Mantuan," is quoted by Holofernes in *Love's Labour's Lost.* The other was the equally familiar *Colloquia Scholastica,* a collection of Latin dialogues for beginners, by the French schoolmaster Mathurin Cordier.[38]

Thomas Dudley also owned a "Diction Lat," perhaps A *Dictionarie English and Latine,* published in London in 1623. So it is apparent that he kept up his knowledge of that language, and he may have used it, with the help of the two old favorites Mantuanus and Corderius, to teach his younger children during the long voyage across the Atlantic in 1630, and before schools were established in the Massachusetts Bay settlements.

Mather's *MS. Life* continues:

> So soon as ever he had passed his childhood he was, by those that stood his best friends, preferred to be a page to the Earl of Northampton, under whom he had opportunity to learn courtship and whatever belonged to civility and good behaviour; with that Earl he tarried till he was ripe for higher services.

This indicates that when Thomas was fourteen years old, the customary age for leaving grammar school, he went from his student's lodging in Northampton, and the modest manor house at Faxton, to become a member of a highly sophisticated household, one of whose centers of activity was the splendid new mansion of Castle Ashby, only a mile and a half from Yardley Hastings.

William, Lord Compton, who in 1618 became Earl of North-

37. Printed in London by Wynkin de Worde, 1526, and many times reprinted for readers that included generations of Elizabethan and Jacobean schoolboys.
38. First printed in Geneva in 1563.

ampton, was in 1590 a young man who had just inherited his title and the estates of Castle Ashby and of Compton Wynyates in Warwickshire. When he was not at one or the other of these properties he was studying at Cambridge University, where he took his M.A. in 1595, or leading the life of a courtier in London, from his "town house" in Tottenham, then a village on the outskirts of the city. In 1599 he kidnapped the daughter of the rich Sir John Spencer, ex-Lord Mayor of London, by carrying her out of her father's house in a bread-basket, and they were married. Queen Elizabeth persuaded his furious father-in-law to accept the situation, so the Spencer fortune was inherited, when Sir John died in 1610, by Lady Compton, his only child, and her husband.

The great Italianate Elizabethan house of Castle Ashby was begun in 1574, by Lord Compton's father, and not finally completed until 1616. In that year the household retinue consisted of eighty-three servants, four chaplains, three musicians, and "The Gardener of Ashby." [39] A quarter-century earlier, when young Thomas Dudley went to serve his pageship there, the number of retainers was probably considerably smaller, but the general style of life would have been the same. Every one of the noble domains, like this, that were scattered thickly throughout sixteenth- and early seventeenth-century England, was a complex social unit in itself; a little world in the image of the whole intricate Elizabethan pattern of society.

In *Knole and the Sackvilles,* Victoria Sackville-West quotes in its entirety a "Catalogue of the Household and Family of the Right Honourable Richard, Earl of Dorset, in the year of our Lord 1613," which contains one hundred and nineteen names, beginning with "My Lord" and ending with "John Morockoe, a

---

39. William Bingham Compton, Sixth Marquess of Northampton, kindly lent me a copy of his privately printed *History of the Comptons,* 1930, from which these notes about the family are taken.

Blackamoor of the Scullery." The list is compiled according to the importance or usefulness of each person named, and notes his or her position at one of the seven dining tables in the house. The three pages are called "Master," and placed at the "Parlour Table," next after "My Lord's," with the Chaplain, the Steward, the Secretary, "My Lord's favourite," and others in responsible posts.[40]

The institution of pageship was an ancient and privileged one, designed to train youths of aristocratic background to take their places with capability in military, political, or court life. Far cry as it seems from the luxurious and stately household of Lord Compton to the austerity of Puritan life in colonial Massachusetts, Thomas Dudley must have learned a great deal, during his years of service to the young nobleman, that helped him in his subsequent career in England and made him one of the most worldly-wise and far-seeing of the pioneer leaders.

Dudley probably remained with Lord Compton until 1594, when he was eighteen years old, then "having fitted himself to do many other Benefits unto the World," as Cotton Mather put it in the *Magnalia,*

> he next became a *Clerk* unto Judge *Nichols,* who being his Kinsman by the Mother's Side, therefore took the more special notice of him. From his Relation to this *Judge,* he had and used an Advantage to attain such a Skill in the *Law,* as was of great Advantage to him in the future changes of his Life; and the *Judge* would have preferred him unto the higher Imployments, . . . if he had not been by Death prevented.
>
> But before he could appear to do much at the *Pen,* . . . he was called upon to do something at the *Sword;* . . . when there were Soldiers to be raised by Order from Queen *Elizabeth* for the *French* Service, in the time of King *Henry* the Fourth, the Young Sparks about *Northampton* were none of them willing to enter into the Service, until a *Commission* was given unto

40. *Knole and the Sackvilles,* 1922, pp. 78–81.

our Young *Dudley* to be their *Captain;* and then presently there were *Fourscore* that Listed under him. At the Head of these he went over into the Low Countries.

Augustine Nicolls, Mrs. Purefoy's son by her first marriage, was admitted to the Middle Temple in 1575, called to the bar in 1583, knighted by King James I in 1603, Judge of the Common Pleas in 1612, and Chancellor to Charles, Prince of Wales, in 1615. He died suddenly in 1616, while on circuit, at the age of fifty-seven. No young man could have had a more excellent patron and employer. Thomas Fuller wrote of him, in his *History of the Worthies of England* (1662):

> He was freely preferred one of the Judges of the Common Pleas. I say freely, King James commonly calling him the Judge that would give no money. . . . He was renowned for his special Judiciary Endowments; Patience to hear both parties all they could say, a happy memory, a singular sagacity, . . . exemplary integrity, even to the rejection of gratuities after judgement given.
>
> His forbearing to travail on the Lord's day, wrought a reformation on some of his own Order. He loved plain and profitable Preaching, being wont to say, "I know not what you call Puritanical Sermons; but they come neerest to my Conscience."

The manor house at Faxton, an unassuming dwelling-place in an isolated hamlet, was yet a center of generous help to those in need, and of hospitality for the serious public men of the county. It was maintained and cherished, after Richard Purefoy's death in 1590, by three generations; John Bridges, in his *History and Antiquities of Northamptonshire* (1791), records the inscription "on the archway fronting the old manor":

> Tres successivi possessores,—
> Anna, Augustinus & Franciscus,

Tribus principibus invicem succedentibus,
Elizabetha, Jacobo & Carolo. MDCXXV.[41]

and another which read: "A.D. 1625—The first year of Charles the
First. Be not displeased with this inadequate structure, for it is
the small work of three blood-relations during three reigns." After
the death of Francis Nicolls, the judge's nephew and heir, the
estate was overtaken by progressive decay, and during World War
II even the road that led to the hamlet was swallowed up by a
giant airfield. In the nineteen-fifties a pilgrim to Faxton, traveling
on foot down one long green slope of pasture-meadow and up
another, could find what was left of the home-base of Thomas
Dudley's early manhood: two inhabited farm cottages, a grassy
mound where the manor house once stood, a derelict row of
almshouses, and the tiny, primitive church of St. Denis, decon-
secrated and vandalized. No trace remained of Mrs. Purefoy's
simple tomb, described by Bridges; the only touch of dignity in the
desecrated nave was the handsome wall-monument where the
effigy of Judge Nicolls, in Elizabethan ruff and scarlet robe, knelt
at a desk, with marble figures of Justice, Wisdom, Fortune, and
Charity attendant on him. Since then the monument has been
removed, presumably to a place of safekeeping, and the little
church has been razed to the ground.

The Judge's papers were scattered and largely lost sight of
when the good days of Faxton came to an end, so there is no
available evidence to corroborate Mather's narrative or clarify the
dates in this period of Thomas Dudley's life.[42]

41. "Three successive possessors, Anne, Augustine and Francis, under
three princes, succeeding one after another, Elizabeth, James and Charles.
1625." (Vol. II, p. 92.)

42. The Marquess of Northampton has informed me that he has no muster-
rolls of 1595–97 for the Yardley Hastings–Castle Ashby area, and the name
of Thomas Dudley does not appear in any of the surviving Northamptonshire musters of that period that I have examined.

It does seem probable, however, that Dudley became the "clerk," or secretary, of Judge Nicolls when he left Lord Compton's service, and continued so until the call came for volunteers to assist King Henry of Navarre against the Spanish enemy. Then, if Mather's account, which was undoubtedly based on the truth, can be credited, he accepted a commission and went off to war at the head of a small detachment. His military experience was brief and bloodless, as the *Magnalia* tells us:

> The Post assigned unto him with his Company, was after at the Siege of *Amiens*, before which the *King* himself was now Encamped; but the Providence of God so Ordered it, that when both Parties were drawn forth in Order to Battel, a Treaty of *Peace* was vigorously set on Foot, which diverted the Battel that was expected. Captain *Dudley* hereupon returned into *England*.

The Spaniards who had occupied Amiens surrendered to the combined forces of the French and English without any serious attempt at resistance in September 1597, and some of the Queen's troops in that sector came home for demobilization. Dudley then, "settling himself about *Northampton*," as the *Magnalia* continues,

> . . . married a Gentlewoman whose Extract and Estate were Considerable; and the Scituation of his Habitation after this helped him to enjoy the Ministry of Mr. *Dod*, Mr. *Cleaver*, Mr. *Winston*, and Mr. *Hildersham*, all of them Excellent and Renowned Men; which *Puritan Ministry* so seasoned his Heart with a Sense of Religion, that he was a Devout and Serious Christian . . . all the rest of his Days. The Spirit of *Real Christianity* in him now also disposed him unto *Sober Non-Conformity*; and from this time, although none more hated the *Fanaticisms* and *Enthusiasms* of Wild *Opinionists*, he became a *Judicious Dissenter* from the *Unscriptural Ceremonies* retained in the Church of *England*.

Thomas probably returned directly to Faxton and resumed his clerkship to Judge Nicolls, lived there until his marriage, and kept the same occupation until the Judge's death in 1616. His wife was the daughter of Edmonde Yorke, a substantial yeoman of Cotton End in the parish of Hardingstone, two miles south of Northampton. The register of the church of St. Edmund contains the entry: "Thomas Dudley and Dorothy Yorke married the 25th of April, 1603."

The young man's character—he was at this time twenty-six years old—appears to have become firmly established by this point in his career. From each of his previous experiences, educational, courtly, legal, and military, he had gained knowledge and training that were to be of value to him throughout his life. He must often, during his pageship and his army service, have been faced with a choice between adventure and sound respectability. Adventure of a most unusual kind awaited him, but he could not have foreseen this in his early years; in these he seemed always to take the step that brought him, at each crossroad of decision, towards a more sober and practical way of life, and that increased his power to accept and fulfill serious responsibility.

It is not surprising that the Puritan leaders mentioned by Mather, whom Dudley would have met at Faxton, influenced him profoundly. For this was a time when his own solid sense of values must have been concerned with the anxieties and perplexities of the world around him, a world which, in his own country at any rate, mourned the passing of the vigorous spirit of Queen Elizabeth's reign and contemplated with some apprehension and disaccord the character of her successor.

The Puritan preacher proferred to a multitude in his own age what seemed enlightenment and a new freedom . . . a counsel of courage, a vision of adventure, . . . a program of

self-discipline for making adventure a success, a prospect of success certain to be attained sooner or later. . . . The Puritan
code . . . was the program of an active, not a monastic or con-
templative life. The saints stripped themselves for battle, and
only as the battle waxed hot or desperate did they degenerate
into the fanatical iconoclasts of familiar tradition. . . .

John Dod, gathering his flock about him, opening his door
to all comers, sitting down at the head of a full table, talking
himself thirsty and calling for a draught of wine and beer
mixed, was no bigoted ascetic, though he did disapprove of
stage plays, dancing and card-playing. The saint had no reason
to fear the world or run away from it. Rather he must go forth
into it and do the will of God there.[43]

Serious-minded as he was, the spiritual excitement implicit in
the teaching of Puritanism must have fascinated the young law-
secretary who, a quarter-century later, at the age of fifty-three,
still had the courage to embark as second in command with the
expedition that was to create another England, on the far shore of
an all-but-uncharted sea. Courage was equally needed by anyone
who felt compelled by conscience to become an acknowledged
Puritan in the early years of King James I's reign. At the Hampton
Court conference in 1604, the king had angrily refused to tolerate
any nonconformity to the established rituals of the Church of
England, saying "I shall make them conform themselves or I
will harry them out of the land." Many of his subjects petitioned
him to reconsider this harsh and dangerous decision, among them
a group of influential citizens and clergy in Northamptonshire.
How well they succeeded is shown in a letter from Sir Dudley
Carleton to Ralph Winwood, dated the 20th February, 1604/5;

The poor Puritan ministers have been ferrited out in all
Corners, and some of them suspended, others deprived of their

43. William Haller, *The Rise of Puritanism*, New York, 1938, pp. 36–37,
123.

Livings. Certaine Lecturers are silenced, and a Crew of Gentlemen of Northampton Shire (who put up a Petition to the King in their Behalfe) told roundly of their Boldness, both at the Councell Table and Star Chamber: And Sir Francis Hastings for drawing the Petition . . . put from his Lieutenancy and Justiceship of Peace in his Shire: Sir Edward Montague and Sir Valentine Knightly, for refusing to subscribe to a Submission, have the like Sentence: The rest upon Acknowledgement of a Fault have no more said to them.[44]

The register of the church of All Saints in Northampton records the next significant event in Dudley's life, the baptism of his first child: "1608. November. *Samuell filius Thome Dudley bapt fuit xxx die.*" From a few of Judge Nicolls's letters, owned by the Northamptonshire Record Society, it can be concluded that, although his work was centered in London, he also concerned himself with legal matters in his own county and spent a good deal of time there. During these years, until the Judge's death in 1616, Dudley was probably living in Northampton and acting as Sir Augustine's agent there, and perhaps attending his employer when he was in London.

No baptismal record has been found to indicate the place and time of birth of the Dudley's second child. She was named Anne, probably in honor of Mrs. Purefoy, and her first dated poem, "Upon a Fit of Sickness. *Anno* 1632. *Aetatis Suae* 19," tells us that she was born either in 1612 or 1613. It is possible that her birthday was on the 20th March, for she used this date twice, in making presentations, that had great personal significance for her, of two major pieces of her work. The first was the dedication to her father, in forty-four lines of verse, of her two long poems, "The Four Elements" and "Of the four Humours in Mans Con-

---

44. *Memorials of Affairs of State in the Reigns of Queen Elizabeth and King James I*, ed. E. Sawyer, 1725, Vol. 2, p. 48.

stitution"; in the second edition of her poems this dedication is followed by the date: "March 20. 1642." The second appearance of this date is at the end of a short letter in which she bequeathed the manuscript of her prose "Meditations Divine and morall" to her son Simon Bradstreet; the letter, in her own hand, is dated "March 20, 1664." There is no other apparent reason why Anne Bradstreet chose the 20th March for the signing of these testimonials, so it seems permissible to guess that this may have been the date of her own birth. It will be remembered that in England and her colonies during the seventeenth century, indeed until 1752, the year was reckoned to begin officially not on the 1st January but on Lady Day, the 25th March, and that the modern method of showing the difference between contemporary and present-day dating of that three-month period is to give both dates, as for example 16th February, 1659/60. Anne Bradstreet indicated that she was nineteen years old in the year 1632; if she was born on the 20th March, 1612/13, her nineteenth birthday would have come on the 20th March, 1631/32, or, as she would have calculated, five days before the beginning of the year 1632. If her birthday *was* on the 20th March she could not have been born in 1611/12, for then her twentieth birthday would have fallen just before the year 1632 began, for her, on the 25th March. I shall therefore take the arbitrary step of supposing that she was born in 1613, as we now reckon it, and shall use that year in referring to her age at any given time during her life.

The first documentary evidence of Anne's existence is in the will of Edmonde Yorke of Cotton End, of which Thomas Dudley was an executor, dated the 16th November, 1614:

Item. I do geve to my three grandchildren, that is to say to Samuell Dudley and Abygaill Greene forty shillinges apeec and one silver spoon a peec and to Anne Dudley twentie shillinges and one silver spone to be delivered unto them at their severall ages of one and twentye yeares or before if my wif shall thincke fytt.[45]

At the age of one and twenty years Anne was three thousand miles away from Northamptonshire, and whether or not she ever received her grandfather's legacy is unlikely to be known. The old symbolism of the silver spoon was not, however, belied in her life, for in spite of the dangers and hardships that were in store for her she was never, in a material sense, poor. And her destiny held two gifts of more worth than worldly riches, a happy and fruitful marriage, and the power to translate her thoughts into verse that was acclaimed in her own time and that is still, three hundred years after her life's end, read with respect and pleasure.

45. *Cal. Northants. and Rutland Wills, 1510–1652; Northants. Registry of Wills*, Series I, Book VIII, p. 137.

CHAPTER TWO

Childhood and Education

"In my young years, . . . I began to make
conscience of my wayes."

(ANNE BRADSTREET—*Religious Experiences
and Occasional Pieces*)

Anne Dudley's earliest childhood was, it appears, spent in North-amptonshire, while her father continued as Judge Nicolls's law-clerk, and for a brief period after the Judge's death in 1616, while he was awaiting his next occupation. Thomas Dudley and his family, although living in Northampton, probably spent a good deal of their time at Faxton, and in both of these places they must have been members of a very serious-minded social group. The land-owning knights and squires of the county who were Judge Nicolls's friends were also in many instances the patrons of the nonconformist clergymen who, as they increased in influence and numbers, were ever more threatened by the authority of the Established Church.

There was neither frivolity nor complacency in the lives of these people, though there was substantial comfort in the great houses and a proverbial hospitality in even the humblest cottages of the clergy. Wealth and energy were both, by scriptural precept, to be devoted to the service of God and the advancement of His kingdom on the earth. The children Samuel and Anne Dudley, born into an atmosphere so weighted with the sense of sober and limitless responsibility, must have become aware of that as soon as they were conscious of anything. What Anne wrote, as a grown woman preparing a spiritual legacy for her own children, about the beginnings of her attitude towards life, may seem overly sanctimonious to a modern reader. But it is a typical affirmation from a seventeenth-century Puritan childhood.

> In my young years about 6. or 7. as I take it I began to make conscience of my wayes, and what I knew was sinfull as lying, disobedience to parents, etc. I avoided it. If at any time I was overtaken with ye like evills, it was a great Trouble. I could not rest 'till by prayer I had confest it unto God. I was also troubled at ye neglect of Private Dutyes tho: too often tardy that way. I also found much comfort in reading ye Scriptures, especially those places I thought most concerned my Condition, and as I grew to have more understanding, so ye more Solace I took in them.[1]

We should not be unduly skeptical of Anne Bradstreet's statement that she was able to read the Bible, and apply its teachings to her own needs, at such a tender age. A book that was published at the time of her birth gives us a clear picture of how children were taught in her day, and shows that she did not exaggerate. John Brinsley, a Puritan schoolmaster of Ashby-de-la-Zouche in Leicestershire, urged in his *Ludus Literarius* (1612), that the "Elementarie," or English reading and spelling lessons, be begun if possible with "a childe not foure yeares old," in a

---

1. MS. of Anne Bradstreet's legacy to her children, in the hand of her son the Reverend Simon Bradstreet, p. 44, Stevens Memorial Library, North Andover, Massachusetts; first printed entire, with the title of "Religious Experiences and Occasional Pieces," in *The Works of Anne Bradstreet,* ed. John Harvard Ellis, Charlestown (Mass.), 1867, p. 3.

class or school that might be conducted by "anyone who can reade":

> Thus may any poore man or woman enter the little ones in a towne together; and make an honest poore living of it, or get somewhat towards helping the same. Also the Parents who have any learning, may enter their little ones, playing with them, at dinners, and suppers, or as they sit by the fire, and find it very pleasant delight. . . .
>
> Thus they may go thorow their Abcie, and Primer. . . . After these they may reade over other English bookes. Amongst which, the Psalmes in metre would be one, because children will learne that booke with most readinesse and delight. . . . Then the Testament, . . . *the Schoole of Vertue* . . . And after it *the Schoole of good manners.*

It is not difficult to imagine Thomas Dudley, who made such excellent use of his own education, as a conscientious father "entering" his son Samuel, and a few years later his daughters, Anne and her young sister Patience who was probably born in 1615 or 1616.

One of Anne Bradstreet's most successful poetic images, introducing the first allegorical speaker in her poem "Of the four Ages of Man," shows how early her mind took cognizance of the inclemencies and perplexities of life:

> Childhood was cloth'd in white & green to show
> His spring was intermixed with some snow;
> Upon his head nature a Garland set
> Of Primrose, Daizy & the Violet.
> Such cold mean flowrs the spring puts forth betime
> Before the sun hath throughly heat the clime.

Orthodox piety then conducts the flower-decked small figure through a melancholy speech on the miseries of infancy and the first stirrings of predestined sin in the hapless child:

In Rattles, Baubles and such toyish stuff,
My then ambitious thoughts were low enough:
My high-born soul so straightly was confin'd,
That its own worth it did not know nor mind:
This little house of flesh did spacious count,
Through ignorance all troubles did surmount;
Yet this advantage had mine ignorance
Freedom from envy and from arrogance.

*   *   *

This was mine innocence, but ah! the seeds
Lay raked up of all the cursed weeds
Which sprouted forth in mine ensuing age,
As he can tel that next comes on the stage:
But yet let me relate before I go
The sins and dangers I am subject to,
Stained from birth with *Adams* sinfull fact,
Thence I began to sin as soon as act:
A perverse will, a love to what's forbid,
A serpents sting in pleasing face lay hid:

*   *   *

As many are my sins, so dangers too;
For sin brings sorrow, sickness death and woe:
And though I miss the tossings of the mind,
Yet griefs in my frail flesh I still do find.

While, as a child, Anne Dudley was absorbing the Calvinist gravity that hung heavy in the air around her, she had her earliest instruction in physical pain. The first of many illnesses, that brought her suffering throughout her life but never embittered her character or kept her from enjoying a full measure of experience, is recorded next in her spiritual memoir:

In a long fitt of sickness which I had on my bed I often communed with my heart, and made my Supplication to the most High who sett me free from that affliction.

Yet Anne must have been a happy child in spite of these sobering impressions. She was living with devoted parents, companioned by a brother and a sister, in as much security as a Puritan family could expect in those days. And she had already made the discovery, which never lost its lustre for her, of the fascination of the printed page.

Thomas Dudley's horizon was also widening during these years. Mather's *MS. Life* tells us that

> Mr. Dudley began to be well known in those places where his abode was, and by being a follower of Mr. Dod, he came into the knowledge of the Lord Say and Lord Compton and other persons of quality, by whose means he was afterwards commended to the service of the Earl of Lincoln, who was then a young man and newly come into the possession of that Earldom.

Dudley probably met the celebrated Puritan preacher John Dod, and was converted by him, soon after his return from the siege of Amiens in 1597. At this time Dod was holding the living of Hanwell in Oxfordshire, near the Northamptonshire border, and also lecturing frequently in Banbury. This man whom John Cotton called "the chief of our people," in a letter written from New England in 1634, had already, at the beginning of the century, attracted a large following. He was an accomplished theologian, trained at Jesus College, Cambridge, tireless in his calling and of a disciplined and holy way of life. At the same time he was full of humor and friendliness. A group of Cambridge undergraduates were so annoyed by his speaking out against drunkenness that they waylaid him on a journey and forced him to dismount and preach to them, with a roadside stump for a pulpit, on a text of their choosing, the word "malt." He did so with such good-natured yet telling argument that his small but rowdy congregation must have been quite nonplussed. His "Sermon on Malt" [2] is well worth reading as a witty homiletic *tour de force.*

Dod began to preach at Hanwell in about 1585, a few years after a son and heir had been born to Sir Richard Fiennes at nearby Broughton Castle. As this child, who was to be the first Viscount Saye and Sele, grew up and had his education at Winchester and at New College, Oxford, he must often have heard John Dod extolling, in his sermons, a life of action and achievement for the Christian pilgrim. Young William Fiennes chose this pattern for his own career, and became one of the most forceful of the Puritan peers in Parliament, later to be known as "Old Subtilty" for his strategic leadership in the Civil War. The Oxford chronicler Anthony Wood, always a staunch Royalist, commented somewhat bitterly on Lord Saye and Sele's early political activities:

The truth is, he being ill natur'd, cholerick, severe and rigid, and withal highly conceited of his own worth, did expect great matters at Court; but they failing, he sided therefore with the discontented party the Puritan, and took all occasions cunningly to promote a Rebellion. For so it was, that several years before the Civil War began, he being looked upon at that time the Godfather of that Party, had meetings of them in his house at Broughton, where was a room and passage thereunto, which his Servants were prohibited to come near; and when they were of a complete number, there would be great noises and talkings heard among them, to the admiration of those that lived in the house, yet could they never discern their Lords Companions. At other times he would be present at their meetings in the house of Knightley at Fawsley in Northamptonshire; where, as at other places in the Kingdom, they had their Council Chambers and chief Speakers.[3]

2. See *A Book of Seventeenth-Century Prose*, ed. R. P. T. Coffin and A. M. Witherspoon, New York, 1929, pp. 456–57.

3. *Athenae Oxonienses*, Vol. II, 1692, p. 178.

Lord Saye and Sele had probably just come into his inheritance when Thomas Dudley was presented to him by John Dod. The fact that there was an early link of blood-relationship between the families of Fiennes and Dudley [4] perhaps made him take an interest in the Puritan secretary of the celebrated Judge Nicolls. That Dudley gained the young nobleman's respect is proven, at any rate, by the important part he was called upon to take, some years later, in the affairs of the family of Fiennes.

At the beginning of King James I's reign John Dod, along with many other prominent Puritan preachers, was "silenced" for non-conformity. That is, he was dismissed from his pulpit at Hanwell by order of Dr. Bridges, the Bishop of Oxford. He was thus, in theory, outlawed from the practice of his profession and the gaining of a livelihood for himself, his wife, and their twelve children. Actually it was impossible to terminate the career of a man with so great a following among all ranks of society in his own territory. Like most of the nonconforming clergymen of this time, he moved from one friendly living, in the gift of a Puritan squire or nobleman, to another, always hounded by Episcopal authority, yet never truly defeated.

According to the Puritan biographer Samuel Clarke, in his *General Martyrologie* (1677), Dod managed to preach for a few years at Fenny Compton in Warwickshire, then went, at the invitation of his friend Sir Erasmus Dryden, to Canons Ashby in Northamptonshire. Here the thirteenth-century church, a surviving fragment of a priory of Austin canons, was a "peculiar," or private family chapel exempt from direct diocesan control. But even in this seclusion the royal displeasure sought him out, as Clarke wrote,

4. See Adlard, *Sutton-Dudleys and Dudleys,* Pedigree A (Part 2); Dean Dudley, *History of the Dudley Family,* Supplement, p. 8.

upon a complaint made against him by Bishop Neal, to King James, who commanded Archbishop Abbott [of Canterbury] to silence him. Then he ceased for some time to preach publiquly . . . being sent for far and near to such as were wounded in spirit, to whom the Lord made him extensively useful.

While Dod was living at Canons Ashby, which is within twenty miles of the city of Northampton, Thomas Dudley would have been able to visit him without difficulty. And it seems possible that Dudley and his wife took Anne soon after her birth to the home of the Drydens to be baptized by the revered minister. All documents of the church at Canons Ashby prior to 1697 have disappeared, perhaps as the result of a Civil War skirmish between Royalist attackers and Parliamentarian defenders that was fought around and actually within the ancient building, causing considerable damage to it. So no local evidence exists to show how often, at the time of Anne's birth, the church was used for services by Dod. But the Archbishop's order to silence him was sent in November 1611 to the Bishop of Peterborough,[5] so it is probable that in the years immediately after this interdiction the hunted clergyman, as Clarke reported, refrained from performing any religious rites except behind the safely closed doors of a private dwelling.

It is a pleasant conjecture that Anne Dudley's unrecorded christening may have taken place in the scarlet-walled Elizabethan drawing-room, with its handsome double-coved ceiling and carved stone chimney-breast, of Canons Ashby House. Two great poets, Edmund Spenser, a friend of Sir Erasmus, and the old knight's grandson John Dryden, are known to have been present at various times in that splendid room. So a child whose thoughts were to be

5. Jeremy Collier, *Ecclesiastical History of Great Britain*, ed. Lathbury, 1852, Vol. IX, p. 37.

so much concerned with poetry could not have been taken, for secret baptism, to a more auspicious place in which to be made a member of the Church of Christ.

Finally, in about 1625, John Dod became the vicar of Fawsley in Northamptonshire, and was able to continue his ministry there until 1645, when he died at the age of ninety-six. The vast Tudor mansion of the Knightleys at Fawsley stands far from the highway in its widespread park, and the nearby church holds a magnificent collection of family tombs. The name of Knightley is a notable one in Puritan annals; as early as 1588 the "Mar-Prelate" press was set up in an attic room at Fawsley, and one of its attacks on the bishops, *Epitome*, was printed there. It is said that the author, John Penry, one of those who wrote under the pseudonym "Martin Mar-Prelate," walked daily in the great park, dressed as a court gallant, to allay suspicion as to what was going on in the house. But the secret leaked out, and Sir Richard Knightley was arraigned before the court of Star Chamber and severely censured for harboring the seditious press. He was summoned again to this court in 1605, with his son Sir Valentine, and they were both fined and deprived of their county offices for signing a petition on behalf of the silenced ministers. Sir Richard died in 1615, and Sir Valentine, his heir, in 1618. The estate descended to another Richard, the Puritan squire who presented the living of Fawsley to John Dod and who, in 1627, was imprisoned for refusing to contribute to the forced loan levied by King Charles I.

The Drydens and the Knightleys, as well as Lord Saye and Sele, were influential advisers for Thomas Dudley to have found as a result of his admiration and friendship for John Dod. Lord Compton, whom Mather included among Dudley's patrons at this time (and who became the Earl of Northampton in 1618), would naturally have remembered him as a page in his household, but the Comptons never swerved from loyalty to the Crown and the Established Church. The second Earl of Northampton was killed, in 1643, fighting for the king at Hopton Heath, and one of his sons was Bishop of London after the Restoration. The first Earl could hardly have approved of the transformation of his erstwhile page into an avowed Puritan, but nevertheless he may have been willing to say a good word for him when the time came.

It must have been largely through Lord Saye and Sele's interest that his cousin, the Earl of Lincoln, engaged Thomas Dudley as his steward when he came into his title and inheritance in 1619. Theophilus Fiennes-Clinton was only nineteen years old when his father died, leaving a large estate in Lincolnshire, with Tattershall Castle and Sempringham Manor as the chief family seats, as well as "town houses" in Boston and London. He also bequeathed to his heir a staggering burden of debts, accumulated by his quarrelsome and extravagant father, Henry, the second Earl of Lincoln, who died in 1615.

Young Theophilus acquired in addition, on his father's death, the titular responsibility for a large family. His mother the dowager Countess, born Elizabeth Knyvet, his younger brothers Charles, Knyvet, and John, and his sisters Frances, Arbella, Susan, Dorcas, and Sara, were all apparently living in the manor house at Sempringham at this time.[6] The youngest of these children must have been about Anne Dudley's age, that is six or seven, when she made the journey with her parents from the Northamptonshire hills to the flat fen-country of Lincolnshire, to begin a new life in the household of the Fiennes-Clinton family. It is not known exactly when Thomas Dudley entered the Earl's service, but the record of the baptism of his third daughter, Sarah, on the 23rd

6. According to *Inquisition post mortem* (397/67), and will of Earl Thomas (P.C.C. 90 Parker), cited in G. E. C[okayne], *Complete Peerage*, ed. H. A. Doubleday and Lord Howard de Walden, 1929, Vol. VII, p. 696, notes (b) and (c).

July, 1620, in the register of St. Andrew's Church at Sempringham, shows that the Dudleys were settled in their new home by that date.

Tattershall Castle, the imposing fortified palace of mediaeval brickwork, built by Ralph Lord Cromwell while he was treasurer to King Henry VI, from 1433 to 1443, came to the Fiennes-Clintons by royal grant in 1551. The second and third Earls of Lincoln are known to have lived there, and Theophilus, the fourth Earl, held it for the Parliament forces through the Civil War, during which it was attacked and severely damaged. After that the buildings around the great central tower fell into ruins, and the tower itself was only a shell by 1912, when Lord Curzon of Kedleston purchased it from the Fiennes-Clinton descendants, restored it admirably, and presented it, in 1914, to the nation.

It is not likely that many days of Anne Dudley's childhood were passed in the rather forbidding castle of Tattershall, for the surviving records, from the ten or eleven years during which Thomas Dudley was in close touch with the Earl of Lincoln, make it appear that the Earl's household was fairly constantly established at Sempringham. Here in the rich farming country on the edge of the fens, the family seat was a manor house of rambling design and mixed architecture. Its oldest parts had been farm-buildings of the great Gilbertine Priory, mother-house of the English order founded by St. Gilbert of Sempringham in or about 1135. The priory flourished for four hundred years, until the dissolution of the monasteries. In 1538 King Henry VIII granted its lands and buildings, after the valuable lead had been stripped from the roofs, to Edward, Lord Clinton, first Earl of Lincoln, who used the monastic ruin as a quarry for the enlarging of the medieval farmhouse into a residence for himself.

Shortly before the Second World War a complete excavation of the site was made, to determine the dimensions of the priory

church, one of the largest, it was found, ever to have been built.[7]
The archaeologists uncovered the foundations of the manor house,
with its medieval core and later additions. They also verified the
existence of a more ambitious project, the "passing fair house" as
it is called in Camden's *Britannia*,[8] which the first Earl began to
build, at the west end of the priory church, but never completed.
Apparently soon after his death, in 1585, the unfinished building
was partly demolished in such a way that its three sides formed
wide terrace-walls around a garden court, directly south of the
manor house. The mounded outline of those walls can still be
seen, a little distance to the southwest of the Norman parish
church where Gilbert of Sempringham worshipped as a boy. That
ancient shrine, which has outlasted its own village, the splendid
priory, and the houses of the Earls of Lincoln, now stands alone
on its gently sloping hill, with not another building in sight in all
the green fields that surround it.

Sempringham manor house, which was occupied by the second
and third Earls, was probably still receiving additions when it
came into the possession of Theophilus, the fourth Earl, in 1619.
The report on the excavation of St. Gilbert's priory mentions
documents in a private collection in Lincolnshire which show
that the building accounts at Sempringham were settled in 1626.[9]
If this is true, it indicates that work on the house was finished,
and the bills were paid, while Thomas Dudley was the Earl's
estate-manager.

On all sides it seems that Lord Lincoln was fortunate in having
been persuaded, as Mather wrote in the *MS. Life*,

7. Rose Graham and Hugh Braun, "Excavations on the Site of Sempringham Priory," in *Journal of the British Archaeological Association*, 3rd Series,
Vol. V, 1940, pp. 73–101.
8. *Britain, or a Chorographicall Description . . . of England, Scotland,
and Ireland, . . .* Written first in Latine by William Camden. . . . Translated newly into English by Philemon Holland, 1610, p. 534.
9. These documents are not at present available for examination.

. . . to entertain Mr. Dudley as his Steward to manage his whole estate, who though it was so involved with many great debts, amounting to near twenty thousand pounds, yet by his prudent, careful, and faithful management of the affairs of that family, he in a few years found means to discharge all of those great debts, wherein the young Earl was so ingulphed, that he saw little hope of ever wading through them all. . . .

And another great and good service he did that family by procuring a match between the daughter of the Lord Say and this Theophilus, . . . who was so wise, virtuous and every way so well an accomplished lady that she proved a great blessing to the whole family.

The arranging of the marriage of the Lady Bridget Fiennes, daughter of his patron and friend Lord Saye and Sele, to her cousin, must have been one of Dudley's first services to the Earl, for by 1622 the young Countess had already borne a child. In that year she received an unusual compliment from her mother-in-law, in the shape of a little book of twenty-one pages, printed at Oxford and entitled *The Countesse of Lincolnes Nurserie*. It is an urgent plea to mothers, on the grounds of health and of religious and moral duty, to nurse their own babies. The dowager Countess dedicated this "first work of mine that ever came into print," to "the right honourable, and approved virtuous Lady, Bridget Countesse of Lincolne," and regretting that she herself had been persuaded to entrust her own eighteen children to the care of largely unsatisfactory wet-nurses, commended her daughter-in-law's behavior:

Your rare example, hath given an excellent approbation to the matter contained in this Booke; for you have passed by all excuses, and have ventured upon, and doe go on with that loving act of a loving mother; in giving the sweete milk of your own breasts, to your owne child.

The most interesting aspect of this curious work is the authorship of its sententious introduction, which begins: "The general consent of too many mothers in an unnatural practise (most Christian Reader) hath caused one of the Noblest and Fairest hands in this land to set pen to paper"; and ends with some lines that are more endowed with feeling than with clarity:

> Blest is the land where Sons of Nobles raigne.
> Blest is the land where Nobles teach their traine.
> To Church for blisse Kings, Queenes, should Nurses be.
> To state its blisse great Dames Babes nurse to see.
> Go then Great booke of Nursing plead the Cause.
> Teach High'st, low'st, all, it's Gods and Natures lawes.

This testimonial is signed "T. L." and is the last known published writing of the Elizabethan poet and physician Thomas Lodge, who in 1622 was a worn-out man of sixty-five, with only three more years to live. C. J. Sisson, in *Thomas Lodge and Other Elizabethans* (1933), makes this comment on his final appearance in print:

> Lodge supports the Countess of Lincoln's thesis with medical and moral argument, and concludes his preface with the last of his verses, poor, angular, and trite. . . . To be invited by so great a lady to give in print his learned sanction to her treatise was the last spark of the almost extinguished glow of his dignity.

From his middle years onwards Lodge was known as a Roman Catholic recusant. This makes one wonder how he came to have an established friendship, as the tone of the preface seems to indicate that it was, with the Puritan Countess. When he was a young man Lodge took part in two free-booting voyages; during the first, to the Canaries in 1588, he wrote his best-known romance, *Rosalynde: Euphues Golden Legacie,* which was published in 1590. On the second expedition, to South America in 1591, one of his companions was Anthony Knyvet; through this association he may have been introduced to Elizabeth Knyvet, the wife of Thomas, third Earl of Lincoln and the mother of Theophilus, the fourth Earl.

During the last decade of his life Lodge was practising medicine in London and was constantly involved in law suits and financial difficulties. In 1621 he published *A Learned Summary upon the Famous Poeme of William of Saluste Lorde of Bartas, Translated out of French*. Here he was dealing, curiously enough for a Roman Catholic, with the work of a Huguenot writer, Guillaume de Salluste, Sieur du Bartas (1544–90), whose long verse-description of the creation of the world was published in Paris in two parts, *La Sepmaine* in 1578 and *La Seconde Sepmaine* in 1584. A commentary on the first part, by Simon Goulart, appeared in Paris in 1582, and it was this work that Lodge translated for the benefit of the many English admirers of Du Bartas. When the whole ponderous epic itself was rendered into English by Joshua Sylvester, as *Bartas: His Devine Weekes and Workes*, in 1605, it gained an immediate popularity that sent it through edition after edition until almost the middle of the century. Spenser's friend Gabriel Harvey called Du Bartas "the French Solomon," Sidney and Milton both showed, at times, his influence, and among the lesser poets who were spellbound by Du Bartas in Sylvester's version was Anne Bradstreet.

The dowager Countess of Lincoln, being sufficiently a woman of letters to have a small book of her own in print, was probably also an admirer of Du Bartas, and familiar with Thomas Lodge's translation of Goulart's commentary on his work. She would have been concerned to provide a suitable early education for her younger children, three sons and five daughters, who remained at home after Theophilus became a student at Queens' College, Cambridge, in 1618, with the Puritan leader and dean of the college, Dr. John Preston, as his tutor.[10] But it must have been difficult in remote Lincolnshire to obtain as needed the services of satisfactory teachers. It seems possible that the Countess, admiring Lodge's literary endowments and knowing the hard circumstances of his later years, offered him the hospitality of Sempringham from time to time and in return received from him some instruction in literature for her children. If this did happen, it is also possible that young Anne Dudley who, judging by her future displays of erudition was a child with an inquiring mind, came to the notice of Lodge, and that it was this old Elizabethan Catholic poet who introduced to the girl who was to become a Puritan writer in New England the work of Du Bartas, and perhaps that of Spenser and Sidney also. He may too, as a translator of Seneca and Josephus, have brought the authors of antiquity to Anne's attention, and as a physician as well as a poet have fired the enthusiasm for scientific study that shows itself in such of her poems as "The Four Elements" and "Of the four Humours in Mans Constitution."

We know from Anne's own writings that at the age of six or seven she was finding "much comfort in reading the Scriptures"; probably by that time she was also engaged in a variety of more secular studies, thanks to the sympathetic interest of her father and to her presence in a household where the training of young minds must have been constantly in progress. The famous Lucy Hutchinson, in her memoirs of herself and her husband, wrote that while she was growing up in the Tower of London, as the daughter of its lieutenant-governor, Sir Allen Apsley, "When I was about seven years of age, I remember I had at one time eight

10. Irvonwy Morgan, *Prince Charles's Puritan Chaplain*, 1957, p. 28.

tutors in several qualities, languages, music, dancing, writing, and needlework." [11] And the eminent schoolmistress of Tottenham High Cross, Mrs. Bathsua Makin, in her small work that was published anonymously in 1673, *An Essay to Revive the Antient Education of Gentlewomen, in Religion, Manners, Arts & Tongues,* wrote of a distinguished pupil:

> The Princess Elizabeth, daughter to King Charles the First, to whom Mrs. Makin was Tutress, at nine Years old could write, read, and in some measure understand, Latin, Greek, Hebrew, French and Italian. Had she lived, what a Miracle would She have been of her Sex.

Both of these quotations concern girls who were born into a higher social sphere than was Anne Dudley. Yet they are applicable to this middle-class Puritan child because of the fortunate circumstances in which she spent her early years, and because the Elizabethan tradition still influenced the education of women. The great Queen had shown to all the world that the capacities of the female mind were far from manifestly inferior. Richard Mulcaster, headmaster of the Merchant Taylors' and St. Paul's schools, spoke for his era in a book, published in 1581, whose long title is generally condensed to *Positions.*

> I set not yong maidens to publike grammar scholes, . . . I send them not to the universities, having no president thereof in my countrie; I allow them learning, with distinction in degrees, with difference of their calling, with respect to their endes. . . . That yong maidens can learne, nature doth give them, and that they have learned, our experience doth teach us, . . . what forraine example can more assure the world, then our diamond at home?

11. Hutchinson, *Memoirs of Colonel Hutchinson,* ed. E. Rhys, Everyman's Library, 1936, Introduction, p. vii.

He allowed the "yong maidens" what we should consider a very limited time, "commonly till they be about thirtene or fouretene yeares old," to make themselves resemble as nearly as possible his ideal portrait:

> Is not a yong gentlewoman, thinke you, thoroughly furnished, which can reade plainly and distinctly, write faire and swiftly, sing cleare and sweetely, play wel and finely, understand and speake the learned languages, and those tongues also which the time most embraseth, with some Logicall helpe to chop, and some Rhetoricke to brave. . . . Now if she be an honest woman, and a good housewife too, were she not worth the wishing, and worthy the shryning?

A knowledge of the "learned languages," Greek, Latin, and Hebrew, meant also a familiarity with the great works of ancient literature. Roger Ascham's description of his pupil the Lady Jane Grey, reading Plato in the original for pleasure and solace, while the rest of the household was out hunting,[12] shows that women, or those of high rank at any rate, were allowed to develop their minds even before the scholarly Elizabeth ascended the throne. But during the century that followed this was not always the case, and the sponsors of well-born young women were sometimes conservative in their attitude towards female education. As an example of what was offered, to satisfy the intellectual curiosity of a mid-seventeenth-century girl, an apt and entertaining document is Sir Ralph Verney's letter, of 1652, to his god-daughter Nancy Denton.

> Good sweet hart bee not soe covitous; beleeve me a Bible (with ye Common prayer) and a good plaine cattichisme in your Mother Tongue being well read and practised is well worth all the rest and much more suitable to your sex; I know your Father

12. Ascham, *The Schoolmaster* (1570), ed. L. V. Ryan, Ithaca (N.Y.), 1967, pp. 35–36.

thinks this false doctrine, but bee confident your husband will bee of my opinion. In French you cannot bee too cunning, for that language affords many admirable bookes fit for you, as Romances, Plays, Poetry, Stories of illustrious (not learned) Woemen, receipts for preserving, makinge creames and all sorts of cookeryes, ordring your gardens and in Breif all manner of good house-wifery. If you please to have a little patience with yourselfe (without Hebrew, Greeke, or Lattin) when I goe to Paris againe I will send you halfe a dozen of the french bookes to begin your Library.[13]

Anne Dudley's education probably began in 1617, when she was four years old, and continued in one form or another until she was married in 1628. The character and extent of her studies can best be judged by an examination of her writings, which are so varied in subject and so filled with the materials of learning that one wonders how, in those eleven growing years, she managed to absorb so much knowledge and retain it so well in her memory. Among the few English women writers before her none displayed so encyclopaedic a mind, and in the seventeenth century only the Duchess of Newcastle, who soon followed her into print, seems to have possessed the same kind of intellectual avidity. But where the work of the eccentric and remarkable Duchess is often marred by an egotistical showmanship, Anne Bradstreet never lost a sense of proportion about herself. Her spirit was as generous as her memory was capacious, and from her own expressions of admiration and gratitude we can discover a great deal about the books she read and the authors she respected.

Her first consciousness of the joy of reading came from the book that was never to fail her, but through her whole life was to be above all others a constant source of guidance, comfort, and inspiration. The Bible that she used was the Geneva version, pre-

13. *Memoirs of the Verney Family*, ed. Frances Parthenope, Lady Verney, and Margaret M. Verney, Vol. III, 1894, pp. 73–74.

pared by the English Protestant exiles living in Switzerland during
Queen Mary's reign, and first printed there in 1560. The Authorized version of the Bible, translated by order of King James I
and published in 1611, did not come into general use until almost
the middle of the century. The Puritans disliked its renderings of
controversial passages and they continued to prefer both the text
and the marginal comments, that had been approved by John
Calvin himself, of the Geneva Bible. The biblical phrases and expressions that occur in Anne Bradstreet's writings are echoes of
the Geneva text, and sometimes also of the old metrical version
of the Psalms, prepared by Thomas Sternhold and John Hopkins,
and first published entire in 1562.

All the younger members of the Earl of Lincoln's Puritan
household must have received a thoroughgoing religious education, perhaps under the guidance of the renowned Dr. Preston
himself. For the brilliant Cambridge dean, who soon became the
Master of Emmanuel College and Preacher to Lincoln's Inn, and
was a friend of King James, the Prince of Wales, and the Duke of
Buckingham, apparently kept in close touch with the young Earl
whom he had tutored at Queens' College. Mather's *MS. Life* tells
us that Dr. Preston preached at Sempringham, and was often
able, through his "frequent intercourse with the Earl of Lincoln's
family," to give valuable and confidential advice to Thomas
Dudley in his management of the Earl's affairs.

One of the books that Dr. Preston would surely have recommended for youthful readers was Sir Walter Raleigh's *History of
the World*, that majestic philosophical study of the ancient king-
doms of man that was written while Sir Walter was a prisoner in
the Tower of London, and published in 1614. The sombre mag-
nificence of style, the vast narratives of dynastic triumph and
decay, and most of all the ever-present recognition of God's will
and authority in the cycles of history, made this monumental

work, which was generally admired, of particular interest and importance to the Puritans.

Anne Bradstreet probably read the *History* as a cornerstone of her education, and kept it beside her in her adult years as a writer. Her longest and most ambitious work, "The Four Monarchies," is largely a paraphrase in verse of Raleigh's dramatic prose. She referred to him several times directly, calling him "our judicious learned Knight" and "wise" and "noble Raileigh."

Anne's earliest memorial tribute, "An Elegie upon that Honourable and renowned Knight Sir Philip Sidney," makes it clear that she had read with thoughtful and somewhat critical interest her kinsman's *Arcadia*, and his *Astrophel and Stella* as well. Another elegy, "In honour of Du Bartas," reflects the continuing pleasure that she gained from his *Divine Weekes and Workes*, as do many other references to him throughout her poems. *The Faerie Queene* must also have been a part of her youthful reading, for she referred to "Spencers poetry" in a long tribute to Queen Elizabeth, and named him again, citing his lament for the dead "Astrophel," in her elegy on Sidney.

The first of her ambitious efforts in verse that were not addressed to the memory of illustrious human beings was the double set of four poems describing, in allegorical form, the elements and the humors. Her material for this scientific exposition would have come, to a large extent, from Du Bartas's epic on the creation of the world, which Douglas Bush has called "a kind of Albert Memorial of encyclopaedic fundamentalism." [14] As an authority on the four humors Anne mentioned "curious learned Crooke"; this was Helkiah Crooke, M.D., whose *Microcosmographia or a Description of the Body of Man*, first published in 1615, is indeed a curious and learned work. And her father owned a copy of the

14. Bush, *English Literature in the Earlier Seventeenth Century, 1600–1660*, Oxford, 1945, p. 73.

"Regimen of Health," a translation of the popular medieval compilation *Regimen Sanitatis Salerni* that was produced by the famous medical school of Salerno, so his daughter may well have delved into this to find her source for references to Galen and Hippocrates.

As the names of Speed, Camden, "learned Pemble," and Archbishop Ussher appear in her work it seems evident that she was familiar with the writings of these historians. John Speed, first a London tailor and then an accomplished mapmaker, published his *Historie of Great Britaine . . . from Julius Caesar, to our most gracious Soveraigne, King James,* in 1611. William Camden's *Britannia* appeared in Latin in 1586 and in Philemon Holland's translation in 1610; his *Annales Rerum Anglicarum et Hibernicarum regnante Elizabetha* (to 1589) was first printed in 1615, and the complete work, continued to the end of Queen Elizabeth's reign, was translated by R. Norton and published in 1630. Anne could not have read this or the Reverend William Pemble's *Period of the Persian Monarchie* (1631) until after her arrival in New England, but the Latin *Annales* of Camden was among her father's books and he may have instructed her from its contents when she was a child. Also belonging to Thomas Dudley was "yᵉ Turkish History," that is Richard Knolles's *Generall Historie of the Turkes* (1603); this work, which David Nichol Smith ranked with Raleigh's *History of the World* "in its conception of the historian's office and in its literary excellence," [15] was apparently the source for a passage, in Anne's long poem on the four seasons, describing the Emperor Bajazet's meeting with a shepherd.

Along with all these books which she is known to have read, it is probable that there were many others that contributed to her

15. Nichol Smith, *Characters of the Seventeenth Century*, Oxford, 1918, Introduction, p. xv.

education. Such widely respected works as Robert Burton's
Anatomy of Melancholy, Bacon's *Essays* and *The Advancement of
Learning,* Captain John Smith's *General History of Virginia, New
England and the Summer Isles,* and the poetry of Michael Drayton, Samuel Daniel, and the Puritan George Wither, may well
have been available to her, since it is permissible to suppose that,
as a member of the household of the Earl of Lincoln, she had
access to a representative library. The religious writings that were
most favored by the Puritans, from John Foxe's Protestant martyr-
ology *Actes and Monuments,* published in 1563, to the controversial tracts and pamphlets that abounded in the early seventeenth century, had a part in the upbringing of every well-taught
nonconformist child. There was one field of study, however, which
she was unlikely to have been permitted to enter. The Puritan
disapproval of both the spirit and purpose of stage plays was so
pronounced that Anne can hardly have had much opportunity to
read the works of the dramatists of her time, although there are
a few images and phrases in her poems that suggest a possible
familiarity with Shakespeare's plays and sonnets. In "Of the four
Ages of Man," as it was first printed in 1650, the allegorical figure
of Youth, acknowledging the threat of early death, says:

> Of Marrow ful my bones, of Milk my breasts,
> Ceas'd by the gripes of Serjeant Death's Arrests.

The metaphor of the fatal officer was twice used by Sylvester in
his translation of Du Bartas, as "Death, dread Serjeant of th'
eternall Judge," and "Serjeant Death's sad warrant." But Anne
Bradstreet's line seems closer to Hamlet's dying words:

> Had I but time (as this fell Sergeant death
> Is strick'd in his Arrest) oh I could tell you . . . .

When "Of the four Ages of Man" was printed for the second time, in 1678, the two lines above had been deleted. Perhaps their author felt that they indicated too obvious a borrowing, from either Shakespeare or Sylvester, or that the image itself was an overworked one.

Towards the end of her own life Anne Bradstreet wrote a short but poignant elegy for a grandchild in which these lines,

> But plants new set to be eradicate,
> And buds new blown, to have so short a date,

do seem to echo strikingly the familiar passage in Shakespeare's Sonnet 18:

> Rough winds do shake the darling buds of May,
> And summer's lease hath all too short a date.

This possible derivation has been commented upon in detail by Hans Galinsky of Mainz, in an essay concerning Anne Bradstreet's literary relationship to both Du Bartas and Shakespeare.[16] The conclusion at which Galinsky arrives, after a thorough examination of the apparent influence of the two European poets on the New England woman, is that there was a "transformation," as well as a "transplantation," of whatever they contributed to her work. The religious faith that animated all of her writings, however secular in subject matter, the intellectual values of her com-

---

16. H. Galinsky, "Anne Bradstreet, Du Bartas und Shakespeare im Zusammenhang kolonialer Verpflanzung and Umformung europäischer Literatur," *Festschrift für Walther Fischer*, Heidelberg, 1959, pp. 145–80. A review of this essay, in *Seventeenth-Century News*, Vol. XXIII, No. 4 (Winter 1965), p. 60, by Astrid v. Muehlenfels, ends as follows: "Though suggestive rather than conclusive, Galinsky's essay is valuable for its comprehensive survey and estimate of Bradstreet scholarship as well as for its imaginative and challenging ideas for new approaches."

munity, and the individual characteristics of her art, had their effects on the memories that were preserved in her mind. Therefore, as Galinsky writes, "The Calvinist Du Bartas could be transplanted and his baroque style could be simplified; Shakespeare too could be transplanted, but the world-picture of his transplanted sonnet had to be transformed by inner necessity." [17]

Anne's writings show that she did not confine her early studies to the works of her own countrymen, or approximate contemporaries like Du Bartas. I have referred to the Elizabethan emphasis on the importance of the "learned languages" in the education of women; Latin still held its own under the early Stuarts, and French, as the second language of the court, had a more than academic vogue. About a fourth of the identifiable books in Thomas Dudley's small library were in Latin, and the inventory notes, rather scornfully perhaps and with no clues as to their titles: "8 french bookes." [18] Cotton Mather dwelt in some detail on how Dudley taught himself proficiency in Latin, using his grammar-school education as a foundation; his knowledge of French would have been helped by his army service abroad, and further developed by his legal training and his advisory role in the Earl of Lincoln's military and court activities.

His daughter probably acquired an elementary understanding of both languages, but it seems unlikely that she went much beyond that with either of them. Only three Latin words, and two familiar tags, occur in her writings, and in spite of her admiration for Du Bartas she was apparently content to read him in Sylvester's version, for nowhere in her work does a sign of French, except for the word "adieu," appear. But she was fortunate to be a student of history and literature at a time when the authors of anti-

17. Galinsky, *op. cit.* p. 180. The essay has not been published in English; the translation here used was prepared for me by Dr. H. G. Schenk of Oxford University.

18. See Appendix: Thomas Dudley's Books.

quity were gaining a second immortality, as it were, in translations as splendid, in some cases, as the best original English works of the period. So in order to mention familiarly, as she does in several of her poems, Homer, Aristotle, Hesiod, and Xenophon; Pliny, Virgil, Seneca, Ovid, Thucydides, and Plutarch, it was not necessary for her to have read them in the original Greek or Latin.

George Chapman's translations of *The Iliad* and *The Odyssey* were published together in 1616. Anne Bradstreet's knowledge of Aristotle probably came to her not from direct translations of his works but rather from the contemporary cosmology, distilled from his writings by the medieval Scholastic interpreters, which she would have found in Raleigh's *History of the World*, Burton's *Anatomy of Melancholy*, and the poetry of Spenser, Du Bartas, and Sir John Davies. Virgil's *Aeneid*, *Eclogues*, and *Georgics* appeared in a series of English versions, by different hands, from the mid-sixteenth century onwards, and Plutarch's *Lives* had its great rendering by Sir Thomas North in 1579. Philemon Holland, called "the Translator Generall in his Age," presented his Livy in 1600, Pliny's *Natural History* in 1601, Suetonius' *Lives of the Caesars* in 1606, and Xenophon's *Cyropaedia* in 1632. Chapman's Homer was followed in 1618 by his version of the *Georgics* of Hesiod. Ovid's *Metamorphoses* appeared in 1567, as translated by Arthur Golding, and again in 1626, in the rendering which George Sandys, treasurer of the Virginia Company, had worked on during his sojourn in the Jamestown colony from 1621 to 1625. Seneca's tragedies were translated or paraphrased by various writers in the later sixteenth century, and his prose works, in a fine translation by Thomas Lodge, appeared in 1614. The first published work of Thomas Hobbes was his rendering into English, in 1629, of Thucydides' *History of the Peloponnesian War*.

Anne Bradstreet's two references to Plutarch, in "The Four Monarchies," occur in the second, not the first, printing of the long

poem; this has been taken, by John Harvard Ellis in the introduction to his edition of *The Works of Anne Bradstreet* (1867), to
indicate that she did not read the *Lives* until after she had been
in New England for some years, and had written "The Four Monarchies" as it first appeared in 1650. Ellis also cites a revised passage describing the murder of Clitus by Alexander, two lines of
which, that are not in the first edition, are clearly borrowed from
Plutarch's account of the episode. However, Ellis may have been
mistaken in his assumption, for the lines beginning "The Roman
Monarchy," as printed in *The Tenth Muse* in 1650,

> Stout *Romulus, Romes* Founder, and first King,
> Whom vestall *Rhea,* into th' world did bring
> His Father was not *Mars,* as some devis'd,
> But *Aemulus,* in Armour all disguis'd.
> Thus he deceiv'd his Neece, she might not know
> The double injury, he then did doe:

must descend directly from North's Plutarch's story of the usurper
Amulius who, fearing the vengeance of his brother's progeny, first
made his niece a Vestal Virgin and then raped her to ensure her
destruction:

> . . . the mother . . . affirmed she was conceyved of those two
> children, by the god Mars. Howbeit some thincke she was
> deceyved in her opinion: for Amulius that had her maidenhead,
> went to her all armed, and perforce dyd ravishe her.[19]

So it seems more probable that the *Lives* was a part of Anne's
early experience, and that she referred to it again, with the result-

---

19. *The Lives of the Noble Grecians and Romanes . . . By that Grave
Learned Philosopher and Historiographer Plutarke of Chaeronea,* Translated
out of Greeke into French by James Amyot: and out of French into
Englishe by Thomas North. The Nonesuch Press, 1929, Vol. I, p. 35.

ing additional echoes, while editing her text for a second printing.

The names of the other classical authors that she mentioned occur in the first edition of her poems, showing that she encountered these as well in her earlier years. She may have read any or all of the translations I have listed, but on the other hand she could have gleaned a more superficial knowledge of the original authors from her reading of Raleigh and other historians, from collections of old tales like William Painter's *Palace of Pleasure* (1566–67), or from such familiar books as the *Bucolica* of Mantuanus or the *Colloquia Scholastica* of Corderius, both of which, we have noted, were in her father's library. The evidence to be found in her work points to the probability that her discovery and exploration of the masters of antiquity lay somewhere between the popular compilations and the whole galaxy of the great translations.

There is a passage in Anne Bradstreet's poem "In Honour of Du Bartas, 1641," which describes in lively metaphor how she had felt on first reading the *Devine Weekes and Workes*. It makes a fitting conclusion to this largely conjectural discussion of young Anne Dudley's education, for in its almost tongue-tied eagerness, its purely seventeenth-century appraisal of the poet's attainments, and its ingenuous admiration, it can serve as her own affirmation of the delight that she took, even from the beginning, in the general search for knowledge.

> My muse unto a Child I may compare,
> Who sees the riches of some famous Fair,
> He feeds his Eyes, but understanding lacks
> To comprehend the worth of all those knacks:
> The glittering plate and Jewels he admires,
> The Hats and Fans, the Plumes and Ladies tires,
> And thousand times his mazed mind doth wish
> Some part (at least) of that brave wealth was his,
> But seeing empty wishes nought obtain,

At night turns to his Mothers cot again,
And tells her tales, (his full heart over-glad)
Of all the glorious sights his Eyes have had:
But finds too soon his want of Eloquence,
The silly pratler speaks no word of sense;
But seeing utterance fail his great desires,
Sits down in silence, deeply he admires:
Thus weak brain'd I, reading thy lofty stile,
Thy profound learning, viewing other while;
Thy Art in natural Philosophy,
Thy Saint like mind in grave Divinity;
Thy piercing skill in high Astronomy,
And curious insight in Anatomy:
Thy Physick, musick and state policy,
Valour in warr, in peace good husbandry.
Sure lib'ral Nature did with Art not small,
In all the arts make thee most liberal.

CHAPTER THREE

The Prelude to Emigration

"Gather my Saints together unto me, those that
make a covenant with mee with sacrifice."

(PSALMS—L, 5, *Geneva version*)

While Anne Dudley was occupied with her studies, both private
and public circumstances in her world were shaping themselves in
significant ways. Another daughter, Mercy, was born to the Dudleys, probably in 1621, which was also the year of the birth of the
Earl and Countess of Lincoln's first child. And soon after that two
young men, both destined to be among the founders of New
England, came to join the household at Sempringham.

The elder of the two was Isaac Johnson, born in 1600 into a
prominent landowning family of Rutlandshire, and by 1621 an
M.A. of Emmanuel College, Cambridge, and an ordained clergyman. He was endowed with high qualities of mind and spirit, and
with substantial material wealth, but his blood was not noble,
therefore his own father refused to sanction his marriage to the
Earl of Lincoln's sister. The wedding took place, however, and was
recorded in *The Allegation Book of the Bishop of Lincoln:*

April 5, 1623. Isaack Johnson of Sempringham, gent, 22, and
Lady Arbella Fynes of same, spinster, 22. His grandfather,

Rob. Johnson, B.D., Archdeacon of Leicester, consents; also her
mother, the Countess of Lincoln.[1]

Isaac Johnson received valuable lands and property from his
grandfather, and became the leading financial investor in the
colonial enterprise, when plans for this were being made by the
Massachusetts Bay Company. We know very little about the Lady
Arbella, except that the flagship of the migration to New England
was named in her honor, and that she and her husband were
among the first, and best-beloved, to pay with their lives for the
freedom of wild America.

The other young man was Simon Bradstreet, son of the vicar of
Horbling, a nearby Lincolnshire village where he was baptized in
St. Andrew's Church on the 18th March, 1603/4. He entered Emmanuel College in 1617 and took his B.A. in 1621.[2] Cotton Mather's account of his life, in the *Magnalia*, tells us that his father died
while he was at Cambridge, having designated Dr. Preston, who
became Master of Emmanuel in 1622, as his guardian. Through
this connection young Simon was introduced to the Earl of
Lincoln, and came soon after to live at Sempringham as Thomas
Dudley's assistant.

By 1624 Dudley had decided, as Mather's *MS. Life* records,

> to retire himself into a more private capacity, for which end he
> left the Earl's family and hired a habitation at Boston, under
> Mr. Cotton, with whom he became intimately acquainted ever
> after; but it was not many years before the necessity of the Earl
> of Lincoln's affairs required his intermeddling therein a second
> time, for he had been in a manner unto him as Joseph was to

1. Dean Dudley, *History of the Dudley Family*, Supplement, p. 46; also
New England Historical and Genealogical Register, Vol. VIII, pp. 360–61.
2. J. and J. A. Venn, eds., *Alumni Cantabrigienses*, Part I, Vol. I, Cambridge, 1923, p. 203.

Pharaoh in Egypt, without whose assistance he could carry on no matter of moment.

Considering Mather's general vagueness about dates and periods of time, we may reasonably assume that Dudley never really left the Earl's service, until just before his departure for America, but that his move from Sempringham to Boston was undertaken not only for his own convenience, but for the Earl's as well. He left Simon Bradstreet in charge of estate matters on the home front, and settled where he and his family could have more personal independence while he was still better able, in the central town of that area, to manage the Earl's over-all financial interests.

An example of the sort of thing he was called upon to do occurred in the autumn of 1624, in connection with an abortive plan to rescue the Protestant kingdom of Bohemia for its deposed ruler, Frederick V, Elector Palatine of the Rhine and husband of the Princess Elizabeth of England. King James I had agreed to raise an army to be led into Germany by Count Mansfeld, a former commander of Frederick's forces, and in spite of the fact that men and money were scarce and the expedition was badly planned (and destined to fail), the younger men of the court were eagerly volunteering as officers. In November King James granted the Earl of Lincoln a regiment, and directed that his lady should "keep hospitality" in the country, rather than spend the winter in London, during the absence of her lord.[3]

Apparently the Earl had misgivings about the organization of the campaign, for he resolved, says Mather's *MS. Life*, "not to go without Mr. Dudley's advice and company, and therefore he sent down to Boston, in Lincolnshire, where Mr. Dudley then sojourned, to come forthwith to London, to order matters for this

3. *Calendar of State Papers, Domestic*—James I, 1624, p. 378.

enterprise, and to be ready to accompany him therein." Dudley, cautious and without enthusiasm in this instance, "sought the best counsel he could" and therefore resolved

> . . . in his passing up to London, to take Cambridge in his way, that he might advise with Dr. Preston about the design, (who was a great statesman as well as a great divine . . .) and he altogether dissuaded Mr. Dudley, or the Earl, from having anything to do in that expedition, laying before them the grounds of his apprehensions, on which he foresaw the sad events of the whole, as did really soon after come to pass. Dr. Preston, by reason of his frequent intercourse with the Earl of Lincoln's family, was free to discover to Mr. Dudley all that he knew, and he improved it thoroughly to take off the Earl's mind from the enterprise; although he was so far engaged therein as having kept a whole troop of horse upon that account, and one brave horse for himself, valued at four-score or a hundred pieces.

Mather's passage evokes a pleasant picture, of the sober man of business stopping in Cambridge to confer in his academic study with the Master of Emmanuel, old in wisdom and distinction at thirty-seven and with but four more years to live, then going on to London to join his employer and friend, the young courtier with a taste for adventure, eager to use his fine horse in battle for the Protestant cause. The Earl showed his good sense in being willing to abandon the whole project, on the advice of these two men whose judgment he respected.

The MS. *Life* gives another glimpse of the high-spiritedness of Lord Lincoln, "who it seems was wont to be very quick in his notions sometimes." Learning at short notice that there was to be a brilliant gathering of "great princes" at the Hague, where the Elector Palatine and his family were in exile, he decided to attend it, with a suitable retinue, and gave Dudley the difficult task of arranging to transport the whole group from Sempringham to Holland in two days. This feat being accomplished,

> . . . when they came there, the Earl's spirits arose to such an height that he would by no means address himself to the Count Palatine upon the knees, although he had been crowned King of Bohemia. Mr. Dudley began now to think that the last error was worse than the first; however, he was forced to find out the best way he could to excuse it, which he did to the Palsgrave's satisfaction.

Endowed as he was with a share of the arrogance that seems to have been generously distributed among his fellow-noblemen, the Earl also possessed courage and firmness of purpose, as we shall see in following him through a formidable experience that was soon to occur.

Thomas Dudley's sojourn in Boston gave him the opportunity to hear the sermons, and gain the friendship, of another founder-to-be of New England, the Reverend John Cotton, vicar of St. Botolph's Church. This energetic nonconformist divine had come to Boston from Emmanuel College, where he was head-lecturer, in 1612. For twenty years he filled the splendid church with a devoted congregation, but when William Laud became Archbishop of Canterbury in 1633, and refused any longer to tolerate Cotton's unorthodoxy, he took ship for America and there became an outstanding religious leader in the colony of Massachusetts Bay.

The Dudleys' eldest child, Samuel, was admitted to Emmanuel College as an undergraduate in the spring of 1626.[4] His sister Anne recorded in later life, in the spiritual legacy that she prepared for her children, her memories of these years in few but earnest words. After noting the "long fitt of sicknes" which she had as a child, she went on to say:

4. *Alumni Cantabrigienses*, Part I, Vol. II, p. 72.

But as I grew up to bee about 14 or 15 I found my heart more
carnall, and sitting loose from God, vanity and the follyes of
Youth take hold of me.

The early serious illness mentioned here was the first of many
that Anne Bradstreet chronicled, in her private writings in prose
and verse, throughout her life. It probably happened when she was
eleven or twelve years old; its nature is not described, but judging
by the symptoms of fever, fainting spells, and lameness that she
noted as afflicting her recurrently from early middle age onwards,
it may have been an attack of acute rheumatic fever, which damaged her heart and left her vulnerable to periods of collapse when
the demands of her strenuous life became too extreme for her endurance. At any rate, she recovered from this first seizure so satis-
factorily that within a few years she was feeling the stirrings of a
normal adolescent.

Life in the prosperous town of Boston, with its markets and
fairs, ships coming to its port on the river Witham, fine houses of
the nobility and gentry, and the great church from which John
Cotton's sermons reverberated throughout the Puritan world, must
have held many temptations to "vanity and the follyes of Youth"
for Anne Dudley. But it was not in her nature, even at this early
age, to become entirely preoccupied with worldly matters. John
Cotton was a preacher and lecturer of enormous energy; it is
recorded that he, "on Lord's day, on afternoons, went over thrice
the whole body of divinity in a catechistical way, and gave the
heads of his discourse to those that were young scholars, . . . to
answer to his questions in public in that great congregation." [5]
Anne was most probably one of the children who attended these
sessions of instruction, for the character of her lifelong religious

5. Samuel Whiting, "The Life of John Cotton," in *Chronicles of the First
Planters of Massachusetts Bay*, ed. Alexander Young, Boston, 1856, p. 424.

faith, with its trust in the wisdom and mercy of God, its belief in the eventual triumph of Christ's kingdom on earth, and its devotion to the apocalyptic poetry of the books of Revelation and Daniel, and the philosophic message of Ecclesiastes, seems to be the result of the influence of Cottons's sermons and teachings on her developing mind.

There is a plausible reason why, in spite of the generous spiritual nourishment that she was receiving, Anne felt her heart to be "more carnall" at this time. Simon Bradstreet, her father's assistant from 1621 to 1624, was no longer a member of the family circle. Not only had he been left behind at Sempringham, as Lord Lincoln's steward, when the Dudleys changed their place of residence, but he had, within a year or so, gone off to another post, and perhaps in Anne's awakening consciousness his image was beginning to take a place that increased in importance as their separation widened. Cotton Mather tells us that "Mr. *Bradstreet* . . . with much ado obtained the Earl's leave to Answer the Desires of the Aged and Pious Countess of *Warwick*, that he would accept the *Stewardship* of her noble Family, which as the former he discharged with an Exemplary Discretion and Fidelity." [6]

The "Aged and Pious" Countess, who can hardly have been more than sixty years old at this time, was the step-mother of Robert Rich, second Earl of Warwick, one of the leading Puritan peers and an investor from the beginning in the various companies formed to colonize North America. The dowager Countess was a woman of wealth and power, born Frances Wray, daughter of Sir Christopher Wray of Glentworth, Lincolnshire, married first to Sir George St. Paul, of Snarford in the same county, and second, in 1616, to the Baron Rich, thirteen years after his divorce from the romantic and notorious Penelope Devereux. The letter-writer John Chamberlain commented on this latter marriage: "The Lord

6. "The Life of Simon Bradstreet, Esq.," *Magnalia*, Book II, p. 19.

Rich, after much wooing and severall attempts in divers places hath at last lighted on the Lady Sainpoll a rich widow of Lincolnshire." And again about a year later, in October of 1617, in both instances writing to his friend Sir Dudley Carleton, ambassador at the Hague: "The Lord Rich is saide to be in great perplexitie, or rather crased in braine, to see himself overreacht by his new wife, who hath so conveyed her estate that he is little or nothing the better by her." [7]

The disappointed nobleman was created Earl of Warwick in August 1618 and died in the following March, at Warwick House in London. His widow survived him until 1634, when she died at Hackney, Middlesex, and was buried with the Earl in his family chapel at Felstead in Essex. She was a much-memorialized lady, for in the little church of St. Lawrence, in Snarford, Lincolnshire, she and her first husband, with their only child, Mattathia, who died in infancy, lie in effigy on a handsome table-tomb, and a wall-monument in the same church displays her medallion-portrait beside that of the Earl of Warwick.

While Simon Bradstreet was employed by the substantial Countess, he was probably obliged to divide his time between her estates in Lincolnshire and the Rich family mansions in London, Hackney, and Essex. So he ceased for the time being to have much if any contact with the Dudleys in Boston, and his place as Lord Lincoln's steward was taken by John Holland, whose son Jeremy was baptized at Sempringham in June of 1625. Soon after this the Earl became involved in a political situation that brought serious trouble to himself and his household, and contributed indirectly but significantly to the formation of the Massachusetts Bay Company.

When Count Mansfeld's expedition met with disaster, and the

7. *Letters of John Chamberlain,* ed. N. E. McClure, Philadelphia, 1939, Vol. II, pp. 44, 101.

English attempt to rescue the Palatinate for the Elector Frederick was virtually abandoned, James I was an ailing and disheartened man. He died in the spring of 1625, leaving his crown, his notorious favorite the Duke of Buckingham, and his hatred of the Puritans to his handsome, fastidious, and self-willed son. Even as King Charles I came to the throne, and welcomed as his queen the Roman Catholic French princess Henrietta Maria, Buckingham was preparing a series of ill-fated military adventures, in the name of Protestantism, against both France and Spain. Money for these undertakings, as well as for the maintenance of the elaborate court-life, was constantly needed. Various shifts were tried for about a year, with increasing lack of success, to raise the necessary sums by voluntary gifts or loans, until the king was persuaded to take the first of those arbitrary steps that led at last to tragedy for himself and his people. In September 1626 he established, in a letter addressed to the leaders of Church and State, a "Commision to require and collect a loan for the King's use from persons able to lend," and issued a set of instructions which the commissioners for the forced loan in all counties were "exactly to observe and ffollow." [8]

Resistance to this unlawful infringement of the prerogative of Parliament and the rights of the subject soon made itself felt over all the country. For example, the justices of the peace in Cornwall reported that, when asked to subscribe to the loan, "the parishes replied, if they had but two kine, they would sell one of them for the supply of his Majesty and the kingdom's occasions *in a Parliamentary way.*" [9] Men in high and low places refused the demand of the commissioners, and among the most active of the resisters was the Earl of Lincoln. We can follow his individual role in this bitter political episode, at times almost from day to day, as it is

8. *Calendar of State Papers, Domestic*—Charles I, 1625–26, pp. 435–36.
9. *Ibid.* p. 450.

noted in contemporary letters and records. The diarist Walter Yonge wrote, summarizing the first few months of the loan's chequered progress:

> December 1626. The King having determined heretofore to demand of all his subjects so much money by way of loan as they are set in subsidy, [that is, listed according to their ability to meet any special tax or assessment levied by act of Parliament], . . . the judges were urged to subscribe. They paid their money, but refused to subscribe to the same as a legal course: for which Sir Randall Crewe, Chief Justice of England, had his patent taken from him, and he was displaced. . . . The privy council subscribed; the lords and peers subscribed, all except 14, whereof six were Earls: viz. Earl of Essex, Earl of Warwick, Earl of Clare, Earl of Huntington, Earl of Lincoln, and the Earl of Bolingbroke, being Lord St. John.[10]

In the same month Sir Benjamin Rudyerd wrote to Sir Francis Nethersole at the Hague, after naming the resisting earls: "And it is thought that theare will be 15 or 16 lordes in this Recusancye, which with the Judges Denyenge to subscribe, will give a greate blowe to this Designe." [11]

On the 6th February, 1626/27, Walter Yonge recorded:

> In Norfolk such as subscribed to the loan do refuse to pay the same. So Cumberland refuse. Lincolnshire also refuse; and the Earls of Lincoln County, and Bolingbroke, two commissioners, are sent for, and a new commission granted for that county.[12]

The Venetian ambassador, Alvise Contarini, kept the Doge and Senate thoroughly informed as to events in England at this time.

10. *Diary of Walter Yonge, Esq., 1604–1628,* ed. Roberts, Camden Society, 1848, p. 98.
11. *State Papers, Domestic, Charles I,* Vol. XLI, No. 3.
12. *Diary,* p. 100.

His letters of February and March 1626/27 add a number of details to the story of the loan. He wrote that the Earl of Rutland, father-in-law of the Duke of Buckingham and Lord Lieutenant of Lincolnshire, had returned hurriedly to London to report that in the whole county of Lincoln only three persons had subscribed, "all the rest having tumultuously joined in the refusal, giving signs of almost open rebellion, venting their rage on the house in which the Royal Commissioners were assembled." The Earl of Rutland, whose daughter was a Roman Catholic and whose interests were entirely those of the king, can have felt nothing but hostility towards a Puritan peer who was publicly resisting the loan. As a result of his accusations, according to Contarini, Lord Lincoln was summoned to join the two hundred or more refusers who were required to present themselves before the Privy Council to explain their behavior. He duly appeared, "in answer to a charge of evil speaking among his servants against this new form of exacting money," and was then "committed to the Tower, for reasons already given, and may possibly remain there a long time without hope of release." [13]

The Privy Council records show that the Earl was summoned on the 13th February, and on the 9th March was deprived of his freedom by "A warrante upon significacion of his Majestie's pleasure to commit the Earle of Lincolne safe prisoner to the Tower." [14] Another source tells us that a charge was preferred against him in the Court of Star Chamber by Sir Henry Fines (perhaps a relative) "for divers riots and other misdemeanours," and that he had "taken a commission forth to put in his answer." [15]

It must be acknowledged that while the Earl of Lincoln and

13. *Calendar of State Papers, Venetian*—Charles I, 1626–28, pp. 119, 126, 130, 154, 161.

14. *Acts of the Privy Council*, 1626–27, Vol. II, Part 2, pp. 61, 128.

15. Sir George Croke, *Reports of Select Cases in the Reign of Charles I*, revised by Sir Harbottle Grimston, Dublin, 1793, Vol. III, p. 64.

many other noblemen and substantial citizens, throughout the land, were suffering for their resistance to the forced loan, the majority of the king's subjects obeyed his command and subscribed, however reluctantly, the sums that the commissioners required them to pay. It is recorded that by the end of 1627 the loan had brought in £236,000, only £52,000 less than it had been expected to yield.[16] In itself, this royal levy was a comparatively unimportant short-term device for the acquiring of urgently needed money; its historic significance lies in the fact that it was King Charles's first open seizure of the authority legally vested, by the people of the realm, in Parliament. The arbitrary acts that followed it increased so rapidly in scope and seriousness, in their fateful progress towards civil war, that the forced loan itself has generally been dealt with rather briefly by the historians of the period, simply as the minor opening scene in a drama of developing tragedy. But its impact on the resisting Puritan noblemen, particularly among them the young Earl of Lincoln, precipitated a secondary series of events that led rapidly to the formation of the Massachusetts Bay Company and the Great Migration to New England, and had a decisive effect on the fortunes of Thomas Dudley and his family.

In the early spring of 1627, when Lord Lincoln was committed to prison, Anne Dudley was presumably just approaching her fourteenth birthday. But she must have been well aware of the political tensions around her and of the perilous position in which her father was placed, not only because of his religious nonconformity, but also as the known retainer and counsellor of a man of substance and title who had dared to defy the king's edict. Although she left no personal comment on her response to this situation, Anne's formal verse reveals an interest in politics, generally of a controversial kind, that is remarkable for a woman of her time. It is reasonable to conclude that this interest sprang from her con-

16. S. R. Gardiner, *History of England, 1603–1642,* 1884, Vol. VI, p. 219.

sciousness, during the first five years of King Charles's reign, of being a member of a dissident and threatened minority.

To return to the account of the Earl's experience: during the month of March 1627 a petition was laid before the king, "That the Countesse of Lincolne may have accesse to her husband now a prisoner in the Tower." [17] On the 17th March the Reverend Joseph Mead wrote from Cambridge to Sir Martin Stuteville, informing him of Lord Lincoln's imprisonment and adding: "He desired to know his charge and accusers, but obtained no more at that time than this general, that he had showed himself an enemy to the king's proceedings, and done harm to others, both by his example and speeches." [18]

King Charles was in an awkward position in relation to the several peers, and far more numerous knights, squires, and wealthy merchants who were either in prison, or awaiting the pleasure of the Privy Council, because they had refused to subscribe to the loan. In the Ambassador Contarini's letter, reporting that the Earl of Lincoln was accused of "evil speaking among his servants against this new form of exacting money," is the significant comment: "Such is the pretext for not punishing those who refuse payment, amongst whom he is one of the chief, and as they are many, chastisement might cause some great disturbance." [19]

The royal anger could vent itself with impunity, however, against humbler citizens, and three retainers of the Earl were singled out for prosecution even before their master was committed to the Tower. Warrants for the arrest of John Holland, "gent.," his steward at this date, Robert Blow, "clarke of the kitching," and John Good, "groom of the stable," were issued on the 21st February by

17. *State Papers Domestic, Charles I*, Vol. LVIII, No. 85.

18. Thomas Birch, D.D., *The Court and Times of Charles I*, ed. R. F. Williams, 1848, Vol. I, p. 207.

19. *Calendar of State Papers, Venetian*—Charles I, 1626–28, p. 154.

the Privy Council,[20] and these were followed by a printed proclamation, one month later, "by the King." The language of this
document, even in abridged form, shows Charles's mounting rage
towards any who had the temerity to disobey his "Regall authori-
tie," and in itself goes far to explain why so many of his subjects,
within the next fourteen years, left their homeland to seek a less
oppressive political air.

> Forasmuch as John Holland and Robert Blow, late servants to
> the Earle of Lincolne . . . have lately committed divers notable
> misdemeanours, to the danger of this State, and happy peace
> thereof contrary to that duety and Allegiance which they ought
> to beare unto Us doe now lurke and keepe themselves close in
> some secret place or places, and will not submit themselves to
> Justice, to the great abuse and insufferable contempt of Us, and
> our Regall authoritie; . . . Wee doe hereby charge and com-
> maund all . . . Our officers, Ministers and Subiects whatsoever
> to be diligent in inquiring and searching for the said John Hol-
> land and Robert Blow . . . whom, . . . if they shal happen to
> teke, Our will & pleasure is that they cause him or them so
> apprehended, to be safely carried to the Sheriffe of that Countie,
> . . . and the Shiriffe safely to convey him or them . . . unto
> the Lords of Our Privy Counsel, there to answere such things as
> shall be obiected against him or them, . . . And . . . that if
> any person or persons, after this Our Proclamation published
> shall directly or indirectly conceale, harbour, keep, reteine or
> maintaine the said John Holland and Robert Blow, . . . Wee
> will (as there is just cause) proceed against them that shall so
> neglect Our Commandement, in all severity.
> Given at Our Court at White-Hall, the one and twentieth
> day of March in the second yeere of Our Reigne of Great
> Britaine, France and Ireland.
> God Save the King.[21]

20. *Acts of the Privy Council*, 1626–27, Vol. II, Part 2, p. 74.
21. *State Papers Domestic, Charles I*, Vol. LVII, No. 79(a); *Entry Books*,
S.P. 45/10, f° 63.

There is no indication, in this ominous pronouncement, what crime or crimes these obscure men were alleged to have committed. Private sources give the reason why the Earl and his dependents were being so energetically proceeded against by their monarch. A letter written by an unnamed person, in London in this same month of March, contains a revealing passage:

> An accident of evil tidings to the Earl of Lincoln is lately happened, concerning letters dispersed among the freeholders, by a servant of his now discovered, and sent for by a pursuivant, and like to prove a case of doubtful issue. Many of the letters were inscribed, *To all true-hearted Englishmen.*[22]

And Walter Yonge noted in his diary, under the 30th March, 1627:

> Such as refuse to subscribe to the loan are to be censured in the Star Chamber. . . . A proclamation for the apprehending of one Jo. Holland and Rob. Blow, the one steward, the other clerk of the kitchen, to the Earl of Lincoln, for dispensing some abridgements of statutes concerning the freedom of the subject from loans and impositions.[23]

The insidious weapon of propaganda was greatly feared and resented by the king and his counsellors, for where it was used, by determined men of power and influence, it made whole counties refuse to support the loan, sometimes with violence as was the case in Lincolnshire. "This scattering of letters is grown rife in divers parts, and they are but ill symptoms," wrote Mead to Stuteville, reporting that Essex was one of the generally resisting counties.[24] Yet no immediate action was taken against the Earl of Lincoln, or

22. Birch, *The Court and Times of Charles I,* Vol. I, p. 202.
23. *Diary,* p. 102.
24. Birch, *op. cit.* p. 207.

such other Puritan stalwarts as Lord Saye and Sele, Sir Erasmus Dryden, and Richard Knightley, M.P. for Northamptonshire, all of whom, along with many others, were either in prison or under summons to appear before the Privy Council. A letter of the 6th April, 1627, addressed to Mead in London, says: "We hear not any more of the Earl of Lincoln's coming to the Star Chamber; but he still remains close prisoner in the Tower." [25]

The punishment of these eminent citizens had to be administered by proxy, as it were, because of the clear and present danger that, as Contarini wrote to his Venetian superiors, "chastisement might cause some great disturbance." Two examples of this procedure are recorded; the first concerns the apprehended fugitive John Good and appears in "A Letter from London," dated May 1627:

> On Wednesday last a poor fellow, who had been some years since a groom to the Earl of Lincoln, was censured in the Star Chamber for scattering of those papers, which it seems the two fled gentleman belonging to the same Earl had written. He was fined by the judges £300, being not worth £5 in all the world, and imprisoned during the King's pleasure.[26]

The second is an even more shocking case of penalizing a rich man, who in this instance is not even identified, through one of his servants:

> The Attorney Gen'l, . . . *versus* Thomas Perkins. When the Commissioners for collecting the Loan Money were to sit at Nottingham, the defendant scattered in the highway seditious letters to dissuade the Freeholders from subscribing, stating that all the Commissioners in Lincolnshire, but two or three, had refused to give money except by way of Parliament, &c. Committed to the Fleet and fined £3000.[27]

25. *Ibid.* pp. 213–14.
26. *Ibid.* p. 222.
27. John Southerden Burn, *The Star Chamber*, 1870, p. 103 (under the heading "Star Chamber reports for the years 1625–28").

Up to this point Thomas Dudley does not appear to have been involved in the campaign of prosecution that was directed against Lord Lincoln and his retainers. He was living in Boston, presumably going about his business there in a respected and unobtrusive way, and very wisely not making an outward show of his deep concern on the Earl's behalf. But observant informers were busy in this troubled time, and one of them, a Lincolnshire justice of the peace named Sir Edward Heron, who was probably also a commissioner for the loan, addressed an obsequious letter in July to Sir Humphrey May, chancellor of the duchy of Lancaster.

Right honorable
   I had rather offende in too much officiousness, then negligence, especially to the Kings majestie: I have hearde, that Mr Hollande whoe attended the earle of Lincolne hath beene in quest by the state, yf it be soe, I doe heare for certeine, that he was seene dyvers tymes, about a month, or six weekes past upon the tarras-walkes at Sempringham; but since that tyme it is privately whispered, that he is nowe removed to the house of one Mr Thomas Dudlye in Boston, whoe did allsoe of late tymes wayte upon the sayde earle; and it is verye probable, because Mr Hollands wyfe is observed to make often viages frome Sempringham unto Boston, and there to abide, sometyme 2 or 3 dayes, sometyme a weeke together; this is all I understande therein, and this all I take my duetie to enforme unto your honor; neither am I scrupulous, yf to anye purpose, except thereby I have beene troublesome to your important affayres; and therefore after my humble salutations I rest

at your Commande
Edward Heron.

Cressye this 28 of July 1627.

   Yet maye you please further to understande that this Mr Dudlye beynge reported to have £300 per annum, some saye £400, refused upon our earnest request to beare 30 shillings towards the loane . . . as we have informed in our certificatts unto the lords of the Councell.[28]

This must have been an anxious summer for the Dudley household, of Thomas and Dorothy and their three daughters, with perhaps Samuel also, on vacation from Cambridge. The well-to-do Thomas had annoyed the authorities by his refusal to subscribe to the loan, and the frequent comings and goings of Mrs. Holland had given rise to the rumor that he was harboring her husband, a fugitive from justice, under his roof. It is curious that Cotton Mather made no mention, in either of his accounts of Dudley's life, of this tense episode of the forced loan; he simply commented, in the *MS. Life,* perhaps with untypical discretion, that "the times began to look black and cloudy upon the Noncomformists, of which Mr. Dudley was one to the full."

The much larger household at Sempringham was undoubtedly in a state of apprehension and practical confusion, for the Earl was still in prison, and his steward, in constant danger of arrest, can hardly have been able to conduct the business of the estate with efficiency. However, as the year ended, the general situation showed signs of improvement. The compulsory loan had served its purpose by bringing in almost as much revenue as had been expected from it, and the king was embarrassed by the fact that more than seventy of the leading resisters were still awaiting their trials in confinement.

On the 2nd January, 1627/28, it was ordered that those who had refused to pay the loan should be released.[29] But Lord Lincoln, as one whose part in the resistance was considered more serious and culpable, was detained until February, when the Council permitted him "to goe abroad in the companie of his keeper . . . to prepare

28. *State Papers Domestic, Charles I,* Vol. LXXII, No. 36.
29. Gardiner, *History of England,* Vol. VI, p. 225.

his answere to an informacion preferred in the Star Chamber by his Majestie's Atturney Gen'l." [30] It does not appear that he was ever actually brought to trial, for on the 15th March a warrant directed the Lieutenant of the Tower:

> Whereas his Majestie hath signified his gracious pleasure for the enlargement of the Erle of Lincolne . . . these are therefore . . . expressly to require you . . . accordingly to discharge and sett free the sayde Erle.[31]

John Holland's daughter, baptized at Sempringham on the 7th December, 1628, was given the name of Deliverance. This was a symbolic word, not only for Lord Lincoln's household but for the Dudleys in Boston as well. For Anne recorded, in her personal memoirs, that

> About 16, the Lord layd his hand sore upon me and smott mee with the small pox. When I was in my affliction, I besought the Lord, and confessed my Pride and Vanity and he was entreated of me, and again restored me. But I rendered not to him according to the benefitt received.
> After a short time I changed my condition and was marryed.

The child whom Simon Bradstreet had known at Sempringham, preoccupied with her studies and her religious faith, yet sometimes, undoubtedly, enticed into gaiety by what she called "vanitye and the follyes of youth," was stricken, probably towards the end of 1628, by the cruel disease that killed more often than it spared. When the news of her illness came to the Countess of Warwick's steward, perhaps he realized all at once that during their separation Anne had grown from childhood to young womanhood, that

30. *Acts of the Privy Council,* 1627–28, p. 265.
31. *Ibid.* p. 350.

she was threatened by death, and that he loved her and wished her for his wife.

Again, as in the case of her baptism, no church record of Anne Dudley's marriage has been found. Cotton Mather simply noted, in the *Magnalia*, in telling of Simon Bradstreet's stewardship to Lady Warwick, "Here he married the daughter of Mr. Dudley." It is most probable, because of the recent danger to which Thomas Dudley had exposed himself, that the ceremony took place privately, in the house of Anne's parents in Boston, and it is also probable that the minister who united the two young Puritans was John Cotton, himself already under sharp episcopal surveillance for his nonconformist practices. It has been assumed by New England biographers and historians that the marriage occurred in 1628, perhaps while Anne was still convalescent from her illness; the episode is reminiscent of a celebrated one of a decade later, when John Hutchinson married the eighteen-year-old Lucy Apsley, another smallpox victim, in 1638,

> as soon as she was able to quit the chamber, when the priest and all that saw her were affrighted to look on her; but God recompensed his justice and constancy by restoring her, though she was longer than ordinary before she recovered to be as well as before.[32]

While Lord Lincoln was a prisoner in the Tower, and Thomas Dudley under suspicion of harboring the wanted fugitive John Holland, a group of troubled men came together in the seclusion of Sempringham, and from their meetings grew the vision of a bold and majestic solution to the problems that tormented them. When that vision had become a reality, and the Massachusetts Bay colony had endured its first winter in the American wilderness, Thomas

32. Lucy Hutchinson, *Memoirs of Colonel Hutchinson*, Everyman's Library, 1936, p. 51.

Dudley wrote an account of the whole experience and addressed it on the 28th March, 1631, as "the thankfullest present I had to send over the seas," to the Countess of Lincoln. His words on the conception of the colony are concise and significant:

> Touching the Plantation which we here have begun, it fell out thus. About the year 1627, some friends being together in Lincolnshire, fell into discourse about New-England, and the planting of the Gospel there; and after some deliberation we imparted our reasons, by letters and messages, to some in London and the west country; where it was likewise deliberately thought upon, and at length with often negotiation so ripened, that in the year 1628 we procured a patent from his Majesty for our planting between the Mattachusetts Bay and Charles River on the south, and the river of Merrimack on the north, and three miles on either side of those rivers and bay; as also for the government of those who did or should inhabit within that compass.[33]

The first planners in Lincolnshire were closely bound together, not only by their religious convictions but also by ties of relationship with the imprisoned Earl of Lincoln. Isaac Johnson, Lord Saye

33. Thomas Dudley's *Letter to the Countess of Lincoln* was actually his official narrative, as deputy governor, of the creation and first ten months of existence of the Massachusetts Bay colony. He sent it to the wife of his former employer in token of affection and gratitude, and also as a factual report that could be circulated among the financial backers and sponsors of the colony. It was first printed in 1696, in *Massachusetts or the First Planters of New England* (Boston, Mass.), a collection of documents assembled by the Boston merchant and antiquarian Joshua Scottow. Alexander Young included Dudley's *Letter* in his *Chronicles of the First Planters of Massachusetts Bay, 1623–1636*, Boston, 1846; in an editorial note he called it "the most interesting as well as authentic document in our early annals." It was reprinted in *The Force Tracts*, ed. Farmer, Vol. II, No. 4, Washington, D.C., 1838, and Rochester, N.Y., 1898, and in Augustine Jones's *Thomas Dudley, Second Governor of Massachusetts*, Boston, 1899 (Appendix A). The passage quoted above is taken from Young's *Chronicles* (as subsequent ones will be), pp. 309–10.

and Sele, John Cotton, Thomas Dudley, and Samuel Skelton, a silenced minister who had become the chaplain at Sempringham, were joined by a man who formed a connecting link with a leading colonizer in the west country. John Humfry of Dorset took the Lady Susan, Lord Lincoln's sister, as his third wife in 1626; their son was baptized at St. Botolph's Church in Boston on the 3rd May, 1627. Before coming to Lincolnshire Humfry had assisted the Reverend John White of Dorchester, author of *The Planter's Plea* (first printed in 1630), in sending a small group of settlers to the Massachusetts Bay territory, so he was able to contribute practical knowledge to the East Anglian discussions.

There had been great interest, since the beginning of the Elizabethan voyages of exploration, in the establishment of settlements along the eastern coast of North America. Noblemen and merchants, ambitious for the glory of the kingdom and the increase of trade, had joined with pioneers in religious independence to form corporations and obtain charters for colonization. The Virginia Company, organized in 1606 as the result of Sir Walter Raleigh's earlier efforts, established the colony of Jamestown in 1607. A subsidiary, known as the Plymouth Company, granted a patent to the separatist Pilgrims, who crossed the Atlantic in the *Mayflower* in the autumn of 1620, and founded the first permanent settlement in New England, at Plymouth on Cape Cod.

The Council for New England was then formed, and from it, in 1623, the Reverend John White of Dorchester and his associates received a patent for the planting of a colony on Cape Ann, which should occupy itself with fishing, farming, trading for furs, and bringing the Christian faith to the savage natives of the New World. But this program was too ambitious for the fifty-odd "Dorchester Adventurers," whose primitive settlement did not prosper and was abandoned in 1625. A stalwart handful of the adventurers remained, however, when the rest returned to England, and these, the "Old Planters" of the Massachusetts Bay territory, moved with their families and cattle to the Indian camp-site known as Nahum-Keike or Naumkeag, "the place of peace." Here they founded, and later christened with the Hebrew version of its Indian name, a pioneer village which was to become the historic city of Salem.

In England, John White and the members of the Council, men of power and substance like the Earl of Warwick, Sir Ferdinando Gorges, Matthew Cradock of London, and Sir Richard Saltonstall of Yorkshire, were anxious to salvage and sustain the remnant of the Dorchester venture. To this end there was formed yet another corporation, the New England Company, which dispatched one of its members, John Endecott, in June 1628, with about forty settlers and a full cargo of mixed provisions, in the *Abigail* from Weymouth, to encourage the plantation at Salem.

The New England Company's charter was granted on the 19th March, 1627/28; four days prior to this the Earl of Lincoln was released from prison, and on his return to Sempringham he must have found the colonial planners hard at work, assisted by Thomas Dudley and probably Simon Bradstreet as well. The names of Isaac Johnson, John Humfry, and Richard Bellingham, the recorder, or chief justice, of Boston, are included in the first membership list of the company.[34] Two others, master-builders second to none in the creation of New England, joined the conferences at Sempringham at about this time, and each has left a glimpse of himself on the long road that led to North America.

Roger Williams, the young clergyman from Essex whose passion for religious freedom of conscience brought him to defy the theocracy of Massachusetts Bay and to found his own colony, which became the state of Rhode Island, wrote in one of his many controversial works, *The Bloudy Tenent yet more Bloudy* (1652):

34. Charles M. Andrews, *The Colonial Period of American History*, New Haven, Vol. I, *The Settlements*, 1935, pp. 359–60.

Master Cotton may call to minde, that the discusser (riding
with himself and one other of precious memorie, Master Thomas
Hooker, to and from Sempringham) presented his Arguments
from Scripture, why he durst not join with them in their use of
Common prayer.

And John Winthrop, the Suffolk squire and lawyer who was to be
the first governor of the Massachusetts Bay colony, noted in his
private journal, under the date of 28th July, 1629:

My Bro: Downing & myselfe ridinge into Lincolnshire by Ely,
my horse fell under me in a bogge in the fennes, so as I was
allmost to the waiste in water; but the Lorde preserved me from
further danger. Blessed be his name.[35]

Time, that has all but obliterated the identity of many early
New Englanders, has generously preserved the image, character,
and life-record of Winthrop, archetype of the Puritan leaders of
the migration. In a portrait owned by the American Antiquarian
Society he is shown at about the age of forty-three, shortly before
his departure for America. The long, sensitive, anxious face ends
in a reddish-brown pointed beard, which rests on a standing ruff
edged with fine lace, as does the dark hair that falls to below the
ears. A black cloak envelops the figure, but reveals the large powerful hands, one of them holding a pair of light gauntlet gloves, and
deep cuffs also edged with lace. It is the likeness of a serious, successful man of the world, which Winthrop surely was, having been
educated at Cambridge and in the law, endowed with an ample
landed estate, and appointed an attorney in the Court of Wards
and Liveries in London. But above all this, his chief concern, as
his voluminous surviving letters and journals show, was with the

35. R. C. Winthrop, *Life and Letters of John Winthrop*, Boston, 1869,
Vol. I, p. 304.

state of his spirit as one of those elected, in the Calvinist sense, to be God's deputy on earth.

Winthrop's religious experience began when he was fourteen years old, and suffering from a fever at Cambridge, but not until his thirtieth year, when he was in despair at the death of his young wife, did he become fully aware of "the covenant of free grace"; then

> . . . the good Spirit of the Lord breathed upon my soul, and said I should live. Then every promise I thought upon held forth Christ unto mee saying I am thy salvation. Now could my soule close with Christ, and rest there with sweet content, so ravished with his Love, as I desired nothing nor feared any thing, but was filled with joy unspeakable and glorious and with a spirit of Adoption.[36]

This was the transforming revelation of oneness with God that came, sooner or later, to every dedicated Puritan, bringing with it the assurance of predestined election, the promise of eternal redemption, and the demand for perfect allegiance throughout every hour and every circumstance of earthly life.

Ideally, it is the privilege of every conscientious Christian to experience such a sense of unity with the infinite. What distinguished the Calvinist in his awareness of "election" was the belief that God had leaned earthward to execute a solemn contract with the individual human being, and that thenceforward there was a living bond of shared responsibility between them. For the earthly creature, it was an affiliation of immeasurable glory and all but insuperable challenge. The Puritan was not at liberty to find true peace or fulfillment in the world; he was a front-line soldier, constantly in action not only against every move of the ancient enemy

36. *Winthrop Papers*, Boston (Massachusetts Historical Society), Vol. III, 1943, pp. 342–43.

on the battlefield around him, but also against the temptations
that lurked like insidious traitors in his own breast.

John Winthrop's personal record of his service in the army of
Christ covers many pages, and is one of the most moving and revealing of devotional documents to survive from that richly introspective age. The exaltation of his union with God was not continuous, but suffered anguished lapses for which he blamed his
preoccupation with worldly affairs, vanity, and slothfulness, and
even too much pleasure in a rich diet and the use of tobacco. With
the help of his faith he fought these weaknesses and overcame
them, and through victory over self he gained the strength and
power to be foremost among the planners of a great spiritual
crusade. Perry Miller has written, of Winthrop and his colleagues:

> They were performers in the main action, in international
> Calvinism, in Protestantism. They were not colonials, and never
> would become colonial; though they died in America, they were
> never to be Americanized. . . . Americans would be English-
> men who attained in America what their English and European
> brethren were seeking. . . . That purification for which Calvin-
> ists on the Continent and Puritans in England had striven for
> three generations was to be wrought in a twinkling upon virgin
> soil.[37]

Many able historians have discussed and weighed, in analytic
detail, the balance of motives that sent so many English men and
women to North America between the years 1620 and 1642. The
persons with whom this study is concerned, Anne Bradstreet and
her immediate family, who from the start were centrally involved
in the Massachusetts Bay enterprise, found their material security
in the homeland seriously hampered and threatened, while at the

37. P. Miller, *The New England Mind: From Colony to Province,* Cambridge (Mass.), 1953, pp. 6 and 8.

same time they conceived the vision of another England planted in a new and all but empty world, where a holy and ordered society, governed by the precepts of Scripture, could grow untrammelled and be a glorious example to the time-corrupted nations of the old world. They accordingly undertook to sacrifice such peace and safety as they still enjoyed in their native land, and to devote their lives to the making of God's kingdom across the sea, with the unquestioning conviction that as it was His will that sent them, so He would prosper the enterprise. Winthrop spoke for them all, in the entirely Puritan language of his tract, *A Modell of Christian Charity*, written on the voyage to America.

> Thus stands the cause betweene God and us, wee are entered into Covenant with him for this worke, wee have taken out a Commission, the Lord hath given us leave to drawe our owne Articles . . . wee have hereupon besought him of favour and blessing: Now if the Lord shall please to heare us, and bring us in peace to the place wee desire, then hath hee ratified this Covenant and sealed our Commission, and will expect a strickt performance of the Articles contained in it, but if wee shall neglect the observacion of these Articles, . . . shall fall to embrace this present world and prosecute our carnall intencions, . . . the Lord will surely breake out in wrathe against us, be revenged of such a perjured people and make us knowe the price of the breache of such a Covenant.[38]

During 1628, because there appeared to be some flaws in the New England Company's patent, the incorporators decided to appeal to the king for a charter, under the Great Seal, in the name of the Massachusetts Bay Company. This was obtained, with considerable effort and expense, on the 4th March, 1628/29, and it gave specifically to a group of twenty-six men, among whom were Thomas Dudley and Simon Bradstreet, " 'one body politique and

38. *Winthrop Papers*, Vol. II, 1931, p. 294.

corporate in Deede, Facte and Name' . . . something that had
not existed before, the right of these men as a corporate body to
rule and administer the territory under their authority and to exercise complete sway over any colonies or plantations that might be
set up on its soil." [39]

The territory granted to "the Governor and Company of the
Mattachusetts Bay in Newe-England" extended from three miles
north of the Merrimack River to three miles south of the Charles
River, a distance of about sixty miles, and from the Atlantic Ocean
on the east to the "South Sea," or Pacific, on the west. It was not
of course realized how vast a length, in contrast to its breadth,
the grant possessed, for it was believed in 1629 that the continent
of North America did not stretch far to the west and that the two
oceans would therefore form boundaries as logical as they were
convenient.

Andrews gives this picture of the business in hand:

On March 23, [1628/29], the Massachusetts Bay Company
was formally organized, with the officials named in the charter
in their respective places, Matthew Cradock, governor, Thomas
Goffe, deputy governor, eleven assistants, a secretary, a treasurer,
and a beadle; and from this time forward, these officials, sitting
in the deputy governor's house at the corner of Philpot Lane,
[in London] . . . performed the necessary work of settling and
equipping the first plantation and of other plantations to follow.
They . . . hired vessels, gathered ordnance and ammunition,
provided provisions, soap, candles, implements and utensils, beer,
wine, and liquor, and purchased steel, iron, merchandise for trading with the Indians, clothing, shoes, house furnishings, sail
cloth, hay for fodder, and cattle. They arranged suitable terms
with men who were hired to go as artisans and craftsmen, and
with a minister, a teacher, and a surgeon. They secured laborers
of all sorts, contracted with indentured servants and made

39. Andrews, *The Settlements*, pp. 364–68.

arrangements for women and maids. They discussed the best way of dividing lands and gathered books for transmission to the colony, among them the Book of Common Prayer. At last, in full control of the situation, the Massachusetts Bay Company was ready to carry forward its work in an efficient and constructive manner.[40]

The first act of the new company was to dispatch an advance group of settlers, under the leadership of two ministers, Francis Higginson and Samuel Skelton, to the Salem colony, which was approximately in the center of their allotted territory. This was the largest expedition that had hitherto been sent to New England, and consisted of five ships, carrying men and women, cattle, and various supplies, that sailed at different dates through April and May of 1629. They all arrived safely, and on the 20th July Skelton and Higginson, both of whom had been silenced for nonconformity in their mother-country, established at Salem the first church in the Massachusetts Bay colony.

A month after this, in England, the company took an unprecedented step. At a meeting held in Cambridge on the 26th August Winthrop, Saltonstall, Johnson, Humfry, Thomas Dudley, and seven others signed a document, thereafter to be known as the Cambridge Agreement, in which they bound themselves

ready in our persons and with such of our severall familyes as are to go with us and such provision as we are able conveniently to furnish ourselves withall, to embark for the said plantacion by the first of March next, at such port or ports of this land as shall be agreed upon by the Company, to the end to passe the Seas (under God's protection) to inhabite and continue in New England. Provided, always that before the last of September next the whole government together with the Patent for the said plantacion bee first by an order of Court legally transferred and

40. *Ibid.* pp. 373–74.

established to remayne with us and others which shall inhabite upon the said plantacion.[41]

Up to this time all the colonial enterprises had been managed by their respective companies in England, the governing boards of which had appointed the plantation officers, directed the extent and character of the settlers' activities, and provided them with the necessary supplies and equipment. That is, in return for financing the projects the companies expected to retain control of their operations. But in the case of the Massachusetts Bay Company the potential settlers themselves demanded, and obtained, the right to carry with them across the sea, and hold in perpetuity, the charter and the "whole government" of the colony.

The Massachusetts Bay Company was an efficient and well-financed joint-stock corporation, and its members who planned to migrate had no particular reason to doubt its ability to supply their practical requirements in full. But the signers of the Cambridge Agreement, who represented the strongest Puritan element in the company, had more than material needs in mind. Their first concern was for the spiritual integrity of the settlement, and if they could not control the religious architecture of the New Jerusalem that they hoped to build in the wilderness, but were at the mercy of every changing mood of the stockholders in London, their great vision could become no more substantial than a mirage.

The Cambridge Agreement was presented to a general court of the company and promptly authorized, on the 29th August, by a small and predominantly Puritan minority of the company's membership.[42] The legality of the whole procedure has been

41. *Massachusetts Historical Society Proceedings*, Boston, Vol. 62, 1930, pp. 279–80.

42. This, and succeeding references, in this chapter, to meetings of the company, are from *Records of the Governor and Company of Massachusetts Bay in New England*, ed. Nathaniel B. Shurtleff, Boston, 1853–54, Vol. I (1628–41).

argued, *pro* and *con*, by many historians, but it has never been denied that among all the tempered axes and adzes, the plough-shares and kegs of nails that were loaded for North America, no ship carried a more powerful instrument for building and sustaining, after the Bible, than His Majesty's Charter to the Governor and Company of Massachusetts Bay in New England.

Thomas Dudley was noted as present at "A Court of Assistants at the Deputies House, on Fryday, the 16 of Octo., 1629"; this was shortly after his fifty-third birthday. At the next general court, on the 20th October, it was decided to replace the existing officers, in conformity with the Cambridge Agreement, by men who had signified their intention of migrating to New England. Accordingly John Winthrop was chosen as governor, and John Humfry as deputy governor, and through the winter these two directed the preparations for the great expedition that was planned for the following spring.

In February 1629/30 Simon Bradstreet took on the duties of secretary to the company, and on the 18th March, at a meeting held at Southampton, he was made an assistant, with two others, to replace three who had decided not to leave their mother-country. The time for departure drew near, but there was one important change still to be made.

> Att a Court of Assistants aboard the Arbella, March 23rd, . . . Mr John Humfrey (in regard hee was to stay behinde in England) was discharged of his Deputy-shipp, & Mr Thomas Dudley chosen Deputy in his place.

Also aboard the *Arbella*, with her parents, husband, and brother and sisters, was the seventeen-year-old Anne Bradstreet. Her childhood left behind, in quiet Lincolnshire where she had lived and studied, she made ready, armed with her faith and as a woman sharing with her men the challenge of the unknown, to find a new life in the strange world across the sea.

CHAPTER FOUR

The Settlement of Massachusetts Bay

". . . in this sharp winter."

(THOMAS DUDLEY—*Letter to the Countess of Lincoln*)

John Milton wrote in 1641, in his anti-episcopal pamphlet *Of Reformation touching Church Discipline in England:*

> What numbers of faithful and freeborn Englishmen, and good Christians, have been constrained to forsake their dearest home, their friends and kindred, whom nothing but the wide ocean, and the savage deserts of America, could hide and shelter from the fury of the bishops. O if we could but see the shape of our dear mother England, as poets are wont to give a personal form to what they please, how would she appear, think ye, but in a mourning weed, with ashes upon her head, and tears abundantly flowing from her eyes, to behold so many of her children exposed at once, and thrust from things of dearest necessity, because their conscience could not assent to things which the bishops thought indifferent.

When this was written more than 21,000 English colonists had already settled in New England, driven by the whip of Archbishop Laud's ecclesiastical authority, and by the inner impetus of the intent to re-create Christ's kingdom in the wilderness. The Angli-can priest and poet George Herbert had earlier, in "The Church Militant," sounded a warning that may possibly have been in-spired by the preparations for the great migration of 1630.

> Religion stands on tiptoe in our land
> Ready to pass to the American strand.

The assembling of the Winthrop Fleet, as it has come to be called, certainly marked the beginning of large-scale colonial enter-prise in New England. The previous undertakings had been ex-perimental, restricted as to numbers of settlers and financial back-ing, but with the founding of Salem and its re-inforcement by the expeditions of 1628 and 1629, the basis for a strong and expanding colony was established. The initiating company in England in-cluded noblemen, lawyers, clergymen, landed gentry, and prosper-ous city merchants, and represented a great many of the English counties, so there must have been general awareness of the am-bitious plan that was afoot, and recognition, fostered by the lead-ing Puritan members of the company, of the zealously religious nature of the project.

The *Arbella*, in which Anne Bradstreet and her family made the voyage to America, was the flag-ship, or admiral, of the fleet of eleven vessels that carried seven hundred colonists to the shores of Massachusetts. John Winthrop described the *Arbella* as a ship "of three hundred and fifty tons . . . being manned with fifty-two seamen, and twenty-eight pieces of ordnance." [1] She had been the *Eagle,* leader of Sir Kenelm Digby's privateers in the Mediter-ranean, and was renamed in honor of the Lady Arbella Johnson, who was also aboard with her husband Isaac Johnson, one of the five "undertakers," or chief financial investors, for the colony.

1. John Winthrop, *History of New England, 1630–1649,* ed. James Savage, Boston, 1853, Vol. I, pp. 1–2.

All the vessels of the fleet were originally designed as merchant freighters, for no passenger ships as such existed in those days. The ones that carried the human cargo of colonists were the "sweet ships," which were kept well caulked and dry, of the wine trade. In each of these, temporary quarters for about one hundred men, women, and children were arranged "between decks," that is in the space between the main deck and the roof of the hold; it is thought that roughly partitioned compartments were built for the women and children, and that the men slept in hammocks slung from every available point. The crew occupied the forecastle cabin in the bow, and in the high poop a-stern were the officers' quarters, the "great cabin," which was used for divine services and other meetings, and probably on the *Arbella*, the largest vessel, a few tiny cabins which were fitted in for the use of the more distinguished women passengers. The galley was between decks, near a hatchway to the hold where the firewood was stored. The only heat on the ship came from the cooking-stove, and since no artificial lighting was allowed, because of the danger of fire, the passengers went to their uneasy beds with the going down of the sun.[2]

The *Arbella*, of which no exact description has survived, is believed to have been about one hundred and fifty feet in length, with a hold eighteen to twenty feet deep. In this space were stored the personal possessions of the colonists, as much furniture, household equipment, and other provisions for a self-sustaining future as the individual family could afford to transport at the cost of £4 per ton. Also in the hold were the company's supplies for the colony, firearms, ammunition, and tools and materials for build-

2. Charles Edward Banks's *The Winthrop Fleet of 1630* (Boston, 1930) is a thorough study of the ships, their passengers and cargoes, and the voyage itself, compiled from Winthrop's *History* and other contemporary writings. Much of the material in this chapter concerning the journey to Massachusetts Bay is based on his work.

ing and farming, as well as the food and drink with which each passenger was furnished in return for the adult fare of £5.

Winthrop listed the provender put aboard the *Arbella*; she carried ten thousand gallons of beer, but only thirty-five hundred gallons of water, which could not be kept potable for very long; two hogsheads of "syder," and one of vinegar, completed the fluid ration for a voyage that might last as long as twelve weeks. The solid food consisted of sixteen hogsheads of dried or powdered meat, six hundred pounds of "haberdyne" or salt codfish, twenty thousand biscuits, one barrel of flour, thirty bushels of oatmeal, and forty bushels of dried peas. For seasonings and cooking fats to improve this unpalatable diet there were eleven firkins of butter, one barrel of salt, one hundred pounds of suet, and a bushel and a half of mustard seed. No mention is made of sugar, so it is presumed that the passengers were expected to bring their own supplies of this, along with such other luxuries as dried fruits, spices, and medicinal cordials. Nor, unfortunately, was the *Arbella* provided with limes or lemons for the prevention of scurvy, consequently a number of the colonists fell ill on the voyage with this dreaded wasting disease, and did not long survive their landing in New England.

Three or four of the ships carried animals instead of human passengers. Winthrop listed two hundred and forty cows and "about sixty horses"; these were kept in pens on the open decks, and a good many of them were lost because of the cruelly buffetting storms the fleet encountered.

In the middle of March 1629/30 the ships began to assemble at Southampton, and those who were to take passage gathered for the embarkation. John Cotton, the beloved pastor of many of the colonists, came from Boston to take leave of his friends and preached to them the farewell sermon, *God's Promise to His*

Plantation,[3] on the text from II Samuel, 7, 10 (Geneva version):
"Also I will appoint a place for my people Israel, and will plant
it, that they may dwell in a place of their own, and move no
more."

When the *Arbella, Ambrose, Talbot,* and *Jewel* were ready to
sail, it was decided that they should set forth on the voyage and
leave the other seven ships, still loading and preparing, to follow
when they could. The four leaders thereupon sailed across Southampton Water and the Solent to Cowes, at the Isle of Wight,
where contrary winds forced them to remain for some days. On
the 28th March Governor Winthrop wrote to his wife, "from
aboard the *Arbella,* riding at the Cowes":

> It pleaseth God, that thou shouldst once again hear from me
> before our departure, and I hope this shall come safe to thy
> hands. . . . The wind hath been against us this week and more;
> but this day it is come fair to the north, so as we are preparing
> (by God's assistance) to set sail in the morning. . . . And now
> (my sweet soul) I must once again take my last farewell of thee
> in Old England. It goeth very near to my heart to leave thee; but
> I know to whom I have committed thee, even to him who loves
> thee much better than any husband can, who hath taken ac-
> count of the hairs of thy head, and puts all thy tears in his
> bottle, who can, and (if it be for his glory) will bring us together
> again with peace and comfort. . . . I hope the course we have
> agreed upon will be some ease to us both. Mondays and Fridays,
> at five of the clock at night, we shall meet in spirit till we meet
> in person. . . . Therefore I will only take thee now and my
> sweet children in mine arms, and kiss and embrace you all, and
> so leave you with my God. Farewell, farewell. I bless you all in
> the name of the Lord Jesus. . . . Pray all for us. Farewell.[4]

On the following day the governor began to write the journal
which he continued with characteristic faithfulness until the year

3. Printed in London, 1630 and 1634.
4. Winthrop, *History,* Vol. I, Appendix, pp. 442–43.

of his death, 1649. This precious document, called *Winthrop's History of New England, 1630–1649* in the editions of 1825–26 and 1853, prepared by James Savage, gives us a day-to-day account of the voyage of the *Arbella* and her three companions. Their departure was an interrupted one, for when they sailed again, on the 29th March, it was only from Cowes to Yarmouth, where they were obliged to take shelter for nine days from heavy storms of wind and rain from the southwest. On the 6th April Winthrop wrote: "The lady Arbella and the gentlewomen, and Mr. Johnson and some others went on shore to refresh themselves"; probably Anne Bradstreet was among them, feeling for the last time the solid earth of England beneath her feet. The captain of Yarmouth Castle, and Matthew Cradock, the former governor of the company, came aboard the flag-ship to wish the colonists God-speed, and the ship's guns fired salutes when they returned to shore.

On the 7th April the voyagers addressed a formal message of leave-taking to the church of their homeland, in *The Humble Request of His Majesties loyall Subjects . . . late gone for New-England; to the rest of their Brethren, in and of the Church of England,* saying in part:

> . . . we desire you would be pleased to take notice of the principals, and body of our company, as those who esteeme it our honour, to call the *Church* of *England*, from whence wee rise, our deare Mother, and cannot part from our native Country, where she specially resideth, without much sadness of heart, and many teares in our eyes. . . . If any there be, who through want of cleare intelligence of our course, or tendernesse of affection towards us, cannot conceive so well of our way as we could desire, we would intreat such not to despise us, nor to desert us in their prayers & affections. . . .
>
> What goodness you shall extend to us in this or any other Christian kindnesse, we your Brethren in CHRIST IESUS shall labour to repay in what dutie wee are or shall be able to per-

forme, promising so far as God shall enable us to give him no
rest on your behalfes, wishing our heads and hearts may be as
fountaines of teares for your everlasting welfare, when wee shall
be in our poore Cottages in the wildernesse, over-shadowed
with the spirit of supplication, through the manifold necessities
and tribulations which may not altogether unexpectedly, nor,
we hope, unprofitably, befall us.[5]

At last, the farewells completed and the weather being clear
with a north-east wind on the following day, Thursday the 8th
April, "about six in the morning," Winthrop wrote, "we weighed
anchor and set sail." Thus began, for Thomas Dudley and his
family, Simon Bradstreet and his young wife Anne, and all the
other souls in the four small ships, a voyage of almost three
thousand miles across the lonely wastes of the Atlantic. There was
no loneliness on the first day at sea, however, for early in the
morning of the 9th April eight sails were sighted astern, and the
captain of the *Arbella,* fearing that they were Spanish privateers
from Dunkirk, ordered the decks cleared and the guns made ready
for action. As the strangers drew near, every man on the ship was
given a musket or a crossbow, some of the temporary cabins were
demolished and "such bed-matters as were subject to fire," though
so much needed for the long cold journey, were thrown over-
board.

The lady Arbella and the other women and children were removed into the lower deck, that they might be out of danger.
All things being thus fitted, we went to prayer upon the upper
deck.[6]

5. Printed in London for John Bellamie, 1630, and reprinted in facsimile,
with an introduction by G. P. Winship, by the New England Society, New
York, 1912. The Reverend John White of Dorchester is believed to be the
author of this document.
6. Winthrop, *History*, Vol. I, p. 7.

The captain, whose courage seems to have given heart to all in his charge, finally stood about to face the enemy, when it was soon discovered that they were not privateers, but friendly vessels bound for various destinations. Cheerful salutes were exchanged, and the relieved governor gave thanks to God for deliverance from fear and danger.

The first Sunday at sea was so rough and stormy that most of the passengers were laid low, and the religious services could not be held. Winthrop described the measures that were taken on the Monday, when the storm had abated, to help the miserable voyagers gain their sea legs.

> Our children and others, that were sick, and lay groaning in the cabins, we fetched out, and having stretched a rope from the steerage to the mainmast, we made them stand, some of one side and some of the other, and sway it up and down till they were warm, and by this means they soon grew well and merry.

Thereafter through the long days and nights the small ships sailed on, encountering much stormy weather, rain, and fog, interspersed by delaying calms and welcome intervals of fair winds and skies. The passengers endured the prevailing cold, the misery of their cramped quarters, and the wretched diet of salt meat or fish and hard biscuit. There were no serious casualties aboard the *Arbella*, except that a woman had a stillborn child, but among the other three ships there were seventeen deaths, and many of the colonists arrived ill and weakened by malnutrition.

On the 8th June, the sixty-second day after they had sailed from Yarmouth, Winthrop wrote in his journal:

> . . . about three in the afternoon, we had sight of land to the N.W. about ten leagues. . . . We had now fair sunshine weather, and so pleasant a sweet air as did much refresh us, and

there came a smell off the shore like the smell of a garden. There came a wild pigeon into our ship, and another small land bird.

After cruising to the southwest for three more days, the *Arbella* cast anchor in the outer harbor of Salem on Saturday, the 12th June, 1630. John Endecott and the Reverend Samuel Skelton came aboard to welcome the new settlers, and the governor and assistants,

> . . . some other gentlemen, and some of the women, and our captain, returned with them to Nahumkeck, where we supped with a good venison pasty and good beer, and at night we returned to our ship, but some of the women stayed behind.
>
> In the mean time most of our people went on shore upon the land of Cape Ann, which lay very near us, and gathered store of fine strawberries.
>
> An Indian came aboard us and lay there all night.[7]

The *Jewel* arrived on the 13th June and the *Ambrose* on the 17th. The eight remaining ships of the fleet, including the *Talbot* which had been driven off course by a storm in mid-April, and had lost fourteen passengers, came into harbor between the 1st and the 6th July.

What the sea-weary travelers found when they disembarked at Salem plantation cannot have brought much comfort or encouragement to them. The settlement consisted of no more than forty dwellings; of these only about a third had the semblance of houses, being built of oak frames and pine boards roughly hewn and sawn from the abundant standing timber. "The faire house for the Governor," as the Reverend Francis Higginson described the headquarters of John Endecott, the chief officer of the Salem colony, was of four rooms and an attic, with a huge central chimney of

7. Winthrop, *History*, Vol. I, p. 31.

field-stone and brick, a shingled roof, and probably small leaded windows of diamond-paned glass brought from England. The other houses were thatch-roofed cabins of one or two rooms, with stone fireplaces and wattle-and-daub or log chimneys and windows made of oiled paper. These were for the more substantial families among the settlers; the rest of the community lived, as best they could, either in cave-like dugouts burrowed into hillsides and roofed with timber and thatch, or in "English wigwams," copied from Indian shelters, that were, in Higginson's words, "verie little and homely, but made with small poles prick't into the ground and so bended and fastened at the tops and on the side, they are matted with boughs and covered with sedge and old mats." [8] Each of these dens of wood and straw had a wattle-and-daub chimney, a wooden door and one small paper window; the earth floor was padded with rushes in a pitiful effort to mitigate the cold and damp.[9]

The primitive village was overcrowded; provisions were in very short supply, and such necessities of life as were not still on hand, from stores brought over from England, had to be produced in the most immediate and rudimentary fashion. The colonists of Winthrop's company realized without delay that they would do bet-

8. Higginson, *New Englands Plantation*, 1630; reprinted in Young, *Chronicles of the First Planters of Massachusetts Bay*, Boston, 1846, pp. 239–59.

9. In 1930, to mark the Massachusetts Bay Tercentenary, the City of Salem constructed a model, as representative as possible, of the original settlement as the Winthrop company found it. The "Pioneers' Village," in park land beside the harbor, with its garden of English flowers and herbs, its crude equipment for making salt, soap, and bricks, the forge and saw pit, stocks and pillory, and a replica of the *Arbella* permanently moored at the small pier, is an impressive memorial to the physical endurance of the early colonists. All building construction, to the smallest detail, was done by hand, with such tools and materials as the founders themselves used. This authenticity of reproduction, combined with the effects of almost half a century of New England weather, gives the silent village a semblance of reality that is very moving.

ter to establish their own plantations, either on virgin land or where small groups from Salem had already begun to settle, in the surrounding area.

Thomas Dudley's remarkable newsletter, which he addressed in March 1631 to "the Right Honorable, my very good Lady, the Lady Bridget, Countess of Lincoln," gives us the most compact and straightforward account, of any that has survived, of what happened during the first summer, autumn, and winter after his arrival in the New World.[10] The beginning of the letter shows how close was the association between the family of Lord Lincoln and "Your Honor's old thankful servant, T.D.," as he signed himself.

> MADAM,
>   Your letters (which are not common nor cheap,) following me hither into New-England, and bringing with them renewed testimonies of the accustomed favors you honored me with in the Old, have drawn from me this narrative retribution, . . . the thankfullest present I had to send over the seas. . . .
>   I have, in the throng of domestic, and not altogether free from public business, thought fit to commit to memory our present condition, and what hath befallen us . . . which I will do shortly, after my usual manner, and must do rudely, having yet no table, nor other room to write in than by the fireside upon my knee, in this sharp winter; to which my family must have leave to resort, though they break good manners, and make me many times forget what I would say, and say what I would not.

Dudley's story opens with a brief description of the territory and its Indian inhabitants, and a review of the English settlement projects from 1620 onwards. Then follows a sombre account of what awaited the Winthrop company at the end of their voyage.

10. See p. 91 above.

Our four ships which set out in April arrived here in June
and July, where we found the Colony in a sad and unexpected
condition, above eighty of them being dead the winter before;
and many of those alive weak and sick; all the corn and bread
amongst them all hardly sufficient to feed them a fortnight. . . .

But bearing these things as we might, we began to consult
of the place of our sitting down; for Salem, where we landed,
pleased us not. And to that purpose, some were sent to the Bay,
to search up the rivers for a convenient place; . . . but some
other of us . . . unshipped our goods into other vessels, and
with much cost and labor brought them in July to Charlestown.

This small plantation, begun in 1628 by some of Endecott's
company, was about fifteen miles to the southwest of Salem,
where the mouth of the Charles River forms a part of what is
now the inner harbor of the city of Boston. A considerable number
of the newly arrived colonists, among them the governor, Isaac
Johnson and Dudley and Bradstreet, decided to settle there, while
other groups established encampments, to which they gave the
names of Roxbury, Watertown, Medford, and Dorchester, at
other sites in the vicinity of the harbor. "This dispersion," wrote
Dudley, "troubled some of us; but help it we could not, wanting
ability to remove to any place fit to build a town upon, and the
time too short to deliberate any longer, lest the winter should
surprise us before we had builded our houses."

At Charlestown the settlers found only one substantial dwelling,
modeled on the "faire house" at Salem; here Governor Winthrop
and the other officers were installed, while "the multitude," according to the early records of Charlestown,[11] "set up cottages,
booths and tents about the Town Hill." Captain Edward Johnson,
one of the colonists, noted that "the Lady *Arrabella* and some
other godly Women aboad at *Salem,* but their Husbands con-

11. Young, *Chronicles of First Planters of Massachusetts Bay,* pp. 371–87.

tinued at *Charles* Town, both for the settling the civill Government, and gathering another Church of *Christ*." [12]

In steadfast dedication to their vision of the New Jerusalem, a
small company of weary men stood in the forest clearing, among
the roughly built little houses, and covenanted together on Sunday the 1st August, 1630,

> . . . to unite our selves into one Congregation, or Church, under
> the Lord Jesus Christ our Head, in such sort as becometh all
> those whom He hath Redeemed, and Sanctifyed to Himselfe,
> . . . and bind our selves, to walke in all our wayes according
> to the Rule of the Gospell, and in all sincere Conformity to
> His holy Ordinaunces, and in mutuall love, and respect each
> to other, so neere as God shall give us grace.[13]

The names of John Winthrop, Thomas Dudley, Isaac Johnson,
and the Reverend John Wilson, who was chosen as pastor, head
the list of church members, and after two others comes that of
Simon Bradstreet. Then there is an indication that the settlement
was soon ready to welcome its leading women to their first homes,
such as they were, in the wilderness, for the twelfth and thir-
teenth names on the list are:

> Dorothy Dudley y[e] wife of Tho: Dudley
> Anne Bradstreete y[e] wife of Simon Bradstreete.

But the most honored of all their women did not come with
them. The Lady Arbella Johnson had arrived in the New World
exhausted by the long voyage in the ship that bore her name.

---

12. *Wonder-Working Providence of Sions Saviour in New England*, ed.
Poole, Andover (Mass.), 1867, p. 37.

13. MS. Transcript of the original records of the First Church in Boston,
1630–87, collection of the Massachusetts Historical Society, Boston; John Gorham Palfrey, *History of New England*, Boston, 1859, Vol. I, p. 316.

Unable to recover her strength in the two months of hard living that followed, she died in Salem and was laid to rest in an unmarked grave in that primitive community.

Anne Bradstreet, with the economy of words that is characteristic of her prose writings, put all her experience of this fateful year into a few lines of her private memoirs:

> I . . . came into this Country, where I found a new world and new manners, at which my heart rose. But after I was convinced it was the way of God, I submitted to it and joined to the church at Boston.

She wrote "the church at Boston" because that is what it shortly became. During the hot summer many of the settlers at Charlestown fell ill, and it was generally felt that the plantation did not have an adequate supply of fresh water. A solitary Englishman named William Blackstone had been living for several years on a point across the river, called Shawmut or Trimountain, where there were several excellent springs; at his suggestion the governor, with John Wilson and a number of others, decided to move from Charlestown to this place. They named the new settlement Boston, in honor of the Earl of Lincoln, Isaac Johnson, and the Reverend John Cotton; as the elected pastor was with them their church was established here, and those who had remained behind were obliged for two years, until they acquired a minister of their own, "generally to go to Boston on the Lord's day to hear the word and enjoy the sacraments," as the early records of Charlestown put it.

There was good reason for Anne Bradstreet's heart to rise in dread and dismay during those first months in the Massachusetts territory. She and her father both referred sadly to the "manners" that the pioneering life engendered. This may seem a trivial cause for complaint to us who look back over the centuries at what was essentially a struggle for survival. The amenities of gracious behavior could hardly be expected to flourish in the midst of the damp and dirt of the hastily built, overcrowded shelters, the crippling illnesses, and the spiritual disabilities of homesickness, sorrow, and discouragement. But the Puritan's code of good manners was an integral part of his standard of Christian conduct, and for these devout colonists, especially those among them who had been privileged to live gently in England, it must have been disheartening to see the formality of every-day communication, the respect for individual privacy, the quick concern for a troubled neighbor, and the dignity of innate self-possession, too often falter and fail under the weight of outrageous circumstance.

Thomas Dudley wrote with some severity of those whose hearts failed them at the outset, while the hard task of shelter-raising was being hurried forward:

> . . . they who had health to labor fell to building, wherein many were interrupted with sickness, and many died weekly, yea, almost daily. . . . Insomuch that the ships being now upon their return, some for England, some for Ireland, there was, as I take it, not much less than a hundred, . . . which returned back again; and glad were we so to be rid of them.

Yet what he went on to relate makes their retreat seem not altogether contemptible.

> The ships being gone, victuals wasting, and mortality increasing, we held divers fasts in our several congregations. But the Lord would not yet be deprecated; for about the beginning of September died Mr. Gager, . . . a skilful chirurgeon, . . . and Mr. Higginson, . . . a zealous and a profitable preacher—this of a consumption, that of a fever; and on the 30th of September died Mr. JOHNSON, another of the five undertakers, (the lady ARBELLA, his wife, being dead a month before.)

. . . He made a most godly end, dying willingly, professing his life better spent in promoting this Plantation than it could have been any other way. He left to us a loss greater than the most conceived. . . .

So that now there were left of the five undertakers but the Governor, Sir Richard Saltonstall, and myself, and seven other of the Assistants. And of the people who came over with us, from the time of their setting sail from England in April, 1630, until December following, there died by estimation about two hundred at the least: so low hath the Lord brought us!

Anne Bradstreet was still an adolescent in age, having presumably just passed her seventeenth birthday, when she left England with her family. But the rigors of that eighteenth year of her life must have brought to her character, with great rapidity, the sober maturity of adulthood. Her youth had been spent among kindly people and pleasant surroundings; although she had had two serious illnesses and was well aware of the religious and political persecution that threatened her family and friends, her world had been, on the whole, an orderly and happy one. Then came the obligation to bid that part of her life farewell, the wearisome voyage, and the grinding sadness of the battle against hunger, cold, and disease in the forests of Massachusetts, while death took one after another of her companions. We are told by all their contemporary recorders that these brief sojourners died bravely, with unshaken faith in God and in the validity of their purpose. But we know that they died miserably too, burning with fever or wasted by scurvy, in the draughty cottages and smoke-filled wigwams, and that even the dignities of burial, so important to the seventeenth-century mind, were denied them. The inquisitive, thieving Indians were all about, waiting to disturb the rest of any who were not hurriedly hidden away in unmarked graves.

Few of the colonists were so fortunate as Anne Bradstreet, who did not lose any member of her family circle. Yet she must have been closely touched by the general grief for the deaths of the Lady Arbella and her husband. Lord Lincoln's sister was eleven years older than his steward's daughter, but shared memories of the good days at Sempringham may have created a bond of friendship between them. Thomas Dudley did not allow his personal sense of loss to appear in his letter to the Countess, which was intended for public circulation among those who were interested in the colony. But two generations later Cotton Mather, in the *Magnalia*, recalled the poignancy of the Lady Arbella's early death, writing that she

> . . . left an earthly paradise in the family of an Earldom, to encounter the sorrows of a wilderness, for the entertainment of a pure worship in the house of God; and then immediately left that wilderness for the heavenly paradise.

"Well," continues Dudley's narrative," "yet they who survived were not discouraged, but bearing God's corrections with humility, and trusting in his mercies, . . . we began again in December to consult about a fit place to build a town upon." Charlestown still suffered from the lack of a good water supply; also, the early records tell us, the settlement was thought to be too vulnerable to attack by the Indians.

> Now after all this, the Indians' treachery being feared, it was judged meet the English should place their towns as near together as could be. For which end Mr. Dudley and Mr. Broadstreet, with some others, went and built and planted between Charlestown and Waterton; who called it Newtown, which was afterwards called Cambridge.[14]

14. Young, *Chronicles of First Planters of Massachusetts Bay*, p. 381.

The founders of Cambridge did not attempt their move in the cold months, but remained in Charlestown during a period of near-starvation, when

> . . . people were necessitated to live upon clams, and muscles, and ground-nuts, and acorns, and these got with much difficulty in the winter time. . . . The Governor himself had the last batch of bread in the oven. . . . But God, who delights to appear in greatest straights, did work marvellously at this time; for . . . about the month of February or March, in comes Mr. Pearce, laden with provisions.[15]

For the safe and timely return of the ship *Lyon,* Captain William Pierce, Master, which had been sent to Ireland for desperately needed supplies, a day of thanksgiving was held throughout the colony on the 22nd February.

In the spring of 1631 Dudley and Bradstreet received their house-lots in the new settlement a few miles up the Charles River. These were recorded in *The Registere Booke of the Landes and Houses in the Newtowne, 1635,*[16] and are now a part of the wide area occupied by Harvard University. Here at last, having weathered their first year in New England, and learned some harsh lessons from it, the two families were able to provide themselves with houses that were sturdily built, against the searching climate, and sizable enough to give them some semblance of fitness for decent living.

Anne Bradstreet had apparently managed to escape, up to this time, the various diseases that took so heavy a toll from the Winthrop company. But her turn came during the second year in Newtown, and later she wrote of the experience:

15. *Ibid.* p. 385.
16. Cambridge (Mass.), printed by order of the City Council, 1896.

After some time I fell into a lingering sicknes like a consumption, together with a lamenesse, which correction I saw the Lord sent to humble and try me and doe mee Good: and it was not altogether ineffectual.

A significant result of this illness was the short poem that provides the only known evidence as to the date of her birth, and was undoubtedly one of her earliest experiments in the writing of verse.

UPON A FIT OF SICKNESS, *Anno.* 1632.
Aetatis suae, 19.

> Twice ten years old, not fully told
>   Since nature gave me breath,
> My race is run, my thread is spun,
>   lo here is fatal Death.
> All men must dye, and so must I
>   this cannot be revok'd
> For Adams sake, this word God spake
>   When he so high provok'd.
> Yet live I shall, this life's but small,
>   in place of highest bliss,
> Where I shall have all I can crave,
>   no life is like to this.
> For what's this life, but care and strife?
>   since first we came from womb,
> Our strength doth waste, our time doth hast,
>   and then we go to th' Tomb.
> O Bubble blast, how long can'st last?
>   that always art a breaking,
> No sooner blown, but dead and gone,
>   ev'n as a word that's speaking.
> O whil'st I live this grace me give,
>   I doing good may be.
> Then deaths arrest I shall count best,
>   because it's thy decree;

Bestow much cost there's nothing lost,
    to make Salvation sure,
O great's the gain, though got with pain,
    comes by profession pure.
The race is run, the field is won,
    the victory's mine I see,
For ever know, thou envious foe,
    the foyle belongs to thee.

This imitative and awkward piece of doggerel verse (which Anne Bradstreet's family thought well enough of to have included in the second edition of her poems, in 1678) is without a redeeming touch of felicity, save possibly in the phrase "ev'n as a word that's speaking," and holds no suggestion of the vigorous and expressive style that its author would eventually master. It is one among the thousands of private devotional exercises written in the early seventeenth century by men and women of all denominations of the Christian faith. Those who were brought up from infancy on the literature of nonconformist piety, with its recurrent theme of direct communication between the elected believer and God, were perhaps particularly inclined to record their deepest feelings in heartfelt, if halting, verse. Kenneth Murdock has pointed out that

> New England Puritans constantly read poetry—or at least verse—and hundreds of them tried their hands at writing it. Anyone who explores Puritan diaries, journals, histories and biographies will find in them many bits of pious rhyme. . . . It is safe to say that the New England Puritans, far from being hostile to poetry, both needed and loved it.[17]

For this testing of her hand, Anne Bradstreet chose a humble and familiar meter, the old ballad form. Originally written in long,

17. *Literature and Theology in Colonial New England*, Cambridge (Mass.), 1949, pp. 140–41.

seven-stressed iambic lines, called "fourteeners," the jog-trot rhythm was shaped into couplets, of alternate eight- and six-syllabled lines, by the Scottish, Welsh, and Irish minstrels and the writers of broadside verse. George Saintsbury, in his *History of English Prosody*, commented on its timeless popularity:

> The ballad quatrain, or common measure, is perhaps the most definitely English . . . of all English metres. It comes the most naturally of all to an English tongue or an English ear; it adapts itself with sublime indifference to the highest poetry and to the lowest doggerel.

The "Sternhold and Hopkins" version of the *Psalms,* first printed in 1562 and long used thereafter by the Puritans, provided the churches with a rhyming, ballad-like psalter that included such questionable hymnody as:

> My shepheard is the living Lord,
>   nothing therefore I neede;
> In pastures faire with waters calme,
>   he sets me forth to feed.

Boston's first pastor, John Wilson, had edified his earlier congregation in England with a long verse-history, in broken fourteeners, of the blessings of Protestantism. This pious achievement, called *A Song, or Story, For the Lasting Remembrance of diverse famous works, which God hath done in our time,* was printed in London in 1626; a passage describing the plague of 1625 will serve to illustrate its qualities.

> In one yeares space, or lesse than so,
>   (From time the Plague began)
> To what a number did they grow,
>   That death grip't in his spanne?

Sixtie two thousand at the least,
Sixe hundred seventy seven,
Were made appeare by deaths arrest,
Before the God of heaven.

Anne Bradstreet had read great and beautiful poems, but she had also undoubtedly worked her way through Wilson's pretentious numbers. The occurrence of the figure of speech "deaths arrest," in both her lines and Wilson's stanza, is significant; it may also remind us of the "Serjeant Death" passage already quoted from one of her long formal poems, that has been made much of by commentators as a possible indication that she had read *Hamlet*.[18] She would have heard the sailors on the *Arbella* singing their sea ballads, and the monotonous rhythm of the Sternhold and Hopkins *Psalms* was with her constantly in New England. So that when she was deeply moved by the thought of approaching death, in 1632, she fell naturally into a commonplace meter and a hackneyed phraseology to express her fear and resignation and sense of final triumph.

There are only two hints of self-conscious literary craftsmanship in this short experiment in verse. Anne's use of the Latin formula "*Anno—Aetatis suae—*" has a touch of the "learned lady"; no more than an occasional phrase or tag in Latin occurs throughout the whole body of her writing, so the appearance of it in the title of this very early poem seems to be a deliberate intellectual gesture, intended to echo the solemn wording of an epitaph. There is evidence too of a studied approach in the internal rhyming of the eight-syllabled lines; this is a form of poetic trickery which has the disadvantage of making every phrase sound like a cliché, as indeed in this small effort of Anne Bradstreet's practically all of them are. Ancestors of her poem are the anonymous "Nut-Brown Maid" and John Still's "Jolly Good Ale and Old," neither of them

18. See pp. 64–65 above.

in the least concerned with piety, though the author of the latter was Bishop of Bath and Wells. And thirty years later the internal-rhymed broken fourteeners made a grisly reappearance in that formidable New England "best seller," Michael Wigglesworth's *The Day of Doom*.[19]

Anne Bradstreet's critical sense was apparently awakened by this initial venture, for never again, in any of her surviving poems, did she use the double-rhyming line. The ballad meter occurs again in ten devotional lyrics, or prayers in verse, but these are among her private writings that were not intended for general circulation. From the beginning of her serious preoccupation with the craft of letters, Anne Bradstreet seems to have employed a selective judgment in the choice of metrical forms for her more ambitious poems. She was limited to some extent by the literary conventions of her day, but her instinct for the suitability of form to matter was certainly superior to that of any other seventeenth-century New England versifier with the exception of Edward Taylor, whose remarkable devotional lyrics were unpublished, and apparently unknown even to those around him, during his lifetime.

If the thought of becoming a poet ever occurred to Anne before she left England, there is no surviving suggestion of it. What seems probable is that she grew up as a delighted reader, with a true love for poetry but without a suspicion that she would one day take up the creative pen herself. Then when she had been deeply stirred by the strange adventures of the migration, and felt her own death near at hand in 1632, a predominantly emotional impulse produced the naïve and stumbling lines that may well have been her first. Perhaps she made a few other attempts at verse-writing soon after this; towards the beginning of the collection of spiritual reminiscences that she made for her children are two or three undated lyrics that seem clearly experimental. At any rate it may be supposed that when she saw lines of verse of

19. See pp. 322–25 below.

her own composition, on paper before her, and felt the beat of metrical rhythms in her head, Anne Bradstreet discovered that she had an urgent desire to be something more than a private versifier.

Another six years were to go by before the first of her poems intended for public circulation was completed. The experiences and influences of these years had a great deal to do with the appearance on the New England scene, in 1638, of young Mistress Bradstreet as a writer of poetry. Respected as she was by her fellow-colonists, because of her social position, and apparently genuinely loved for the grace and excellence of her character, she must nevertheless have been the target of some quizzical glances, and not a few sharp words, for permitting herself to do such an extraordinary thing. The courage that was engendered in her by her desire to write was surely extraordinary, for no Puritan of her time took up a literary vocation without accepting a heavy responsibility, and there was no precedent in the history of Puritanism for a woman to shoulder such a burden. Perry Miller has clearly stated the extent of this obligation, in telling us that

> . . . verse was simply a heightened form of eloquence, . . . like the oration, its function was to carry inartificial arguments from man to man. . . . Poetry existed primarily for its utility, it was foredoomed to didacticism, and because it was the most highly ornate of the arts, it was always in grave danger of overstepping proper limits and becoming pleasing for its own sake. . . . Poetry in Puritan eyes, therefore, was a species of rhetoric, a dress for great truths, a sugar for the pill.
>
> Only some two persons in seventeenth-century New England have left any evidence that they were deeply imbued with a true poetic insight; the greater of these [was] the Reverend Edward Taylor, . . . [whose] verse combines into one motif the themes of the limitation of human faculties and of the theological necessity for a plain style even in poetry. . . . The other of the true New England poets, Anne Bradstreet, expressed the gist of

the matter more succinctly: "I have not studied in this you read to show my skill, but to declare the Truth—not to sett forth myself, but the Glory of God." [20]

From a study of her works one draws the conclusion that Anne Bradstreet remained fully aware, throughout her life as a writer, of the challenging position she had chosen to occupy. So much so that she seems to emerge from her history with two distinct facets of personality, one being that of the fulfilled and integrated woman, the other that of the somewhat self-conscious poet. These two come together and are fused into a whole only occasionally, but when they do her surest and most moving poetry is the result.

In the brief spiritual autobiography that she bequeathed to her children, there is no mention of the fact that her leisure hours in New England were devoted to the composition of a large body of verse. If this legacy alone, among all her writings, had survived, it would appear that she was a thoughtful, steadfast Christian, a devoted wife and mother, and the writer of clear, vigorous prose and some ingenuous pieces of private and reverential verse, only two of which have enough poetic merit to give them lasting interest. But nothing in the little volume of personal memoirs suggests that Anne Bradstreet had a serious vocation as a poet. On the other hand her more formal or public poems, especially those written from 1638 to 1644, while she was getting into her literary stride and wrestling with the technical problems that her craft presented, are full of references, many of them critical, to herself as a poet. This quality of objectivity is one of the main supports in the fabric of her writing. It permitted her to express diffidence as to her own powers, at the start, then to turn briskly defiant, when she felt more confident. And it gave her always a healthy sense of the extent and limitations of her talent.

20. P. Miller, *The New England Mind: The Seventeenth Century*, New York, 1939, pp. 360–62.

CHAPTER FIVE

The Apprentice Writer

"My muse unto a Child I may compare."
(ANNE BRADSTREET—*In honour of Du Bartas*)

After her recovery from the "lingering sicknes" of 1632, Anne Bradstreet was for a time preoccupied with other than literary creation. Her gratitude for the birth of her first-born, Samuel, at Newtown in 1633 or 1634, is recorded in her private journal:

> It pleased God to keep me a long time without a child, which was a great greif to me, and cost mee many prayers and tears before I obtaind one, and after him gave mee many more.

She could not have been more than twenty-one years old when Samuel was born, but five or six years of marriage without motherhood had distressed and alarmed her. When her son was a grown man she remembered her earlier anxiety in the presence of a fresh one, and wrote in the verse-prayer, "Upon my Son Samuel his going for England, Novem. 6, 1647":

> Thou mighty God of Sea and Land,
> I here resigne into thy hand

> The Son of Prayers, of Vowes, of teares,
> The child I stay'd for many yeares.
> Thou heard'st me then and gav'st him me;
> Hear me again, I give him Thee.

Seven more children were born to the Bradstreets between 1635 and 1652, so in spite of recurring intervals of ill health Anne had no further cause for concern about her ability to bear a child.

Thomas Dudley was elected the second governor of the colony in May 1634. John Winthrop had held the office continuously since 1630, but his domineering ways had made him somewhat less popular than during the strenuous early period of settlement, when his authority had been accepted without question. Winthrop and Dudley had quarreled in 1632, the governor accusing his deputy of usury in the sale of corn, and of extravagant ostentation in the decorating of his house at Newtown with what appeared to be wainscoting. As to the house, Dudley replied that he had simply ordered some extra boarding nailed to the walls to keep out the cold drafts, but he was so angered by these criticisms that he asked to be relieved of the deputyship. The general court considered his resignation and refused to accept it, and peace was apparently restored. There were other disagreements between these two proud men, but the marriage of Winthrop's daughter Mary to Samuel Dudley, the deputy's eldest child, in this same year of 1632, seems to have brought about a genuine reconciliation. At any rate the two leaders continued to work together, for the good of the colony, until Winthrop's death in 1649, even though the first governor's instinctive assumption of authority, and Dudley's irascibility and uncompromising sense of justice, occasionally created sharp differences of opinion between them.

Dudley served as governor for only a year, but during his term of office two serious problems confronted the colony. The first was an order from the Privy Council in England for the return of the Royal Charter, so that it might be revoked and a new government for the colony, under the jurisdiction of Archbishop Laud, be then appointed. King Charles had taken alarm at the number and substance of those who were emigrating to New England, and wished to assume a stronger economic and religious control over the growing settlements.

The general court of the Massachusetts Bay colony made no other answer to this unpalatable summons than to agree among themselves to defend their legal rights to the land and authority that the king had granted them, to strengthen the fortifications of Boston harbor, and to train a militia. Fortunately the king's increasing troubles in England prevented his pressing the colonists further, and by the end of 1635 the threat to the charter had lost its power.[1]

The second problem that troubled Dudley's tenure was the unorthodox teaching of the Reverend Roger Williams (*c.* 1603–83), which endangered the religious and political structure of the whole colony. Williams, one of the most interesting and controversial figures in New England's early history, was educated for the law at Cambridge, under the patronage of Sir Edward Coke, but became a nonconformist minister and emigrated to Massachusetts in 1631. He assisted, then succeeded, Samuel Skelton as pastor of Salem, and was loved and revered by his congregation. But he made an enemy of the general court by consistently preaching that the civil state had no justifiable power in spiritual matters, and that every man's conscience should be free to select its own form of worship. He also held that the king had no authority to give land in the New World to the colonists, and that they could claim honest title to their territory only by purchasing it from the Indians. These, and others of his doctrines that appeared dangerously defiant of the rigid theocratic system of the colony,

1. Palfrey, *History of New England*, Vol. I, pp. 370–71, 386–405.

had begun to divide the churches and cause bitter factionalism, at a time when unity, in purpose and performance, was essential.

Williams was called before Governor Dudley and the magistrates, early in 1635, and publicly censured for his opinions. But he refused to abandon them, and later in the year, when John Haynes had become governor, the erring pastor was formally tried and banished from the colony. After much hardship he and his family, with some faithful followers from Salem, settled in the country of the Narragansett Indians, near the Plymouth colony. Here they established, upon the basis of individual freedom of conscience in matters of religion, the plantation of Providence, now the capital city of the state of Rhode Island.

In the autumn of 1635, perhaps as the result of the problems and tensions of the past year, Dudley decided to move to the most remote plantation in the Bay Colony. This was Agawam, or Ipswich, on the coast, about forty miles north of the settlements along the Charles River. In 1633, when the governor's son, John Winthrop, Jr., and twelve other pioneers were raising the first cabins on the site of the new community, a visiting colonist described it as

> one of the most spacious for a plantation, being neare the sea, it aboundeth with fish, and flesh of fowles and beasts, great Meads and Marshes and plaine plowing grounds, many good rivers and harbours and no rattle snakes.[2]

Thomas Dudley, with his wife and two unmarried daughters, Sarah and Mercy, left the well-built house in Newtown with its controversial wainscoting and took the overnight journey, through rough unsettled country, that led them to yet another temporary frontier shelter. They did not go alone, for Samuel Dudley and

2. William Wood, *New England's Prospect* (1634), ed. Boynton, Boston, 1898, p. 46.

his wife Mary, with one or two children, Patience Dudley and her soldier husband Captain Daniel Denison, and Simon and Anne Bradstreet, with their son Samuel and perhaps their infant daughter Dorothy (who was born in 1635 or 1636), chose family solidarity instead of the briefly enjoyed comforts of life in Newtown, and traveled with the elder Dudleys to the new settlement.

Two small monuments, beside the quiet tree-shaded street in modern Ipswich that was the original center of the town, mark the actual homesites shown in the early records:

> Thomas Dudley, Esq., granted a parcel of 9 acres, in Ipswich, adjoining a lott intended to Mr. Broadstreet.[3]

The first householders were required by the general court to build within a half-mile radius of the meetinghouse, to carry arms at all times and to keep continuous watches; Captain Denison was put in charge of the military defense of the settlement.[4] These precautions were thought necessary because the Indians of the frontier had not yet become accustomed to English neighbors, and there was constant danger that they might launch an attack on the newcomers.

Ipswich plantation was established by men whose minds were trained for more sophisticated occupations than the clearing of virgin forest and the laying of roads across wild countryside. Governor Winthrop's eldest son and namesake, educated at Trinity College, Dublin, and the Inner Temple, was a soldier and scientist, a friend of Sir Kenelm Digby, and a future member of the Royal Society and governor of the colony of Connecticut. He left Ipswich in 1634, after the death of his young wife, but there remained as leaders of the settlement such men as Richard Salton-

3. Thomas F. Waters, *Ipswich in the Massachusetts Bay Colony*, Ipswich, 1905, Vol. I, p. 375.

4. *Massachusetts Colony Records*, Vol. I, pp. 157, 190–91.

stall, son of Sir Richard Saltonstall of Yorkshire, and the ministers Nathaniel Ward and Nathaniel Rogers, all three, like Simon Bradstreet and Samuel Dudley, old students of Emmanuel College, Cambridge. Saltonstall was an assistant, or magistrate, of the Bay Colony, as was also Richard Bellingham, former recorder of Boston in Lincolnshire, soon to be chosen as governor and also, along with Thomas Dudley, as one of the four non-university members of the Board of Overseers of Harvard College.

The wives of these men must have found the first year or two of life in Ipswich very demanding, for they had once again to settle their families in new dwellings and assemble the stores of provisions for the winter months, and they were also expected to furnish the reciprocal hospitality that such "a remarkably cultivated society for a frontier town," as Samuel Eliot Morison describes it,[5] surely required. Domestic workers were apparently plentiful, but that they were often uncouth and ill-mannered is shown by these distressful lines from a letter that Samuel Dudley's wife sent to her stepmother, Mrs. John Winthrop, in Boston:

> I thought it convenient to acquaint you and my father, what a great affliction I have met withal by my maide servant, . . . through mine and my husbands forbearance . . . shee hath got such a head and is growen soe insolent, that her carriage towards us especially myselfe is insufferable. if I bid her doe a thing shee will bid me to doe it myselfe, and she says, how shee can give content as wel as any servant but shee will not. . . . If I should write to you of all the reviling speeches, and filthie language shee hath used towards me I should but greive you. My husband hath used all meanes for to reforme her, reasons and perswasions, but shee doth professe that her heart and her nature will not suffer her to confesse her faults; . . . so that we know not how to proceede against her: but my husband now hath hired another maide and is resolved to put her away the next weeke.[6]

5. *Builders of the Bay Colony*, Boston, 1930, p. 235.
6. *Winthrop Papers*, Vol. III, 1943, p. 221.

When Anne Bradstreet was not occupied by the many tasks of ordering her house and caring for her children, she would have joined her husband in receiving and entertaining his guests. At such times she may have taken part in, or at any rate listened to, the serious talk of men whose thoughts ranged far beyond the borders of the Bay Colony, to examine and discuss the literary, theological, and scientific trends of the European world, and to dwell with anxiety on the widening rift between king and parliament in their old home. These intelligent conversations no doubt inspired Anne to spend her leisure hours in reading and study of whatever books she had brought with her or could borrow from the relatives and friends around her. This in turn may have brought her to the adventurous point of trying her hand at the writing of formal verse. It must again be emphasized that only a conscious and ardent desire to become a poet, combined with a strong sense of spiritual dedication, could give the necessary courage for such an act to a Puritan woman of 1636. She had deliberately to defy the conventions of her day concerning the conduct of women, who could be forgiven almost anything before an attempt to challenge the intellectual superiority of men. And she had to reconcile her need for self-expression with her loyalty to the requirements of her hard-working husband and growing family of children, personal responsibilities that already made continual demands on her limited physical strength.

She could with impunity have written as much private, unpublicized verse, in her free time, as she wished, like her near contemporary Edward Taylor or a later New England woman poet, Emily Dickinson. But her individual pattern of character made it essential, apparently, that her major literary efforts should be expended for the sake of those around her, family, friends, and the members of the zealously crusading community of which she was a part. Yet with all her inner resolution she might never have persisted in such a course if she had not had the sympathetic support of two enlightened men, her father and her husband, and the flattering encouragement of another, the author of a curious little work called *The Simple Cobler of Aggawam.*

Neither a cobbler nor in the least simple, the Reverend Nathaniel Ward was a lawyer, as well as a clergyman, who emigrated to America in 1634, when he was fifty-five years old. He was educated at Emmanuel College, Cambridge, studied and practised law in London, then traveled on the Continent, where he made his headquarters at the court of the Elector Palatine and often, as he said, held the little Prince Rupert, Charles I's nephew, in his arms. At Heidelberg he came under the influence of the learned Calvinist David Pareus and entered the ministry; soon after this he returned to England and preached as a vigorous nonconformist in London and Essex, protected by powerful friends, for about ten years, until Archbishop Laud's expedient patience was exhausted and Ward had to flee the country.

In Ipswich, he served as pastor from 1634 to 1636, then left that post to devote himself to his great work for the colony, the drafting of an urgently needed code of laws, "The Body of Liberties," which was adopted in 1641 and used as the basis of the more inclusive *Lawes and Liberties concerning the Inhabitants of the Massachusets,* printed at Boston in 1648. Ward continued to live in Ipswich, and there wrote an extravagant and witty commentary on what he felt, with profound concern, were the major evils of his day. *The Simple Cobler of Aggawam in America, Willing to help 'mend his Native Country, lamentably tattered, both in the upper-Leather and sole, with all the honest stitches he can take . . . by Theodore de la Guard,* appeared in London in 1647, and went through five editions by the end of that year. The publisher was Stephen Bowtell, who three years later presented Anne Bradstreet's poems to the world, and on the title-page of Ward's book is printed one of the only two Latin proverbs that Anne quoted: "Ne Sutor quidem ultra crepidam." [7]

Nathaniel Ward was an Elizabethan in age and spirit, like his contemporary Thomas Dudley, and as passionate a patriot as he was a Christian. His innate respect for authority led him to attack the signs of its breaking down, as he observed them in the perils of religious toleration, the increasing worldliness of women, and the tragic conflict between the king and a large proportion of his subjects. He "hath in a jesting way," wrote Thomas Fuller, "de-delivered much Smart-Truth of this present Times." [8] His packed and angular prose is intensely individual in its wry twists of phrase and use of strange compound words. There is nothing quite like it in colonial New England writing.

> My heart hath naturally detested . . . Toleration of divers Religions, or of one Religion in segregant shapes: He that willingly assents to the last . . . is either an Atheist, or an Heretique, or an Hypocrite, or at best a captive to some lust: Polypiety is the greatest impiety in the world. . . . I lived in a City, where a Papist preached in one Church, a Lutheran in another, a Calvinist in a third; . . . the Religion of that place was but motly and meagre, their affections Leopard-like.
>
> . . . let all considerate men beware of ungrounded opinions in Religion: Since I knew what to feare, my timerous heart hath dreaded three things: a blazing starre appearing in the aire: a State Comet, I mean a favourite rising in a Kingdome, a new Opinion spreading in Religion: these are Exorbitancies: which is a formidable word: a vacuum and an exorbitancy, are mundicidious evils.
>
> If all be true we heare, Never was any People under the Sun,

7. This familiar tag, which Pliny the Elder rendered as "Ne supra crepidam judicaret," and Erasmus as "Ne sutor ultra crepidam," is usually translated: "Shoemaker, stick to your last." See Hoyt's *New Cyclopedia of Practical Quotations*, ed. K. L. Roberts, New York, 1922, p. 706.

8. *The Worthies of England*, 1662, Part 3, p. 71.

so sick of new Opinions as English-men nor of new fashions as English-women: if God helpe not the one, and the devill leave not helping the other, a blind man may easily foresee what will become of both. . . . I honour the woman that can honour her selfe with her attire: a good Text always deserves a fair Margent . . . but when I heare a nugiperous Gentledame inquire what dresse the Queen is in this week; what the nudiustertian fashion of the court . . . I look at her as the very gizzard of a trifle, the product of a quarter of a cypher, the epitome of nothing. . . . I can make my selfe sicke at any time, with comparing the dazling splender wherewith our Gentlewomen were embellished in some former habits, with the gut-foundred goosdom, wherewith they are now surcingled and debauched. Wee have about five or six of them in our Colony: if I see any of them accidentally, I cannot cleanse my phansie of them for a moneth after. . . .

My Dearest Lord, and my more than dearest King . . . give me leave to inquire of your Majesty, what you make in fields of blood, when you should be amidst your Parliament of peace: . . . Doth it become you, the King of the stateliest Island the world hath, to forsake your Throne, and take up the manufacture of cutting your Subjects throats, for no other sin, but for Deifying you so over-much, that you cannot be quiet in your Spirit, till they have pluckt you down as over-low? . . . Is no Bishop no King, such an oraculous Truth, that you will pawne your Crowne and life upon it? . . . Have you not driven good Subjects enough abroad, but you will also slaughter them that stay at home? . . .

If my tongue should reach your eares, which I little hope for; Let it be once said; the great King of great Britaine, took advice of a simple Cobler, as will not exchange either his blood or his pride, with any Shoo-maker or Tanner in your Realme, nor with any of your late Bishops which have flattered you thus in peeces. . . .[9]

There are few readers in these days who glance at the Simple Cobler's pages, to find beneath their crotchety language the de-

9. *The Simple Cobler of Aggawam* (1647), ed. David Pulsifer, Boston, 1843, pp. 5, 21, 23, 26–27, 56–57, 61, 64.

votion to a self-defeating king and the solicitude for a homeland in crisis. But their words were of immediate significance when they were written, and in Anne Bradstreet's work of this period there are indications that she was influenced by the convictions of the sharp-witted minister. She probably read some parts of Ward's manuscript in the early stages of its composition, but she did not, fortunately, take his style as a model; her prose is as clear and direct as his is crabbed and oblique. And the subject of her first surviving poem of a consciously literary nature may not, perhaps, have seemed well chosen to the hidebound Puritan, even though he was cosmopolitan enough to write, or quote from another source, the satiric couplet:

> The world is full of care, much like unto a bubble;
> Women and care, and care and women, and women and care and trouble.

"An Elegie upon that Honourable and renowned Knight, Sir *Philip Sidney*, who was untimely slaine at the Seige of *Zutphon*, Anno 1586. By A.B., in the yeare, 1638." is an ambitious tribute in the classic style, consisting of one hundred and forty-two lines of rhyming iambic couplets. It is the earliest dated of the poems that were published in *The Tenth Muse* in 1650, and judging by its chaotic composition it is a beginner's effort at formal verse-writing. It is also the most severely altered and emended, of any of those poems, by the author when she was preparing her text for a second edition.

The elegy in its first printing opens with a four-line salutation to Sidney as

> No lesse an Honour to our *British* Land,
> Then she that sway'd the Scepter with her hand:

next we find that the scene is Parnassus, where the speaker is haranguing a formidable company on the subject of England's "brave Achilles" and "noble Scipio." Mars, Minerva, Mercury, and five of the Muses are ready to agree that Sidney was pre-eminent in all the accomplishments under their sway. But then the visitor from New England goes a little too far in tactlessly suggesting, to Thalia and Melpomene, that their sisterhood's "nine-fold wit" had been exhausted in the creation of the *Arcadia*. She continues with a critical estimate of this pastoral romance, praises Sidney's military career and valiant death, and devotes a long passage to his love for the famous Stella. During this recital, which begins bravely enough with the self-assertive lines

> Let then, none dis-allow of these my straines,
> Which have the self-same blood yet in my veines;

the author shows an increasing lack of confidence, makes several apologies for her want of skill and, too late, finds herself literally hoisted into a very awkward position:

> Goodwill, did make my head-long pen to run,
> Like unwise *Phaeton* his ill guided sonne,
>
> 　　　*　　　*　　　*
>
> So proudly foolish I, with *Phaeton* strive,
> Fame's flaming Chariot for to drive.
> Till terrour-struck for my too weighty charge,
> I leave't in brief, *Apollo* do't at large.

Apollo laughs kindly and rescues her, because of his own regard for Sidney's fame, but the Muses, angered by the presumption of one of their own sex, sarcastically refuse to help her:

> With high disdain, they said they gave no more,
> Since *Sydney* had exhausted all their store.

They snatch the bewildered writer's "scribling pen" and drive her from Parnassus; when she sits down in despair, Erato (whose name is here given the punning spelling of *Errata*) relents and throws her the pen so she may finish her poem, which she does with the conventional and rather well-knit postscript of

HIS EPITAPH
Here lies intomb'd in fame, under this stone,
Philip and *Alexander* both in one.
Heire to the Muses, the Son of *Mars* in truth,
Learning, valour, beauty, all in vertuous youth:
His praise is much, this shall suffice my pen,
That *Sidney* dy'd the quintessence of men.

In spite of its absurdity, and its lack of any marked poetic felicity, the elegy has some interesting passages, and a generally disarming quality in its revelation of the author's own awareness of her beginner's awkwardness. Her boldness in introducing her human self, with the purpose of celebrating a human hero, into the company of the classical divinities, was not as far-fetched in her own day as it seems to be in ours. There are many poems of the period, for example, Aurelian Townshend's lovely lyric "A Dialogue betwixt Time and a Pilgrime," in which the writer converses with an allegorical or mythical being, and eminent thinkers like Sir Thomas Browne believed in the existence of "spiritual creatures" who could manifest themselves, in spectral or even seemingly corporeal form, to those who were perceptive enough to recognize them. But Anne Bradstreet, as she discovered in writing this poem, was not able to meet the challenge of so august an assemblage. At any rate the encounter taught her a lesson, for although she used the device of personification frequently in her later poems, she never again put herself in the position of having an argument with any symbolical personage.

After the author makes her untactful suggestion to Thalia and Melpomene "That this one Volume should exhaust your store," she adds insult to injury by beginning her remarks on the *Arcadia* with a sanctimonious attack on its frivolity:

> I praise thee not for this, it is unfit,
> This was thy shame, O miracle of wit;
> Yet doth thy shame (with all) purchase renown,
> What doe thy vertues then? Oh, honours crown!
>
> *   *   *
>
> Thy wiser dayes, condemn'd thy witty works,
> Who knowes the Spels that in thy Rethorick lurks?
> But some infatuate fooles soone caught therein,
> Found *Cupids* Dam, had never such a Gin;
> Which makes severer eyes but scorn thy Story,
> And modest Maids, and Wives, blush at thy glory.

What Milton called "the vaine, amatorious Poem of Sir Philip Sidney's *Arcadia*" [10] was equally scorned by the earlier Puritans, Anne Bradstreet tells us emphatically, as licentious and dangerous. But the lines that follow immediately, of praise for the *Arcadia's* good qualities, are an early and striking example of Anne's stalwart independence of mind.

> Yet, he's a beetle head, that cann't discry
> A world of treasure, in that rubbish lye;
> And doth thy selfe, thy worke, and honour wrong,
> (O brave Refiner of our *Brittish* Tongue;)
> That sees not learning, valour, and morality,
> Justice, friendship, and kind hospitality;
> Yea, and Divinity within thy Book,
> Such were prejudicate, and did not look:
> But to say truth, thy worth I shall but staine,
> Thy fame, and praise, is farre beyond my straine.

If she had not been reared in the culturally liberal atmosphere of the Earl of Lincoln's household, Anne Bradstreet might not

10. *Eikonoklastes,* 1649, p. 12.

have been permitted even a glimpse of Sidney's romance. As it was, her Puritan rectitude perceived the peril to "infatuate fooles" in the elaborate love story, yet her generous spirit could not but recognize the noble aspects of the work. Some of the "severer eyes" in the colony may have looked askance at her defense of the *Arcadia,* but it is significant that her poem was included, probably because of the universal respect for Sidney as a man, among those printed in *The Tenth Muse.* It is the only seventeenth-century New England tribute, so far as I have been able to discover, to that Elizabethan paragon of courtly valor and grace.

In the succeeding lines, on Sidney's military achievements and early death, he is compared to Achilles, Hector, and Scipio. Then a contemporary soldier-poet appears:

> Noble *Bartas,* this to thy praise adds more,
> In sad, sweet verse, thou didst his death deplore.

Du Bartas's lines on Sidney are in *La Seconde Sepmaine,* "Deuxième Jour, II, Babylone," where he salutes three "piliers" of the English tongue:

> Tomas More et Baccon, tous deux grands chancelliers,
>
> *   *   *
>
> Et le milor Cydné qui, cigne doux-chantant,
> Va les flots orgueilleux de Tamise flatant;
> Ce fleuve, gros d'honneur, emporte sa faconde
> Dans le sein de Thetis, et Thetis par la monde.[11]

In praising Sidney's swan-like eloquence in these somewhat water-logged lines Du Bartas did not, and for a very good reason, deplore

11. *The Works of Guillaume de Salluste Sieur Du Bartas,* ed. U. T. Holmes, Jr., J. C. Lyons, and R. W. Linker, Chapel Hill (N. C.), 1940, Vol. III, p. 141.

his death. *La Seconde Sepmaine* was published in 1584, and Sidney was alive for two years after that. So it is apparent that Anne Bradstreet had not read Du Bartas in the original French, and that her reference was based on Sylvester's translation, in which the tribute to Sidney was rendered as:

> And (World-mourn'd) *Sidney*, warbling to the *Thames*
> His Swan-like tunes, so courts her coy proud streams,
> That (all with-childe with Fame) his fame they bear
> To *Thetis* lap; and *Thetis*, every-where.[12]

Sylvester's undoubted chagrin at not being able to translate the French poet's contrived pun of "Cydné—cigne" perhaps found some solace in the ridiculous biological conceit that he forced into the lines. Sidney seems to have warbled only once to the proud river; the elaborate imagery of the introductory passage in Sonnet CIII of *Astrophel and Stella* probably charmed Du Bartas and also gave him the idea of twisting the good English name into the fanciful semblance of a swan.

> O Happie *Thames* that didst my *Stella* beare,
> I saw thee with full many a smiling line
> Upon thy cheerful face Joves Livery weare:
> While those faire Plannets on thy streames did shine,
> The boat for joy could not to dance forbeare.[13]

Anne Bradstreet shared the enthusiasm of her time for the symbolical name or word that could be employed to set off a whole chain of interrelated images, suggestions, and meanings; she had a promising pun at hand for her lines on the lady for whom

12. *Du Bartas His Divine Weekes and Workes . . . Translated . . . by . . . Joshua Sylvester*, 1621, p. 265.
13. *The Works of Sir Philip Sidney*, ed. Albert Feuillerat, Cambridge, 1922, Vol. II, p. 369.

Tattershall Castle, Tattershall, Lincolnshire.

St. Andrew's Church, Sempringham, Lincolnshire.

John Winthrop.

THE *John Brand*
1795.
TENTH MUSE

Lately fprung up in AMERICA.

OR

Severall Poems, compiled
with great variety of VVit
and Learning, full of delight.
Wherein efpecially is contained a compleat difcourfe and defcription of

The Four { *Elements,*
Conftitutions,
Ages of Man,
Seafons of the Year.

Together with an Exact Epitomie of
the Four Monarchies, *viz.*

The { *Affyrian,*
Perfian,
Grecian,
Roman.

Alfo a Dialogue between Old *England* and
New, concerning the late troubles.

With divers other pleafant and ferious Poems.

By a Gentlewoman in thofe parts.

Printed at *London* for *Stephen Bowtell* at the figne of the
Bible in Popes Head-Alley. 1650.

Title-page of *The Tenth Muse,* 1650.

SEVERAL
POEMS

Compiled with great variety of Wit and
Learning, full of Delight;
Wherein especially is contained a compleat
Discourse, and Description of

The Four { ELEMENTS.
CONSTITUTIONS,
AGES of Man,
SEASONS of the Year.

Together with an exact Epitome of
the three first *Monarchyes*

Viz. The { ASSYRIAN,
PERSIAN,
GRECIAN.

And beginning of the Romane Common-wealth
to the end of their last King :

With diverse other pleasant & serious *Poems,*

By a Gentlewoman in *New-England.*

The second Edition, Corrected by the Author
and enlarged by an Addition of several other
Poems found amongst her Papers
after her Death.

Boston, Printed by *John Foster,* 1678.

Title-page of *Several Poems*, 1678.

Simon Bradstreet in old age. Nineteenth-century copy,
by Hannah Crowninshield, of an earlier, probably lost, portrait.

63

He that would keep a pure heart
and lead a blamlesse Life, must
set himselfe alway in the carefull
presence of god, the considera
-tion of his allseeing eye will
be able to restrain from
evill and as spur, to quicken
on to good dutys, we certainly
dreame of some remotnes betwixt
god and us, or else we should not
so often faile in our whole
Course of life as we doe, but he
that with David, sets the lord alway in his sight will not sinne
against him.

64

We see in orchards, some trees soe
fruitfull, that the waight of
their Burden is the breaking of
their Limbes, some againe are but
meanly loaden, and some haue
nothing to shew but leaues only,
and some among them are dry stocks
so is it in the church which is gods
orchard, there are some

eminent Christians, that are soe
frequent in good dutys, that many
times, the waight therof impares
both their bodys and estates, and ther
are some (and they sincere ones too)
who haue not attained to that frui
fullnes, altho they aime at perfection
And againe there are others that haue
nothing to Commend them, but only
a gay proffession, and these are but
Leauie christians, which are in as much
danger of being Cut down, as the dry
stock, for both Cumber the ground

65

we se in the firmament there is but one
Sun, among a multitude of starres
and those starres also, to differ much
one from the other, in regard of bignes
and brightnes yet all receiue their light
from that one Sun, so is it in the church
both militant and triumphant, there
is but one christ, who is the Sun of
righteousnes, in the midest of an innu
merable Company of Saints, and those
Saints haue their degrees, euen in this

Pages 30 and 31 of Anne Bradstreet's autograph manuscript
of "Meditations Divine and morall."

The first burial-ground in old Andover,
now North Andover, Massachusetts.

Sidney's sonnet sequence was supposedly written, and she made good use of its possibilities.

> Illustrious *Stella,* thou didst [shine] [14] full well,
> If thine aspect was milde to *Astrophell;*
> I feare thou wert a Commet, did portend
> Such prince as he, his race should shortly end:
> If such Stars as these, sad presages be,
> I wish no more such Blazers we may see;
> But thou art gone, such Meteors never last,
> And as thy beauty, so thy name would wast,
> But that it is record by *Philips* hand,
> That such an omen once was in our land,
> O Princely *Philip,* rather *Alexander,*
> Who wert of honours band, the chief Commander.
> How could that *Stella,* so confine thy will?
> To wait till she, her influence distill,
> I rather judg'd thee of his mind that wept,
> To be within the bounds of one world kept,
> But *Omphala,* set *Hercules* to spin,
> And *Mars* himself was ta'n by *Venus* gin;
> Then wonder lesse, if warlike *Philip* yield
> When such a *Hero* shoots him out o' th' field,
> Yet this preheminence thou hast above,
> That thine was true, but theirs adult'rate love.

In 1575, when Sidney was at the beginning of his career as a courtier and soldier, he met the twelve-year-old Lady Penelope, daughter of Walter Devereux, first Earl of Essex, and shortly after that a contract of marriage between the two young people was drawn up with the approval of both fathers.[15] Sidney was, however, much occupied with travel, court life, and diplomacy at this

14. Printed as "thine" in *The Tenth Muse,* 1650 (the only contemporary appearance of this passage), but surely a typographical error.

15. *Letters and Memorials of State,* ed. Collins, 1746, Vol. I, Part 2, p. 147.

time, and there is no record of any further plans for the match. In 1581 Penelope Devereux was married to Robert Rich, third Baron Rich and later Earl of Warwick, and in 1583 the newly knighted Sir Philip took as his wife Frances, the daughter of his patron Sir Francis Walsingham. It is believed, by many authorities on Sidney's life and work, that the collection of songs and sonnets known as *Astrophel and Stella* (first printed in 1591), was begun as an exercise in the writing of elegant love-poems but that from the twenty-fourth sonnet, an angry and cynical juggling with the word "rich," they are addressed to the Lady Penelope. The poetic account of Astrophel's love for Stella moves from passionate hope through rejection and despair, to final renunciation, and while there is no evidence that Penelope ever encouraged this devotion, numerous allusions in other contemporary works show that Sidney's romantic pursuit of her, up to the time of his own marriage, was accepted as a matter of fact.

After Sir Philip's death at the age of thirty-two, following the battle of Zutphen in 1586, Penelope's life became increasingly notorious. Her marriage to Lord Rich was not a happy one, and she lived so openly with her lover Charles Blount, Lord Mountjoy, that her husband divorced her in 1601. She and Mountjoy, who had been created Earl of Devonshire, were married in 1605; for this breach of the canon law they were banished from court, and Penelope died in 1607, penitent at the end of her meteoric career. Lord Rich became the Earl of Warwick in 1618, and took as his second wife Frances St. Paul, who, it will be remembered, was the "aged and pious Countess of Warwick" by whom Simon Bradstreet was employed as steward at the time of his marriage to Anne Dudley, shortly before their emigration to North America.

An interesting comment on Anne's lines about Stella is included in Hoyt H. Hudson's essay, *Penelope Devereux as Sidney's Stella,* in which he examines the contemporary references to this dramatic association.

> Exactly how Sidney's love (whether assumed or real) for Stella was regarded by moralists in his family a generation later, we may learn from Anne Bradstreet's "An Elegie upon that Honourable and renowned Knight, Sir *Philip Sidney* . . . ," printed in *The Tenth Muse* (1650), but dated 1638. It will be recalled that Anne Bradstreet was born Anne Dudley, the daughter of Thomas Dudley . . . , a relative of Sidney through Mary Dudley, Sidney's mother. Mrs. Bradstreet mentions the relationship, . . . finds a defence for the *Arcadia* . . . [and] deals with Stella, [in the passage quoted above].
>
> The account is clear. Stella was a comet or a meteor rather than a star; she presaged the end of the man who loved her; her name would be forgotten except for the poems in which Sidney celebrated her; Sidney's love for her kept him from more important matters. On the other hand, we may console ourselves with the fact that the two never committed adultery together, as did other famous lovers; and . . . we may hope that Sidney received some happiness from loving Stella.
>
> Mrs. Bradstreet does not say that Stella was Penelope Devereux. Yet that lady exactly fulfills the demands of this account. "I wish no more such Blazers we may see," says the poetess. She can hardly have in mind Frances Walsingham, Sidney's wife; . . . That Penelope was a "Blazer" was sufficiently well known to have caused the circulation of scurrilous epigrams about her.[16]

During her brief sojourn in the Countess of Warwick's household, if not before that, Anne would have heard the story of the first Lady Rich's life. Its elements of drama and tragedy must have appealed to her, and she was well enough aware of a popular belief, that a sudden comet or meteor in the heavens was a portent of disaster on earth, to make the most of the lady's poetic name. The

16. *Huntington Library Bulletin*, No. 7, 1935, pp. 89–129.

passage on Stella is the most successfully constructed in the poem, and must have given its author some satisfaction, so it is significant that she cancelled it entirely when she revised the elegy for its second printing, and replaced it with the lines:

> And *Phoenix Spencer* doth unto his life,
> His death present in sable to his wife,
> *Stella* the fair, whose streams from Conduits fell
> For the sad loss of her dear *Astrophel*.

Anne had two good reasons for being disconcerted when she saw the original passage in print, and for preferring to echo Spenser's elegiac "Astrophel" of 1595, which was dedicated to Sidney's widow and in which she is clearly identified as "Stella the faire, the fairest star in skie." Robert Rich, second Earl of Warwick, admiral of the fleet for Parliament and one of the Massachusetts Bay colony's most powerful friends and promoters, was Penelope Devereux's son by her first husband Baron Rich, and if he had taken offense at this obvious reference to his mother the consequences for the author and her family might have been extremely embarrassing. Also, Sidney had become with the passing years a symbol of Protestant virtue and heroism, particularly among the Puritan writers, who generally avoided any mention of his love-poetry or the veiled romance of his youth. So it is apparent that Anne Bradstreet tried to correct her *gaffe,* for future printings at any rate, by striking out the whole indiscreet Stella passage and substituting, with the great poet and friend of Sidney as her authority, the brief conventional image of the mourning wife.

Joshua Sylvester, in an introductory sonnet to his "Elegiac Epistle for Sir William Sidney" (Sir Philip's nephew), recognized his own incompetence to eulogize that splendid family.

> Although I know none, but a Sidney's Muse,
> Worthy to sing a Sidney's Worthinesse.

Anne Bradstreet, a more tasteful if less prolific versifier than the translator of Du Bartas, encountered all the pitfalls of the beginner in her attempt to pay homage to Sir Philip and finally had to admit that

> Fain would I shew, how thou fame's path didst tread,
> But now into such Lab'rinths am I led
> With endlesse turnes, the way I find not out,
> For to persist, my muse is more in doubt:
> Calls me ambitious fool, that durst aspire,
> Enough for me to look, and so admire.
> And makes me now with *Sylvester* confesse,
> But *Sydney's* Muse, can sing his worthinesse.

If, as I have suggested, Anne encountered the English Du Bartas as a child, she may very well have used the handsome new edition of 1621, entitled in full *Du Bartas His Divine Weekes and Workes, with a Compleate Collection of all the other most delight-full Workes Translated and written by y^t famous Philomusus, Joshua Sylvester, Gent.* This elaborately printed storehouse of metrical lumber must have fascinated the young reader, as it did many of her older and more critically sophisticated contemporaries. F. P. Wilson has analyzed the appeal, and the shortcomings for present-day readers, of the ponderous work:

> The patriotic and Protestant fervor, the usefulness of the *Divine Weekes and Workes* as an encyclopaedia of current views . . . on the marvels of natural history and the wonders of science, the elaborate similes which bring the reader the latest popular news of geographical discovery or everyday life, the strident and fantastic wit, . . . these ingredients may explain the popularity of the English Du Bartas in and long after Sylvester's generation . . . but the critic is still baffled by the hold which he had upon the youthful Milton and the youthful Dryden.

Those who do not confuse poetry with piety may ask if there ever was a poet with such admirers who showed such insensitiveness to word and cadence as did Sylvester in "the grave-sweet warbles of his native style." He abused his mother tongue as Du Bartas abused his; and his original verses are only worse than his translations because he showed in them (as Drayton said) such poverty of invention that he "still wrote less in striving to write more." [17]

When Anne Bradstreet crossed the ocean to the New World she must have brought with her, among her personal possessions, a copy of the *Divine Weekes and Workes,* along with her Geneva Bible and the collected writings of Sidney and Spenser, possibly those published in 1621 and 1617 respectively. And when she first undertook to compose a formal elegy, and discovered the difficulties it involved, she was probably somewhat comforted by Sylvester's confession that he, too, was unable to celebrate a Sidney in worthy terms.

Twelve years later, when Anne saw her tribute to Sir Philip in print, she obviously realized the extent of its faults, in taste and composition. The drastic revision of the poem, before its second appearance in 1678, shows that she did her best to clarify the argument and to throw the emphasis more on Sidney and less on herself, by deleting several passages that did not concern him. Sixty-one lines are struck out altogether; these include, as well as the ill-starred criticism of Stella, the *contretemps* with Phaeton's chariot and Apollo, and the greater part of the censorious remarks preceding the defense of the *Arcadia.* The author's claim to kinship with her hero is altered (as noted earlier in this study [18]) to "Whilst English blood yet runs within my veins," and her muse no longer calls her "ambitious fool." Yet she still apologizes fre-

17. *Elizabethan and Jacobean,* Oxford, 1945, pp. 65–70.
18. See pp. 11–12 above.

quently for her insufficiency, and the final quarrel with the Muses remains, partly because the poem would be only a fragment without it, but largely, it would seem, because it symbolized, beyond its outward silliness, the aspiring poet's determination, in spite of rebuffs and discouragement, to continue the struggle for acknowledged accomplishment.

With all its falterings the elegy probably gave Anne Bradstreet a sense of some kind of achievement, which spurred her ambition and led her to plan, and begin to write, during the next few years, the elaborate series of "fours" which are the longest of her individual works and which were not completed until considerably later. Meanwhile the next surviving dated poem, after the Sidney elegy, shows so much improvement in organization, emphasis, and expression that it must surely be the result of a self-imposed and conscientious period of apprenticeship.

It was inevitable that she should compose a formal tribute to the author of the monumental work which had so captivated her youthful imagination. "In honour of *Du Bartas*, 1641," is also a commemorative eulogy, of eighty-four lines and an eight-line "Epitaph," in heroic couplets. It succeeds in expressing profound feeling in an articulate and orderly way, and although we cannot share the author's admiration for her immediate subject, we can follow with interest, and even pleasure, her ingenuous account of her own poetic awakening.

> Among the happy wits this age hath shown,
> Great, dear, sweet *Bartas* thou art matchless known;
> My ravish'd Eyes and heart with faltering tongue,
> In humble wise have vow'd their service long,
> But knowing th' task so great, & strength but small,
> Gave o're the work, before begun withal.
> My dazled sight of late review'd thy lines,
> Where Art, and more then Art, in nature shines,

Reflection from their beaming Altitude,
Did thaw my frozen hearts ingratitude;
Which Rayes darting upon some richer ground,
Had caused flours and fruits soon to abound;
But barren I my Dasey here do bring,
A homely flour in this my latter Spring,
If Summer, or my Autumn age do yield,
Flours, fruits, in Garden, Orchard, or in Field,
They shall be consecrated in my Verse,
And prostrate offered at great *Bartas* Herse.

The sixth line can be read in two ways: that she had begun in the past to write her praise of Du Bartas, but had abandoned the effort through discouragement, or that, paradoxically, her lack of confidence had made her give up the project before she even attempted it. I believe that the latter meaning was what she intended, for it carries out the sense of the whole statement: that from her first meeting with the French poet, presumably as a child, she was fascinated and longed to give concrete expression to her delight, but felt incapable of doing so. Then, when she was older, she read the *Divine Weekes and Workes* again, and felt their sunlike power not only dazzling her eyes but also warming her heart, so that her desire to write could at last bear fruit, though of a humble and unpretentious kind. Therefore she laid a simple early flower of her verse as an offering at the tomb of Du Bartas, and dedicated to his memory whatever else she might create.

This rather commonplace little speech is made alive and warm by the presence of an image that had great significance for Anne Bradstreet, and that she used again and again, in its direct sense and also to illustrate both the mystery of faith and the cycle of man's experience. That is, the life-giving virtue of the sun, reviving the frozen earth so that it could bring forth the flowers and fruits of God's creation in their seasons. In 1641, in her "latter Spring," Anne was twenty-eight years old.

Following the opening section of the poem comes the twenty-six-line passage that has already been quoted [19] in connection with a review of Anne Bradstreet's probable education. The comparison of her muse to a child at a "famous" fair, fascinated by the rich merchandise though unable to comprehend its real value, vainly wishing to possess some of it and then as vainly trying to describe its glories to his mother at the end of the day, is a typical Du Bartas device. In an imaginative essay on Edward Taylor, the critic Austin Warren writes of Du Bartas:

> His characteristic analogies compare not the less to the greater but the greater to the less, domesticating the wild or grand things into familiar properties of chamber, hearth and barnyard. But the trait which most obviously differentiates his conceits from those of Donne is their externality: Donne is a psychologist and casuist whose remembered conceits are poetic correlatives for inner states. Du Bartas' conceits couple disjunct worlds —heaven and earth, animate and inanimate; but they do so only superficially, for his heaven is as material and external as his earth, and the images conjoined lie within a single dimension.

Commenting on "the simple, unfigured, unpretentious Tudor verse of the Tenth Muse," Warren continues:

> In spite of her contemporary celebration as a "Du Bartas girl," Anne Bradstreet's long "moralities" have nothing in common with the *Weeks* except their run-on couplets and their panoramic scope. But the humbler baroque ingenuities the New Englanders could reproduce.[20]

19. See pp. 69–70 above.
20. A. Warren, *Rage for Order*, Chicago, 1948, pp. 4–5, 11.

Anne *did* compare the greater to the less with the homely illustration of her muse as the spellbound and inarticulate child at the
fair. But with the line that ends the passage: "Thus weak brain'd
I, reading thy lofty stile," and the impressive list of Du Bartas's
intellectual attainments that follows, she made the analogy soar
up again from the frivolous to the majestic, and restored the dignity of tone that the poem requires.

The next ten lines are a naïve but genuine description of a state
well known to every poet or would-be poet.

> A thousand thousand times my sensless sences
> Moveless stand charm'd by thy sweet influences;
> More sensless then the stones to *Amphions* Lute,
> Mine eyes are sightless, and my tongue is mute,
> My full astonish'd heart doth pant to break,
> Through grief it wants a faculty to speak:
> Volleyes of praises could I echo then,
> Had I an Angels voice, or *Bartas* pen:
> But wishes can't accomplish my desire,
> Pardon if I adore, when I admire.

Anne Bradstreet was here recording, while protesting that she was
incapable of doing so, the overwhelming experience of total response to the power of poetry. The impact was so violent as to be
physical as well as emotional, and with it came the equally overwhelming desire to be a poet herself. What she was adoring, with
an abandon that is very rare in her writing, was not so much the
actual work of Du Bartas, or any other specific poet, but rather the
miraculous ability of certain human minds to transmute intangible
thoughts into measured words of enduring beauty and meaning.

The poets of Anne Bradstreet's time were, almost all of them,
men who had studied their craft from early youth and who wrote
as experienced technicians as well as deeply sentient beings: they

would have thought it unnecessary and unsuitable to give vent to such feelings as Anne Bradstreet did in the passage just quoted. To be sure Sir Philip Sidney himself complained, though more as a lover than a poet, in the famous first sonnet of *Astrophel and Stella,* that he was

> . . . great with child to speak, and helpless in my throes,
> Biting my truant pen, beating myself for spite,
> "Fool," said my Muse to me, "look in thy heart and write."

And Anne Bradstreet's contemporary, Margaret Cavendish, Duchess of Newcastle, whose literary outpourings began to appear in print in 1653, confessed in "The Claspe":

> When I did write this Booke, I took great paines,
> For I did walke, and thinke, and breake my Braines.
> My Thoughts run out of Breath, then downe would lye,
> And panting with short wind, like those that dye.
> When Time had given Ease, and lent them strength,
> Then up would get, and run another length.[21]

But this is complacent, as was the Duchess's attitude in all of her productions, compared with the anguish and ecstasy that cry out from Anne's ingenuous lines. She used the scientific language of her day to describe, in graphic detail, her physiological reaction to the poetry that moved her so deeply. Admiration, ambition, and desire, all of which she felt, were included among the "concupiscible passions" which "arise when the imagination or the reasonable will perceives or conceives an object which appeals to it as pleasing or repellent." [22] In *The Anatomy of Melancholy,* a classic

---

21. Margaret Newcastle, *Poems and Fancies,* 1653, p. 47.
22. Lawrence Babb, *The Elizabethan Malady,* East Lansing (Mich.), 1951, p. 4.

work with which Anne may well have been familiar, Robert Burton aptly defined her state:

> This Concupiscible appetite, howsoever it may seem to carry with it a show of pleasure and delight, and our concupiscences most part affect us with content . . . yet if they be in extreams, they rack and wring us on the other side.

And possibly she had also read Pierre de la Primaudaye's diagnosis, in his translated work *The French Academie* (1618), of the end-result of what we now call shock, accompanying a sudden access of violent emotion, when "all the blood retiring to the heart choaketh it, and utterly extinguisheth naturall heat and the spirits, so that death must needs ensue thereof."

Fortunately Anne's "full astonish'd heart" did not, like the too-long-tormented Duke of Gloucester's " 'Twixt two extremes of passion, joy and greefe, / Burst smilingly." After the passage of emotional revelation she resumed the formal tone of the poem, and apostrophized France as having gained more glory from the achievement of Du Bartas than from all the conquests of her martial kings. In this closing section, before the epitaph, the eulogy is brought to a successfully monumental end, the effect of scale being accomplished with an almost sly ingenuity by the reappearance of the author and her final word.

> Unto each man his riches is assign'd
> Of Name, of State, of Body and of Mind:
> Thou hadst thy part of all, but of the last,
> O pregnant brain, O comprehension vast:
> Thy haughty Stile and rapted wit sublime
> All ages wondring at, shall never climb.
> Thy sacred works are not for imitation,
> But Monuments to future Admiration.
> Thus *Bartas* fame shall last while starrs do stand,

And whilst there's Air or Fire, or Sea or Land.
But least mine ignorance should do thee wrong,
To celebrate thy merits in my Song,
I'le leave thy praise to those shal do thee right,
Good will, not skill, did cause me bring my Mite.

Even in so exalted a passage she could not resist the temptation of
the pun in "Stile," which certainly, like Du Bartas, compares the
greater to the lesser! But otherwise the vocabulary is sound, and the
introduction of the four elements hints that she was already at
work on her long poem on the quaternions in nature.

The "Epitaph" celebrates Du Bartas as the masterpiece of
humanity and the immortal child of fame:

But Nature vanquish'd Art, so *Bartas* dy'd;
But Fame out-living both, he is reviv'd.

Though the rhyme is false, the concluding recurrence of the
poem's chief argument is technically appropriate. In this whole
elegiac tribute, as compared to the one she addressed to Sir Philip
Sidney, the author was able to keep her material within the bounds
of decorous continuity, and to show considerable skill in the
handling of the two contrasting figures, the universally acclaimed
French warrior-poet and the diffident New England woman who,
though longing to be his disciple, is still aware that "Thy sacred
works are not for imitation."

This poem, which apparently satisfied Anne Bradstreet since she
made only minor word-changes in preparation for its second printing, seems to mark the end of her tentative start as a writer. During
the next six years the amount of verse she produced was so substantial that one cannot but marvel at her determination, in spite
of constant personal obligations and recurrent ill health, to find
the necessary time for the exercise of her chosen vocation.

CHAPTER SIX

Family Life and Literary Development

"Now say, have women worth? or have they none?
Or had they some, but with our Queen is't gone?

*   *   *

Let such as say our Sex is void of Reason,
Know tis a Slander now, but once was Treason."

(ANNE BRADSTREET—*In Honour of Queen Elizabeth*)

By 1641 the Massachusetts Bay colony had entered the second period of its development. A continuous procession of ships across the Atlantic had brought colonists and supplies to strengthen the wilderness plantations of 1628–30 and push the frontiers of settlement ever further inland and up and down the coast. The Great Migration ceased abruptly in 1642, when every English Puritan was committed to his part in the civil strife at home, but by that time the exertions of more than 20,000 settlers had, as the anonymous author of *New Englands First Fruits* [1] wrote, "planted fifty towns and villages, built thirty or forty churches, and more ministers' houses, a castle, a college, prisons, forts, cartways, causeys many, . . . having comfortable houses, gardens, orchards, grounds fenced, corn-fields, &c."

1. A 26-page tract, published in London in 1643, describing the benefits and opportunities of life in the New World, and particularly promoting Harvard College, from which the first class was graduated in 1642. Reprinted in Samuel Eliot Morison's *The Founding of Harvard College*, Cambridge (Mass.), 1935, Appendix D.

The New Jerusalem of Winthrop's company, for which many lives were sacrificed and where every survivor was a hero of almost Biblical proportions, had settled into a substantial human community, sure of its continuing existence and full of practical ambitions for the future. The men and women of the planting generation, whose essential task had been to preserve their own and their children's lives, could look around them with pride and with humble thanksgiving at the solid results of their victory over famine, the extremes of climate, and the threat of Indian savagery. The intensity of the first offensive against the wilderness could be permitted to slacken, and the winter soldiers of Christ could become individual citizens again, with a chance to develop their varying abilities and incentives in comparative security.

There was still hard work for everyone, and the precepts of the scriptural kingdom as an inflexible rule of conduct. But several kinds of practical industry had begun to operate, and while the farmers tilled their fields and the artisans plied their trades, young Harvard College, which was formally established in 1639, began to produce its harvest of intellectual leaders for the New World. Stephen Daye arrived in the colony and set up its first printing press; the midnight oil shone, in the studies of scholarly ministers and governing officials, on multiplying pages of manuscript; and in the house of Simon Bradstreet, in Ipswich, the literature of English North America had its birth.

The activities of personal, domestic, and family life were at their zenith for Anne Bradstreet, while at the same time she somehow or other contrived to become a serious poet. Her husband's duties, as a permanent member of the Court of Assistants, became more complex and demanding as the colony grew. His good offices were required over a wide area, for the settling of disputes and solving of technical problems, and he was often absent from Ipswich for prolonged periods. From 1638 to the end of 1643 he was one of those primarily responsible for the formation of the confederacy, under the title of "The United Colonies of New England," of Massachusetts, Plymouth, Connecticut, and New Haven, a great forward step in political maturity by what had been four isolated and self-centered territorial entities.

At home, the Bradstreets' nursery of two children, Samuel and Dorothy, was increased by Sarah, probably born in 1638, and Simon, whose birthday was the 28th September, 1640. During these years Anne's two unmarried sisters changed their estate; Sarah Dudley, who was baptized at Sempringham in 1620, became the wife of Major Benjamin Keanye of Boston, and Mercy Dudley, born in 1621, married in 1638 John Woodbridge, of Newbury near Ipswich, a man whose friendship and admiration were to be of great significance in the life of his sister-in-law Anne Bradstreet.

Thomas Dudley, who had his sixtieth birthday in 1636, remained second only to Winthrop among the leaders of the colony. He served as deputy governor in 1638 and 1639, and in the latter year, probably after Mercy's marriage, moved his small household from Ipswich to the village of Roxbury, two miles from Boston, in order to be nearer to the center of colonial administration. He was again elected governor in 1640, 1645, and 1650, was a member of the first Board of Overseers of Harvard College, and made a substantial gift, a perpetual share of the value of his house and land, to the Roxbury Latin School when it was founded in 1646.

While life in the Bay Colony followed its generally sober and orderly pattern of development, events in the mother-country across the sea were moving rapidly towards the disastrous climax of civil war. These events were anxiously watched by the Massachusetts colonists, as they received the news of them from friends and supporters in England. Three days after King Charles I had dissolved the Short Parliament, on the 5th May, 1640, because it refused to provide him with funds for a campaign against the Scots, John Winthrop's nephew Benjamin Gostlin wrote to him from London:

> . . . the Lord be mercyfull unto us and turne the Kings hart or else to this Land in my foolish Iudgment is nothing to be expected but confushion . . . therefore I beseech you to pray for us for if ever mother had neede of Dawghters helps now it hath. . . .[2]

In the mid-summer of 1642, when the war had begun "casually and dispersedly," as C. V. Wedgwood writes, "over all England," [3] the General Court of Massachusetts Bay ordered that the 21st July "should bee kept as a day of publike humiliation throughout this jurisdiction, in regard of our owne straites . . . and the distractions of our native country, Ireland, Holland, and other parts of Europe." [4] There were many other occasions of public fasting and prayer as the months and years of the war multiplied, and we have already noted the private distress of one colonist, as it is revealed in the curious language of *The Simple Cobler of Agawam*. It seems possible that Anne Bradstreet read Benjamin Gostlin's letter of 1640, which must have been circulated among the government officials of the colony, and noted its simile of the mother having need of the "Dawghters helps," for she employed this same allegorical comparision at considerable length in "A Dialogue between old *England* and New; concerning their present Troubles, *Anno*, 1642."

This poem, which may well be the earliest, and most revealing, literary expression of the emotional relationship between the war-torn parent country and its colonial offspring, is in divided sections

2. *Winthrop Papers*, Vol. IV, pp. 235–36.
3. *The King's War*, Vol. II, 1958, of *The Great Rebellion*, p. 107.
4. *Massachusetts Colony Records*, Vol. II, p. 16.

of heroic couplets, two hundred and ninety-five lines of them in
the first printing, and two hundred and eighty-nine in the second,
the odd line being added by a triplet. The author here makes her
first successful use of the device of personification, in contrast to
the acrimonious muddle that occurs in the elegy on Sir Philip
Sidney. The reader is made clearly aware of the two symbolical
female figures, the elder sitting dejected in the rags of regal
splendor, while the younger in her tidy homespun dress sends
words of didactic encouragement across the dividing ocean. The
poem is essentially feminine, for although the ladies employ the
language of preacher, politician, and soldier in their conversation,
one is constantly reminded that this is an outspoken discussion of a
family crisis, between a mother and daughter who are as closely
bound in affection as they are in blood. "New-England" speaks
first:

> Alas dear Mother, fairest Queen and best,
> With honour, wealth, and peace, happy and blest;
> What ails thee hang thy head, and cross thine arms?
> And sit i' th' dust, to sigh these sad alarms?
>
> *   *   *
>
> What means this wailing tone, this mournful guise?
> Ah, tell thy daughter, she may sympathize.

Old England

> Art ignorant indeed of these my woes?
> Or must my forced tongue these griefs disclose?
> And must myself dissect my tatter'd state,
> Which 'mazed Christendome stands wondring at?
> And thou a Child, a Limbe, and dost not feel
> My fainting weakned body now to reel?
>
> *   *   *

New-England

And thus (alas) your state you much deplore
In general terms, but will not say wherefore:
What medicine shall I seek to cure this woe,
If th'wound so dangerous I may not know.
But you perhaps, would have me ghess it out:

Is it, the daughter asks, the invasions of the Saxons, Danes, or Normans, or the "Intestine warrs" of Maud and Stephen or the rebellious Barons, that cause the mother's distress. Or is it the deposition of Edward II, and imprisonment of Richard II, or the outbreak of the war "That from the red white pricking roses sprung," which ended when Richmond came and broke "the Tushes of the Boar"? Or is it fear of "Spains bragging Armado," or of the false friendship of France and Scotland or the ingratitude of Holland, or have drought, famine, and pestilence brought suffering to the country? "Old England" replies that it is not ". . . forreign foe, nor feigned friend I fear"; Spain's fleet has been sunk, France has learned to respect the power of English arms, and Scotland and Holland offer no present threats. "Famine and Plague, two Sisters of the Sword," are more to be dreaded, "Unless our tears prevent it speedily."

But yet I Answer not what you demand,
To shew the grievance of my troubled Land?
Before I tell th' Effect, I'le shew the Cause
Which are my sins the breach of sacred Laws,
Idolatry supplanter of a Nation,
With foolish Superstitious Adoration.

*   *   *

Church Offices were sold and bought for gain,
That Pope had hope to find, *Rome* here again.

*   *   *

And thou poor soul, wert jeer'd among the rest,
Thy flying for the truth was made a jest.
For Sabbath-breaking, and for drunkenness,
Did ever land profaness more express?

This passage reveals that for Anne Bradstreet, and for those around her, the real danger to the motherland was seen to lie in the weakness of the Established Church, which seemed to be moving towards a return to the old religion. It has been said that

> The New England Puritans . . . were just as patriotic as Englishmen who remained at home. They hated Spain like poison, and France only a little less. In their eyes, as in those of Anglicans, the most important issue in the western world was the struggle between Catholicism and Protestantism.[5]

As the poem's dramatic (and, it must be admitted, somewhat pedantic) introductory section unfolds it can be seen that its two chief arguments are the menace of Roman Catholicism and the tragedy of a nation divided and threatening violence against royal authority. "From crying blood yet cleansed am not I," continues "Old England," citing the execution of Lady Jane Grey and the murder of Richard III's nephews in the Tower, whose only crime was that they had royal blood, and the fate of other martyrs "dying causelessly." Those leaders of the Puritan movement who spoke out, from the pulpit and in print, against the continuing abuses and oppressions, were harshly dealt with.

The Sermons yet upon Record do stand
That cri'd destruction to my wicked land:
These Prophets mouthes (alas the while) was stopt,

5. Perry Miller and Thomas H. Johnson, eds., *The Puritans*, New York, 1938, Introduction, p. 8.

Unworthily, some backs whipt, and eares cropt;
Their reverent cheeks, did beare the glorious markes
Of stinking, stigmatizing, Romish Clerkes.

The last four lines above were deleted from the second printing of the poem. They refer to the punishments inflicted, at the behest of Archbishop Laud, on such writers as William Prynne, Henry Burton, and John Bastwick. Although the Court of Star Chamber, in which these men were tried, imposed many cruel sentences on nonconformists before its abolition in 1640, it never admittedly contained "Romish Clerkes," and Anne Bradstreet was well advised to cancel these lines while preparing the poem for its second appearance.

The description of the mother-country's sorrows continues: religious persecution at home, and warnings from abroad in the loss of the Palatinate in the Thirty Years War, the defeat of the Huguenots at La Rochelle, and the massacre of thousands of Protestants in the Irish Rebellion of 1641. When "Old England" ends her long speech the daughter still asks, sympathetically but with a touch of impatience,

Pray in plain terms, what is your present grief?
Then lets join heads and hearts for your relief.

And finally the lamenting parent comes to the point:

Well to the matter then, there's grown of late
'Twixt King and Peers a Question of State,
Which is the chief, the Law, or else the King.

*   *   *

Old customes, new Prerogatives stood on,
Had they not held Law fast all had been gone:
Which by their prudence stood them in such stead

They took high *Strafford* lower by the head.
And to their *Laud* be't spoke, they held i' th' tower
All *Englands* Metropolitane that hour.

After the execution of the king's most influential minister, Thomas Wentworth, Earl of Strafford, and the imprisonment of Archbishop Laud, "Old England" relates that King Charles, baffled by the defiance of the House of Commons and the increasing dissensions among his subjects in London, fled with his family to the north and established the headquarters of the Royalist cause at York. Thus the civil conflict began in earnest, in August of 1642, and the mother-country bewails the fact that she is "now destroy'd and slaught'red" by her own people.

Oh pity me in this sad perturbation,
My plundred Towns, my houses devastation,
My weeping Virgins and my young men slain;
My wealthy trading fall'n, my dearth of grain,
The seed-times come, but ploughman hath no hope
Because he knows not who shall inn his Crop.

The penultimate line above shows that the "Dialogue" was finished, and dated "1642," in the early spring of 1643, just before the 25th of March, that is, on which day the year 1643 began for Anne Bradstreet. News of the war as it developed through the autumn and winter of 1642–43, with its costly battles and its disruption of trade, resulting in scarcities of food and the threatened collapse of the whole farming system of the country, came regularly, though often belatedly, to New England in the ships that reached her ports. And the contents of these news-despatches would have been made known to Anne as soon as they were communicated to her husband and her father. The poem in which she expressed her deep concern for her native land does not reveal any

of the studied "literary" quality of most of her longer compositions; it has instead a sense of immediacy and urgency that is quite
appropriate to the subject. This is sharply contemporary, though
not "on the spot," reporting of a crisis in the lives of men and
women, in England, that shook their colonial counterparts profoundly. The cruel witticism describing Strafford's beheading, and
the harsh pun on Archbishop Laud's incarceration, illustrate C. V.
Wedgwood's statement that

> The supporters of each side in the political struggle recognised
> the need for propaganda that would strike home quickly to
> men's minds. . . . From the outbreak of the war even some
> poets who were highly skilled in the fashionable manner of the
> 1630's adopted a simple, even a crude, form of writing when
> their intention was to defend a cause . . . to as wide a public
> as possible.[6]

When "Old England" ends the description of her woes, the
colonial daughter completes the poem with a long speech of encouragement and advice. "Your griefs I pity," she says, "but soon
hope to see / Out of your troubles much good fruit to be," and
the admonition that follows shows that although the religious
struggle was of paramount importance to Anne Bradstreet, as it
was to those around her, she was also thoroughly aware of the
political conflict between the royal prerogative and the rights
of the people.

> After dark Popery the day did clear,
> But now the Sun in's brightness shall appear.
> Blest be the Nobles of thy noble Land,
> With ventur'd lives for Truths defence that stand.
> Blest be thy Commons, who for common good,
> And thy infringed Laws have boldly stood.

6. *Poetry and Politics under the Stuarts*, Cambridge, 1960, pp. 71 and 73.

> Blest be thy Counties, who did aid thee still,
> With hearts and States to testifie their will.
> Blest be thy Preachers, who do chear thee on,
> O cry the Sword of God, and *Gideon*;
>
>   *   *   *
>
> These are the dayes the Churches foes to crush,
> To root out Popelings head, tail, branch and rush;
> Let's bring *Baals* vestments forth to make a fire,
> Their Mytires, Surplices, and all their Tire,
> Copes, Rotchets, Crossiers, and such empty trash,
> And let their Names consume, but let the flash
> Light Christendome, and all the world to see
> We hate *Romes* whore, with all her trumpery.
> Go on brave *Essex*, with a Loyal heart,
> Not false to King, nor to the better part;
> But those that hurt his people and his Crown,
> As duty binds, expel and tread them down.
> Let Gaoles be fill'd with th' remnant of that pack,
> And sturdy *Tyburn* loaded till it crack.

The last two lines did not appear in the second printing of the poem. After the restoration of the monarchy extreme penalties were inflicted on the Regicides and other Puritan leaders, a number of whom were arrested and executed. In view of these vengeful acts, which shocked the New Englanders, Anne Bradstreet probably thought it best to delete so vindictive a wish from her comments on the Civil War itself.

The description of "brave Essex" as "not false to King, nor to the better part" shows how accurately the character of Robert Devereux, third Earl of Essex and Commander of the Parliamentary army from 1642 to 1645, was appraised by a citizen of faraway Massachusetts even during the first months of the war. G. M. Trevelyan's judgement of him is in harmony with Anne Bradstreet's words.

The formula of rebellion in these early months was the oath "to live and die with the Earl of Essex." But the good Earl was only a figure-head, not a motive power. He belongs to that type of man, faithful and honourable, who is put at the head of armies when a civil war begins, but has to be removed before it can end. He shrank unconsciously from beating up the royal camp, and this political instinct was not counteracted by the promptings of an active military genius. In the last week of August and the first fortnight of September, 1642, Essex delayed to march on Nottingham at the head of a regular force, against which Charles had then nothing to oppose save a few thousand horsemen without discipline, and a few hundred pikemen without pikes.[7]

"New-England's" speech continues:

> And ye brave Nobles chase away all fear,
> And to this hopeful Cause closely adhere·

> *   *   *

> These, these are they I trust, with *Charles* our King,
> Out of all mists such glorious dayes shall bring;
> That dazled eyes beholding much shall wonder
> At that thy setled peace, thy wealth and splendor.
> Thy Church and weal establish'd in such manner,
> That all shall joy, that thou display'dst thy Banner;
> And discipline erected so I trust,
> That nursing Kings shall come and lick thy dust.

Like the instinctively loyal Earl of Essex, the majority of thoughtful New Englanders could not bring themselves to believe that the king was their arch-enemy, even though their allegiance was entirely given to the Parliamentary cause. They found plausible refuge in blaming the "High Church" party, with the alien Roman Catholic queen as its leader, for all the troubles of the

7. *History of England*, 1947, Vol. V., *England Under the Stuarts*, p. 195.

nation and its misguided monarch. When Anne Bradstreet wrote of "those that hurt his people and his Crown" she was surely matching the quaintly expressed but none the less earnest conviction of Nathaniel Ward:

> I am sure, a King cannot hold by Copy, at the will of other Lords; the law calls that base tenure, inconsistent with Royalty; much more base it is, to hold at the will of Ladies: Apron-string tenure is very weak, tyed but of a slipping knot, which a childe may undoe, much more a King. It stands not with our Queens honour to weare an Apron, much lesse her Husband, in the strings; that were to ensnare both him and her self in many unsafeties. . . . To speak English, Books and tongues tell us, I wish they tell us true, that the Error of these Wars on our Kings part proceeds only from ill Counsellors.[8]

It was not difficult for the Puritans to argue that the English Papists and the High Anglican extremists were in complete agreement, and to categorize them all as "ill Counsellors." They believed that these in their entirety must be rooted out and destroyed, that only thus could peace be restored between the king, grown war-weary and wiser, and his people, and that the great crusade of Protestantism against Roman Catholicism should then go on to victory in the whole civilized world. "New-England" brings her admonitory advice to the mother-country, and the poem, to an end with a fiery rallying-call to the wider conflict:

> So shall thy happy Nation ever flourish,
> When truth & righteousnes they thus shall nourish.
> When thus in peace, thine Armies brave send out,
> To sack proud *Rome*, and all her Vassals rout;
>
> *   *   *
>
> Bring forth the Beast that rul'd the World with's beck,
> And tear his flesh, & set your feet on's neck;

8. *The Simple Cobler of Aggawam*, p. 69.

And make his filthy Den so desolate,
To th'stonishment of all that knew his state:
This done with brandish'd Swords to *Turky* goe,
For then what is't, but English blades dare do,
And lay her waste for so's the sacred Doom,
And do to *Gog* as thou hast done to *Rome.*

*   *   *

Then fulness of the Nations in shall flow,
And Jew and Gentile to one worship go;
Then follows dayes of happiness and rest;
Whose lot doth fall, to live therein is blest:
No Canaanite shall then be found i'th' Land,
And holiness on horses bells shall stand.

*   *   *

Farewel dear Mother, Parliament prevail,
And in a while, you'le tell another tale.

The word "Parliament" in the penultimate line is altered to "rightest cause" in the second edition; the obvious inference is that the author felt the modification advisable because of the restoration of the monarchy. But it is also possible, if the poem was edited during the Commonwealth period, that the change reflects the feeling among conservative Puritans that the victorious party in the war had gone to unwarranted extremes of cruelty in the name of Parliament.

The scriptural climax of the poem paraphrases Zechariah's account of the exaltation of Jerusalem, and St. Paul's teachings (in Romans, II and III, and I Corinthians, XII), concerning the common spiritual heritage of Christian and Jew. An echoing thought-sequence occurs in Edward Johnson's *Wonder-Working Providence of Sion's Saviour . . . in New England,* written when the Civil War was ending and published in London in 1654.

The Forlorne hopes of Antichrists Army, were the proud Prelates of *England:* the Forlorne of Christs Armies, were these

N.E. people. . . . Here is a people not onely praying but fighting for you, . . . that they with you may enjoy that glorious resurrection-day, . . . when not only the Bridegroom shall appear to his Churches both of *Jews* and *Gentiles,* (which are his spouse) in a more brighter array than ever heretofore, but also his Bride shall be clothed by him in the richest garments that ever the Sons of men put on.[9]

The compiler of a bibliography of colonial verse has made this comment on the poem:

Of decided merit and interest is Anne Bradstreet's "Dialogue between Old England and New," . . . This poem clearly contains the typical New England attitude toward the English civil war, most interestingly in the closing section, where the Cromwellian revolution is seen as the expansion of the New England experiment, eventually tending toward the reformation of the whole world.[10]

The foremost preacher in Massachusetts, at this time, of the doctrine of the millennium, or the Church triumphant on earth for a thousand years after which Christ would come again for "that glorious resurrection-day," was the Reverend John Cotton, who had emigrated, from Boston in Lincolnshire, in 1633 to become the teacher, or assistant to the pastor, of the First Church in colonial Boston. Thomas Dudley and his family, in nearby Newtown, must have welcomed their friend and neighbor of the Lincolnshire years, and it is likely that Anne Bradstreet attended his lectures and sermons as often as she could. After the move to Ipswich in 1635 she would have been able to read his teachings

9. *Wonder-Working Providence,* ed. W. F. Poole, Andover (Mass.), 1867, pp. 232–33.
10. Harold S. Jantz, *The First Century of New England Verse,* Worcester (Mass.), 1944, Introduction, p. 37.

in manuscript copies, as they must have been widely circulated in the colony before being published in London. The final section of the "Dialogue" strongly reflects Cotton's influence on Anne's convictions, and there is a clear echo, in her hopeful picture of England's spiritual future, from one of Cotton's works on church discipline.

> Hence it is prophesied by *Isaiah*, that Kings and Queens, who are nursing fathers and mothers to the church, *shall bow down to the Church, with their faces to the earth*. . . . That is, they shall walk in professed subjection to the Ordinances of Christ in his Church.[11]

Anne Bradstreet's lively metrical commentary on the Civil War, an event of intense significance to English people everywhere, was (as we have noted) composed during the early years of her most fruitful period of writing. It differs from all her other ambitious poems in that its subject is neither elegiac, traditional nor rhetorical, but one requiring a treatment in which narration and explication are predominant. In presenting this challenge to the author it provided an alternative to the weighty rhythms of Sylvester that had affected Anne's ear while she was composing her tributes to Sidney and Du Bartas. In the "Dialogue" she had to convey an urgent message as clearly and forcefully as possible, without too much concern for the purely decorative quality of the verse, and if consequently the poem is lacking in poetic grace, it has true documentary distinction, and the added virtue that it gave its author a vigorous push in the direction of developing her own verbal economies and a fresher and less monotonous iambic tempo.

The "Dialogue" also provides the first revelation of a somewhat surprising quality in Anne Bradstreet's nature. This is the strain of

11. John Cotton, *The Keyes of the Kingdom of Heaven* (1644), Boston, 1843, p. 100.

violence that here breaks out into fury against the Roman Catholic Church, and that reappears startlingly in some of her later work. A comment by Harold Jantz would seem to belie this; he notes "the perennial charm and modest whimsicality of Anne Bradstreet's verse," and continues, "She is a genuine poet, even though not a great one. . . . In sad contrast to her beautifully balanced and essentially happy personality is that of Anne Yale Hopkins, the wife of Governor Edward Hopkins of Connecticut, whose literary career was cut short by insanity in the early 1640's." [12] But if the important word "balanced" had not been justifiably present in his summation, the contrast between these two women might not have been so great. For unquestionably there were strong and conflicting forces in Anne Bradstreet's character which, if they had not been controlled by her innate sense of proportion and her faculty of objectivity, and had not found a safe outlet in the writing of verse, might have brought her into disastrous contention with her rigid environment. A further glance at the fate of poor Mrs. Hopkins, and of two other New England women whose lives were wrecked by their inability to conform to the dictatorial pattern of their society, will illustrate this point.

John Winthrop wrote, under the date of 13th April, 1645:

> Mr. Hopkins, the governour of Hartford upon Connecticut, came to Boston, and brought his wife with him, (a godly young woman, and of special parts), who was fallen into a sad infirmity, the loss of her understanding and reason, which had been growing upon her divers years, by occasion of her giving herself wholly to reading and writing, and had written many books. Her husband, being very loving and tender of her, was loath to grieve her; but he saw his error, when it was too late. For if she had attended her household affairs, and such things as belong to women, and not gone out of her way and calling to meddle in such things as are proper for men, whose minds are

12. *First Century of New England Verse*, Introduction, p. 36.

stronger, etc., she had kept her wits, and might have improved them usefully and honourably in the place God had set her. He brought her to Boston, and left her with her brother, one Mr. Yale, a merchant, to try what means might be had here for her. But no help could be had.[13]

The unfortunate lady lived, apparently without recovering her reason, until 1698; no trace has ever appeared of the "many books" she is said to have written.

A more celebrated tragedy was that of Anne Hutchinson, the wife of a prosperous citizen of Lincolnshire, who came to Massachusetts Bay in 1634 with her husband and eight children. She was a capable and resolute woman, but she had come to hold certain personal religious convictions that were contrary to the established Calvinist doctrines of the colony. Winthrop recorded that she "brought over with her two dangerous errors: 1. That the person of the Holy Ghost dwells in a justified person. 2. That no sanctification can help to evidence to us our justification." [14] This means that Mrs. Hutchinson was publicly professing the dreaded heresy of Antinomian enthusiasm, believing herself to be "in direct communication with the God-head, and . . . prepared to follow the promptings of the voice within against all the precepts of the Bible, the churches, reason, or the government of Massachusetts Bay." [15] She gathered around her a large group of Boston women, and her weekly lectures were so compelling that the Reverend John Cotton, the young governor Henry Vane, and other leading citizens became her supporters. By 1636 she had created an alarming division among the churches of the colony.

When Winthrop and Dudley were again serving as governor

---

13. J. Winthrop, *History of New England*, Vol. II, pp. 265–66.

14. *Ibid.* Vol. I, p. 239.

15. Perry Miller and Thomas H. Johnson, eds., *The Puritans*, Introduction, p. 10.

and deputy, in 1637, Mrs. Hutchinson and some of her followers were brought to trial for the dissemination of heretical opinions. The court proceedings were long and harsh, and in the end Anne Hutchinson was sentenced to depart from the colony, which she did in the early spring of 1638. Five years later she and her family, who had settled near the Dutch plantations on the Long Island Sound, were massacred by the Indians, except for one daughter who was carried away into captivity.

The danger of "enthusiasm" among the women of the colony was apparently not quite eliminated by the martyrdom of Mrs. Hutchinson. Anne Bradstreet's younger sister Sarah, who married in 1638 Major Benjamin Keanye, the son of a prominent Boston merchant, began some years later to behave in such an irrational way that she would seem to have been really unbalanced. Her husband went to England on business for his father, and it appears that Sarah accompanied him, for the first sign of her trouble is in a letter sent from London by Stephen Winthrop (whose sister Mary had married Samuel Dudley) to his brother John Winthrop, Jr. This is dated 27th March, 1646, and contains the curious statement, without further explanation: "My she Cosin Keane is growne a great preacher." [16] Perhaps the intense atmosphere of London, during those middle years of the Civil War, had an unfortunate effect on an already unstable personality.

The next recorded event in Sarah's case occurred in November of the same year, after she had returned to Massachusetts without her husband. At the First Church in Boston she was "in open Assembly Admonished of hir Irregular Prophesying in mixt Assemblies and for Refusing ordinarily to heare in yᵉ Churches of Christ." [17] During the early spring of 1647 Thomas Dudley re-

---

16. *Winthrop Papers*, Vol. V, p. 70.
17. Transcript of MS. Records of First Church in Boston, 1630–87 (at Massachusetts Historical Society, Boston), p. 24.

ceived a series of extremely unpleasant letters from London, which strangely enough have survived, in which Benjamin Keanye accused his wife of gross immorality as well as religious incontinence. In the last, and least offensive, of these communications he wrote:

> But most of all it greeves mee, that shee has runne so faste from that highth of error in judgement, to that extremitie of error in practisse . . . that shee has not lefte mee any roome or way of reconsciliation: And theirefoare as you desier, I do plainely declare my resolution, never againe to live with her as a Husband.[18]

It was apparently Dudley's wish to obtain this written repudiation of the wife by the husband, for he was then able, before the summer was over, to persuade the colonial court to take the unusual step of ending his daughter's marriage by divorce. There is no question but that Dudley's august position—he was again deputy governor from 1646 to 1649—made this possible, and that it caused consternation on both sides of the Atlantic is shown by a troubled postscript, in a letter of November 1647 from the Reverend Ezekiel Rogers of Rowley (a small settlement near Ipswich) to Governor Winthrop.

> Sir, since the writing of this, I thought myselfe bounde to acquaint you that there is not a little discourse raised, & by some, offense taken, at the late Divorce granted by the Court. How waighty a business it is, as I neede not tell you, so I would humbly desire that some course may be taken so to cleere the Courts proceeding, as that rumors might be stopped, & letters of mistake with England prevented.[19]

18. *Winthrop Papers*, Vol. V, p. 144. (Three of the letters are in *Suffolk County Deeds*, i, 83–84, in the State House, Boston.)
19. *Winthrop Papers*, Vol. V, p. 189.

This drastic action did not solve the problem of Sarah Dudley. In October, shortly after her divorce, she was excommunicated by the church in Boston, not only for her "Irregular Prophecying" but also for having fallen into "odious, lewd, & scandalous uncleane behavior with . . . an Excommunicate person." [20] The public scandal that she was causing must have brought infinite distress to her family, probably the second in prominence after the Winthrops in the whole colony, and therefore keenly conscious of their obligation to be an example of uprightness in all ways to those around them.

In the face of all this unsavory evidence the harassed deputy governor seems to have managed to convince the court that his daughter was mentally irresponsible rather than deliberately profligate, and that what she needed was a strong man to watch over her and control her actions. At any rate she was permitted to marry again, in spite of the facts that her first husband was still living and that the laws of Massachusetts dealt very severely with sexual offenses, the penalty for proven adultery being death. [21] The man who was chosen for this honor was one Thomas Pacey of Boston, about whom nothing is known save that he was of lower social station than his wife. Sarah lived until 1659, her fortieth year, and died apparently in poverty, for her father's will of 1653 required that his other heirs should provide her with a yearly payment of £6, and even if necessary with "diett & lodgeing." [22] The will of her ex-father-in-law Robert Keanye, proved in May 1656, made provision for his granddaughter Anne, or Hannah, the only child of Benjamin and Sarah, but specifically prohibits her mother, to whom he refers as Mrs. Pacey, from having any part of her daughter's portion. [23]

20. MS. Records of First Church in Boston, p. 25.
21. *Massachusetts Colony Records*, Vol. I, p. 225.
22. Will of Thomas Dudley, *Suffolk County, Massachusetts, Probate Court Records*, Vol. I, p. 90.
23. *Boston Record Commissioner's Report*, Boston, 1886, Vol. X, p. 48.

Although Sarah undoubtedly lacked both intelligence and stability of character, her history might not have been so melancholy if she had lived in a more tolerant world. Calvinist inflexibility, it would seem, soon warped into a state of religious hysteria the strong imagination that sought public self-expression at all cost, and hounded an overly emotional nature into a disgrace that it may never have truly deserved.

Anne Bradstreet must have been fond of her younger sister, for her second daughter, born about 1638, was named Sarah. But there is no mention in her writings of this family tragedy, nor of the other two contemporaries at whose misfortunes we have glanced. Yet it may be supposed that her heart bled for all of them, with understanding and with sympathy for their sorrows, since she herself had to govern an independence of mind, an appetite for reading and writing, and a need for an audience that encroached dangerously on the masculine preserves of her time. She too was Thomas Dudley's daughter, and from that proud, uncompromising, irascible pioneer she had the blood of an ardent family that had paid with a number of lives the price of its endless ambition.

Outwardly, according to what we are told of her, Anne Bradstreet's life was a model of graciousness and devotion; her deep love for her kindred was as deeply returned, and she was apparently respected by all who really knew her. It is in her writings that we find evidence that her faith was not always serene and unshaken, and that she could be possessed by a sort of mental rage that might, if once allowed to break out from the intellectual discipline under which she kept it, have caused irreparable damage. In the straightforward prose of her private journal she wrote:

Many times hath Satan troubled me concerning the verity of the Scriptures, many times by Atheisme how I could know whether there was a God; I never saw any miracles to confirm me, and those which I read of how did I know but they were feigned. That there is a God my Reason would soon tell me by the wondrous workes that I see, the vast frame of the Heaven and the Earth, the order of all things, night and day, Summer and Winter, Spring and Autumn, the dayly providing for this great household upon the Earth, the preserving and directing of All to its proper End. The consideration of these things would with amazement certainly resolve me that there is an Eternall Being.

But how should I know he is such a God as I worship in Trinity, and such a Saviour as I rely upon? tho: this hath thousands of Times been suggested to mee, yet God hath helped me over. . . .

When I have gott over this Block, then have I another putt in my way. That admitt this bee the true God whom wee worship, and that bee his word, yet why may not the Popish Religion bee the right? They have the same God, the same Christ, the same word. They only enterprett it one way wee another.

This hath sometimes stuck with me, and more it would, but the vain fooleries that are in their Religion, together with their lying miracles, and cruell persecutions of the Saints, which admitt were they as they terme them yet not so to bee dealt withall.

From these unorthodox thoughts she would revert, as though in horror at her own questioning tolerance, to such outbursts as the fire-and-sword passages of the "Dialogue between Old England and New." The compassionate admonition, "yet not so to bee dealt withall," was forgotten, at least for the time being, when she wrote her exhortation for the ruthless destruction of "Rome's whore with all her trumpery."

A circumstance that probably gave an added stimulus to her work, and perhaps also contributed to her growth in maturity and self-reliance, at about this time, was the removal of her parents from Ipswich to Roxbury in 1639. Since their arrival in Massachusetts the senior Dudleys and the Bradstreets had always lived close together, as in Ipswich for example, where their houses stood side by side. Anne's child-rearing and home-keeping cares must often have been made easier by her mother's presence, but it was her father's companionship and his understanding of her intellectual aspirations that would have given her constant pleasure and support. So that when he moved away, forty miles down the coast, to be nearer to his official duties in Boston, she must have missed him sorely, in spite of the fullness of her life with her husband and children.

Therefore much of her writing at this time was done for direct presentation to Thomas Dudley, who it seems had already provided her with a literary pattern that she spent a great deal of creative labor in following. Dudley's surviving poetic remains consist only of a bit of valedictory doggerel said to have been found in his pocket after his death, but we have two references to his more substantial verse-making. One of them is from Cotton Mather's summation of his character, in the *MS. Life:*

> He was a man of great spirit, as well as of great understanding; suitable to the family he was, by his father, descended from; . . . he was endowed with many excellent abilities . . . for he was known to be well skilled in the law, . . . he was likewise a great historian. . . . He had an excellent pen, as was accounted by all; nor was he a mean poet; mention is made by some of his relations of a paper of verses, describing the state of Europe in his time, which . . . passed the royal test in King James's time, who was himself not meanly learned, and so no unmeet judge of such matters.

The other allusion is in Anne Bradstreet's forty-four line dedication of the first two of her recurrent "fours": "The Four Elements" and "Of the four Humours in Mans Constitution." I quote a number of lines from this, as it was first printed in 1650, because it reveals so much of the author's hopes and fears, her pleasure in her uniquely seventeenth-century poetic project, and her true love for her father.

To her most Honoured Father *Thomas Dudley* Esq; *these humbly presented*

Deare Sir, of late delighted with the sight,
Of your four sisters, deckt in black & white
Of fairer Dames, the sun near saw the face,
(though made a pedestall for *Adams* Race)
Their worth so shines, in those rich lines you show,
Their paralells to find I scarcely know,
To climbe their Climes I have nor strength, nor skill,
To mount so high, requires an Eagles quill:
Yet view thereof, did cause my thoughts to soare,
My lowly pen, might wait upon those four,
I bring my four; and four, now meanly clad,
To do their homage unto yours most glad.

> T. D. on the four parts of the world

*   *   *

These same are they, of whom we being have,
These are of all, the life, the nurse, the grave,
These are, the hot, the cold, the moist, the dry,
That sinke, that swim, that fill, that upwards flye,
Of these consists, our bodyes, cloathes, and food,
The world, the usefull, hurtfull, and the good:

These eight integral parts of nature must keep "Sweet harmony," and yet, the author says, they "jar oft times"; she will make them describe their individual powers and show that, although sometimes they dangerously disagree, in the end their "divers natures, make one unity."

Something of all (though mean) I did intend,
But fear'd you'ld judge, one *Bartas* was my friend,

I honour him, but dare not wear his wealth,
My goods are true (though poor) I love no stealth,
But if I did, I durst not send them you;
Who must reward a theife, but with his due.
I shall not need my innocence to clear,
These ragged lines, will do't, when they appear.
On what they are, your mild aspect I crave,
Accept my best, my worst vouchsafe a grave.

> From her, that to your selfe more duty owes,
> Then waters, in the boundlesse Ocean flowes.

This is boldly signed "ANNE BRADSTREET" in both the first and second editions of the poems; the date "March 20, 1642," which was added in the second printing, indicates that this section of the multiple pageant of nature was finished in the early spring of 1642/43, at the same time as the "Dialogue between Old England and New." In the dedication the description "my four; and four" was altered to read "my four times four" in *Several Poems,* 1678, so as to make the introductory presentation embrace "Of the four Ages of Man" and "The four Seasons of the Year" as well. These two latter parts, of what may be considered one long poem, were not completed until a few years later and will be examined in the next chapter.

It is a pity, though not perhaps a serious loss to literature, that neither of Thomas Dudley's above-mentioned verse-productions has ever come to light. Cotton Mather is, as usual, tantalizingly oblique in his allusion to the "paper of verses, describing the state of Europe . . . which . . . passed the royal test in King James's time." The censorship of printing in London was under the control of the Archbishop of Canterbury, [24] not the Crown itself, and all approved publications were supposed to be listed

24. Douglas Bush, *English Literature in the Earlier Seventeenth Century,* p. 27.

in the registers of the guild of printers, called the Stationers' Company. Nothing identifiable as Dudley's description of Europe has been found in the *Stationers' Register;* it may have been issued as a broadside, now lost, or appeared in one of the early "corantos," or news-letters, that has not survived. Anne Bradstreet's salutation to "T. D. on the four parts of the world" as "deckt in black & white" encourages the assumption that this poetic effort, surely a separate and later piece of work by Dudley, was actually printed, but this too seems to have vanished completely.

Anne admittedly used her father's poem as the inspiration and model for her ambitious series of "fours." It would be interesting to be able to compare the influence of his literary style, with that of her acknowledged masters Spenser, Sidney, and the English Du Bartas, on his daughter's work. But her own vigorous statement that her "goods" are not stolen, from the affluent Frenchman or anyone else, shows that she was already anxious to avoid dependence on other poets and aware that, in spite of her protestations, she would be called a "Du Bartas Girle" *ad nauseam.*

The present-day reader of Anne's dedication, and of the two four-part poems on the elements and the humors that follow, is likely to be somewhat bewildered by the consequential characters who march forward to present their speeches, and incidentally to honor Thomas Dudley's geographical ladies. Yet, even though rather breathlessly displayed by their author, they would have been recognized at once by her contemporaries as the apt personifications of the eight substances from which all physical life, as interpreted by the Aristotelian, or "old" cosmology, was formed. The world and all that it contained, according to this philosophy, were made up of the four elements, earth, water, air, and fire, and the world's miniature, man, was a compound of the elements vitalized by the four humors, blood, choler, melancholy, and phlegm.

The old cosmology held that the earth was fixed at the center of the universe, and around it revolved the sun, moon, and stars. As God reigned in Heaven, over a host of angelic beings of varying degrees of sublimity, so man was supreme on earth, only a little lower than the angels and lord of all the world's creatures, from the lion, the eagle, and Leviathan, the whale, down to the minutest living organisms of land and sea. This was the concept of the Great Chain of Being, "the vast system of gradations which linked everything in the Universe from the merest stone on Earth to the Almighty Himself, in an infinite series of progressive stages. Based on the fundamental principles of the Plenitude of God and the Continuity of His Creation, it permitted no exceptions, no disruptions in its orderly sequence of ascending powers." [25] Satan existed, in the extreme depths of sublunary space, to bring evil and temptation into the world, so that man's rational soul should be endlessly engaged in the struggle to triumph over his baser nature. When the pattern of the elements was upset by the Powers of Darkness, dreadful storms and natural disasters occurred, and when the humors in man's body became unbalanced, illness, madness, and all kinds of wickedness were the result. This was the argument of Ulysses in his great speech in *Troilus and Cressida:*

> Take but degree away, untune that string,
> And hark, what discord follows!

It was the accepted Renaissance view of the universe, and it only gave way, slowly and reluctantly in the sixteenth and seventeenth

25. J. B. Bamborough, *The Little World of Man*, 1952, p. 13.

centuries, before the realistic examinations of nature by such men as Kepler, Galileo, Sir Francis Bacon, and William Harvey, whose studies eventually brought about the so-called Scientific Revolution and the abandonment, for all practical purposes, of the dogmas of the Aristotelian cosmology.

Anne Bradstreet was a child of the Renaissance, thoroughly indoctrinated, as many of her poems attest, with the old conception of the universe. She was, so far as I have been able to discover, the first English woman who wrote verse based on the traditional scientific theories of her time. But the elements and humors, symbolizing the complex yet harmonious interrelation of nature and mankind, had a special significance for poets and had figured in English verse from its beginnings. Anonymous medieval lyrics described the humors; [26] Spenser, Sidney, Sir John Davies, and John Donne all introduced the elements into their poems, and Du Bartas's long account of the order brought from original Chaos, in "The First Weeke," was the forerunner of a beautiful passage in *Paradise Lost*:

> Till at his second bidding darkness fled.
> Light shon, and order from disorder sprung:
> Swift to their several quarters hasted then
> The cumbrous Elements, Earth, Flood, Aire, Fire,

which was probably written about twenty years later than Anne Bradstreet's poem on the elements.

The method of presentation that she chose for her "fours" was a popular one in her time. Douglas Bush comments on it:

> Of great importance for poetry was a special development of the religious view of nature and, in some sense, of the scientific

26. *Secular Lyrics of the XIVth and XVth Centuries*, ed. R. H. Robbins, Oxford, 1952, pp. 71–73.

view as well: that was the allegorical or emblematic conception. Because God maintains an active and intimate connection with his works . . . there is an unlimited network of correspondences binding together the physical and the spiritual, the earthly and the human and the celestial. . . . Because of this general belief in the divine unity of all creation, natural objects were seen not so much in themselves but as emblems or allegories of moral, religious and metaphysical truth.[27]

Art as well as poetry took delight in the creation of these symbolic and idealized human forms, which appear so often in the engraved title-pages of the period, and as guardians, representing every kind of virtue, to the human beings in effigy on the proud and splendid family tombs. And we know, from an inventory, that Sir Edward Coke, Chief Justice of England under King James I, had in his house "eight faire pictures whereof foure are of the elements and foure of the 4 seasons of the yeare." [28]

Sixteen separate allegorical figures make up the cast of Anne Bradstreet's pageant of the elements, humors, ages, and seasons. Her purpose was to show these characters first as individuals, then as corresponding, related aspects of the four divisions of nature, and these four in turn as parts of an essential whole. While the device may seem tedious to a modern reader, and the language and similes often too ingenuous for so ambitious a scheme, it is safe to assume that Thomas Dudley, and others close to the author, were moved to admiration and pleasure by this allegorical morality, into which so much stored-up learning and so many wise conclusions had found their way.

"The Four Elements" and "Of the four Humours in Mans Constitution" have, respectively, four hundred and eighty-four lines and six hundred and five lines, in heroic couplets with one

27. D. Bush, *Science and English Poetry*, New York, 1950, p. 11.
28. Catherine Drinker Bowen, *The Lion and the Throne*, 1957, p. 454.

triplet. A few quotations, with a synopsis of the arguments of the separate parts of each poem, will suffice to show how far the author succeeded in carrying out her grandiose plan. A short but turbulent introduction sets the stage for the recitatives of the elemental sisters.

> The Fire, Air, Earth and water did contest
> Which was the strongest, noblest and the best,
> Who was of greatest use and might'est force;
> In placide Terms, they thought now to discourse,
> That in due order each her turn should speak;
> But enmity this amity did break.

Each element was so determined to be the chief speaker that their disciplined organization was broken and their jealousy produced thunderstorms, earthquakes, and floods, until

> All looked like a Chaos or new birth:
>
> *   *   *
>
> The rumbling, hissing, puffing was so great
> The worlds confusion it did seem to threat
> Till gentle Air, Contention so abated
> That betwixt hot and cold, she arbitrated:

and the sisters finally agreed to give first place to "Fire . . . the noblest and most active Element."

"Fire" then spiritedly describes her powers, claiming control over the making of all tools, for the arts, war, agriculture, cooking, and chemistry. She aids the alchemists in their efforts to transmute base metals into gold, she provides the silversmiths with their shining ore, and on high she fills the sun with his life-giving heat, and governs a colorfully described assemblage of constellations and planets. She lists the cities of antiquity destroyed by volcanoes or burned by victorious armies, and here for the second printing two couplets were added, telling of the Great Fire of London in 1666. The "correspondence" relationships of "Fire" are stated, to the humor choler, the season of summer, and the prime age, between thirty and fifty, of man. She ends her speech by promising

> And in a word, the world I shall consume
> And all therein, at that great day of Doom.

"Earth" comes next, and of course claims all growing things and every country and city of the world. She ranges from classical geography through the beasts of jungle and plain, to the medicinal plants of the "Galenists" and the materials for building ships and houses. Gold and jewels are hers, and the mineral and botanical poisons, and she controls drought and famine, earthquakes and sandstorms, though her "windy Sister" is partly responsible for the latter. Her correspondence is to the humor melancholy, the autumnal season, and the old age of man, and she reminds all her children that they are of earth and to earth must return in the end.

Then "Water" takes the stage, declaring that she is the cause of all the fruitfulness of the earth, which without her would be a desert, and that she gives life as well to animals and men. She cites Egypt's fertile valley of the Nile, goes on to describe the riches of her rivers, lakes, and oceans, and in one of the poem's most pleasing passages challenges the claim of "Earth" to all gold and jewels.

> My pearles that dangle at thy Darlings ears,
> Not thou, but shel-fish yield, as *Pliny* clears.
> Was ever gem so rich found in thy trunk,
> As *Egypts* wanton, *Cleopatra* drunk?
> Or hast thou any colour can come nigh
> The Roman purple, double *Tirian* Dye?

> Which *Caesars* Consuls, Tribunes all adorn,
> For it to search my waves they thought no scorn.
> Thy gallant rich perfuming Amber-greece
> I lightly cast ashore as frothy fleece:
> With rowling grains of purest massie gold,
> Which *Spains Americans* do gladly hold.

Here the word "Americans" refers to the native Indian peoples of the Spanish colonies; not until well into the eighteenth century was it used to designate any of the white, European-descended, inhabitants of the New World.

"Water" continues, telling of her sway over medicinal cordials, human tears, and all the waterways of commerce, and of her correspondences to the humor phlegm, winter, and the age of childhood. The power to send hail and snow, ice and floods is hers; she recalls the ocean's swallowing of Atlantis and the great deluge of "Noe," but ends her speech on a reassuring note with the promise of the rainbow.

"I am the breath of every living soul," proclaims the last speaker, "Air." Words and songs, the sound of drums and trumpets and the report of guns, the wind that fills sails and drives mills, and the airy properties of fire and steam, are hers, as well as birds and all flying creatures, and she is linked to youth and springtime and the sanguine humor, blood. She confesses also her dominion over plagues and pestilence, hurricanes and destroying storms, and that it is by her struggles, when imprisoned underground, that earthquakes are caused. She alone among the elements claims supernatural powers, boasting, as her speech and the whole poem end, of those celestial omens that were so awe-inspiring to the seventeenth-century world.

> Then what prodigious sights I sometimes show,
> As battles pitcht in th' air, as countryes know,

Their joyning fighting, forcing and retreat,
That earth appears in heaven, O wonder great!
Sometimes red flaming swords and blazing stars,
Portentous signs of famines, plagues and wars.
Which make the mighty Monarchs fear their fates
By death or great mutation of their States.

The four sisters who speak their parts in the second quaternion
are much more contentious than the elements, a circumstance
which might not seem incongruous to a present-day psychiatrist.
"Of the four Humours in Mans Constitution" is so much a *tour
de force* that it cannot avoid being ridiculous at times, yet it is
also interesting as a distillation of the considerable knowledge of
contemporary physiological and psychological theories that Anne
Bradstreet had acquired. Its nearest literary counterpart must be
Phineas Fletcher's geographical allegory of human anatomy, *The
Purple Island* of 1633, in which rivers represent the veins, moun-
tains and hills the bones, and so on, and the intellectual qualities
are personified as the inhabitants of the island. Douglas Bush
writes of this "notorious poem":

> The medieval theme of "the castle of the body," which had
> been grotesque enough in Du Bartas and in Spenser, becomes
> still more grotesque in becoming more laboriously scientific.
> Fletcher may be called the Jacobean or Caroline Erasmus
> Darwin. . . . [His] zeal was of course religious and ethical as
> well as scientific . . . and if we survive the anatomy (which
> attracted James Joyce), we reach a catalogue and a battle of the
> vices and virtues. It is, however, a static mixture of decorative
> abstraction and satirical realism.[29]

Anne Bradstreet's four humors, though inevitably somewhat
grotesque, are not at all static. Their self-assertive energy and their

29. *English Literature in the Earlier Seventeenth Century*, p. 88.

antagonistic attitudes towards one another give a welcome liveliness to what could otherwise be a monotonous recital of anatomical facts. In both of the long poems the speakers address each other in language that is direct and simple, even though many technical terms are used and quite a few historical and mythical personages or events appear as illustrations of particular points that the ladies wish to make. Anne's lines are not overloaded, as Sylvester's are, with cumbersome compound epithets and complex metaphors, and the iambic rhythm trots along at a fairly nimble pace.

There is again an introductory quarrel, as to which of the humors deserves the first place, until "Choler," through sheer impetuosity, wins the stage. She proudly claims control over the heart and the vital spirits, "Arms and Arts" and "The princely qualities befitting Kings," and says that without her heat neither muscles, nor nerves, nor stomach would function, nor the differences of sex be established. She spends a great deal of her alloted time in belittling the other three, so insultingly that "Blood" comes on highly offended, and argues vigorously not only her own case but that of the essential co-operation of all the humors, mixed together in proper balance, to maintain health in man's body and mind.

This is a correct attitude for the speaker, since it was believed that the humors, "distilled by concoction" in the liver, were then mingled and carried by the blood to the different parts of the body. "Blood" asserts that she gives the soldier his manliness and nobility, to compensate for "Choler's" ferocity, and that those of "sanguine" temperament are known to excel in the arts and sciences and to be kind, liberal, and courteous.

The next speaker is "Melancholy," who grumbles at being called black and sad and the "sinke" of the other three humors. She claims the noble qualities of wisdom, patience, constancy, temperance, and chastity, and describes in detail her functional importance to the bones, liver, stomach, and spleen. She is not subject to the many diseases that associate themselves with the other humors, but acknowledges that

> My sickness in conceit chiefly doth lye,
> What I imagine that's my malady.
> Chymeraes strange are in my phantasy,
> And things that never were, nor shall I see.

Lastly, "mild Flegme" appears, and explains with long-suffering patience that, although she must depend on the other three for heat and energy, she is primarily responsible for the brain, "the noblest member," and therefore guides reason, fancy, and memory, and the five senses. Her passage on the sight, though its physical content is directly paraphrased from Dr. Helkiah Crooke's *Microcosmographia, or a Description of the Body of Man,*[30] has a dramatic note that is the author's own.

> The optick Nerve, Coats, humours all are mine,
> The watry, glassie, and the Chrystaline;
> O mixture strange! O colour colourless,
> Thy perfect temperament who can express:
> He was no fool who thought the soul lay there,
> Whence her affections passions speak so clear.
> O good, O bad, O true, O traiterous eyes
> What wonderments within your Balls there lyes,
> Of all the Senses sight shall be the Queen;
> Yet some may wish, O had mine eyes ne're seen.

30. See Helen McMahon, "Anne Bradstreet, Jean Bertault, and Dr. Crooke," in *Early American Literature*, Vol. 3, No. 2, Fall 1968, pp. 118–23; this essay presents a careful analysis of the considerable use that A. B. made of Dr. Crooke's work in her poem on the humors, and also points out that the strategy of debate in the poem, and some of its images, may be derived from Sylvester's translation of "Panaretus" by the French poet Jean Bertault.

"Flegme" fittingly ends this debate of the humors by an appeal to her sisters to join hands and work peacefully together, for, she says:

> Unless we agree, all falls into confusion.
> Let Sanguine with her hot hand Choler hold,
> To take her moist my moisture will be bold:
> My cold, cold melancholys hand shall clasp;
> Her dry, dry Cholers other hand shall grasp.
> Two hot, two moist, two cold, two dry here be,
> A golden Ring, the Posey UNITY.
> Nor jarrs nor scoffs, let none hereafter see,
> But all admire our perfect Amity
> Nor be discern'd, here's water, earth, air, fire,
> But here's a compact body, whole intire.
> This loving counsel, pleas'd them all so well
> That flegm was judg'd for kindness to excell.

The reminder that man is a blend of the elements seems to bring these two "fours" together as a completed whole; apparently Anne Bradstreet thought so when she presented them to her father in the early spring of 1643. She may have been already at work on her sequel-sets, the ages and seasons, but the wording in the dedication's first printing, as we have noted, makes it clear that these were not offered to Thomas Dudley until somewhat later.

Two other poems were finished, and dated, during this year. Both are descriptive of women, but of genuine flesh-and-blood human beings who were of personal significance to the author, rather than of abstract females whom she created to serve as purveyors of her own erudition. These tributes are, therefore, warmer and more spontaneous than the studied "fours," even though the first delves into ancient history for its comparisons with the greatest woman of Anne Bradstreet's cultural era.

"In Honour of that High and Mighty Princess, Queen Elizabeth, OF HAPPY MEMORY" is a poem that Anne was bound to write; why she wrote it at this particular time requires a little investigation. Perhaps the increasing awareness of her own public reputation as a "learned lady," which brought the perils of criticism along with the pleasures of praise, directed her thoughts towards that unassailable model of intellectual distinction as well as regal pre-eminence. Thomas Dudley owned a copy of the Latin biography of the queen whom he had served as a soldier, William Camden's *Annales Rerum Anglicarum, et Hibernicarum, regnante Elizabetha;* it is not very likely that Anne could have read this word for word, but the English translation, first published complete in 1630, may have come into her hands in the early 1640's, as the poem suggests some recent reading about the great queen. Also, while the first year of the Civil War was revealing, in all its horrors, the enmity between the king and a multitude of his subjects, many of the latter must have recalled a monarch who said to her Parliament, as her long reign drew towards its close,

> And though God hath raised me high, yet this I account the glory of my crown, that I have reigned with your loves. This makes me that I do not so much rejoice that God hath made me to be a Queen, as to be a Queen over so thankful a people, and to be the means under God to conserve you in safety and to preserve you from danger.

Anne Bradstreet's elegiac tribute begins with a "Proeme" of eighteen lines, in which Elizabeth's fame is saluted as resounding perpetually throughout the world, so that

> . . . men account it no impiety,
> To say thou wert a fleshy Diety:
> Thousands bring offerings (though out of date)
> Thy world of honours to accumulate,

'Mongst hundred Hecatombs of roaring verse,
Mine bleating stands before thy royal Herse.
Thou never didst, nor canst thou now disdain
T'accept the tribute of a loyal brain.

"The Poem" then tells, in ninety-two lines followed by two six-line epitaphs, of the achievements of the glorious reign and the "personal perfections" of the queen, who is likened to Minerva and exalted over such female wonders of the past as Dido, Cleopatra, and Zenobia.

No *Phoenix* pen, nor *Spencers* poetry,
No *Speeds* nor *Cambdens* learned History,
Elizahs works, warrs praise, can e're compact,
The World's the Theatre where she did act.
No memoryes nor volumes can contain
The 'leven Olympiads of her happy reign:
Who was so good, so just, so learn'd so wise,
From all the Kings on earth she won the prize.

* * *

She hath wip'd off th'aspersion of her Sex,
That women wisdome lack to play the Rex:

* * *

Was ever people better rul'd than hers?
Was ever land more happy freed from stirrs?
Did ever wealth in *England* more abound?
Her victoryes in forreign Coasts resound,
Ships more invincible then *Spains* her foe
She wrackt, she sackt, she sunk his Armado:

* * *

Fierce *Tomris,* (*Cyrus* heads-man) *Scythians* queen,
Had put her harness off, had shee but seen
Our Amazon in th'Camp of *Tilbury,*

Judging all valour and all Majesty
Within that Princess to have residence,
And prostrate yielded to her excellence.

The verbal briskness and eager tempo of the poem reflect the author's enthusiasm for her subject, and show how far she had advanced in freeing herself from the prosodical chains of the Du Bartas-Sylvester style. A staccato device of repetition is used effectively, in several forms, and the climax of the poem is reached in the passage which names the "Phoenix Queen" as the great advocate of female intelligence, and which stands as the chapter-heading and keynote for this period of Anne Bradstreet's literary coming-of-age.

Now say, have women worth? or have they none?
Or had they some, but with our Queen is't gone?
Nay Masculines, you have thus taxt us long,
But she, though dead, will vindicate our wrong.
Let such as say our Sex is void of Reason,
Know tis a Slander now, but once was Treason.

*   *   *

Full fraught with honour, riches and with dayes
She set, she set, like *Titan* in his rayes.
No more shall rise or set so glorious sun
Untill the heavens great revolution,
If then new things their old forms shall retain,
Eliza shall rule *Albion* once again.

Her Epitaph

Here sleeps THE Queen, this is the Royal Bed,
Of th' Damask Rose, sprung from the white and red,
Whose sweet perfume fills the all-filling Air:
This Rose is wither'd, once so lovely fair.

On neither tree did grow such Rose before,
The greater was our gain, our loss the more.

ANOTHER

Here lyes the pride of Queens, Pattern of Kings,
So blaze it Fame, here's feathers for thy wings.
Here lyes the envi'd, yet unparalled Prince,
Whose living virtues speak, (though dead long since)
If many worlds, as that Fantastick fram'd,
In every one be her great glory fam'd.

The last two lines undoubtedly refer to the "new cosmology" which, among its revolutionary astronomical theories, propounded the possibility that there might be many other celestial bodies, besides the world itself, that were inhabited by thinking beings. Anne Bradstreet was obviously skeptical of this newfangled idea, but she made the most of poetic license by supposing that, if such worlds did exist, the high repute of Queen Elizabeth I would in due course have found its way to them.

After the two contrived but attractive verse-memorials the date "1643" appears in the first printing. No editorial changes were made in the epitaphs, and only a few minor ones in the rest of the poem, for the second printing in 1678.

During the Christmas season of 1643 another woman must have been predominant in Anne Bradstreet's thoughts, and she wrote, with decorous restraint but genuine feeling:

AN EPITAPH
On my dear and ever honoured Mother

Mrs. Dorothy Dudley,
who deceased DECEMB. 27. 1643. *and of her age* 61.

Here lyes,
A Worthy Matron of unspotted life,
A loving Mother and obedient wife,

A friendly Neighbor, pitiful to poor,
Whom oft she fed, and clothed with her store;
To Servants wisely aweful, but yet kind,
And as they did, so they reward did find:
A true Instructer of her Family,
The which she ordered with dexterity.
The publick meetings ever did frequent,
And in her Closet constant hours she spent;
Religious in all her words and wayes,
Preparing still for death, till end of dayes:
Of all her Children, Children, liv'd to see,
Then dying, left a blessed memory.

This brief memorial was not among the poems printed in *The Tenth Muse* in 1650, but was included with the later and more personal writings that appeared in *Several Poems* in 1678. Behind its conventional yet precisely biographical phrases we can glimpse the steadfast Northamptonshire personality of that "gentlewoman both of good estate and good extraction," Dorothy Yorke, who had shared her husband's busy life in England, his troubles at the time of the forced loan, and his resolve to emigrate to the strange world of North America, and had shepherded their family beyond the first decade of life in the colony. Along with the outward anxieties and hardships she had also to cope with some inward problems, for the character of Thomas Dudley can hardly have been compatible at all times with domestic tranquility, and in two of their children at least there were, as I have already pointed out, traits of temperament that must have shown their disturbing nature at an early age.

It is a tribute to Mrs. Dudley's intelligence and ability that all of her children grew to maturity, and all but one of them had useful and successful lives. The eldest, Samuel, educated at Emmanuel College, Cambridge, became a minister in the colony of New Hampshire; he was thrice married, firstly to Mary, the daughter of Governor Winthrop, and had eighteen children.

After Anne Bradstreet the next daughter, Patience, married Major General Daniel Denison, had two children, and lived until 1691. Mercy, the youngest, was the wife of the Reverend John Woodbridge; she became the mother of twelve children and lived to the age of seventy. The life of Sarah, the third daughter, was ruined by her religious and sexual irresponsibility; it was her mother's good fortune that she did not live to experience the humiliation of Sarah's divorce and excommunication.

Not only Anne Bradstreet's elegiac stanza but also, in a sense, her whole life testify to the affectionate understanding and sound instruction that she had, to the age of thirty, from her mother. Having lost so dependable and beloved a parent, she was from this time forward a woman on her own, and as her self-reliance as a human being grew, so did her scope and ability as a writer.

CHAPTER SEVEN

The Maturing Writer

> "And oh ye high flown quills that soar the Skies,
> And ever with your prey still catch your praise,
> If e're you daigne these lowly lines your eyes
> Give Thyme or Parsley wreath, I ask no bayes."

> (ANNE BRADSTREET—*The Prologue*)

There are no dated poems of a personal nature surviving from the period of Anne Bradstreet's greatest literary activity, that is, the years 1642 to 1647 when the bulk of her formal verse was written. Both the dedication to Thomas Dudley, of the first two sets of her "fours," and the epitaph on Dorothy Dudley are public rather than private tributes, even though they reflect their author's affection and esteem for her parents.

However, a group of thirteen personal lyrics, written between 1632 and 1670, was added to the second edition of Anne Bradstreet's poems, with the general heading: "Several other Poems made by the Author upon Diverse Occasions, were found among her Papers after her Death, which she never meant should come to publick view; amongst which, these following (at the desire of some friends that knew her well) are here inserted." Among these are five undated short pieces, all addressed to her husband, which may be approximately assigned to the years 1642 to 1647. The finest of these lyrics, written at a time of great physical and

emotional stress, is one in which the woman and the poet are
wholly fused.

BEFORE THE BIRTH OF ONE OF HER CHILDREN.

All things within this fading world hath end,
Adversity doth still our joyes attend;
No tyes so strong, no friends so dear and sweet,
But with deaths parting blow is sure to meet.
The sentence past is most irrovocable,
A common thing, yet oh inevitable;
How soon, my Dear, death may my steps attend,
How soon't may be thy Lot to lose thy friend,
We both are ignorant, yet love bids me
These farewell lines to recommend to thee,
That when that knot's unty'd that made us one,
I may seem thine, who in effect am none.
And if I see not half my dayes that's due,
What nature would, God grant to yours and you;
The many faults that well you know I have,
Let be interr'd in my oblivious [1] grave;
If any worth or virtue were in me,
Let that live freshly in thy memory
And when thou feel'st no grief, as I no harms,
Yet love thy dead, who long lay in thine arms:
And when thy loss shall be repaid with gains
Look to my little babes my dear remains.
And if thou love thy self, or loved'st me
These O protect from step Dames injury.
And if chance to thine eyes shall bring this verse,
With some sad sighs honour my absent Herse;
And kiss this paper for thy loves dear sake,
Who with salt tears this last Farewel did take.

A.B.

1. This word appears as "oblivions" in the first (1678) printing of the
poem, and is given thus in subsequent reprints, but I have corrected it as
indicated by the *errata* leaf that survives only in the Prince copy, at the Boston (Mass.) Public Library, of *Several Poems*, 1678.

The line "And if I see not half my dayes that's due" must date the poem as written before the spring of 1647, when Anne presumably reached her thirty-fifth year, half the scriptural allotment, that is, of three score years and ten. The Bradstreets' fifth child, Hannah, was probably born in 1642, and the sixth, Mercy, in 1646, so the lyric undoubtedly relates to one of these births.

Anne Bradstreet never achieved a purer expression of deep feeling than in the twenty-eight lines of this simple poem. Without any recourse to conceits or contrivance, from its introductory quiet acceptance of the transience of life's joys, to its poignant final note of farewell, the lyric conveys with clear economy of language the sorrow of parting from a beloved companion, with whom the perfection of emotional fulfillment has been experienced. The writer did not describe herself as "thy friend" simply for the sake of rhyme; in that single familiar word are expressed the trust and pride and devotion of a supremely happy marriage. Its use by Anne Bradstreet recalls these lines from Bishop Henry King's celebrated lament for his wife:

> Accept thou Shrine of my dead Saint,
> Instead of Dirges this complaint;
> And for sweet flowres to crown thy hearse,
> Receive a strew of weeping verse
> From thy griev'd friend, whom thou might'st see
> Quite melted into tears for thee.

The kinship of the two poems has twice been pointed out, in private correspondence, by distinguished men of letters: Alexander Witherspoon of Yale University wrote, on the 27th August, 1951:

> I was much touched by Mrs. Bradstreet's lines to her husband. . . . I must say that the four lines [17–20] particularly have no

equal for genuine pathos and simple sincerity except in Henry King's *Exequy* to his dead wife. And no century in English literature could have produced either set of verses but the seventeenth!

And the poet Walter de la Mare commented, in a letter of 13th December, 1951:

> The crystal-clear beauty and truth of the lines to her husband . . . bring to mind nothing less moving and treasurable than Bishop King's "Exequy."

To compare this poem of Anne Bradstreet's with her own piece of doggerel verse, written under somewhat similar circumstances, "Upon a Fit of Sickness, Anno. 1632," is to recognize at once how far her native poetic gift had developed in the intervening years. The lines to her husband were surely composed as a private expression, without any idea of public approval; their excellence lies in the sensitive reticence with which the pathos of their message is conveyed. In sober phrases, without striking imagery or simile, in simple end-stopped couplets rhyming mainly on monosyllables, the writer says what it is imperative for her to say. The only two vivid touches in the poem are the use of the sharp adjective "salt" in the final line, and the skilful alliteration which reaches its climax in the moving appeal,

> Yet love thy dead, who long lay in thine arms.

In light-hearted constrast to this intensely serious poem are three verse-epistles, printed in sequence under the heading: "A Letter to her Husband, absent upon Publick employment." These were no doubt written for actual delivery to Simon Bradstreet while he was attending the General Court in Boston, or had gone even further afield on the increasingly complicated business of the federated colonies. If he was in truth the perfect husband that the poems eulogize, he must have received these offerings with delight, for they are charming exercises in affectionate virtuosity, without a hint of bitterness or reproach. The first two "letters" make use of one of Anne Bradstreet's favorite images, the sun.

> My head, my heart, mine Eyes, my life, nay more,
> My joy, my Magazine of earthly store,
> If two be one, as surely thou and I,
> How stayest thou there, whilst I at *Ipswich* lye?
> So many steps, head from the heart to sever
> If but a neck, soon should we be together:
> I like the earth this season, mourn in black,
> My Sun is gone so far in's Zodiack,
> Whom whilst I 'joy'd, nor storms, nor frosts I felt,
> His warmth such frigid colds did cause to melt.
> My chilled limbs now nummed lie forlorn;
> Return, return sweet *Sol* from *Capricorn*;
> In this dead time, alas, what can I more
> Then view those fruits which through thy heat I bore?
> Which sweet contentment yield me for a space,
> True living Pictures of their Fathers face.
> O strange effect! now thou art *Southward* gone,
> I weary grow, the tedious day so long;
> But when thou *Northward* to me shalt return,
> I wish my Sun may never set, but burn
> Within the Cancer of my glowing breast,
> The welcome house of him my dearest guest.
> Where ever, ever stay, and go not thence,
> Till natures sad decree shall call thee hence;
> Flesh of thy flesh, bone of thy bone,
> I here, thou there, yet both but one.
>
> *A.B.*

This and the two following verse-letters are the only examples we have of Anne Bradstreet's deliberate experimenting with the "conceited" style, that was so brilliantly developed by the so-called metaphysical school of seventeenth-century English poets. The contemporary term for the style was "strong lines," a good description of this packed and allusive manner of writing which forces the reader to follow an argument or an analogy worked out at length. Anne's natural style of composition was far removed from this intricately designed and essentially masculine type of versification; she was at once too forthright and too ingenuous to be capable of any sustained performance of such mental gymnastics, even though she made generous use of the more obvious kinds of comparisons and metaphors. But in these private *billets-doux* to her husband, written for her pleasure in the sending as well as for his in the receiving, she apparently felt tempted to try her hand at what must have seemed to her a very sophisticated, even rather daring, manner of expression.

That she was erudite enough at least to play with the metaphysical style is shown by her development of the image of the sun as the counterpart of Simon Bradstreet; the recital of "Sol's" activities is based on the ancient Ptolemaic astronomy, which held that the sun, moon, planets, and starry concourse all moved in their ordered circles around the central motionless earth. The sun's progress through the months and seasons of the year was plotted by its changing positions in relation to the constellations of the zodiacal circle; so Anne Bradstreet's poem tells us that her "Sun" had gone southward, probably to Boston, in December or January, the time of Capricorn, and begs him to return and make a perpetual summer in her "glowing breast."

The next and longer letter, of forty lines, is more elaborate and also more confused in its imagery. The appeal to Phoebus has some of the absurdity of the author's brush with Apollo in the first version of the "Elegie upon Sir Philip Sidney," and at one point she seems to be simultaneously invoking the pagan sun-

god and the Christian deity. But the exercise is entertaining, and
strikes one spark at least from its elemental materials.

> *Phoebus* make haste, the day's too long, be gone,
> The silent night's the fittest time for moan;
> But stay this once, unto my suit give ear,
> And tell my griefs in either Hemisphere:

*   *   *

> Commend me to the man more lov'd then life,
> Shew him the sorrows of his widdowed wife;
> My dumpish thoughts, my groans, my brakish tears
> My sobs, my longing hopes, my doubting fears,
> And if he love, how can he there abide?
> My Interest's more then all the world beside.
> He that can tell the starrs or Ocean sand,
> Or all the grass that in the Meads do stand,
> The leaves in th' woods, the hail or drops of rain,
> Or in a corn-field number every grain,
> Or every mote that in the sun-shine hops,
> May count my sighs, and number all my drops:
> Tell him, the countless steps that thou dost trace,
> That once a day, thy Spouse thou mayst imbrace;

*   *   *

> O *Phoebus*, hadst thou but thus long from thine
> Restrain'd the beams of thy beloved shine,
> At thy return, if so thou could'st or durst
> Behold a Chaos blacker then the first.
> Tell him here's worse then a confused matter,
> His little world's a fathom under water,
> Naught but the fervor of his ardent beams
> Hath power to dry the torrent of these streams.
> Tell him I would say more, but cannot well,
> Oppressed minds, abruptest tales do tell.
> Now post with double speed, mark what I say,
> By all our loves conjure him not to stay.

The third letter, taking its cast of characters from the woods and streams, is fanciful rather than grandly arbitrary in the comparisons it employs, and reflects Anne Bradstreet's familiarity with the traditions of fidelity in the animal world. It seems to be the most easily and spontaneously composed of the three, and pleases by its playful punning and lively imagery.

> As loving Hind that (Hartless) wants her Deer,
> Scuds through the wood and Fern with harkning ear,
> Perplext, in every bush & nook doth pry,
> Her dearest Deer, might answer ear or eye;
> So doth my anxious soul, which now doth miss,
> A dearer Dear (far dearer Heart) then this.
> Still wait with doubts, and hopes, and failing eye,
> His voice to hear, or person to discry.
> Or as the pensive Dove doth all alone
> (On withered bough) most uncouthly bemoan
> The absence of her Love, and loving Mate,
> Whose loss hath made her so unfortunate:
> Ev'n thus doe I, with many a deep sad groan
> Bewail my turtle true, who now is gone,
> His presence and his safe return, still wooes,
> With thousand dolefull sighs & mournfull Cooes.
> Or as the loving Mullet, that true Fish,
> Her fellow lost, nor joy nor life do wish,
> But lanches on that shore, there for to dye,
> Where she her captive husband doth espy.
> Mine being gone, I lead a joyless life,
> I have a loving phere,[2] yet seem no wife:
> But worst of all, to him can't steer my course,
> I here, he there, alas, both kept by force:
> Return my Dear, my joy, my only Love,
> Unto thy Hinde, thy Mullet and thy Dove,
> Who neither joyes in pasture, house nor streams,
> The substance gone, O me, these are but dreams.

2. "Phere," an alternative spelling for "fere": mate.

Together at one Tree, oh let us brouze,
And like two Turtles roost within one house,
And like the Mullets in one River glide,
Let's still remain but one, till death divide.

Thy loving Love and Dearest Dear,
At home, abroad, and everywhere.

A.B.

A short uncomplicated lyric completes the group of tributes to Simon Bradstreet included in the edition of 1678. It is undoubtedly the most often quoted of Anne's poems, and its quiet, joyful intensity sounds the keynote to the whole of her personal life.

To my Dear and Loving Husband

If ever two were one, then surely we.
If ever man were lov'd by wife, then thee;
If ever wife was happy in a man,
Compare with me ye women if you can.
I prize thy love more then whole Mines of gold,
Or all the riches that the East doth hold.
My love is such that Rivers cannot quench,
Nor aught but love from thee, give recompense.
Thy love is such I can no way repay,
The heavens reward thee manifold I pray.
Then while we live, in love lets so persever,
That when we live no more, we may live ever.

Samuel Eliot Morison has commented that these lines are "so human, simple, yet inevitable in language, so devoid of contemporary conceits or religious dogma. Save for one obsolete accent (persever instead of persevere) they might have been written at any time during the last three centuries." [3]

3. S. E. Morison, *The Intellectual Life of Colonial New England*, New York, 1956, p. 222.

At the beginning of the period to which these personal poems would seem to belong, that is 1642 to 1647, Anne Bradstreet had completed "The Four Elements" and "Of the four Humours in Mans Constitution," which as we have seen were presented to Thomas Dudley in March 1642/43. She then proceeded to write the two long poems, on the ages and seasons, that formed the second half of her fourfold composition.

"Of the four Ages of Man" is undoubtedly, for a present-day reader at any rate, the most intelligible and acceptable part of the quaternion. Its characters, one small boy and three men, are human beings representing their own kind, rather than symbolical impersonators of the moods and materials of nature. And the poem gives us some interesting glimpses of society and its values in the seventeenth century in England. Harold S. Jantz has expressed the opinion that "the section on 'Old Age' . . . is obviously a versification of personal reminiscences and political attitudes of her father." [4] The poem has four hundred and forty-four lines in the first printing; eight more were added, and a number of editorial changes were made, for the second edition. An introduction tells how the four ages are severally related, according to the system of "correspondences," to the elements and the humors, then the characters themselves are brought onto the stage.

> Childhood was cloth'd in white & green to show
> His spring was intermixed with some snow:
> Upon his head nature a Garland set
> Of Primrose, Daizy & the Violet.
> Such cold mean flowrs the spring puts forth betime
> Before the sun hath throughly heat the clime.
> His Hobby striding did not ride but run,
> And in his hand an hour-glass new begun,

4. H. S. Jantz, *The First Century of New England Verse*, p. 37.

*   *   *

Next Youth came up in gorgeous attire,
(As that fond age doth most of all desire)
His Suit of Crimson and his scarfe of green,
His pride in's countenance was quickly seen,

*   *   *

No wooden horse, but one of mettal try'd
He seems to fly or swim, and not to ride,
Then prancing on the stage, about he wheels,
But as he went death waited at his heels.
The next came up in a much graver sort,
As one that cared for a good report,
His sword by's side, and choler in his eyes,
But neither us'd as yet, for he was wise:
Of Autumns fruits a basket on his arm,
His golden God in's purse, which was his charm.
And last of all to act upon this stage
Leaning upon his staff came up Old Age,
Under his arm a sheaf of wheat he bore,
An harvest of the best, what needs he more?
In's other hand a glass ev'n almost run,
Thus writ about *This out then am I done.*

Though "Childhood" is an appealing figure, he has a melancholy tale to tell of "The sins and dangers I am subject to." A revealing part of his speech has already been quoted [5] to illustrate the austerity of the atmosphere in which even comfortably circumstanced Puritan children were reared, at the time of Anne Bradstreet's birth and infancy in England. The next character, however, is far from puritanical. The figure of "Youth" suggests a composite, of the author's adolescent memories of the arrogant young men who jeered at the staidness of her family and friends, with her more immediate response to the reports, from Parlia-

5. See p. 45 above.

mentary sources and therefore often exaggerated, of the cruelty
and license of some of the Royalist officers in the Civil War.

"Youth's" account of himself begins auspiciously, with a
description of his handsome appearance and his fine education,
academically and in courtly manners and the arts of war.

> My wit, my bounty, and my courtesie,
> Makes all to place their future hopes on me.[6]

Then the self-portrait deteriorates:

> This is my best, but Youth is known, Alas!
> To be as wild as is the snuffing Ass:
> As vain as froth, or vanity can be,
> That who would see vain man, may look on me.
> My gifts abused, my education lost,
> My wofull Parents longing hopes are crost,
> My wit evaporates in merriment,
> My valour in some beastly quarrell's spent:
> My lust doth hurry me to all that's ill:
> I know no law nor reason but my will.

> *   *   *

> If any care I take, 'tis to be fine,
> For sure my suit, more then my virtues shine
> If time from leud Companions I can spare,
> 'Tis spent in curling, frisling up my hair.
> Some new *Adonis* I do strive to be;
> *Sardanapalus* now survives in me.
> Cards, Dice and Oathes concomitant I love,
> To playes, to masques, to Taverns still I move.
> And in a word, if what I am you'd hear,
> Seek out a *Brittish* bruitish Cavaleer.

6. See Ann Stanford, "Anne Bradstreet's Portrait of Sir Philip Sidney,"
Early American Literature Newsletter, I (Winter 1966–67), pp. 11–13, for
a suggestion that the picture of "Youth" as an ideal young man is based on
the character of Sidney.

The line about "curling, frisling up my hair" was replaced in the second printing by " 'Tis spent to curle and pounce my new-bought hair"; this alteration could hardly have been made until after 1660, for the fashion of powdered wigs for men appears to have come to England with King Charles II on his return from exile in France. The comparison with Sardanapalus, a degenerate Assyrian ruler, seems to indicate that Anne was already hard at work, during the 1640's, on her *magnum opus* "The Four Monarchies."

The long account of "Youth's" crimes and misdemeanors, and the list of hideous diseases to which he may fall victim,[7] sombrely concludes:

> Thus I have said, and what I've been, you see
> Childhood and Youth are vain yea vanity.

A more substantial character next appears, "Middle Age," who tells of his rejection of the wildness of youth and his determination to redeem the time.

> Then with both hands I graspt the world together
> Thus out of one extream into another:
> But yet laid hold on virtue seemingly,
> Who climbs without hold climbs dangerously.

His story is one of hard and serious endeavor, whether as a poor laborer, a powerful nobleman, a "Pastor" or a soldier, sometimes oppressed by failure, and often exposed to the perils of ambition.

> If happiness my sordidness hath found,
> 'Twas in the Crop of my manured ground.

7. See above, pp. 64–65 for a discussion of the line in the first printing of "Youth's" speech that suggests the possibility that Anne Bradstreet had read *Hamlet*.

My thriving Cattle and my new-milch-Cow,
My fleeced Sheep, and fruitful farrowing Sow:
To greater things I never did aspire,
My dunghill thoughts or hopes could reach no higher.
If to be rich or great it was my fate
How was I broyl'd with envy and with hate?
Greater then was the great'st was my desire,
And thirst for honour, set my heart on fire:

*   *   *

My thirst was higher then nobility,
I oft long'd sore to tast on Royalty:
Whence poyson, Pistols, and dread instruments,
Have been curst furtherers of mine intents.
Nor Brothers, Nephewes, Sons, nor Sires I've spar'd,
When to a Monarchy, my way they barr'd.

The four last lines above, which hark back to the long "crying blood" passage, describing the martyrdoms and murders of several claimants to royal power, in "A Dialogue between Old England and New," were deleted from the second printing of the poem. The couplet that replaced them: "Then Kings must be depos'd or put to flight/ I might possess that Throne which was their right," is clearly a more up-to-date, post-Restoration comment on the usurpation that many good Puritans were unable to accept with enthusiasm. "Middle Age" acknowledges his vulnerability to gout, sciatica, and lunacy, among many less familiar maladies, and ends with the recurrent refrain: "Man at his best estate is vanity."

The personification of "Old Age" speaks as a man of accomplishment, with a serious sense of values, and his review of historical events fits the life-span of Anne Bradstreet's father, who was nearly seventy years old when the poem was written.

It's not my valour, honour, nor my gold,
My ruin'd house now falling can uphold.
It's not my learning Rhetorick wit so large,
Hath now the power, death's warfare to discharge.
It's not my goodly state, nor bed of downe
That can refresh, or ease, if Conscience frown.
Nor from Alliance can I now have hope,
But what I have done well, that is my prop;
He that in youth is godly, wise and sage,
Provides a staff then to support his Age.
Mutations great, some joyful and some sad,
In this short pilgrimage I oft have had.

* * *

Such private changes oft mine eyes have seen,
In various times of state I've also been.
I've seen a Kingdome flourish like a tree,
When it was rul'd by that Celestial she;

* * *

I saw all peace at home, terror to foes,
But ah, I saw at last those eyes to close,
And then methought the day at noon grew dark
When it had lost that radiant Sun-like Spark.

The tribute to Queen Elizabeth I introduces an historical passage, of thirty-four lines in the first printing, altered and expanded to fifty lines for the second edition. The first version mentions King James I only as the destroyer of the Puritans' hopes for religious toleration and the intended victim of the Gunpowder Plot, then lists the military disasters in the Bay of Cadiz in 1625, at the Isle of Rhé in 1627, and those on the Continent from 1620 to 1625 which resulted in the defeat and exile of the protestant Elector Palatine, the husband of England's Princess Elizabeth. The revision refers more tactfully to James I,

> . . . under whose rayes
> We joy'd in many blest and prosperous dayes.

And a lament is added for the accomplished and popular Henry, Prince of Wales, who died in 1612 in his nineteenth year.

After this the earlier version points to the downfall of many from high places, among them Buckingham and Strafford:

> I've seen one stab'd, another loose his head:
> And others fly their Country, through their dread.

The final line of the couplet, which might be interpreted as a reference to the Puritan Exodus of 1630–42, appears in the second printing as "And others fly, struck both with gilt and dread." This alteration makes it clear that the author was thinking of the refugees to the Continent, from Roman Catholic and High Church circles, following the decisive defeat of the Royalist army at the Battle of Naseby in 1645.

The original text of the poem then describes in general terms, in a passage of eight lines, the tragic state of the country rent by civil war. In her revision Anne Bradstreet inserted a four-line description, in language of extraordinary violence, of the Irish Rebellion of 1641 "By bloudy Popish, hellish miscreants." The amended passage concerning the war in England is un-doubtedly post-Restoration in sentiment; nevertheless it seems to echo the respect for the anointed monarch that sounds clearly in "A Dialogue between Old England and New," and also to reflect the dislike of Cromwell, as an ambitious extremist, that appears to have been felt by many of the Massachusetts colonists.

The final couplet, an addition, sounds a note of caution relevant to any period of extreme political unrest and transition.

> I've seen a King by force thrust from his throne,
> And an Usurper subt'ly mount thereon.
> I've seen a state unmoulded, rent in twain,
> But ye may live to see't made up again.
> I've seen it plunder'd, taxt and soak'd in bloud,
> But out of evill you may see much good.
> What are my thoughts, this is no time to say,
> Men may more freely speak another day.

Even so forthright a mind as Anne Bradstreet's must have been rather disconcerted when her personal opinions on the Civil War and other recent events in England appeared unexpectedly in print. And after the Restoration she had every reason to appreciate the delicacy of the colonial Puritans' relationship with King Charles II. It is apparent, therefore, that many of her editorial changes were made in the interests of discretion, though of necessity they had to be of a come-lately nature.

After the historical passage "Old Age" conducts his own pilgrimage, and the whole poem, to a close with a long paraphrase of the twelfth chapter of Ecclesiastes, and the final affirmation:

> And I shall see with these same very eyes,
> My strong Redeemer coming in the Skies.
> Triumph I shall o're sin, o're death, o're Hell,
> And in that hope I bid you all farewel.

"The Four Seasons of the Year," which Anne Bradstreet designated as "Of four times four the last *Quaternion*," is also the most conventional, derivative, and, it must be admitted, the lamest and dullest of the entire composition. "Spring," a young woman "With smiling face and garments somewhat green," launches into a description of her allotted months, March, April, and May, and we soon find ourselves perusing a metrical farmers' almanac. The sun, according to the old cosmology which we have already encountered in the verse-letters to Simon Bradstreet, enters Aries on the tenth of March, and thereafter we follow his progress around the earth through the twelve houses of the zodiac, with appropriate temperature-notes for each month of the year. The "correspondences" are carefully identified, as when "Summer" appears,

> With melted tauny face, and garments thin,
> Resembling Fire, Choler, and Middle Age,
> As *Spring* did Air, Blood, Youth in's equipage;

and, in a ludicrously Du Bartasian image:

> Cold, moist, young flegmy winter now doth lye
> In swadling Clouts, like new born Infancy
> Bound up with frosts, and furr'd with hail & snows,
> And like an Infant, still it taller grows.

The reader will by now have become aware that Anne Bradstreet was not by inclination a pastoral or landscape poet; perhaps she herself, however, did not realize this until she undertook to compose an orderly description of the natural world, in its outward and seasonal aspects, in order to complete her sixteenfold poetic project. At any rate she did not use the obvious material, the impressions of her own fifteen wild Decembers and burning summers in New England. Samuel Eliot Morison, Perry Miller, and Harold Jantz, in their commentaries on Anne Bradstreet's work, have noted sadly that her nature-imagery, at least until after the publication of *The Tenth Muse*, derives from a blend of her memories of the English countryside with the stylized vocabulary of the literary-pastoral scene, which, used with charm and freshness by Spenser and Sidney, became elaborately artificial in the pages of Sylvester's Du Bartas.[8] Thus, in "The Four Seasons," nightingales tune their lays, the meads are dight with cowslips, oranges and pomegranates dangle on the trees, and finally, "The Northern winter-blasts begin to hiss." Yet even among the two hundred and fifty-two lines of "The Four Seasons" we may glimpse the tidy, extremely feminine, and observant character of their author, as in this short passage from the description of April:

> The Primrose pale, and azure violet
> Among the virduous grass hath nature set,
> That when the Sun on's Love (the earth) doth shine
> These might as lace set out her garment fine.
> The fearfull bird his little house now builds
> In trees and walls, in Cities and in fields,
> The outside strong, the inside warm and neat;
> A natural Artificer compleat.

As though in rueful anticipation of future criticisms of her poem, Anne Bradstreet addressed a brief apology, signed in the first printing, "Your dutifull Daughter A.B.," to the earliest and most revered of her critics.

> My Subjects bare, my Brain is bad,
> Or better Lines you should have had;
> The first fell in so nat'rally,
> I knew not how to pass it by;
> The last, though bad I could not mend,

8. See Morison, *Builders of the Bay Colony*, Boston, 1930, pp. 329–30; Miller, "Errand into the Wilderness," *William and Mary Quarterly*, 3rd Series, Vol. X, No. 1 (January 1953), p. 12; Jantz, *First Century of New England Verse*, p. 31.

Accept therefore of what is pen'd,
And all the faults that you shall spy
Shall at your feet for pardon cry.

If one looks at this rhetorical "four times four" as a composite whole, which indeed it is, its development in the author's mind may be discerned. The intellectual curiosity which she inherited from her father responded eagerly to the dramatized symbolism of the writers whom she most admired, and, as she tells us in the dedication of "The Four Elements" and "The Four Humours," Thomas Dudley's own fashionable experiment with a quartet of personifications inspired her to undertake an even more ambitious project.

Having selected her curious and in many ways awkward cast of characters, she organized and presented them with an enthusiasm that brings vitality and even occasional charm into the didactic monologues of the eight abstract ladies. The original dedication makes clear that she considered the twofold poem on the elements and humors to be complete in itself; the idea of continuing the system of "correspondences," so as to round out the composition into a tetralogy, obviously came as an afterthought, possibly even as the result of a suggestion made by her father or some other reader of the first two parts.

So Anne set to work on "Of the Four Ages of Man," which "fell in so nat'rally,/ I knew not how to pass it by," and created a set of reasonably life-sized male actors of her own time, in contrast to the statuesque and vaguely classical females of the earlier half of the pageant. The attributes and experiences of the four ages are all taken from the contemporary scene, and it is quite possible, as Harold Jantz has suggested, that the typical reminiscences of "Old Age" are echoes from Thomas Dudley's memories of the political events of his lifetime. If so, the absence of any reference to the colonization of New England seems peculiar, but the probable reason for this is that Anne Bradstreet was following a strict literary formula, and could not permit any one of her allegorical personages to become even remotely identifiable with an individual human being.

Although the experimental exuberance with which she juggled the elements and humors is lacking in the more pedestrian procession of the ages, Anne Bradstreet's native interest in the flow of history and the behavior of mankind brought some zest and color into this third part of her long project. Not so, unfortunately, with the final section on the four seasons; the figures are mere pasteboard cutouts, borrowed from secondhand stock, and the author herself was the first to acknowledge that the poem was "bad." It may be mentioned again, in slight extenuation, that the conventional limits within which she was writing gave no scope for her personal comments on the natural scene around her. That she could look perceptively at the world's seasonal wonders is shown by the brief passage already quoted from the speech of "Spring," by the description of "Childhood" in the introduction to "The Four Ages," and by the three verse-letters to her husband. But it was not until after a good many more years had passed that Anne Bradstreet achieved true spiritual unity, in her finest single poem, with the wonder and mystery of nature.

Two drastic and far-reaching changes occurred in Anne Bradstreet's personal life between 1643 and 1646. The first was her father's remarriage, on the 14th April, 1644, less than four months after her mother's death, to Katherine (*née* Dighton), the widow of Samuel Hackburne of Roxbury.

There were three children of this marriage, Deborah, Joseph, and Paul, and in Joseph, who lived from 1647 to 1720, the characteristic ambition, ability, and arrogance of the Dudleys flourished again. He began to study for the ministry, but soon found that he preferred a political career, and after holding several posts in Massachusetts he was sent to England, in 1682, to negotiate with the government on behalf of the colonists. He made influential friends at court and in Parliamentary circles, and in 1685 was commissioned by King James II as president of the colonies of Maine, New Hampshire, Massachusetts, and Rhode Island. The independent-minded New Englanders greatly resented having one of their own sons placed in the position of royal authority over them, and Dudley's regime was brief and unpopular, even though many of his acts were beneficial to the colonists. In less than a year he was succeeded by Sir Edmund Andros, but became president of the Royal Governor's council and so shared the mounting hatred of what was considered the tyranny of the Stuart king.

When news came of the abdication of James II and the accession of King William and Queen Mary, in the spring of 1689, the Andros government was briskly overturned and its leaders, including Joseph Dudley, were imprisoned for some months in Boston and then deported to England. There once more the clever and worldly Dudley fared well; he was made lieutenant-governor of the Isle of Wight, a post which he held for eight years, and for a part of that time he was also a member of Parliament, the first native-born English American to sit in the House of Commons. In 1702 he returned to New England, commissioned by Queen Anne as governor of Massachusetts, and, under the improved relations between the monarch and her colonial subjects, he fulfilled this office successfully for the rest of his active life.

Joseph Dudley's proud, dark face, surrounded by a vast Restoration wig, stares aggressively from the portrait, privately owned by his descendants, that is believed to have been painted by

Kneller in the 1690's. It is interesting to compare his career with that of his father; whereas the pioneer governor, harsh and authoritarian as he may often have been, never swerved from his selfless dedication to the ideals of Calvinistic spiritual righteousness, civil probity, and the creation and preservation of the New Jerusalem in New England, his intelligent and able son Joseph seems to have been primarily concerned with the acquisition of power, money, and position for his own aggrandizement. In a very real sense he betrayed his native community by making himself a tool of the crumbling Stuart dynasty as it sought to exploit the vigorous colonies in the New World.

A dramatic postscript to Anne Bradstreet's life occurred, seventeen years after her death, at a critical point in Joseph Dudley's career. When the government of Sir Edmund Andros was deposed, and Anne's lordly half-brother was bundled off to prison along with the other hated royal officials, it was the aged Simon Bradstreet, "the Nestor of New England" as Cotton Mather called him, then in his eighty-seventh year, who accepted the post of governor and served, under the old charter granted by Charles I, until a more acceptable royal commissioner arrived in 1692.

To return to somewhat earlier days: Thomas Dudley's preoccupation with his new marriage and with his continuing official duties—he was appointed sergeant major general of the military forces of the colony for 1644, was again governor in 1645, and deputy governor from 1646 to 1650—must inevitably have caused a break in the close relationship that had existed between himself and his daughter Anne. The second change that came into her life at this time was the complete uprooting of the Bradstreet household, in 1645 or 1646, and its removal to a recently established outpost settlement.

Ipswich had been the family's home for almost a decade, but

even while the town was growing into a substantial community, and the comforts and stability of domestic life had increased, plans for further expansion into the wilderness were brewing in the minds of Simon Bradstreet and his colleagues. As early as 1634 the General Court had ordered

> . . . that the land aboute Cochichowicke shalbe reserved for an inland plantacion, and that whosoever will goe to inhabite there shall have three yeares immunity from all taxes, levyes, publique charges & services whatsoever, (military dissipline onely excepted). John Winthrop, Rich: Bellingham, & William Coddington, Esq, are chosen a committee to licence any that they thinke meete to inhabite there, & that it shalbe lawfull for no person to go thither without their consent, or the maior parte of them.[9]

About fifteen miles west of Ipswich, between the Merrimack River, its tributary the Shawsheen, and the small Lake Cochichewick (as its Indian name appears in present-day spelling), was an area of undulating, wooded, and well-watered land, parts of which had been roughly cleared by the Indians for their annual plantings of field-corn, or maize. The colony's explorers had apparently reported that it was an excellent site for a new settlement, and consequently the General Court had officially designated it as such. On the 6th September, 1638, the same body voted that

> Mr. Bradstreete, Mr. Dudley, Iunior, Captain Dennison, Mr. Clarke, of Newberry, Mr. Woodbridge, and seven others, are alowed (upon their petition) to begin a plantation at Merrimack, & shall have liberty to associate to them such others as they can agree upon.[10]

9. *Massachusetts Colony Records*, Vol. I, p. 141.
10. *Ibid.*, Vol. I, p. 237.

So there must have been much discussion, in Ipswich and the nearby coastal towns, of the founding of this inland settlement. In December 1638 Anne Bradstreet's friend Nathaniel Ward, then in his sixty-second year, wrote to John Winthrop concerning his interest in the "plantation at Quichichacke," where he wished to settle with his son, a minister lately arrived from England, and his son-in-law, the physician Giles Firmin.[11] But a little later he decided that his health would not stand the rigors of frontier life, and he remained in Ipswich until his return to England in 1647.

John Woodbridge, who married Anne Bradstreet's sister Mercy in 1639, was also corresponding with John Winthrop about "Quichichuick." [12] This young man, from a substantial Wiltshire family, had left his training for the ministry at Oxford when Chancellor Laud's harsh measures against nonconformity made it impossible for him to remain there. He emigrated to Massachusetts in 1634 and settled at Newbury where his uncle was the pastor, and where he lived for several years as a farmer and held offices in the town government. But he was ambitious, not only to share in the founding of a new community but also to be its minister, so with the help of his father-in-law Thomas Dudley, who wrote him in 1642, "I think you were best redeem what time you may without hurt of your estate in perfecting your former studies," [13] he became a schoolmaster in Boston. There he was also able to finish his preparation for the Church, and in 1645 he was ordained and chosen as the first minister of Andover (by which good old English name the unwieldy title of Cochichewick had been replaced).

During these years the new plantation near the Merrimack

11. *Winthrop Papers*, Vol. IV, pp. 162–64.
12. *Ibid.* Vol. IV, p. 327.
13. John Winthrop, *History of New England*, ed. Savage, Vol. II, pp. 309–10 (note).

River had been developing, from a handful of forest shelters, into an orderly village with some substantial houses and a small unadorned meetinghouse for church services and public gatherings. Firewood was stacked to season for the winter, and all around the village the fields had been cleared of stumps and boulders, and fenced in the hope of discouraging the Indians and wild animals. Beyond the settlement, for empty, trail-less miles on every hand, stretched the virgin woodland, its density broken only by the clustered wigwams of an occasional Indian plantation or camp. The original manuscript *Book of Land Records and Town Meetings*, preserved in the archives of Andover, gives a sharp indication of how persistent, as well as formidable, the wilderness of this countryside was. At a meeting in January 1695, fifty years after the town's settlement, it was voted "that whosoever shall catch any wolf and carry ye head to the constable as ye law directs shall have of ye towne twenty shillings in pay & this act to continue 2 years from ye date hereof." So princely a bounty proves the seriousness of the wolf-menace, even after Andover had been in existence for half a century.

There is a tradition, cited in 1829 in Abiel Abbott's *History of Andover*, that in 1644 Simon Bradstreet built the first sawmill on the Cochichewick Brook, where later a thriving industrial area developed. Undoubtedly he also saw to the building of a reasonably sturdy and comfortable house for his large family, before the actual move from Ipswich took place. The town records begin with "The names of all the free House houlders in order as they came to Towne"; the list is headed by "Mr. Simon Bradstreet," then come twenty-two others, none of whom, incidentally, has the title of "Mr." It appears that Bradstreet was the most prominent civil founder of the settlement, as John Woodbridge was its ecclesiastical leader; this is borne out by

Edward Johnson's account, published in 1654 in his *Wonder-working Providence of Sions Saviour in New-England:*

> . . . there was a Town founded about one or two mile distant
> from the place where the goodly river of Merrimeck receives her
> branches into her own body, hard upon the river of Shawshin
> . . . the honored Mr. Simon Broadstreet taking up his last
> setling there, hath been a great means to further the work, it
> being well fitted for the husbandmans hand, were it not that the
> remoteness of the place from Towns of trade, bringeth some
> inconveniencies upon the planters, who are inforced to carry
> their corn far to market; this Town is called Andover, and hath
> good store of land improved for the bigness of it, they soon
> gathered into a Church, having the reverend Mr. Woodbridg
> to instruct them in the wayes of Christ.

There follows one of the metrical passages with which Johnson's work is generously larded, and which typifies the homiletic verse that echoed from New England pulpits, and adorned the pages of Puritan writings, while Anne Bradstreet was practicing her own craft of letters.

> Thou Sister young, Christ is to thee a wall
> Of flaming fire, to hurt thee none may come
> In slipp'ry paths, and dark wayes shall they fall,
> His Angels might shall chase their countless sum.
> Thy *Shepheard* with full cups and table spread,
> Before thy foes in Wilderness thee feeds,
> Increasing thy young lambs in bosom bred,
> Of Churches by his wonder-working deeds:
> To countless number must Christ's Churches reach,
> The day's at hand, both Jew and Gentile shall
> Come crowding in his Churches, Christ to preach,
> And last for aye, none can cause them to fall.

The completing ceremony in the creation of Andover took place at a General Court in Boston, on 6th May, 1646, when

> Cutshamakin, sagamore of ye massatusetts, came into ye Courte, & acknowledged that for ye somme of sixe pounds, & a coate, which he had already received, he had sold to Mr. John Woodbridge, in ye behalfe of ye inhabitants of Chochichawicke, now called Andevor, all his right, interest, & priviledg in ye land sixe miles southward from ye toune, two miles eastward to Rowley bounds, be the same more or lesse, northward to Merrimacke River; provided, y^t ye Indian, called Roger, & his company, may have liberty to take alewifes in Chochichawicke River for their oune eating; but if they either spoyle or steale any corne, or other fruits of ye inhabitants there, to any considerarble valew, this liberty of taking fish shall for ever cease; & ye said Roger is still to enjoy 4 acres of ground where now he plants.[14]

Simon Bradstreet's house-lot, as noted in the town records, consisted of twenty acres. This land has been recently identified as lying across the road from a fine three-story, central-chimneyed, "salt-box" house that was long believed to have been built by Simon Bradstreet in 1667, and to have been Anne's home until her death in 1672. But it has been clearly established that the house could not have been constructed before 1715, and that it was built for and lived in by the Reverend Thomas Barnard, pastor of the North Parish Church in Andover.[15]

Although no roof-tree survives that gave shelter to the Bradstreet family during Anne's lifetime, we know on which plot of ground in the original settlement, now called North Andover, the successive houses of the Bradstreets stood. And documentary

14. *Massachusetts Colony Records*, Vol. III, pp. 73–74.
15. Abbott Lowell Cummings, "The Parson Barnard House, formerly known as the Bradstreet House," *Old-Time New England* (Society for Preservation of New England Antiquities), Vol. XLVII, No. 2, Fall 1956, pp. 29–40.

evidence shows that their move to Andover took place sometime between the spring of 1645 and the autumn of 1646: on 14th May, 1645, the General Court commissioned Simon Bradstreet, his brother-in-law Captain Daniel Dennison, and others, to form a "Military Company" for the towns of Ipswich and Newbury and their smaller neighbors,[16] and on 23rd November, 1646, "Symon Bradstreete of Andover, gent." sold to one Edward Jackson a farm of five hundred acres in Cambridge, which he had lately purchased from Thomas Mayhew.[17] This land-transaction was one of many in which Bradstreet was engaged at this time, and is the first to be found on record in which he is identified as being "of Andover." [18]

The Bradstreet household that was established in the new settlement consisted of Simon and Anne, their three daughters, Dorothy, Sarah, and Hannah, aged about eleven to four years old, and Simon, Junior, who was five or six. The eldest son, Samuel, who was twelve or thirteen in 1646, was being prepared to enter Harvard College within three years, probably at the Latin School in Boston. Simon, the younger son, recorded in his diary that he was sent to Ipswich for his grammar-school education:

> 1640. I was borne in N. England, at Ipswitch Septem. 28, being Munday 1640.
> 1651. I had my Education in the same Town at the free School, the master of w'ch was my ever respected friend Mr. Ezekiell Cheevers. My Father was removed from Ipsw. to Andover, before I was putt to school, so y^t my schooling was more chargeable.[19]

16. *Massachusetts Colony Records*, Vol. II, p. 111.
17. *Suffolk County, Massachusetts, Deeds*, Vol. I (79).
18. I am indebted for this information to Mr. Forbes Rockwell of North Andover, who kindly brought these two references to my attention.
19. *New England Historical and Genealogical Register*, Boston, Vol. IX, 1855, p. 118. This manuscript record of family and domestic data, written

As soon as Anne Bradstreet had accomplished the task of unpacking the family's belongings, arranging their furniture, and organizing her domestic helpers into their new routine, she must, with considerable relief, have opened her boxes of papers and resumed the literary work that was so meaningful a part of her life. By this time she was probably deeply engaged on "The Four Monarchies," her longest and most ambitious composition, a metrical review of about fifteen centuries of ancient history, conceived with the intent to show how dark and turbulent were the first ages of man's existence, before the coming of Christ brought light and hope to the world.

It seems likely that Anne began to work on this ponderous project soon after she came to think of herself as a serious poet. Her muse was essentially scholastic rather than lyrical, so it appears that, in the manner of Spenser and Du Bartas before her, and of Milton directly after her, she sought for, and eventually selected, a monumental theme for the epic poem that she had resolved to write. Perhaps her admiration for Sir Walter Raleigh's *History of the World* led to her choice of subject, with this passage from his splendid preface as the keynote of her inspiration:

> For who hath not observed, what labour, practice, peril, bloodshed, and cruelty, the Kings and Princes of the World have undergone, exercised, taken on them, and committed; to make themselves and their Issues Masters of the World? And yet hath Babylon, Persia, Egypt, Syria, Macedon, Carthage, Rome, and the rest, no fruit, no flower, grass, nor leaf, springing upon the face of the earth, of those seeds: No, their very roots and ruines do hardly remain.

by the Reverend Simon Bradstreet of New London, Connecticut, was in the possession of his descendants until late in the nineteenth century, but its present location is unknown.

The perished glory of pagan antiquity was a beguiling theme to the seventeenth-century mind, as was also the greater concept of God's everlasting timelessness enfolding the little span of earthly time. Never were these two thoughts so wonderfully mingled as in John Donne's sermon on the text "In my Father's house are many mansions," preached to the king in April 1626.

> . . . A state but of one Day, because no Night shall overtake, or determine it, . . . yesterday doth not usher it in, nor to morrow shall not drive it out. *Methusalem*, with all his hundreds of yeares, was but a Mushrome of a nights growth, to this day. And all the foure Monarchies, with all their thousands of yeares, And all the powerfull Kings, and all the beautifull Queenes of this world, were but as a bed of flowers, some gathered at six, some at seaven, some at eight, All in one Morning, in respect of this Day.[20]

But to write a successful epic on the four monarchies was, as she realized before her work drew to its halting close, beyond Anne Bradstreet's power. All the hours of patient, dogged labor, stretched over perhaps as much as ten years, produced only a rhymed paraphrase, in more than five thousand lines of heroic couplets, of the chronicles of ancient history as she had read them in the works of Raleigh and his contemporaries, translations of the authors of antiquity, and the Old Testament.

The chronology of the long poem progresses from the Assyrian monarchy, "Beginning under *Nimrod*, 131 Years after the Flood," through the Persian kings and their wars with Greece and Egypt, and the reign of Alexander the Great and the struggles of his successors, to the Roman conquest of Greece. The Roman monarchy, "beginning *Anno Mundi*, 3213," comes to an abrupt and early end with "Tarquinius Superbus, the

20. *Sermons of John Donne*, ed. Simpson and Potter, University of California Press, Vol. III, 1954, p. 138.

last King of the Romans," in 510 B.C. So far as it is possible to reconstruct the time-sequence of the composition of "The Four Monarchies," it was probably begun in the late 1630's, in Ipswich, and continued there through the Assyrian, Persian, and just over half of the Grecian histories. A couplet ending a long passage on the death of Alexander,

> What troubles and contentions did ensue
> We may hereafter shew in season due,

suggests that an interruption, caused by the move to Andover, occurred at this point. Then as soon as Anne was able to resume her literary work, in the family's new home, she completed the Grecian monarchy, with a bewilderingly tangled account of the conflicts between Alexander's successors and the eventual subjection of the Greek world to the power of Rome. Here she added an epilogue of forty-four lines presenting, with imagery largely borrowed from the Prophet Daniel, an allegorical synopsis of the whole monumental project, followed by a confession of her own weariness after the long trek through the wilderness of ancient times.

> The *Assyrian* Monarchy long time did stand,
> But yet the *Persian* got the upper hand;
> The *Grecian* them did utterly subdue,
> And millions were subjected unto few:
> The *Grecian* longer then the *Persian* stood,
> Then came the *Roman* like a raging flood;
>
> *   *   *
>
> The first a Lion, second was a Bear,
> The third a Leopard, which four wings did rear;
> The last more strong and dreadful then the rest,
> Whose Iron teeth devoured every Beast,

*   *   *

Yet shall this Lion, Bear, this Leopard, Ram,
All trembling stand before the powerful Lamb.
With these three Monarchyes now have I done,
But how the fourth, their Kingdomes from them won,
And how from small beginnings it did grow,
To fill the world with terrour and with woe;
My tyred brain leavs to some better pen,
This task befits not women like to men:
For what is past, I blush, excuse to make
But humbly stand, some grave reproof to take;
Pardon to crave for errours, is but vain,
The Subject was too high, beyond my strain,
To frame Apology for some offence,
Converts our boldness into impudence;
This my presumption, some now to requite,
Ne sutor ultra crepidam may write.

With this old precept that the shoemaker should stick to his last (which also appears on the 1647 title-page of Nathaniel Ward's *The Simple Cobler of Aggawam*), Anne Bradstreet announced her decision to abandon, three-quarters of the way through, her effort to chronicle in verse the four great episodes of the antique world. But perseverance, inherited and cultivated, was a strong trait in her character; so next we find a very feminine postscript directly following the seemingly valedictory lines above.

After some dayes of rest, my restless heart
To finish what's begun, new thoughts impart,
And maugre all resolves, my fancy wrought
This fourth to th' other three, now might be brought:
Shortness of time and inability,
Will force me to a confus'd brevity.
Yet in this Chaos, one shall easily spy

> The vast Limbs of a mighty Monarchy,
> What e're is found amiss take in good part,
> As faults proceeding from my head, not heart.

Therefore she embarked, probably during the winter of 1646–47, on the last of her monarchies. She had obviously grown weary of the project itself, but the misgivings and discouragement she felt at this time were due not so much to that as to the many pressures and strains of an extremely difficult period in her life.

Anne was undoubtedly already pregnant with her sixth child, Mercy, when she had to supervise the wearisome task of dismantling the house in Ipswich and moving all of its contents, along with four young children, over the wilderness trail to Andover. The heavy demands on her strength may have brought on one of the attacks of "my old Distemper of weaknes and fainting," as she called it, from which she suffered increasingly as she grew older. And perhaps it was at this point in her experience, when she was beset by both physical and mental dejection, that she wrote the farewell lyric to her husband, "Before the Birth of one of her Children," quoted at the beginning of this chapter.

Simon Bradstreet's role as one of the founders, and subsequently the leading settler, of Andover did not prevent him from carrying on widespread activities elsewhere. He was required to be present at the meetings of the General Court in Boston, sometimes had to travel as far afield as to Connecticut, or other distant points in New England, as Commissioner for the United Colonies, and was continually engaged, on his own behalf, in complicated land-transactions throughout the settled areas of Massachusetts.

So his wife must often have been left alone, in charge of the children and of a group of servants who were perhaps unruly and not always trustworthy, in an unfamiliar house in a rough frontier village. With nightfall there would have come the ever-present threat of wolves and Indians, lurking in the dark woods around the little settlement, and gloomy thoughts, maybe, crowding into the mind of lonely Mistress Bradstreet: nostalgia for the graciousness and comfort of life in old England, anxiety for her husband's safety, fears that her own days might soon end in illness and exhaustion, memories of companionship with her parents mixed with some bitter feelings about the new house-hold in Roxbury, and heartsick concern for her sister Sarah, whose unbalanced behavior was leading directly towards the tragedy of public disgrace.

The modern poet John Berryman, in *Homage to Mistress Bradstreet*, has distilled the essence of Anne's ordeal of pioneer-ing into these lines:

> Outside the New World winters in grand dark
> white air lashing high thro' the virgin stands
> foxes down foxholes sigh,
> surely the English heart quails, stunned.

> *   *   *

> Winter than summer worse, that first, like a file
> on a quick, or the poison suck of a thrilled tooth;
> and still we may unpack.
> Wolves & storms among, uncouth
> board-pieces, boxes, barrels vanish, grow
> houses, rise. Motes that hop in sunlight slow
> indoors, and I am Ruth
> away: . . .[21]

This was certainly a time of severe physical and spiritual trial for Anne Bradstreet, and it is small wonder that she had neither

21. Berryman, *Homage to Mistress Bradstreet*, New York, 1956, stanzas 2 and 9. Copyright © 1956 by John Berryman. Reprinted by permission of Farrar, Straus & Giroux, Inc., and Faber and Faber Ltd., London.

the strength nor the enthusiasm, after doggedly completing her Grecian monarchy, to pursue the history of Rome beyond the fall of Tarquinius Superbus, five centuries before the birth of Christ. But when the whole work appeared in print, in 1650, and Anne could see what short shrift she had given to the majestic story of the Roman world, she was apparently chagrined at her failure "To finish what's begun." Perhaps she reread the final section of Raleigh's *History*, and found his epilogue to the Roman monarchy, which he had chronicled through the Punic wars and the fall of Carthage to about 130 B.C.

> By this which we have alreadie set downe, is seene the beginning and end of the three first Monarchies of the world; whereof the Founders and Erectours thought, that they could never have ended. That of *Rome* which made the fourth, was also at this time almost at the highest. We have left it flourishing in the middle of the field; . . . But after some continuance, it shall begin to lose the beauty it had; the stormes of ambition shal beat her great boughes and branches one against another; her leaves shall fall off, her limbes wither, and a rabble of barbarous Nations enter the field, and cut her downe.[22]

At any rate, Anne did make another attempt to complete her major project, and in a twenty-line "Apology," printed in the second edition of her poems at the end of "The Four Monarchies," she tells what happened to her effort, after she

> At length resolv'd, when many years had past,
> To prosecute my story to the last;
> And for the same, I hours not few did spend,
> And weary lines (though lanke) I many pen'd:
> But 'fore I could accomplish my desire,

22. Sir Walter Raleigh, *History of the World*, 1614, Book 5, Chapter 6, p. 775.

My papers fell a prey to th' raging fire.
And thus my pains (with better things) I lost,
Which none had cause to wail, nor I to boast.
No more I'le do sith I have suffer'd wrack,
Although my Monarchies their legs do lack:
Nor matter is't——[23] this last, the world now sees,
Hath many Ages been upon his knees

In the final line we have a pleasant example of Anne Brad-street's individual turn of humor, that deftly twists a punning dig at popery out of her own misfortune. The fire that destroyed her home and its contents in 1666 did not consume all of her papers, as a number of her personal poems, dated or datable before that year, and the little manuscript books containing her prose meditations and spiritual memoirs, survived to be printed in 1678 or later. But she gave up her last monarchy when its many "weary lines" were burned, and took what satiric Calvinist comfort she could in leaving Rome, the idolatrous, metaphorically "upon his knees."

One example is enough to show how devotedly Anne followed Sir Walter Raleigh as her guide through the world of antiquity. In her "Assyrian Monarchy" the great Queen Semiramis leads a vast army against the eastern King Staurobates, only to suffer devastating defeat:

But this is wonderful, of all those men,
They say, but twenty e're came back agen.
The River *Indus* swept them half away,
The rest *Staurobates* in fight did slay;
This was last progress of this mighty Queen,
Who in her Country never more was seen.
The Poets feign'd her turn'd into a Dove,
Leaving the world to *Venus* soar'd above:

23. Dash supplied.

> Which made the *Assyrians* many a day,
> A Dove within their Ensigns to display.

From Raleigh's account she took the substance, but left the poetry of his measured prose behind.

> But of what multitude soever the Armie of *Semiramis* consisted: the same being broken and overthrown by *Staurobates* upon the banks of *Indus, canticum cantavit extremum: she sang her last song;* and (as Antiquity hath fained) was changed by the Gods into a Dove, (the bird of *Venus*) whence it came that the *Babylonians* gave a Dove in their ensignes.[24]

While the author of *The Tenth Muse* was carefully revising her printed text in anticipation of another edition, she made many minor changes, of a word or phrase, throughout "The Four Monarchies," and at several points we find whole passages, of as many as twelve lines, altered or suppressed. These latter emendations seem to have been largely inspired by her rereading, after 1650, of Plutarch's *Lives* in its fine rendering into English by Sir Thomas North, first printed in 1579, and her familiarity with Archbishop Ussher's *Annals of the World*, in its translation, of 1658, from the original Latin.

What Anne Bradstreet set out to accomplish in "The Four Monarchies" is quite apparent: she wished to produce a metrical argument, modeled on her father's poem on the four parts of the world, that would demonstrate the vanity and degradation of the long dark ages of antiquity, compared with the enlightenment, even in strife and adversity, of the Christian era. The end result of her perseverance is no more than a barren exercise in rhetorical ingenuity, unreadable by present-day standards, whatever her contemporaries may have thought of its grandiose scheme and moral usefulness. It is sad, if commendable, that the

24. *History of the World*, Book I, Chapter 12, p. 216.

author herself realized at last how unsuited to her ability was this arduous excursion through ancient history, and we must give her credit for the succinct admission which sums up the character, and the composition, of the whole poem; "And weary lines (though lanke) I many pen'd."

There is a question about this tedious work which remains to be answered. Why did this gentle woman select, in the first place, so grim and unfeminine a subject, and then persistently keep faith with it throughout almost the whole of her literary lifetime? We have already noted that a strain of violence is occasionally revealed in Anne Bradstreet's poetry; I believe that it was to a certain extent this trait in her character that drew her to a close study, with the help of Raleigh and other historians, of the ferocious early dynasties. There is not a sin of the flesh or the spirit that is not described, often with revolting detail, in her account of the ambitions, conquests, cruelties, and licentious self-indulgences of the monarchs of antiquity. And her narrations of murder or death in action, such as this episode from the Battle of Marathon, are invested with a savage glee that is quite alarming.

> The *Persians* to their galleys post with speed
> Where an *Athenian* shew'd a valiant deed,
> Pursues his flying foes then on the sand,
> He stays a lanching gally with his hand,
> Which soon cut off, inrag'd, he with his left,
> Renews his hold, and when of that bereft,
> His whetted teeth he claps in the firm wood,
> Off flyes his head, down showres his frolick bloud,
> Go *Persians*, carry home that angry piece,
> As the best Trophe which ye won in *Greece.*

It seems likely that "The Four Monarchies" provided Anne Bradstreet with a legitimate outlet for what, if indeed she was consciously aware of its presence, she would have called the choleric humor of her constitution. This, in modern perspective, we may recognize as the tension resulting from the confinement of her adventurous spirit within a narrow code of life, a quality that Kenneth Murdock notices even in her later poetry and describes as "the strain set up between the essential instinctive emotion and the bonds drawn tight against full expression by elements in the Puritan's way of thought." [25]

While it is to be regretted that Anne poured so much cerebral energy into the bottomless pit of "The Four Monarchies," it remains that a great deal of technical discipline was required for the accomplishment of this ambitious task. So, as the exercise may well have been psychologically useful, in helping its author to gain increased tranquility of spirit through the release of inner tension, the actual writing of so many lines of verse surely contributed to her ability to handle the tools of her literary trade.

One of the liveliest and most pleasing of her shorter poems, and more than any other her personal manifesto as a poet, was a by-product of "The Four Monarchies." Entitled "The Prologue" and signed "A.B.," in its first printing, it undoubtedly accompanied the manuscript of her long verse-history when that was finally put into the hands of her father and her circle of close friends.

THE PROLOGUE

> To sing of Wars, of Captains, and of Kings,
> Of Cities founded, Common-wealths begun,
> For my mean pen are too superior things:
> Or how they all, or each their dates have run
> Let Poets and Historians set these forth,
> My obscure Lines shall not so dim their worth.

25. Murdock, *Literature and Theology in Colonial New England*, Cambridge (Mass.), 1949, p. 151.

But when my wondring eyes and envious heart
Great *Bartas* sugar'd lines, do but read o're
Fool I do grudg the Muses did not part
'Twixt him and me that overfluent store;
A *Bartas* can, do what a *Bartas* will
But simple I according to my skill.

From school-boyes tongue no rhet'rick we expect
Nor yet a sweet Consort from broken strings,
Nor perfect beauty, where's a main defect:
My foolish, broken, blemish'd Muse so sings
And this to mend, alas, no Art is able,
'Cause nature, made it so irreparable.

Nor can I, like that fluent sweet tongu'd Greek,
Who lisp'd at first, in future times speak plain
By Art he gladly found what he did seek
A full requital of his, striving pain
Art can do much, but this maxime's most sure
A weak or wounded brain admits no cure.

I am obnoxious to each carping tongue
Who says my hand a needle better fits,
A Poets pen all scorn I should thus wrong,
For such despite they cast on Female wits:
If what I do prove well, it won't advance,
They'l say it's stoln, or else it was by chance.

But sure the Antique Greeks were far more mild
Else of our Sexe, why feigned they those Nine
And poesy made, *Calliope's* own Child;
So 'mongst the rest they placed the Arts Divine,
But this weak knot, they will full soon untie,
The Greeks did nought, but play the fools & lye.

Let Greeks be Greeks, and women what they are
Men have precedency and still excell,
It is but vain unjustly to wage warre;
Men can do best, and women know it well
Preheminence in all and each is yours;
Yet grant some small acknowledgment of ours.

And oh ye high flown quills that soar the Skies,
And ever with your prey still catch your praise,
If e're you daigne these lowly lines your eyes
Give Thyme or Parsley wreath, I ask no bayes,
This mean and unrefined ore [26] of mine
Will make your glistering gold, but more to shine.

This, in spite of its outward gaiety of expression, and the welcome change from the prevailing heroic couplets to the lighter six-line stanza with its pleasant rhyme-scheme, is a very serious poem. The author's merciless self-denigration, in the first four stanzas, reveals how passionately she longed for poetic excellence, still symbolized, in her loyal mind (though fortunately not in her actual writing), by the "sugar'd lines" of Du Bartas. The stern discipline of her Puritan faith forced her, spent and discouraged after the ordeal of "The Four Monarchies," to look her "foolish, broken, blemish'd Muse" in the face and acknowledge, with the psychiatric fatalism of her day, that "A weak or wounded brain admits no cure."

Then the tone of the poem changes; the author rallies and turns to attack those, and they must have been many and busy in that tightly-banded community, whose tongues wagged viciously against the governor's daughter, the rich assistant's wife, who had the effrontery to write long poems on presumptuously lofty subjects and hand them round to be read and discussed in public. She answers them back in a way that no weak or wounded brain would have the courage to do, with classic scorn as her weapon and the Sacred Nine as her allies.

But soon her feminine intuition recognizes that only with the subtle arms of tact and persuasiveness can she win any respect from the superior world of men. The final stanza is a triumph

26. As in the third edition of A. B.'s poems, 1758; corrected from "stuffe," 1650, and "ure," 1678.

of deliberate and whimsical archness. She exalts her literary preceptors only to entangle them in a diverting multiple pun, that cannot have failed to please even the most critical of her readers. She asks with sly humility, in a line of great charm, for seemingly homely herbs as a reward instead of the symbolic crown of Laurel, or Bay; yet she knew from her study of ancient times, as many of her audience would also have known, that the Greeks honored Thyme as an emblem of vitality and courage, and made, from what Anacreon called the "fadeless foliage" of Parsley, wreaths for the victors at the Isthmian games and garlands in homage to the virtuous dead.[27] And finally she offers, to the whole company of poets, the precious but unpurified metal of her own verse as a foil to the shining perfection of their works.

Thus Anne Bradstreet, after some fourteen years of serious literary endeavor, stated her diffident yet positive *anch'io son poeta* to the small world around her, giving notice that she expected a just appraisal and acceptance of the work she had done. At least one man among the readers of "The Prologue," her brother-in-law John Woodbridge, gave to her modest demand his complete agreement, and the answer to it that he brought about, when her poems were printed for the whole English-speaking world to see, was recognition and reward beyond anything she could have anticipated.

Two more fairly short formal poems, both of scriptural derivation and both undated, are known to belong to this period of Anne Bradstreet's writing, as they were included in the contents of *The Tenth Muse*. "David's Lamentation for Saul and Jonathan" we shall examine, for reasons that will there be seen, at the end of this chapter. The final poem in the book, "Of the

27. Eleanour Sinclair Rohde, A *Garden of Herbs*, 1926, pp. 112–13, 170; Mrs. M. Grieve, A *Modern Herbal*, 1931, Vol. II, pp. 611, 809.

vanity of all worldly creatures," is also the first direct expression of personal religious faith that Anne made available to the readers around her. While its language is of biblical derivation, its argument, in the fifty-six lines of rhymed couplets, has an immediacy of conviction which gives the impression that it was written all at once, in contrast to her longer and more studied pieces, and in answer to an inner need for re-examination of spiritual values.

There were continuing reasons why Anne's mood of melancholy and world-weariness should have persisted during the early years of her life in Andover. The honor of the Dudley family was seriously blemished by Sarah's divorce, in the summer of 1647, followed by her excommunication from the church in Boston, in October of that year.[28] Anne was probably again pregnant at this time, as her seventh child, Dudley, was born in 1648; her sister's degradation must have been a shocking blow to her loyal heart and upright character, and she can hardly have felt unmixed pleasure at the birth of her half-brother, Joseph Dudley, in September of 1647.

So she turned to the book that was her unfailing support whenever she was beset by distress or sorrow, and, beginning with the *contemptus mundi* of Ecclesiastes, she acknowledged the emptiness of all earthly hope and glory, then reaffirmed her own belief in the great promise of Revelation.

> As he said vanity, so vain say I,
> Oh! vanity, O vain all under Sky;
> Where is the man can say, lo I have found
> On brittle Earth a Consolation sound?
> What is't in honour to be set on high?
> No, they like Beasts and Sons of men shall dye:

28. See pp. 174–76 above.

And whil'st they live, how oft doth turn their fate,
He's now a captive, that was King of late.

* * *

Where is it then, in wisdom, learning arts?
Sure if on earth, it must be in those parts:
Yet these the wisest man of men did find
But vanity, vexation of mind.

* * *

If not in honour, beauty, age nor treasure,
Nor yet in learning, wisdome, youth nor pleasure,
Where shall I climb, sound, seek search or find
That *Summum Bonum* which may stay my mind?
There is a path, no vultures eye hath seen,
Where Lion fierce, nor lions whelps have been,
Which leads unto that living Crystal Fount,
Who drinks thereof, the world doth nought account.

* * *

It brings to honour, which shall ne're decay,
It stores with wealth which time can't wear away.
It yieldeth pleasures far beyond conceit,
And truly beautifies without deceit,
Nor strength, nor wisdome nor fresh youth shall fade
Nor death shall see, but are immortal made.
This pearl of price, this tree of life, this spring
Who is possessed of, shall reign a King.
Nor change of state, nor cares shall ever see
But wear his crown unto eternity:
This satiates the Soul, this stayes the mind,
And all the rest, but Vanity we find.

This is more than a mere paraphrase of the biblical verses; the depth of feeling which animates the poem is Anne Bradstreet's own, and may well have contributed to a vitality of composition which is more marked than in any other poem in *The Tenth Muse*. The iambic rhythm is strengthened by the pronounced caesural pause in many of the lines, interspersed with lines of unbroken flow, and the repeated device of grouping a number of significant nouns, verbs, or phrases, divided by commas or conjunctions, in a single line such as:

Where shall I climb, sound, seek search or find,

produces an onomatopoeic suggestion of actual physical energy expended in the quest for the wisdom and peace that do not perish with the vanities of earthly life.

As the decade of the 1640's was moving towards its close, John Winthrop died at his house in Boston, on the 26th of March, 1649. At the age of sixty-one he was still the prime leader and mentor of the Massachusetts Bay colony, having served as governor for twelve out of the nineteen years of its existence, and it must have seemed to his contemporaries and their families, especially among them the Dudleys and Bradstreets, as though the first chapter of the history of New England had ended with his passing.

During these same years the Civil War in England was dragging out its bitter and costly course. Oliver Cromwell's rise to power as the efficient co-ordinator of the Parliamentary forces and joint commander, with Lord Fairfax, of the New Model Army, had resulted in the decisive Battle of Naseby in 1645, the surrender of Oxford, and King Charles's flight to Scotland in 1646. In the summer of 1647 the king was captured in the north and taken to Hampton Court, from whence he escaped to the Isle of Wight, took refuge in Carisbrooke Castle, and sent word to the Houses of Parliament that he would discuss the terms for peace with their emissaries.

Meanwhile although Massachusetts, as G. M. Trevelyan says, "had since the beginnings of the troubles in England acted as if it were an independent state," [29] some of its most able citizens had crossed the Atlantic in order to accept military, naval, or political posts in the service of Parliament. Among these were two of Anne Bradstreet's closest friends, the ministers Nathaniel Ward and John Woodbridge, and their departure, in the already troubled year of 1647, must have added to her anxieties and brought her increased awareness of the sad state of things in the mother-country. A line from her poem on the vanity of all earthly creatures,

> He's now a slave, that was a Prince of late.

was originally printed as the less specific,

> He's now a slave, that was a Prince of late.

The revision suggests she knew of her own monarch's defeat and capture, and used them to illustrate the hollowness of man's highest worldly hopes.

Nathaniel Ward arrived in London at about the time that his book, *The Simple Cobler of Aggawam,* was published, and found himself immediately famous because of it. But his vigorous defense of his beloved king, when he was called to preach before the House of Commons, brought only a hostile and disapproving response from that assembly. So Ward, who was seventy in 1648, retired to a quiet country parish in Essex, as far away as possible from a world that he felt was changing for the worse, and there died in 1652.

John Woodbridge, on the other hand, had a significant duty

29. *History of England,* 1927, p. 421.

to perform; he was made chaplain to the Commissioners of Parliament who were sent, in December of 1647, to the Isle of Wight to negotiate with the king. Their mission failed completely, because Charles was already scheming with envoys from Scotland who promised the support of their army in restoring him to the throne. Woodbridge's wife, who was Anne Bradstreet's sister Mercy, and their children joined him in England in 1648; from then on he preached at Andover and in Wiltshire until in 1663, after the Restoration, he took his whole family back to New England, where he lived to be eighty-three and died in 1696. Even in his old age he must have remembered clearly the meetings at Carisbrooke Castle, between the stern men who carried the uncompromising demands of Parliament, and the king who was almost a beggar but who never lost his personal dignity nor his belief in the supreme authority of the Crown of England.

It has been generally assumed that John Woodbridge took with him to England, in 1647, manuscript copies of all the poems that appeared in print, three years later, in *The Tenth Muse*. But I should like to suggest that one of these, "David's Lamentation for Saul and Jonathan," was not written until 1649 and then sent across the sea to Woodbridge, or more probably to Nathaniel Ward, as an elegy in scriptural disguise for the king who was beheaded on the 30th of January, 1649.

The poem of lamentation is a close paraphrase, in forty lines of rhymed couplets, of the Geneva Bible's version of II Samuel, Chapter I, verses 19–27.

> Alas slain is the Head of Israel,
> Illustrious *Saul* whose beauty did excell,
> Upon thy places mountainous and high,
> How did the Mighty fall, and falling dye?
> In *Gath* let not this thing be spoken on,

Nor published in streets of *Askalon*,
Lest daughters of the Philistines rejoyce,
Lest the uncircumcis'd lift up their voice.
O *Gilbo* Mounts, let never pearled dew,
Nor fruitfull showres your barren tops bestrew,
Nor fields of offrings ever on you grow,
Nor any pleasant thing e're may you show;
For there the Mighty Ones did soon decay,
The shield of *Saul* was vilely cast away,
There had his dignity so sore a foyle,
As if his head ne're felt the sacred oyle.
Sometimes from crimson, blood of gastly slain,
The bow of *Jonathan* ne're turn'd in vain:
Nor from the fat, and spoils of Mighty men
With bloodless sword did *Saul* turn back agen.

          *   *   *

O Israels Dames, o'reflow your beauteous eyes
For valiant *Saul* who on Mount *Gilbo* lyes,
Who cloathed you in Cloath of richest Dye,
And choice delights, full of variety,
On your array put ornaments of gold,
Which made you yet more beauteous to behold.
O! how in Battle did the mighty fall
In midst of strength not succoured at all.
O lovely *Jonathan!* how wast thou slain?
In places high, full low thou didst remain.

          *   *   *

How are the mighty fall'n into decay?
And warlike weapons perished away?

Taken at its face value this set of verses has no originality and very little poetic merit, save for the dirge-like tone conveyed by the repeated image of the fallen mighty, and there does not seem to be any apparent reason why Anne Bradstreet should have taken the trouble to write it. If, however, we remember that there were many Puritans who were deeply shocked by the judicial murder of their anointed sovereign but who were obliged, under Cromwell's dictatorship, to hide their feelings or to express them only, as the defeated Royalists did, in veiled and secret ways, then it seems that we may have a clue to the meaning and purpose of this sombre poem.

Letters from England brought, at long intervals, the news of the king's execution to the several ports at which the infrequent ships touched. Stephen Winthrop wrote from London, in mid-March, to his brother John Winthrop, Junior, in Connecticut, telling of Cromwell's return with his victorious forces from the north, his quarrel with Parliament, and that

> . . . the Army marched immediately up to Lond. and within two or three dayes in a morning sett guards about the Howse and withheld all those from coming to sitt in the Howse who were for a Treaty with the King and the calling in the Scotts: and the rest voted the Triall of the King who is since beheaded with Duk Hambleton Lord Holand Lord Caple and more I believe will suffer yet. . . . They have voted the Kingly Government downe and Likewise the Lords, and the howse of Comons to be supreame. All is quiett but I know not how Long it will Last. . . . New England seems to be the only safe place where I beleive we must come good store at Length if we cann.[30]

And more than two months later, on 26th May, 1649, a letter from Roger Williams in Rhode Island, to the same recipient, reported:

> Sir, Tidings are high from England; many ships from many parts say, and a Bristoll ship come to the Ile of Shoales within few dayes confirme, that the King and many great Lords and Parlia-

30. *Winthrop Papers*, Vol. V, p. 320.

ment men are beheaded: London was shut up on the Day of Execution, not a dore to be opened etc. . . . It is said mr. Peters preached (after the fashion of England) the funeral Sermon to the King, after sentence, out of the terrible Denunciation to the King of Babilon, Esa [Isaiah]: 14. 18 etc.[31]

The Reverend Hugh Peter, or Peters (as he is interchangeably called), was a fanatical Puritan who had come early to New England and had then returned to work actively for Parliament during the Civil War. He paid with his own head, after the Restoration, for his cruel sermon to the condemned king, as one who had "destroyed his land and slain his people." Yet many sermons of the same nature must have been preached in New England, when word of the execution had spread through the whole colony, so it behoved Anne Bradstreet to be cautious in expressing the grief that I believe she felt for the dead king. It will be remembered that she had grown up in the household of a nobleman who had been a courtier during the reigns of both King James I and his successor. Although the Earl of Lincoln was one of the Puritan peers who resisted the forced loan levied by Charles I and was consequently imprisoned, he was received back into favor after his release, and had a part in obtaining the royal charter for the Massachusetts Bay Company. In New England the pioneers continued to be subjects of the Crown, and were not directly involved in the mother-country's increasingly bitter division, that led to the Civil War, between the king and the greater number of his people. Anne Bradstreet's friend and mentor, in her early years as a serious writer, was the Reverend Nathaniel Ward, her father's contemporary, whose lifelong devotion to his sovereign is the main theme of *The Simple Cobler of Aggawam*. Nowhere in Anne's writing is there a hint of animosity against the king, on the contrary there is a

31. *Ibid.* p. 348.

sense of outrage in the couplet from "Old Age's" speech in "The Four Ages":

> I've seen a King by force thrust from his throne,
> And an Usurper subt'ly mount thereon,

of compassion for martyred royalty in the "crying blood" passage of the "Dialogue between Old England and New," and, in the same poem, a vigorous assertion of loyalty when she addresses the "brave Nobles" and goes on

> These, these are they I trust, with *Charles* our King,
> Out of all mists such glorious days shall bring.

So it seems quite possible that she used the paraphrase from II Samuel to record her sorrow at the long dreadful carnage of the Civil War and her shocked incredulity at its culminating act of violence, the execution of King Charles by his own people, which was a more terrible thing in its way than the death of the mighty Saul in battle against his enemies. If this is so, Anne probably sent the poem directly to Nathaniel Ward in England; her old friend would have recognized at once the veiled message of shared dismay that it carried, and furthermore many of her readers, when *The Tenth Muse* appeared in 1650, would have known without question what meaning the biblical paraphrase was intended to convey. This is, and must remain, a conjecture. But it is interesting to think that this otherwise undistinguished poem, by a New England Puritan, may be eligible for inclusion in the curious and touching medley, known to exist but usually hidden away in the old country mansions of England, of symbolic testimonials to the martyred king.

CHAPTER EIGHT

The Tenth Muse

"My rambling brat (in print) . . ."

(ANNE BRADSTREET—*The Author to her Book*)

Under the date "1st July, 1650" *The Stationers' Register* has this entry:

> Master Bowtell. Entred under the hands of Master Downham and Master Flesher, Warden, a booke called *The tenth muse lately sprung up in America*, written by Ann Bradstreet . . .
> . . . . vj d.[1]

There was a lot of substance for sixpence in the little book, which, although it measures only five and a half by three and three-quarters inches, contains two hundred and twenty pages closely printed in small type. The British Museum's excellent copy is a part of the great collection of Civil War and Commonwealth period books and pamphlets made by the London bookseller George Thomason between 1641 and 1662. Thomason's

---

1. *Transcript of the Registers of the Worshipful Company of Stationers for 1640–1708*, ed. H. R. Plomer, Roxburghe Club, 1913–14, Vol. I, p. 346.

notation in *The Tenth Muse* shows that his copy was acquired on the 5th July, 1650; this must have been within a few days after the actual date of publication.[2]

The neatly printed title-page presents a compendious summary of the book's contents:

> THE TENTH MUSE Lately sprung up in AMERICA. OR Severall Poems, compiled with great variety of Wit and Learning, full of delight. Wherein especially is contained a complete discourse and description of The Four *Elements, Constitutions, Ages of Man, Seasons of the Year.* Together with an Exact Epitomie of the Four Monarchies, *viz.* The *Assyrian, Persian, Grecian, Roman.* Also a Dialogue between Old *England* and New, concerning the late troubles. With divers other pleasant and serious Poems. By a Gentlewoman in those parts.
>
> Printed at *London* for *Stephen Bowtell* at the signe of the Bible in Popes Head-Alley. 1650.

Master Stephen Bowtell was a publisher and bookseller in London from 1643 to 1664; in spite of the implication of his "signe" he was known as the producer of political rather than religious books.[3] What must have been one of his most successful ventures was the publication, in 1647, of *The Simple Cobler of Aggawam in America,* by "Theodore de la Guard" (Nathaniel Ward's punning pseudonym). Bowtell's relations with Anne Bradstreet's old friend must have been thoroughly cordial while *The Simple Cobler* was going through five reprintings in the same year, and it is very likely that Ward recommended Bowtell to John Woodbridge when the publication of Anne's poems was under discussion.

2. B. M., E. 1365(4); *Catalogue of the Thomason Tracts,* ed. G. K. Fortescue, 1908, Vol. I, p. 805.

3. H. R. Plomer, *Dictionary of Booksellers and Printers in England, Scotland and Ireland from 1641 to 1667,* The Bibliographical Society, 1907, p. 31.

The Tenth Muse was introduced to her new and wider public by twelve pages of prefatory material, then come the thirteen formal poems examined in the preceding chapters: the Dedication "To her most Honoured Father" of the "four and four" on the elements and humors, "The Prologue," followed by the four quaternions on the elements, humors, ages, and seasons, "The Four Monarchies," "A Dialogue between Old England and New," "An Elegy upon Sir Philip Sidney," "In Honour of Du Bartas," "In Honour of Queen Elizabeth," "David's Lamentation for Saul and Jonathan," and "Of the Vanity of all Worldly Creatures." There is both chronological and textual confusion in the order in which these poems were printed; if Anne Bradstreet had been in a position to supervise their publication she would undoubtedly have arranged them differently, and it seems that their most logical form of presentation, so far as dating and interrelation are concerned, would be as follows:

"An Elegy upon Sir Philip Sidney," dated 1638.

"In Honour of Du Bartas," dated 1641.

"A Dialogue between Old England and New," dated 1642 (and probably finished in March 1643).

The Dedication "To her most Honoured Father Thomas Dudley, Esq.," dated (in *Several Poems*, 1678) March 20, 1642 (for 1643).

"The Four Elements" ⎱ (both finished before March 20,
"The Four Humours" ⎰ 1643).

"The Four Ages" ⎱ (both probably written 1643–46).
"The Four Seasons" ⎰

"In Honour of Queen Elizabeth," dated 1643.

"The Prologue"

"The Four Monarchies"   (undated but all pre-
                                         sumably written be-
"Of the Vanity of all Worldly   tween 1643 and 1647).
    Creatures"

"David's Lamentation for Saul and Jonathan" (possibly
    written in 1649).

At any rate, even if somewhat muddled under Woodbridge's
and Bowtell's direction, they were all there in print, for the
whole English-reading world to see, between the modest calf
covers of *The Tenth Muse*. Anne's poems were not obliged to
face the public eye alone and unsupported. They were introduced
by a group of testimonials impressive enough to reassure the
potential reader who was asked to exchange his sixpence, a not
inconsiderable sum in those days, for the writings of an unknown
lady in far-off North America.

The prefatory material in *The Tenth Muse* explains how and
why the book came to be published, and also illustrates the
contemporary attitude towards women writers. First comes the
epistle to the reader, unsigned, but almost certainly written by
Anne Bradstreet's brother-in-law, the Reverend John Woodbridge.

Kind Reader:
    Had I opportunity but to borrow some of the Author's wit,
'tis possible I might so trim this curious Work with such quaint
expressions, as that the Preface might bespeake thy further
perusall; but I feare 'twil be a shame for a man that can speak
so little, to be seene in the title page of this Womans Book, lest
by comparing the one with the other, the Reader should passe
his sentence, that it is the gift of women, not only to speak
most, but to speake best; I shall leave therefore to commend

that, which with any ingenious Reader will too much commend the Author, unlesse men turne more peevish then women, to envie the excellency of the inferiour Sex. I doubt not but the Reader will quickly finde more then I can say, and the worst effect of his reading will be unbeleif, which will make him question whether it be a womans Work, and aske, Is it possible? If any doe, take this as an answer from him that dares avow it; It is the Work of a Woman, honoured, and esteemed where she lives, for her gracious demeanour, her eminent parts, her pious conversation, her courteous disposition, her exact diligence in her place, and discreet managing of her family occasions; and more then so, these Poems are the fruit but of some few houres, curtailed from her sleep, and other refreshments. I dare adde little, lest I keepe thee too long, if thou wilt not beleeve the worth of these things (in their kind) when a man sayes it, yet beleeve it from a woman when thou seest it. This only I shall annex, I feare the displeasure of no person in the publishing of these Poems but the Authors, without whose knowledge, and contrary to her expectation, I have presumed to bring to publick view what she resolved should never in such a manner see the Sun; but I found that divers had gotten some scattered papers, affected them wel, were likely to have sent forth broken peices to the Authors prejudice, which I thought to prevent, as well as to pleasure those that earnestly desired the view of the whole.

This is not actually quite so patronizing as it seems to be. John Woodbridge clearly felt deep respect and affection for his sister-in-law, and true admiration for her poems, and there is nothing unmannerly in his presupposing the incredulity of the reader, that such a body of work should spring from the mind of a member of the "inferiour Sex." For no English woman before Anne Bradstreet had, so far as I have been able to discover, offered in print a collection of poems so large in volume or so varied in subject-matter. An examination of the surviving publications of Anne's female verse-making predecessors and contemporaries, further on in this chapter, will, I believe, show that *The Tenth Muse* was the first printed work of poetry by an English woman that was not liable to be viewed as something of a curiosity, because of either the exalted position of the author or the very limited nature of the subject.

Woodbridge was, therefore, doing something unusual, to say the least, in bringing before the public the writings of a woman of unpretentious rank who presumed to handle, in panoramic scope, such hitherto entirely masculine topics as history, war, politics, and the "natural philosophy," or science, of the world and of its microcosm, man. He was avowedly convinced that her poems deserved wider circulation than they had had in New England, and he was anxious lest unauthorized persons should publish them surreptitiously and incorrectly. Although he presents himself as solely responsible for the publication, it seems probable that he acted as a member of a sort of family conspiracy, in which Thomas Dudley and Simon Bradstreet supported him in taking, without her knowledge, a step of great significance to the life of their close relative.

It must be emphasized that this was in no sense a frivolous or ostentatious act. These men of Anne Bradstreet's family, and the other admirers of her poems in the New England community, were serious, thrifty, and self-disciplined people, who weighed every impulse primarily for its value in the sight of God. They must have believed that many others in their world would be both pleased and benefited by reading the work of a woman whom they honored, not only for the exemplary qualities of her character but also for the edifying verse that she had written, in the midst of her busy and sometimes perilous life in the New World's wilderness. It is also quite possible that they felt that the publication of *The Tenth Muse* would prove, to those in England who watched the progress of the colony

with critical appraisal, that opportunities for cultural development and expression, even for women, were not lacking there.

Another friend of Anne's who, as I have suggested, may have
been privy to the publishing plot, contributed the first of the
prefatory rhymes, signed "N. *Ward*," which is an outstanding
example of humorous verse by a Puritan of his period.

> *Mercury* shew'd *Apollo, Bartas* Book,
> *Minerva* this, and wisht him well to look,
> And tell uprightly, which, did which excell;
> He view'd, and view'd, and vow'd he could not tell.
> They bid him Hemisphear his mouldy nose,
> With's crackt leering-glasses, for it would pose
> The best brains he had in's old pudding-pan,
> Sex weigh'd, which best, the Woman, or the Man?
> He peer'd, and por'd, and glar'd, and said for wore,
> I'me even as wise now, as I was before:
> They both 'gan laugh, and said, it was no mar'l
> The Auth'resse was a right *Du Bartas* Girle.
> Good sooth quoth the old *Don*, tel ye me so,
> I muse whither at length these Girls will go;
> It half revives my chil frost-bitten blood,
> To see a woman, once, do ought that's good;
> And chode by *Chaucers* Boots, and *Homers* Furrs,
> Let men look to't, least women weare the Spurs.

Harold S. Jantz calls this a "true early Baroque conceptism,
which shares with the late Renaissance a tightly packed form,
broken line, and telescoped imagery." [4] The caricature of Apollo
seems like a self-portrait of the rugged old clergyman himself,
who, though he never overtly would have written a sentimental
word, has also packed his curious lines with unmistakable affection for his young friend of the Ipswich days, and with warm
pride in her unusual accomplishment.

4. *The First Century of New England Verse*, p. 12.

Nathaniel Ward's tribute is followed by the longest of the prefatory pieces, seventy-four lines in couplets, titled "To my deare Sister, the Author of these Poems" and signed "*I. W.*". In typical cleric's verse of the period Woodbridge apologizes for the product of his "addle braines," repeats the declarations of the prose epistle, and occasionally achieves a felicitous line.

> Yet am I willing, with upright intent,
> To shew my love without a complement.
> There needs no painting to that comely face,
> That in its native beauty hath such grace;

*   *   *

> If women, I with women, may compare,
> Your Works are solid, others weake as aire;
> Some books of Women I have heard of late,
> Perused some, so witlesse, intricate,
> So void of sense, and truth, as if to erre
> Were only wisht (acting above their sphear)

*   *   *

> What you have done, the Sun shall witnesse beare,
> That for a womans Worke 'tis very rare;
> And if the Nine vouchsafe the Tenth a place,
> I think they rightly may yeeld you that grace.

*   *   *

> If you shall think, it will be to your shame
> To be in print, then I must beare the blame:
> If't be a fault, 'tis mine, 'tis shame that might
> Deny so faire an infant of its right,

*   *   *

> 'Tis true, it doth not now so neatly stand,
> As if 'twere pollisht with your owne sweet hand;
> 'Tis not so richly deckt, so trimly tir'd,

Yet it is such as justly is admir'd.
If it be folly, 'tis of both, or neither,
Both you and I, we'l both be fools together.

Woodbridge's elaborate protestations reveal his awareness of the risk he was taking, in thus exposing himself at once to the possibility of public scorn and of the righteous indignation of his strong-minded sister-in-law. His own brother, however, apparently stood by him among the other sponsors of Anne Bradstreet's literary debut. The next offering, "Upon the Author, by a knowne Friend," is unsigned in *The Tenth Muse*, but initialed "B. W." in the second printing, and is believed to be the work of the Reverend Benjamin Woodbridge. This rather restless clergyman came to New England as a very young man and was listed, in 1642, as the first graduate of the newly established Harvard College. He then returned to England, took a doctorate in theology at Magdalen Hall, Oxford, and preached at Salisbury and Newbury until 1666. In that year he was again in Massachusetts, ministering to the church in Amesbury, but in 1669 he went back to his native land and remained there until his death in 1684. Anthony Wood gives an entertaining account of his controversial writings and turbulent career in the Church.[5] He may have accompanied his elder brother to England in 1647; at any rate he was there when *The Tenth Muse* appeared, and was probably the contributor of the twelve stilted lines "by a knowne Friend," with their admonition:

Mankind take up some blushes on the score,
Menopolize perfection no more:
In your owne Arts, confesse your selves out-done,
The Moone hath totally eclips'd the Sun.

5. *Athenae Oxonienses*, Vol. II, p. 586.

The pun in the second line may well be intentional, and not just the result of a typesetter's error!

The remaining five short salutations are, not unexpectedly, quite without any poetic merit; their interest lies in the apparent fact that they were all written, in England, by men who did not know Mistress Bradstreet and who were challenged by the unusual task of commending the literary efforts of a woman. Although each of these verselets is signed by two initials, the identity of the authors is not, and probably never will be, known. However, it is safe to assume that they were, with one possible exception, friends or acquaintances of John Woodbridge among whom he had circulated the manuscripts of Anne's poems and from whom he had received these metrical seals of approval for his project of publishing them.

I have attempted to identify the owners of the initials and, although the results of my search must remain hypothetical, I have found possible candidates for the authorship of four out of these five testimonials. From the years when Woodbridge was at Oxford, about 1628 to 1634, several literary men whom he may have known there are listed in Anthony Wood's *Athenæ Oxonienses, an exact History of all the Writers who have had their Education in the University of Oxford.* The later interests and activities of these men make it conceivable that, when Woodbridge returned to England in 1647, he sought their opinions of Anne Bradstreet's work. At least they may be considered as typical of the sort of scholars who would have been inclined to look with a fair amount of sympathy at this manifestation of female virtuosity.

The first and fourth of these verse-offerings are signed "C. B.". A neo-classic quatrain follows Benjamin Woodbridge's contribution, and the labored pun in the final line seems to suggest that the writer fancied himself to be something of a poet.

I cannot wonder at *Apollo* now
That he with Female Lawrell crown'd his brow,
That made him witty: had I leave to chuse,
My Verse should be a Page unto your Muse.

A little collection of metrical tributes to his friends, very similar in general character to these lines, was published in 1651 by Clement Barksdale, with the title *Nympha Libethris or the Cotswold Muse*. This conforming Church of England clergyman, who was also a schoolmaster, took his B.A. at Merton College in 1629 and his M.A. in 1632. Wood wrote of him:

> He was a good Disputant, . . . a frequent preacher, but very conceited and vain, a great pretender to Poetry and a writer and translator of several little Tracts, most of which are meer Scribbles.[6]

Among these writings, to which Wood gives such scant admiration, is a translation of a "logick exercise" by Anna Maria von Schurman (1607–78), a celebrated bluestocking of Utrecht, entitled *The Learned Maid, or whether a Maid may be a Scholar,* which was published in 1659. Another, which did not appear in print until 1675, is a four-leaf *Letter touching a Colledge of Maides, or a Virgin-Society.* In spite of their religious differences Woodbridge may have known Barksdale at Oxford, and later, being aware of his interest in female education, have sent him the Bradstreet manuscripts and received in return his stiff little commendation.

The other verselet signed "C. B." is, though highly conventional, more forthright and unaffected than the Apollonian quatrain and therefore probably by a different writer.

6. *Athenae Oxonienses*, Vol. II, p. 614.

Upon the Author

Twere extreame folly should I dare attempt,
To praise this Authors worth with complement;
None but her self must dare commend her parts,
Whose sublime brain's the Synopsis of Arts:
Nature and Skil, here both in one agree,
To frame this Master-peice of Poetry:
False Fame, belye their Sex, no more, it can,
Surpasse, or parallel, the best of man.

These lines may possibly have been contributed by Cassibelan Burton (1609–1682), a classicist who made a translation of Martial's epigrams that was, however, never published. He was the son of the Oxford-educated antiquarian William Burton, and the nephew of the much more famous Oxford scholar and psychologist the Reverend Robert Burton, or "Democritus Junior," author of *The Anatomy of Melancholy.*

The second tribute is a refreshingly facetious piece of verse, which must, nevertheless, have annoyed Anne Bradstreet by its sarcastic tone, for it was deleted from the second printing of her poems.

Arme, arme, Soldado's arme, Horse, Horse,
        speed to your Horses,
Gentle-women, make head, they vent their
        plots in Verses;
They write of Monarchies, a most seditious word,
It signifies Oppression, Tyranny, and Sword:
March amain to *London,* they'l rise, for
        there they flock,
But stay a while, they seldome rise till
        ten a clock.

                                                            R.Q.

I have been unable to discover any imaginable candidate for the authorship of these curious lines, with their sly, satiric thrust at the anti-monarchy propaganda of Cromwell's Commonwealth, and yet appearing in a distinctly Puritan publication. Sir Robert Quarles, the elder brother of Francis Quarles, the poet whose *Emblems Divine and Moral* (1635) and other pious works were extremely popular in New England, might have been suggested, except that he died in 1640. There is an Elizabethan note in the call to arms, the galloping broken rhythm and panting commas, of the stanza, and it is conceivable that "R. Q." was an old friend of Nathaniel Ward's, sharing his crotchety attitude towards women and some of the quality of his humorous verse.

Following this is a grandiose offering of fourteen lines, the title of which takes up almost the whole of a page:

In praise of the Author, Mistris *Anne Bradstreet*, Vertue's true and lively Patterne, Wife of the Worshipfull *Simon Bradstreet*, Esquire.
At present residing in the Occidentall parts of the World, in *America*, alias NOV-ANGLIA.[7]

> *What Golden splendent* STAR *is this, so bright,*
> *One thousand miles thrice told, both day and night,*
> *(From th' Orient first sprung) now from the West*
> *That shines; swift-winged* Phoebus, *and the rest,*
> *Of all* Joves *fiery flames surmounting far,*
> *As doth each Planet, every falling Star;*
> *By whose divine, and lucid light most cleare,*
> *Natures darke secret Mysteries appeare;*
> *Heaven's, Earths, admired wonders, noble acts*
> *Of Kings, and Princes most heroyick facts,*

7. It has been pointed out that "the limitation of *America* to the British Colonies of North America is first recorded in 1650, when Mistris Anne Bradstreet was 'residing in America, alias Nov-Anglia' ": R. W. Chapman, *Johnsonian and Other Essays and Reviews*, Oxford, 1953, p. 208 (reprinting: "To What Strange Shores?" a review in "The Times Literary Supplement," 10th Oct., 1936, of *A Dictionary of American English*, by Sir William Craigie, and *The American Language*, by H. L. Mencken).

And what e're else in darkness seem'd to dye,
Revives all things so obvious now to th' eye;
That he who these, its glittering Rayes views o're,
Shall see what's done, in all the world before.

N.H.

The elaborate display of typography in the title, the italicizing of the whole composition, and the facts that Anne Bradstreet's name here first appears in her book, and that her husband is also respectfully mentioned, make it seem that this tribute was considered a particularly gratifying one. Possibly it was written by Nathaniel Holmes, a prominent Calvinist preacher and writer, who received his doctorate in Divinity at Exeter College, Oxford, in 1637. He became associated with the famous Henry Burton, one of the most bitterly persecuted of the nonconformist clergy, in ministering to an independent congregation in London after 1640; both of these men must have taken a lively interest in the progress of the New England colonies, and Holmes may have expressed, albeit in classically pagan phraseology, his approval of the erudition of "a Gentlewoman in those parts."

A rather brisk little commendation entitled "Another to M^ris. *Anne Bradstreete*, Author of this Poem" completes the group of initialed tributes and seems to refer specifically to "The Four Monarchies."

I've read your Poem (Lady) and admire,
Your Sex, to such a pitch should e're aspire;
Goe on to write, continue to relate,
New Histories, of Monarchy and State;
And what the *Romans* to their Poets gave,
Be sure such honour, and esteeme you'l have.

H.S.

Henry Stubbe the elder (1606?–1678), an Oxford-educated nonconforming clergyman whom Woodbridge may have known, had a son of the same name who seems a suitable candidate for the authorship of these lines, though he would have been only sixteen or seventeen when they were written. The younger Henry lived from 1632 to 1676, became a classical scholar, mathematician, physician, and a close friend of Thomas Hobbes, and was called by Anthony Wood "the most noted person of his age that these late times have produced." [8] As a poor student at Westminster School he came to the notice of Sir Henry Vane the younger, who befriended him, sent him to Christ Church at Oxford in 1649, and remained his patron until his own death, by beheading on Tower Hill, in 1662.

Vane, whose father was a trusted adviser to King Charles I, had been sent to Massachusetts Bay as a young man, in 1635, because his father hoped that the experience would cure him of his puritanical leanings. It did not, however, and Vane was so popular in New England that in 1636, in spite of his inexperience and impetuosity, he was elected governor of the colony. He supported Anne Hutchinson in the Antinomian controversy; during her trial the general feeling turned against him, and he went home to England in 1637. He was a Parliamentary leader throughout the Civil War, and one of the Commissioners sent to negotiate with the king at the Isle of Wight in 1648.

Whether or not Vane had encountered John Woodbridge during his brief sojourn in Massachusetts, he would undoubtedly have been interested in the presence of the New Englander as a chaplain for the Commissioners. It is within the realm of possibility that the young prodigy Henry Stubbe was with his patron Sir Henry Vane, acting as a secretary, during the summer of 1648, that Woodbridge showed "The Four Monarchies" to both of them, and that Stubbe was sufficiently impressed to offer the testimonial signed "H. S.".

The prefatory material is completed by two anagrams and

8. *Athenae Oxonienses*, Vol. II, p. 412.

a rhymed couplet, all unsigned. It is almost impossible for a present-day reader to catch even an echo of the enthusiasm felt in Anne Bradstreet's time for that tortuous literary device, the anagram. But Harold S. Jantz, in his comments on colonial New England poetry, deals sympathetically with its use by the Massachusetts ministers John Wilson and John Fiske. He points out that an intricate contrapuntal technique was involved in creating an emblem, or motto, from the letters of a person's name and then expanding and interweaving the theme in the poem, usually elegiac, that followed it. He thinks it likely that Wilson composed the anagrams in *The Tenth Muse*.[9]

> *Anna Bradestreate.*   Deer Neat *An Bartas*.
>
> So *Bartas* like thy fine spun Poems been,
> That *Bartas* name will prove an Epicene.
>
> *Anne Bradstreate.*   Artes bred neat *An*.

As a more developed and interesting example of this technique Jantz quotes an anonymous poem, which he attributes to John Fiske, sent to Governor Thomas Dudley soon after his election in 1645. "It is," he says, "one of the most carefully wrought poems of the period, an aesthetic delight—if one does not allow modern objections as to its contents to obtrude. Its reception did not mean a nasty shock to Thomas Dudley, but a deep delight, and he probably cherished it during the eight years that still remained to him."

> THOMAS DUDLEY
>
> AH! OLD, MUST DYE.
>
> A deaths head on your hand you neede not weare,
> a dying head you on your shoulders beare:

9. *First Century of New England Verse*, pp. 14–15, 30–33.

you need not one to minde you, you must dye,
you in your name may spell mortalitye.
younge men may dye, but old men these dye must,
t'will not be long before you turne to dust.
before you turne to dust! ah! must; old! dye!
what shall younge doe, when old in dust doe lye?
when old in dust lye, what N. England doe?
when old in dust doe lye, it's best dye too.[10]

It was the most dramatic moment of Anne Bradstreet's not uneventful life, we may suppose, when the little book of her own poems, "in black and white," was put into her hands. We are spared the necessity of trying to imagine her feelings, for she recorded them herself, with wry and touching wit, in a short poem which appeared in the second edition of her work.

The Author to her Book

Thou ill-form'd offspring of my feeble brain,
Who after birth did'st by my side remain,
Till snatcht from thence by friends, less wise then true,
Who thee abroad, expos'd to publick view,
Made thee in raggs, halting to th'press to trudg,
Where errors were not lessened (all may judg)
At thy return my blushing was not small,
My rambling brat (in print) should mother call,
I cast thee by as one unfit for light,
Thy Visage was so irksome in my sight;
Yet being mine own, at length affection would
Thy blemishes amend, if so I could:
I wash'd thy face, but more defects I saw,
And rubbing off a spot, still made a flaw.
I stretcht thy joynts to make thee even feet,
Yet still thou run'st more hobling then is meet;
In better dress to trim thee was my mind,

10. *Ibid.* p. 34.

> But nought save home-spun Cloth, i'th'house I find.
> In this array, 'mongst Vulgars mayst thou roam
> In Criticks hands, beware thou dost not come;
> And take thy way where yet thou art not known,
> If for thy Father askt, say, thou hadst none:
> And for thy Mother, she alas is poor,
> Which caus'd her thus to send thee out of door.

This is one of Anne Bradstreet's most spontaneous poems, in which the woman and the writer speak together with a single intent. The simile of parenthood is a natural one; she had the example of Spenser's

> Goe little book: thy selfe present,
> As child whose parent is unkent:

as well as John Woodbridge's apologetic

> If't be a fault, 'tis mine, 'tis shame that might
> Deny so fair an Infant of its right,
> To look abroad;

and always there was the growing family of legitimate children that made it easy for the "carping Tongues" to say that she should stick to motherhood and let poetry alone.

The poem was obviously not written until some years after the publication of *The Tenth Muse*, for the references to the author's attempts to mend the blemishes show that she was already making preparations for a second edition of the "rambling brat." Yet neither passing time nor keen self-criticism could banish, from her lines to her book, the genuine sense of excitement with which she acknowledged it as her own, and the anxious affection with which she made ready to send it forth again "where yet thou art not known."

This consciousness of literary identity had, as one of her most appreciative critics has noted, a marked effect on her later work.

> *The Tenth Muse* did this for Anne Bradstreet: it completely cured her of the Du Bartas disease, and of writing imitative poetry. She was thirty-eight when the book came out in 1650. For the remaining twenty-two years of her life, she wrote lyrical poetry.[11]

Only two of her nine introductory admirers made a point of associating Anne Bradstreet's poetry intimately with that of Du Bartas. These two, Nathaniel Ward and, supposedly, John Wilson, were both members of the first generation of New England settlers, born in the later sixteenth century and educated in the high Renaissance tradition in old England. Ward had instinctively, as his writings clearly show, a very small opinion of the intelligence of women; the conflict between this and his apparently genuine affection for Anne Bradstreet was comfortably solved by having Mercury and Minerva present the "Auth'ress" as a Little Madam Echo, as it were, of Du Bartas.

The other contributors of complimentary verse, aside from the elsuive "R. Q.," were probably of a younger generation, and, with the exception of the Woodbridge brothers, men who had never left their native land to sojourn in the North American colonies. They would therefore have been exposed to the constantly changing trends in literary styles and appreciations, and aware, as the century approached its middle point, that the Huguenot epic of Du Bartas, established by Sylvester as an English classic, was beginning to lose some of its monumental stature. Douglas Bush comments on this development: "Probably one main reason for the poem's eventual eclipse was what had been a main reason for

11. Samuel Eliot Morison, *Builders of the Bay Colony*, p. 331.

its prestige, the religious medievalism of its scientific substance." [12]

Anne Bradstreet has shared with her greatest contemporary, John Milton, the reputation of having been enchanted, encouraged, and inspired by the English Du Bartas. Her early affirmation of passionate devotion, "In honour of Du Bartas," seems to have set the style for her critics, all the way from Nathaniel Ward to Samuel Eliot Morison, who have emphasized her dependence, technical as well as spiritual, in her earlier writings at any rate, on the French poet. What they seem to have consistently disregarded is her own forthright disavowal of any intent to imitate: "My goods are true (though poor) I love no stealth," she firmly wrote in the dedication to her father of her "four times four," and this statement has been finally upheld, in the middle of our century, by Austin Warren's already quoted judgment that Anne's long formal poems have nothing in common with Du Bartas "except their run-on couplets and their panoramic scope." [13]

To be sure there are occasional echoes of Du Bartas in Anne Bradstreet's verse, where a contrived metaphor, a stilted image, or an overelaborate descriptive passage betrays its origin. But what she herself perhaps only partially realized, and many of her critics have failed to observe, is that the qualities inherent in her poetic personality, of objectivity, humor, honest humility, and a sort of downright matter-of-fact-ness, along with a somewhat limited technical scope, made it impossible for her to reproduce, even if she had deliberately tried to do so, the histrionic virtuosity of the ebullient Frenchman.

So while we remember that it was, by her own admission, the overpowering experience of reading *The Divine Weekes and Workes* that kindled in her imagination the determination to

12. D. Bush, *English Literature in the Earlier Seventeenth Century*, p. 74.
13. See p. 151 above.

become a poet, we should also be willing to acknowledge that she did not, even in the most self-conscious of the poems that appeared in *The Tenth Muse*, truly imitate her mentor. And we may presuppose as well, at this point in her literary career, where Anne Bradstreet stands before us, as it were, with the newly printed volume of her own writings in her hands, that the impact of this astonishing event released her from the earlier sense of poetic insecurity, and gave her the confidence to write as she wished, within the compass of her craftmanship, for the rest of her life.

The much-discussed subject of the Du Bartas-Bradstreet relationship has recently received comprehensive treatment by Hans Galinsky of Mainz, to whom we have already referred in connection with his theories about Anne's familiarity with Shakespeare.[14] The greater part of his essay is devoted to a review of the comments of literary historians and critics, covering more than a century in time, on Anne Bradstreet's indebtedness to Du Bartas. He finds that these commentators, until very lately, have been consistently influenced by Anne's lines in praise and honor of Du Bartas, and have neglected her own disavowals of imitation as well as the striking dissimilarities, recently pointed out by Austin Warren, between her unassuming work and that of the sophisticated Frenchman.

The immediate impact of *The Tenth Muse* on the reading, and book-buying, public of the 1650's is not revealed, apparently, by any surviving record. The earliest indication I have found of the book's reception cannot be considered a critical comment, but is nevertheless informative. In 1657 William London, a bookseller of Newcastle-on-Tyne, published an ambitious trade-list with a title that sheds generous light on the popular subjects of his time:

14. See pp. 65–66 above.

A Catalogue of the most Vendible Books in England, Orderly and Alphabetically Digested, under the Heads of Divinity, History, Physick and Chyrurgery, Law, Arithmetic, Geometry, Astrology, Dialling, Measuring Land and Timber, Gageing, Navigation, Architecture, Horsemanship, Faulconry, Merchandize, Limning, Military Discipline, Heraldry, Fortification and Fireworks, Husbandry, Gardening, Romances, Poems, Playes, &c. With Hebrew, Greek and Latin for Schools and Scholars.

All these, along with a stock of globes, papers, and so on, were "to be sold by the Author at his Shop in Newcastle." Of the one hundred and sixty-four pages of the catalogue, following a lengthy "Introduction to the Use of Books," four and one-half are devoted to the "Romances, Poems, Playes." There are ninety-six separate titles in the poetry section; a number of these are translations of the classics, and the English works include those of Cowley, Crashaw, Donne, Drayton, "Dubartas" Herbert's *The Temple*, Herrick's "Poems Humane and Divine," "Mr Milton's Poems with a mask before the Earl of Bridgewater," "Orchestra, a Poem of the Antiquity and Excellency of dancing," "Poems and fancies by the Lady Marg. Newcastle," Quarles, "Mr. Shaksper's Poems," Vaughan's *Poems* and "Silex Scintillans, 2 parts," Waller, and Wither. Anne Bradstreet's book has the distinction of being named twice in the alphabetical list, as:

Mrs. Bradstreet. The 10. Muse, a Poem.

*   *   *

Tenth Muse, or an exact Epitomy of the four monarchies.

This duplication may have been inadvertent; on the other hand, it could indicate that London's shop was overstocked with copies of *The Tenth Muse*. It shows at any rate that the book was in active circulation seven years after its publication.

The inclusion of only two women writers, in so rich a company of English poets, makes one wonder just whom John Woodbridge had in mind when he referred, in his verse-epistle to the author of *The Tenth Muse*, to "Some Books of Women I have heard of late,/ Perused some," which he deemed "so witless, intricate,/ So void of sense, and truth. . . ." This is reminiscent of Ben Jonson's earlier merciless lampooning of the "Would-be" learned lady, in *Volpone* and *Epicene*, yet Woodbridge had the discrimination and courage to bring his sister-in-law's "solid works" to "publick view," and the charity to leave unnamed the "silly Souls" whose writings he compared so unflatteringly with hers. Posterity has no doubt consigned most of these hapless authoresses to oblivion, but a survey of the known women writers of England, of Anne Bradstreet's time and earlier, reveals an impressively large group. This can be narrowed, however, so far as poetry is concerned, by the exclusion of those who wrote only in prose, or as translators of classic or foreign authors, or whose poetic remains consist of no more than one or two pieces. Representative of this number are: the mystic anchoress Julian of Norwich, whose *Revelations of Divine Love*, written at about the end of the fourteenth century, was not printed until 1670; Dame Juliana Berners, prioress of a nunnery and the supposed author of a work on hunting, hawking, and heraldry called *The Boke of St. Albans*, which appeared in 1486, and Margery Kempe of Lynn, who is credited with having written the first autobiography in the English language. This extremely devout and temperamental woman recorded, in about 1436, her religious experiences, visions, and pilgrimages; in 1501 Wynkyn de Worde printed *A shorte treatyse of contemplacyon, taken out of the boke of Margarie Kempe*, but it was not until the 1930's that the complete manuscript was found and published in both a scholarly and a modern language version.[15]

Among the royal and noble ladies of the sixteenth century whose work has come down to us in print were: Margaret Beaufort, Countess of Richmond (died 1509), the mother of King Henry VII, who translated from the French a devotional book called *The Mirroure of Golde for the Synfull Soule*; Queen Catharine Parr, whose *Prayers Stirryng the Mynd unto Heavenlye Medytacions* was many times reprinted after its appearance in 1545, and the accomplished and ill-fated Lady Jane Grey, who left several religious epistles and a poem lamenting her own death. Another woman who suffered a tragic fate was Anne Askew, Lady Kyme, who in 1545 was accused of heresy, imprisoned, tortured repeatedly on the rack, and finally burned at the stake in the following year. Her own very moving account of her "examinacyons" was immediately printed in Germany, to evade the king's censors, and a few years later in London. At least two of the four celebrated intellectual daughters of Sir Anthony Cooke of Essex achieved publication: Anna, the wife of Sir Nicholas Bacon and the mother of Francis Bacon, translated from Italian the sermons of Bernardino Ochino, and from Latin Bishop Jewel's *Apologie for the Church of England*, and Elizabeth, Lady Russell, saw printed in 1605, before her death in 1609, *A Way of Reconciliation of a Good and Learned Man*, her translation of a French devotional work.

The most illustrious woman of her age, Queen Elizabeth I of England, was a scholar before she became a monarch, and took pride throughout her life in her ability to deliver formal addresses

15. *The Book of Margery Kempe*, ed. S. B. Meech and Hope Emily Allen, Early English Text Soc. (212), 1940; *The Book of Margery Kempe, 1436, A Modern Version*, ed. W. Butler-Bowdon, 1936.

in Greek, Latin, French, and Italian. At the tender age of thirteen or fourteen she translated the meditations of Queen Margaret of Navarre, published in 1548 as *A Godly Medytacyon of the Christen Sowle,* and tradition makes her the author, while still a princess, of the famous quatrain with which she replied to a "Popish Priest" who pressed her closely to declare her opinion about transubstantiation:

> Christ was the Word that spake it,
> He took the bread, and brake it,
> And what His Word did make it,
> That I believe, and take it.[16]

Only a handful of occasional verses by the great Queen have survived, but these reflect the vigor of mind and command of language that made Roger Ascham, her tutor, so lavish in his praise of her "singularity of learning." *The Oxford Book of Sixteenth Century Verse* includes the sombre poem on Mary Stuart, "The Daughter of Debate," which appeared in 1589, two years after Mary's execution, in Puttenham's *The Arte of English Poesie,* also another, lighter yet moving lyric, taken from the Rawlinson MS.:

YOUTH AND CUPID

> When I was fair and young, and favour graced me,
> Of many was I sought, their mistress for to be;
> But I did scorn them all, and answered them therefore,
> "Go, go, go, seek some otherwhere,
> Importune me no more!"
>
> How many weeping eyes I made to pine with woe,
> How many sighing hearts, I have no skill to show;

16. George Ballard, *Memoirs of British Ladies,* 1775, p. 152; Alexander Dyce, *Specimens of British Poetesses,* 1827, p. 22.

Yet I the prouder grew, and answered them therefore,
   "Go, go, go, seek some otherwhere,
     Importune me no more!"

Then spake fair Venus' son, that proud victorious boy,
And said: "Fine dame, since that you be so coy,
I will so pluck your plumes that you shall say no more,
   "Go, go, go, seek some otherwhere,
     Importune me no more!"

When he had spake these words, such change grew in my
     breast
That neither night nor day since that, I could take any rest.
Then lo! I did repent that I had said before,
   "Go, go, go, seek some otherwhere,
     Importune me no more!"

Next only in fame, in her time, to Queen Elizabeth, was "Sidney's sister, Pembroke's mother," Mary Sidney (1561–1621), who married William Herbert, Earl of Pembroke, and made his house, Wilton in Wiltshire, a gathering place for poets and men of letters. It was in her honor that her brother Sir Philip Sidney wrote and dedicated *The Countess of Pembroke's Arcadia;* after Sir Philip's early death in 1586 the Countess completed his verse-translation of the Psalms of David, adding one hundred and seven of her own compositions to the forty-three that he had made. This Elizabethan Psalter was praised by Donne, Samuel Daniel, and other contemporary writers, and apparently circulated widely in manuscript, but was not printed until the Chiswick Press produced a limited edition in 1823. Lately it has been republished in a well-edited paperback volume which is its first American appearance.[17]

17. *The Psalms of Sir Philip Sidney and the Countess of Pembroke,* edited with an introduction by J. C. A. Rathmell, New York, Doubleday Anchor Books, 1963.

Works of the Countess that were printed during her lifetime are: "Astrea," a pastoral dialogue in honor of Queen Elizabeth, included in 1602 in Francis Davison's *Poetical Rhapsody*, and two translations from French, Robert Garnier's *The Tragedie of Antonie*, and a prose work, A *Discourse of Life and Death*, by Philip du Plessis-Mornay. These last two were published in one volume in 1529, and frequently reprinted.

The first book of verse by an English woman was, so far as I have been able to discover, the work of an extremely obscure and almost totally forgotten young person named Isabella Whitney. She was the sister of the minor poet and emblem-writer Geoffrey Whitney, who lived from *c.* 1548 to *c.* 1601, and her little publication, A *Sweet Nosgay, or pleasant Posye: contayning a hundred and ten Phylosophicall Flowers, etc.,* "By Is. W., Gent.," seems to have survived in a single imperfect copy of which no part has ever been reprinted. Bohn's edition of W. T. Lowndes's *Bibliographer's Manual* (1869) notes a copy without title-page as "Probably unique. Unknown to bibliographers," and dates it 1573. This is undoubtedly the one that is now in the British Museum, rebound, without provenance, lacking the first three leaves of text, and listed by the *Short-Title Catalogue of English Books, 1475–1640* as the only located copy. It is a tiny octavo of thirty-seven leaves, printed in black letter and italic type, and is dated by the postscript to the dedicatory epistle, addressed to George Mainwaring, Esq., "From Abchurch Lane, the 10 of October, 1573. By your welwillyng Countriwoman. Is. W.".

The author explains in a poetical address to the reader that her "Phylosophicall Flowers" grew from the inspiration of "*Plat* his Plot," to which good fortune had led her after she had studied the works of many writers and found them unrewarding. She refers to a book perhaps even more obscure than her own—it does not appear in the *Short-Title Catalogue*—though by a more celebrated writer: *The Floures of Philosophie, with the Pleasures of Poetrie annexed to them,* a translation in prose and verse of passages from Seneca and others, which was printed in 1572. This was the first literary effort of a young man newly graduated from Cambridge, who later, as Sir Hugh Plat, became the popular author of *Delightes for Ladies, The Jewell House of Art and Nature,* and other books on husbandry, distillation, cookery, and related country matters.

While the flowers in young Plat's plot are not original, Isabella's bouquet of adages and admonitions is apparently her own, though composed in unrelieved doggerel. The only appeal of the jog-trot quatrains is in their quaint and rather touching naïveté, summed up in the "farewell to the reader":

> Good Reader now you tasted have,
>   and smelt of all my flowers:
> The which to get some payne I tooke,
>   and travayled many houres.
> I must request you spoyle them not,
>   nor doo in peeces teare them:
> But if thy selfe doo lothe the sent,
>   geve others leave to weare them.

Following the philosophical nosegay is a group of "Certain familiar Epistles and friendly Letters by the Auctor: with Replies," consisting of ten short poems to her brothers, sisters, and friends, with three replies in verse. The collection ends with two valedictions: "A Communication which the Auctor had to London, before she made her Wyll" and "The maner of her Wyll, and what she left to London: and to all those in it: at her departing."

The verse in this latter part of the little volume is entirely subjective, and reveals Isabella Whitney as well educated, though no poet, and a member of a large and comfortably circumstanced family. She was of sufficiently good birth to be engaged as a maid-in-waiting to a noble lady, and sadly recalls, in a letter to her brother, that for some indiscretion, probably with a young man, she was dismissed from this greatly valued service. She deplores her state of being unwed, seemingly unloved, and haunted by misfortune, and urges "two of her yonger Sisters servinge in London" to be modest, discreet, and conscientious in everything they do, and above all to remember their prayers to God at morning and evening.

At least this melancholy, self-pitying, and apparently neurotic young woman had the satisfaction of seeing her plaintive lines in print, and not for the first time at that, for she had already produced a single poem, also in tedious quatrains: *The copy of a letter, lately written in meeter, by a Yonge Gentilwoman: to her unconstant Lover. With an Admonition to al yong Gentilwomen, and to all other Mayds in general to beware of mennes flattery. By Is. W.* This doleful lament, undated by its printer but assigned to 1567 by the *Short-Title Catalogue*, was given an aid to survival by its inclusion in Edward Arber's collection of rare and fugitive early writings: *An English Garner* (8 volumes, 1877–96).

Elizabeth Jane Weston (1582–1612), a celebrated Latin scholar of her day, was born in Surrey but spent most of her life in Bohemia. Her *Poemata* appeared at Frankfort in 1602, and *Parthenicon* at Prague in 1606; she seems to have left no literary work in English. Another poetess, writing in Scottish was Elizabeth Melville, Lady Colville of Culross, who wrote a Bunyan-like poem on the Last Judgment; *Ane Godlie Dreame, compylit in Scottish Meter* was published in Edinburgh in 1603.

The earliest original poetic drama in English by a woman was apparently *The Tragedie of Mariam, the Faire Queene of Jewry*, *written by that learned, virtuous, and truly noble lady, E.C.,* which was printed in 1613. It has been established [18] that these initials represent the eccentric and determinedly intellectual daughter of Sir Lawrence Tanfield of Burford in Oxfordshire, Chief Baron of the Exchequer in 1625. Elizabeth Tanfield (*c.* 1585–1639) married Sir Henry Cary, Viscount Falkland, bore him numerous children, then, having become a passionate Roman Catholic, separated from him and lived in an unsettled fashion for the rest of her days. Her greatest memorial is that she was the mother of the philosopher-statesman Lucius Cary, Viscount Falkland, beloved and honored in his lifetime and deeply mourned at his early death at the battle of Newbury in 1643.

Lady Falkland's grim, Othello-like tale of the murder of Mariam by her jealousy-maddened husband King Herod was reprinted, as a literary curiosity, by the Malone Society in 1914. It contains one fine poem, a chorus on the nobility of forgiving injuries, from which two stanzas are particularly quoteable:

> The fairest action of our human life
>   Is scorning to revenge an injury;
> For who forgives without a further strife,
>   His adversary's heart to him doth tie.
> And 'tis a firmer conquest truly said,
> To win the heart, than overthrow the head.
>
>   *   *   *
>
> A noble heart doth teach a virtuous scorn.
>   To scorn to owe a duty over-long;
> To scorn to be for benefits foreborne;
>   To scorn to lie; to scorn to do a wrong;
> To scorn to bear an injury in mind;
> To scorn a free-born heart slave-like to bind.

18. Douglas Bush, *English Literature in the Earlier Seventeenth Century,* p. 506; Kenneth Murdock, *The Sun at Noon,* New York, 1939, p. 14.

A high-spirited lady named Rachel Speght, who may have been the daughter of the Chaucerian scholar Thomas Speght, published in 1617 a reply to an attack on "lewd, idle, froward, and unconstant Women" written by one Joseph Swetnam. Her rebuttal is called A *Mouzell for Melastomus, the cynicall Bayter of, and foule-mouthed Barker against Evah's Sex,* "An apologeticall answere to that irreligious and illiterate pamphlet made by Jo. Sw. and by him intituled, *The Arraignment of Women.*" A gentler product of her pen was a poetic memorial to her mother: *Mortalitie's Memorandum, with a Dreame Prefixed, imaginarie in manner, reall in matter;* this was printed in 1621, and contains a stanza that must have echoed the feelings of many intelligent women of her time:

> Both man and woman of three parts consist,
> Which Paul doth bodie, soule and spirit call:
> And from the soule three faculties arise,
> The mind, the will, the power; then wherefore shall
> A woman have her intellect in vain,
> Or not endevour knowledge to attain?

A more pretentious work that appeared in the same year was *The Countess of Montgomerie's Urania,* by Lady Mary Wroth, daughter of the Earl of Leicester and niece of Sir Philip Sidney. Lady Mary and her husband, Sir Robert Wroth, were the friends and patrons of many writers, including Ben Jonson, so it is not surprising that she felt inspired to produce a stylish literary composition. The *Urania* was, however, only an undistinguished imitation of Sidney's *Arcadia,* and as such gained very little praise beyond its authoress's immediate circle.

A small quarto volume of only twenty pages was published in 1630, by a lady of whom nothing apparently is known but her graceful name. This is A *Chaine of Pearle: or, a Memoriall* of the peerless *Graces* and *heroick* Virtues of Queene Elizabeth, of glorious Memory. Composed by the noble lady Diana Primrose. This tribute, which was reprinted in *The Harleian Miscellany* (1808–13), and in John Nichols's *Progresses of Queen Elizabeth* (1823), is presented in ten "Pearls," or short poems each celebrating one of the virtues, after an invocation which ends:

> . . . deign, (O thou star-crowned Queen)
> T'accept these ill-composed pearly rows,
> Wherein thy glory chiefly shall be seen:
> For by these lines, so black and impolite,
> Thy Swan-like lustre shall appear more white.

In 1637 there appeared a work of remarkable ingenuity, *Fame's Roule: or, the Names of K. Charles, Q. Mary and his Posterity; together with the Names of the Dukes, Marquesses, &c. of England, Scotland, and Ireland; anagrammatiz'd and expressed by acrosticke Lines on their Names. By Mistris Mary Fage.* Four hundred examples are here set forth of the popular anagram, each one followed by a poetic tribute developing the anagram's theme, and with the initial letters of each line forming the subject's name. The Reverend Alexander Dyce, in his charmingly printed anthology of 1827, *Specimens of British Poetesses*, includes two of Mary Fage's offerings; they are surprisingly successful as verse considering the intricate artifice that their composition required.

After these products of the literary inclinations of English women, and others perhaps that are even more obscured by the mists of time, there came in 1650, from the transatlantic frontier of English civilization, a compact little book containing thirteen long poems more varied in subject-matter, and more ambitious in scope, than any previously published by a woman. *The Tenth Muse* differed in still another way from its predecessors: it was destined to be reprinted, with the inclusion of Anne Bradstreet's later works, once in its own century and once in the eighteenth, twice in the nineteenth and four times, so far, in our century, so that whoever wished to read Anne's poems could always come upon them, without a great deal of trouble, in a reasonably contemporary edition.

The publication of books by women increased quite markedly in the years directly following the appearance of *The Tenth Muse*. Two members of the mid-seventeenth-century English world of letters left interesting critical comments on the female writers of their time. The eldest, and most didactic, was the learned lady Mrs. Bathsua Makin, who has been mentioned in an earlier chapter as the "Tutress" of the daughter of King Charles I, Princess Elizabeth, and the founder of a school for girls at Tottenham High Cross in London. Her book, *An Essay to Revive the Ancient Education of Gentlewomen in Religion, Manners, Arts & Tongues,* was published anonymously in 1673; in arguing the potential excellence of women in various fields of learning, she had much to say about their ability as poets:

> *Orator fit:* But all the Instruction and Education in the World, all the pains, time and patience imaginable, can never infuse that sublime Fancy, that strong Memory, and excellent Judgement required in one that shall wear the Bayes. If Women have been good Poets, Men injure them Exceedingly, to account them giddy-headed Gossips, fit only to discourse of their Hens, Ducks, and Geese, and not by any means to be suffered to meddle with Arts and Tongues, lest by intollerable pride they should run mad.
>
> If I do make this appear, that Women have been good Poets, it will confirm all I have said before: for, besides natural Endowments, there is required a general and universal improvement in all kinds of Learning. A good Poet, must know things Divine, things Natural, things Moral, things Historical, and things Arti-

ficial; together with the several terms belonging to all Faculties, to which they must allude. Good Poets must be universal Scholars, able to use a pleasing Phrase, and to express themselves with moving Eloquence.

The female poets of antiquity and of foreign countries are commemorated for several pages, then the English catalogue begins:

How excellent a Poet Mrs. Broadstreet is (now in America) her works do testify.

We need no other encomium of Mris. Philips, than what Mr. Cowley gives, he plucks the Laurel from his own Brow, to crown hers, as best deserving it. Besides, her works in print speak for her.

Mrs. Makin also cited Queen Elizabeth I, Lady Jane Grey, Anne Askew, the four accomplished daughters of Sir Anthony Cooke, and the Duchess of Newcastle. It is sad that Anne Bradstreet did not live quite long enough to read this small but impressive work. To know that her poems were still noticed and admired in England, more than twenty years after their publication, would probably have pleased her even more than to see her name heading the list of distinguished and interesting women.

The other commentator was Edward Phillips, John Milton's nephew, who published in 1675 his *Theatrum Poetarum: or a complete Collection of the Poets.* Under the heading, "Women among the Moderns Eminent for Poetry," he noted:

Anne Broadstreet, a New-England Poetess, no less in title, viz. before her Poems, printed in Old England anno 1650; then *The tenth Muse Sprung up in America*, the memory of which Poems, consisting chiefly of Descriptions of the four Elements, the four Humours, the four Ages, the four Seasons, and the four Monarchies, is not yet wholly extinct.[19]

19. *Theatrum Poetarum*, Part II, p. 254.

Phillips gave unstinted praise to one, and rather sarcastic recognition to the other, of the only two women writers of this period whose stature can be considered to rival that of Anne Bradstreet. As different in their own characters and backgrounds as they were both unlike their New England contemporary, they gained more acclaim and attention in their own day and are now, as fate will have it, much less remembered and commented upon than the author of *The Tenth Muse.*

The eldest, first published, and most prolific of these two ladies was born Margaret Lucas in 1623, became the second wife of William Cavendish, Duke of Newcastle, and lived until 1673. Her great energy, combined with eccentricity in dress, manners, opinions, and literary expression, made her notorious as a "Fantastic" as well as admired, by many of her contemporaries, for her writings. From 1645, when they were married in Paris, she and her husband lived abroad, often in financial difficulties, until the restoration of the monarchy in 1660, but like Anne Bradstreet, who was also in a sense an exile from her native land, Margaret Cavendish was supported, fulfilled, and encouraged in her literary labors by an ideally happy marriage. Her first book, *Poems, and Fancies,* appeared in London in 1653; it is prefaced by five epistles and three sets of verses in all of which the authoress apologizes for her presumption and begs understanding indulgence from her readers. The last of these introductory pieces, called "An excuse for so much writ upon my Verses," has a touch of naïve charm which is ordinarily lacking in the Duchess's pedantic and unmusical productions.

> Condemne me not for making such a coyle
> About my *Book,* alas it is my *Childe.*
> Just like a *Bird,* when her *Young* are in Nest,
> Goes in, and out, and hops, and takes no Rest;

But when their *Young* are fledg'd, their heads out peep,
Lord what a chirping does the *Old* one keep.
So I, for feare my *Strengthlesse Childe* should fall
Against a doore, or stoole, aloud I call,
Bid have a care of such a dangerous place:
Thus write I much, to hinder all *disgrace.*

The poems, and a few short prose pieces, that follow, are concerned with nature, science, the virtues and vices, and man's relation to them all, and are the fruits of imaginative speculation
rather than of acquired knowledge. After this curious volume the
Duchess published, within fifteen years, eleven more separate
works, of verse, prose, and plays, and during her lifetime there
appeared second editions, and even a third, of some of her books.
But the only one of all these for which she is, deservedly, remembered with respect is her biography of her husband: *The Life of
the thrice Noble, High and Puissant Prince William Cavendishe,
Duke, Marquess, and Earl of Newcastle; . . . Written by the
thrice Noble, Illustrious, and Excellent Princess, Margaret, Duchess of Newcastle, his wife.* This had its first printing in 1667 and
another in 1675; it was re-edited by Sir Charles Firth, in 1886,
and published as *The Life of William Cavendish, Duke of New-
Castle, to which is added The True Relation of my . . . Life, by
Margaret, Duchess of Newcastle.* Her modern biographer, Douglas Grant, in *Margaret the First* (1957), deals sympathetically
and generously with his unwieldy subject, but in Edward Phillips's entry on her, published two years after her death, there is
a note of irony which points to her being almost as overpowering to her own contemporaries as she seems today.

Margaret, Duchess of New-Castle, lately decreas't, a very ob-
liging Lady to the World; and withall not regardless of her own
future Fame, by so largely and copiously imparting to public

view her studious Endeavours in the Arts and Ingenuities, there being three ample Volumes of her in Print, one of Orations, the other of Philosophical Notions and Discourses, the third of Dramatic and other kinds of Poetry.[20]

And a last word on her, which is also a sharp comment on all the literary ladies of the time, comes from Dorothy Osborne, that woman of letters in the most literal sense, whose private correspondence with her intended husband, never in the least meant for publication, has been a delight to readers for almost a century. "Let me ask you," Dorothy wrote to Sir William Temple, in 1653,

if you have seen a book of poems newly come out, made by my Lady Newcastle? For God's sake if you meet with it send it to me; they say 'tis ten times more extravagant than her dress. Sure, the poor woman is a little distracted, she could never be so ridiculous else as to venture at writing books, and in verse too. If I should not sleep this fortnight I should not come to that.[21]

Born in 1632 and destined to live for only thirty-two years, Katherine Fowler, the wife of James Philips of Cardigan in Wales, was an accomplished and gifted woman whom Douglas Bush calls "the first real English poetess." [22] She was a disciple of the stylish minor poet William Cartwright, and her circle of literary friends and acquaintances included Henry Vaughan, Abraham Cowley, and Bishop Jeremy Taylor. Edward Phillips saluted her as "the most applauded, at this time, Poetess of our Nation . . . her Fame is of a fresh and lively date from the but

20. *Theatrum Poetarum*, Part II, p. 259.
21. *Letters from Dorothy Osborne to Sir William Temple*, ed. E. A. Parry, New York, 1888, pp. 96–97.
22. *English Literature in the Earlier Seventeenth Century*, p. 125.

late publisht Volume of her Poetical works, and those also of a style suitable to the humour and Genius of these times." [23]

Known to her admirers as "the matchless Orinda," Mrs. Philips wrote many fashionable poetic tributes to her husband, "Antenor," and to others close to her who had adopted such classical names as Rosania, Lucasia, Silvander, and so on. She also translated from the French St. Amant's long poem, "La Solitude," and two of Corneille's tragedies, *Pompey* and *Horace.* Her writings were circulated in manuscript and aroused so much interest that a pirated edition of the poems appeared early in 1664. Her friends in London immediately took steps to have this publication suppressed, and when the dismayed authoress herself came up from Wales to pursue the matter, she contracted smallpox and died in London in June of that year. A corrected edition of her poems, with the translations, was published in 1667, in an attractive folio volume; other editions followed in 1669, 1678, and 1710. A selection of her verse, edited by J. R. Tutin, appeared in 1904, and George Saintsbury reprinted the poems from the 1678 text in *Minor Poets of the Caroline Period* (1905). Mrs. Philips is represented in many anthologies, and her work and life were given a thorough study by Philip Webster Souers in *The Matchless Orinda,* (1931). Although her graceful lyrics are more polished and elegant in style than almost all of Anne Bradstreet's poems, they are limited by the somewhat affected Platonism of their composition, and lack the vigor and forthrightness of the New England woman's writing.

Three more literary women, from the latter years of the seventeenth century, may be mentioned. Anne Collins, of whom nothing is known beyond her name on the title-page of a small volume of one hundred and two pages, was the author of *Divine*

23. *Theatrum Poetarum,* Part II, p. 257.

Songs and Meditations in 1653. Of this collection of pious effusions only one copy appears to have survived; this is in the Huntington Library in California, and has lately been given a partial rebirth in the printing of about half of its contents by the Augustan Reprint Society in 1961. Anne Finch, Countess of Winchelsea (1661–1720), was to some extent a follower of "Orinda." Her rather sombre poems, written for her husband, "Daphnis," and her circle of friends, among whom was Alexander Pope, did not appear in print until 1713. Wordsworth's admiration for the Countess's descriptions of nature caused a revival of interest in her almost forgotten work, and eventually an edition of the poems, prepared by Myra Reynolds, was published in Chicago in 1903.

In great contrast to the refinement of all these women writers was the rugged and uninhibited personality of the first professional English authoress, Mrs. Aphra Behn. Born in 1640 of humble parents, she was taken by well-to-do friends to spend her adolescent years in the English colony of Surinam in Guiana. Returning to London she married a Dutch merchant named Behn, and when he died in 1666 she was able to obtain from King Charles II a commission as a secret agent in Holland. But within the year she was back again in London, and so poor that it is believed that she spent some time in prison for debt. She then began to write plays, frankly for money, and with the intricate plots, witty and licentious dialogue, and amorous preoccupations calculated to please the Restoration audiences. Between "The Forced Marriage" of 1670 and "The Rover" in 1677, her greatest success, "the incomparable Astrea," as she was called, became the toast of the literary taverns and coffee-houses, and numbered among her friends the Earl of Rochester, John Dryden, Edmund Waller, and Sir Peter Lely. She also published romances, the most famous of which, *Oroonoko* (1678), is set in the tropical splendors of Guiana. The fine lyric that begins "Love in Fantastique Triumph satt" is the most celebrated of her poems; these range from graceful, sometimes ribald, songs and ballads to solemn elegies for her distinguished friends, and appeared in print in 1684.

Mrs. Behn died in 1689, and was given the honor of a poet's grave in Westminster Abbey, next to that of Abraham Cowley. Her works were increasingly neglected during the eighteenth and most of the nineteenth century, but in our own time she has been revived in the six-volume edition, *The Works of Aphra Behn, with a Memoir*, prepared by the Reverend Montague Summers and published in 1915, and by Victoria Sackville-West's biography, *Aphra Behn: The Incomparable Astrea*, of 1928. A useful paperback, *Selected Writings of the Ingenious Mrs. Aphra Behn*, edited with an introduction by Robert Phelps, appeared in 1950.

Supported by two centuries of published writing by women, and her own irrepressible strength of character, Mrs. Behn won herself a respected place in the man's world of literature. The fact that this place was so long withheld from any woman, and so hard to win, has been commented upon, with insight and feeling, by Virginia Woolf in her essay *A Room of One's Own*. She emphasizes the loneliness and frustration of the women who longed to express themselves in creative writing, and cites the bizarre Duchess of Newcastle and the melancholy Countess of Winchelsea as examples of talented writers whose productions were "disfigured and deformed" by the weight of public opinion against them. As a telling illustration of this attitude Mrs. Woolf quotes Dorothy Osborne's withering words about "a book of poems . . . made by my Lady Newcastle," but, coming to the end of the seventeenth century and of the long struggle of women for acceptance as writers, she says:

All women together ought to let flowers fall on the tomb of Aphra Behn, for it was she who earned them the right to speak their minds.

Mrs. Woolf makes an interesting point which seems to have a relation to the argument, in this study, concerning Anne Bradstreet's position in English literature. Considering the obscurity of women in the sixteenth century, as revealed by the records that have come down to us, she writes:

> Occasionally an individual woman is mentioned, an Elizabeth or a Mary, a queen or a great lady. But by no possible means could middle-class women with nothing but brains and character at their command have taken part in any one of the great movements which, brought together, constitute the historian's view of the past.[24]

This is, however, exactly what Anne Bradstreet did, only about a quarter-century after the death of Queen Elizabeth I. As a middle-class woman, certainly equipped with brains and character, she was privileged to take part in a great movement, the opening up of the new English world of North America. And in so doing she liberated herself not only as a woman and a Puritan, but also as a poet.

It seems reasonable to conclude that Anne Bradstreet wrote more freely, and with less self-consciousness, in the sharp fresh air of Massachusetts than she would have done in the more conventional atmosphere of the mother-country. If she had remained in England she would almost certainly have written verse and had it published, because she was determined to be a poet. But I believe that much of the passion and aspiration that went into what she wrote in New England would have been suppressed,

24. *A Room of One's Own*, 1929, p. 62.

or greatly enfeebled, by the traditional confinements and taboos of the kind of life she would have led in the homeland.

In the Massachusetts Bay colony life was a very different matter; from the start of the venture men, women, and children too, were equally involved in the struggle for survival, equally exposed to the perils of famine, disease, cold, and the ever-lurking Indians. It was inevitable that the women, who stood shoulder to shoulder with their men through the first hard years of settlement, and took their full share of the dangers and discouragements, the responsibilities and even the practical planning, should have come to be judged not as a weak and ineffectual group, but on their merits as individuals, and should have won the respect and privileges that those merits deserved. John Woodbridge's introductory epistle to *The Tenth Muse* is an excellent illustration of this new attitude, superimposing on the time-honored condescension towards "the inferiour Sex" the writer's undisguised admiration for the character and accomplishment of his sister-in-law.

So it would appear that Anne Bradstreet did in a way, although a very different way so far as method and manner were concerned, in New England what Aphra Behn, later in the century, did in old England. That is, the author of *The Tenth Muse*, though her writing was tentative at the start, developed so stalwart an individuality both in her work and in her personal conduct that the attention of the men around her was bound to be focused on her outstanding qualities, and, through her, on the potentialities of her sex; thus she had, undoubtedly, an early and a leading share in earning for the women of the New World "the right to speak their minds."

CHAPTER NINE

Later Poetry and Prose

"My Fathers God, be God of me and mine."
(ANNE BRADSTREET—*To the Memory of . . .*
Thomas Dudley, Esq.)

Three years after the publication of *The Tenth Muse,* on the 31st July, 1653, Anne Bradstreet's beloved and revered father died, at his home in Roxbury, in his seventy-seventh year. The old Elizabethan had served his people faithfully and well; he was in office as deputy governor until the 18th May, only two and a half months before his death. Governor Thomas Hutchinson, in his eighteenth-century *History of the Colony and Province of Massachusetts-Bay,* wrote that Thomas Dudley died

> greatly lamented, being a principal founder of the colony, and having recommended himself by great firmness and fidelity in the discharge of his trust; having never been out of the magistracy, and generally either governor or deputy governor. He was zealous, beyond measure, against all sorts of hereticks.[1]

It is not surprising that so uncompromising a Puritan theocrat should have made lasting enemies, as well as devoted friends and

1. *Hutchinson's History of Massachusetts-Bay* (Boston, 1764), ed. Lawrence Shaw Mayo, Cambridge (Mass.), 1936, Vol. I, p. 156 (note).

followers. His daughter's elegiac tribute of eighty lines, "To the Memory of my dear and ever honoured Father, Thomas Dudley, Esq.," which apeared in the second edition of her poems, recognizes the existence of his critics with her usual honesty, salutes his public achievement with formal dignity, and grieves for him with deep personal feeling. "My mournfull mind," she says,

> Presents my Lamentations at his Herse,
> Who was my Father, Guide, Instructer too,
> To whom I ought whatever I could doe:
>
> *   *   *
>
> Let malice bite, and envy knaw its fill,
> He was my Father, and Ile praise him still.
>
> *   *   *
>
> Well known and lov'd, where'ere he liv'd, by most
> Both in his native, and in foreign coast,
>
> *   *   *
>
> One of thy Founders, him *New-England* know,
> Who staid thy feeble sides when thou wast low,
> Who spent his state, his strength, & years with care
> That After-comers in them might have share.
> True Patriot of this little Commonweal,
> Who is't can tax thee ought, but for thy zeal?
> Truths friend thou wert, to errors still a foe,
> Which caus'd Apostates to maligne so.
> Thy love to true Religion e're shall shine,
> My Fathers God, be God of me and mine.
> Upon the earth he did not build his nest,
> But as a Pilgrim, what he had, possest.
> High thoughts he gave no harbour in his heart,
> Nor honours pufft him up, when he had part:
> Those titles loath'd, which some too much do love
> For truly his ambition lay above.

*   *   *

Now fully ripe, as shock of wheat that's grown,
Death as a Sickle hath him timely mown,
And in celestial Barn hath hous'd him high,
Where storms, nor showrs, nor ought can damnifie.

*   *   *

His pious Footsteps followed by his race,
At last will bring us to that happy place
Where we with joy each others face shall see,
And parted more by death shall never be.

His Epitaph

Within this Tomb a Patriot lyes
That was both pious, just and wise,
To Truth a shield, to right a Wall,
To Sectaryes a whip and Maul,
A Magazine of History,
A Prizer of good Company
In manners pleasant and severe
The Good him lov'd, the bad did fear,
And when his time with years was spent
If some rejoyc'd, more did lament.

Harold Jantz calls this poem "a noble and warm defense of a stern and gentle man," and goes on to say: "The brief concluding epitaph is one of the finest and surest word portraits of the period." [2]

Dudley, who was one of the richest men of the colony, left an estate valued at £1560. 10s. 1d., carefully distributed, in his will, to his children by both marriages, and his grandchildren. [3] A Latin epitaph, attributed to his friend the Reverend Ezekiel

2. *First Century of New Engalnd Verse*, pp. 37–38.
3. Will of Thomas Dudley: *Suffolk County, Massachusetts, Probate Court Records*, Vol. I, p. 90.

Rogers, calls him *"Helluo Librorum, Lectorum Bibliotheca Communis, Sacrae Syllabus Historiae"*;[4] his library, or what was left of it at the time of his death, when he had probably given away many books to his friends and family, is itemized in the inventory of his possessions.[5]

Undoubtedly the strongest of Thomas Dudley's convictions, which he shared with such of the colony's founders as John Winthrop and Nathaniel Ward, was an unswerving devotion to the Calvinist form of worship and way of life; his horror of any sort of religious toleration is strongly expressed in the preamble to his will:

> For my sole I commend it into the hand of my God in whome I have beleved, whome I have loved, which hee hath promised to receive in Jesus Christ my redeemer & saviour, with whome I desire ever to bee, leaveing this testimony behinde mee for the use & example of my posteritie, and any other upon whome it may worke, that I have hated & doe hate every falce way in religion, not onely the Old Idolitry and superstition of Popery, which is weareing away, but much more, (as being much worse), the newe heresies, blasphamies, & errors of late sprange upp in our native Country of England, and secretly received & fostered here more then I wishe they were.

And as though to reiterate this rigid philosophy in a more immediate and personal way, he left, to be "found after his Death, in his Pocket," as Cotton Mather wrote, "these Lines of his own Composing," the only bit of his verse-making that survives from his efforts to prove that he too could be a poet.

> Dim Eyes, Deaf Ears, Cold Stomach, shew
> My Dissolution is in View.

4. C. Mather, *Magnalia*, Book II, p. 17: "A Devourer of books, in himself a choice collector; a compend of sacred history."
5. See Appendix: Thomas Dudley's Books.

Eleven times Seven near liv'd have I,
And now God calls, I willing Die.
My Shuttle's shot, my Race is run,
My Sun is set, my Day is done.
My Span is measur'd, Tale is told,
My Flower is faded, and grown old.
My Dream is vanish'd, Shadow's fled,
My Soul with Christ, my Body Dead.
Farewel Dear Wife, Children and Friends,
Hate Heresie, make Blessed Ends.
Bear Poverty, live with good Men;
So shall we live with Joy agen.
Let Men of God in Courts and Churches watch
O're such as do a *Toleration* hatch,
Lest that Ill Egg bring forth a Cockatrice,
To poison all with Heresie and Vice.
If Men be left, and otherwise Combine,
My *Epitaph's,* I DY'D NO LIBERTINE.[6]

Another example of the family's taste for poetic composition
has survived in one imperfect copy of *An Almanack for the Year
of our Lord 1657 . . . by S. B. Philomathemat,* in the collection
of the American Antiquarian Society in Worcester, Massachusetts.
This was the work of the Bradstreets' eldest son, Samuel, who
graduated from Harvard in 1653. It must have pleased his mother
to see above his name, on the second page of the almanac, a six-
stanza poem celebrating in flowery Spenserian language Apollo's
wooing of the earth-goddess Tellus.[7] In November 1657 Samuel
went to England to study medicine, remaining until the summer
of 1661. Among Anne Bradstreet's private devotional poems is
one on his departure, and another giving thanks for his safe
return.

During the decade after the publication of *The Tenth Muse*

6. *Magnalia,* Book II, p. 17.
7. Reprinted in *The Puritans,* ed. Miller and Johnson, p. 632.

Anne was occupied with personal and family affairs, some of them disturbing and all of them demanding of her time and strength. She did not cease to write, but her writings that have survived from this period are, with the exception of the elegy for her father, entirely subjective and informal, reflecting her absorption in the things that were happening around her, and in her own spiritual and bodily state.

When her father died, her youngest child, John, born the 22nd July, 1652, was just over a year old, and her house was full of adolescents and children. Samuel, just graduated from Harvard, was probably living temporarily at home; the two eldest daughters, Dorothy and Sarah, were beginning to think of marriage; Simon, the only one absent, was in his third year, as his diary has told us, at school in Ipswich. The two younger girls, Hannah and Mercy, were about eleven and seven, and little Dudley was five. The mother of this quiverfull was in her forty-first year, and even with the help of her elder daughters and some domestic servants she must have been endlessly engaged in attending to the needs, activities, and welfare of this large family, particularly as her husband was required to be often away from home on his official duties, thus leaving her in sole charge of the household in Andover.

As a result of all this responsibility, perhaps made more arduous by the onset of her physical climacteric, her health, which for the most part had been reasonably good during her child-bearing years, began to fail. She left an interesting, and very poignant, record of the recurring bouts of illness, in the devotional legacy for her childern which she probably decided to prepare at about this time, under the impression that her life might be drawing to its close. This was the manuscript which was copied by Simon Bradstreet, Junior, from the now lost original, into the little book already containing the "Meditations Divine and morall" which his mother had written for and bequeathed to him.[8]

"A true copy of a Book left by my hon'd & dear mother to her children & found among some papers after her Death" begins:

TO MY DEAR CHILDREN

This Book by Any yet unread
I leave for you when I am dead,
That being gone, here you may find
What was your liveing mothers mind.
Make use of what I leave in Love
And God shall blesse you from above.

A. B.

My dear children,

I knowing by experience that the exhortations of parents make most effect when the speakers leave to speak, and more especially sink deepest which are spoke latest, and being ignorant whether on my death bed I shall have opportunity to speak to any of you, much lesse to All, thought it the best whilst I was able to compose some short matters, (for what else to call them I know not) and bequeath to you, that when I am no more with you, yet I may bee dayly in your remembrance, (Although that is the least in my aim in what I now doe) but that you may gain

---

8. This manuscript book is now in the Anne Bradstreet collection in the Stevens Memorial Library, North Andover, Massachusetts. The portion of it copied by Simon Bradstreet, Junior, was first printed entire, under the title "Religious Experiences and Occasional Pieces," by J. H. Ellis in his edition of Anne Bradstreet's *Works*, Charlestown (Mass.), 1867. It appears again (without the covering title) in *The Works of Anne Bradstreet*, ed. Jeannine Hensley, Cambridge (Mass.), 1967. Another copy of the portion of the manuscript that is in Simon's hand exists; it was made by his sister Sarah Hubbard and is now in the Houghton Library at Harvard University.

some spiritual Advantage by my experience. I have not studied in this you read to shew my skill, but to declare the Truth, not to sett forth my self, but the Glory of God. If I had minded the former it had been perhaps better pleasing to you, but seing the last is the best, let it bee best pleasing to you.

The method I will observe shall bee this—I will begin with Gods dealing with me from my childhood to this Day.

Then follow the various affirmations, which have already been quoted throughout this study, of Anne's increasing awareness, from the age of "about 6 or 7 as I take it," of the importance of religious faith and discipline in her life. She records a serious childhood illness, then the alarming fact that at "about 14 or 15 I found my heart more carnall, . . . vanitye and the follyes of youth take hold of me." After this came in quick succession the chastening attack of smallpox, marriage, and the drastic change to "a new world and new manners, at which my heart rose" in dismay. Then acceptance and endurance of the first two years of settlement, another "lingering sicknes," and finally the longed-for birth of her first child, "and after him . . . many more."

There is not a single reference, in the twenty-three closely written manuscript pages of this spiritual testament, to Anne Bradstreet's vocation as a poet. Although the document contains sixteen sets of verses of varying lengths (besides the few introductory lines), either in the old "fourteeners" of the ballads and paraphrased psalms, or in four-stressed iambic quatrains, these are all metrical prayers, or ejaculations of thankfulness, such as filled the private commonplace books of the literate believers of the period. Anne probably felt that her public writings could speak for themselves, as it were, but that what was behind and around them, as well as behind and around all other aspects of her life, her constant personal relationship with God, should be expressed in words of praise and thanksgiving not only for the fulfillment of her own spirit but also for the benefit of her children's minds and hearts.

Among all my experiences of Gods gratious Dealings with me I have constantly observed this that he hath never suffered me long to sitt loose from him, but by one affliction or other hath made me look home, and search what was amisse. So usually thus it hath been with me that I have no sooner felt my heart out of order, but I have expected correction for it, which most commonly hath been upon my own person, in sicknesse, weaknes, paines, sometimes on my soul, in Doubts and feares of Gods displeasure, and my sincerity towards him. Sometimes he hath smott a child with sicknes, sometimes chasstned by losses in estate, and these Times (through his great mercy) have been the times of my greatest Getting and Advantage, yea I have found them the Times when the Lord hath manifested the most Love to me. . . .

I have been with God like an untoward child, that no longer then the rod has been on my back (or at least in sight) but I have been apt to forgett him and my Self too. Before I was afflicted I went astray, but now I keep thy Statutes. . . .

But some new Troubles I have had since the World has been filled with Blasphemy, and Sectaries, and some who have been accounted sincere Christians have been carryed away with them, that sometimes I have said, Is there ffaith upon the Earth? And I have not known what to think. But then I have remembred the words of Christ that so it must bee, and that if it were possible the very elect should bee deceived. Behold saith our Saviour I have told you before. That hath stayed my heart, and I can now say, Return O my Soul to thy Rest, upon this Rock Christ Jesus will I build my faith, and if I perish, I perish. But I know all the Powers of Hell shall never prevail against it, I know whom I have trusted, and whom I have believed, and that he is able to keep that I have committed to his charge.

Now to the King, Immortall, Eternall and invisible, the only wise God, bee Honoure, and Glory for ever and Ever,

Amen.

This was written in much sicknesse and weaknes, and is very weakly and imperfectly done, but if you can pick any Benefitt out of it, It is the mark which I aimed at.

The long introduction is followed by four "occasionall meditations" in verse and one in prose, giving thanks to God for comfort in sorrow and for deliverance from "a feaver," "a fitt of ffainting," and the fear of death. These are all undated, but on "July 8th, 1656" Anne records:

I had a sore fitt of fainting, which lasted 2 or 3 dayes, but not in that extremity which at first it took me, and so much the sorer it was to me because my dear husband was from home (who is my chiefest comforter on Earth) but my God who never failed me was not absent but helped me. . . .

Again in August of the same year, and in May of 1657:

After much weaknes and sicknes when my spirits were worn out, and many times my faith weak likewise, the Lord was pleased to uphold my drooping heart, and to manifest his Love to me. . . .
I had a sore sicknes and weaknes took hold of me which hath by fitts lasted all this spring till this 11 May, yet hath my God given me many a respite, and some ability to perform the Dutyes I owe to him, and the work of my famely.

Immediately after this comes a short poem of rejoicing, dated "May 13, 1657." Anne's gratitude to her maker, the Sun of Righteousness, seems to reflect the restoration of health to her body and spirit, her pleasure in the beauty of the season, and perhaps the fact that Simon Bradstreet, her earthly Sun, had come home for an extended stay.

As Spring the winter doth succeed
And leaves the naked Trees doe dresse
The earth all black is cloth'd in green
At sun-shine each their joy expresse.

My Suns returned with healing wings
My Soul and Body doth rejoice,
My heart exults and praises sings
To him that heard my wailing Voice.

My winters past my stormes are gone
And former clowdes seem now all fled
But if they must eclipse again
I'le run where I was succoured.

I have a shelter from the storm
A shadow from the fainting heat
I have accesse unto his Throne,
Who is a God so wondrous great.

Finally, the entry for "Sept. 30, 1657" brings this section of the manuscript to an end:

It pleased God to viset me with my old Distemper of weaknes and fainting, but not in that sore manner somtimes he hath. I desire not only willingly but thankfully to submitt to him for I trust it is out of his abundant Love to my straying Soul which in prosperity is too much in love with the World. I have found by experience I can no more live without correction then without food. Lord with thy correction give Instruction and amendment, and then thy stroakes shall bee welcome. I have not been refined in the furnace of affliction as some have been, but have rather been preserved with sugar then brine, yet will he preserve me to his heavenly Kingdom.

Thus (dear children) have yee seen the many sicknesses and

weaknesses that I have passed through: to the end that if you meet with the like you may have recourse to the same God who hath heard and delivered me, and will doe the like for you if you trust in him; And when he shall deliver you out of distresse forgett not to give him thankes, but to walk more closely with him then before, This is the desire of your Loving mother.

A. B.

This private spiritual autobiography contributes greatly to an understanding of Anne Bradstreet's literary personality. Only three of the eighteen poems that she released to "publick view" are specific statements of her own religious faith; one, "Of the vanity of all worldly creatures," was written before 1650 and printed in *The Tenth Muse* [9]; the other two were composed later and will be discussed in the next chapter. These three poems steadfastly argue the supremacy of unearthly values over the transient material offerings of the world; they are orthodox examples of Puritan belief. It is in her private confession, which she wished to share, posthumously, with her children, of the wrestlings of her imagination and human passion with her uncompromising theological heritage, that we find revealed the source of the element of conflict which has been noted earlier in this study,[10] and about which a recent commentator has this to say:

Again and again, during Anne Bradstreet's pilgrimage through the new world, there was the rising of the heart either in dismay or rebellion and the assertion of the self against the dogma she encountered. Next, there was the need for conviction. It was only after persuasion that she could ever submit to the "way." Rebellion and a struggle for or against conviction form a pattern which runs through her writing. It is the statement of dogma

9. See pp. 241–44 above.
10. See pp. 171–72 and 177–78 above.

and the concurrent feeling of resistance to dogma that give much of that writing the vitality we are still conscious of today.[11]

As her father's daughter, Anne could be deeply distressed that the world was filled "with Blasphemy, and Sectaries," but she could also permit herself to think, and even to commit to writing, such heresies as would have horrified Thomas Dudley, that staunch condemner of anything that suggested a "toleration." She recorded that "Satan" had tempted her "many times by Atheisme" to question whether or not there was a God, and if so, "such a God as I worship in Trinity, and such a Saviour as I rely upon?" Then when her contemplation of the earth, the seasons, and "the order of all things" had convinced her that there must be an "Eternall Being," she would wonder if her way of worship was the only true one, and "why may not the Popish Religion bee the right?"

In the end, these doubts and misgivings were always conquered, not so much by a conscientious loyalty to Puritan dogma as by an essential faith in "this Rock Christ Jesus" and the certainty that "he is able to keep that I have committed to his charge." Anne Bradstreet was not the only New Englander who was assailed by hard questions of the spirit; in the middle 1650's, when most of the elder founding fathers, like Winthrop, Dudley, John Cotton, and Thomas Hooker were dead, there came a faltering in the general acceptance of the Covenant of Grace, the individual experience of election and conversion that had united the first wave of the settlers in their aspiration to build a New Jerusalem in the American wilderness.

Norman Pettit, in a recent study of Puritan theology in New England, has pointed out that:

11. Ann Stanford, "Anne Bradstreet, Dogmatist and Rebel," in *The New England Quarterly*, Vol. XXXIX, No. 3 (Sept. 1966), p. 374.

The members of the second generation were naturally not pitched to the high key of piety which had marked the Great Migration to the Bay. However much they may have sympathized with their elders' views, there were many among them who could not honestly claim to have known the unique experience which their parents had described as a gradual change of heart. As a result, there arose a class of people virtually set apart from the regenerate community, people for whom the theories of the founders were far too strenuous and demanding.[12]

Facing this problem, the ministers of the colonial churches, many of whom held divergent opinions themselves as to the efficacy of baptism, the necessity of the believer's conscious preparation for the phenomenon of conversion, and the irrevocability of the conversion itself, came together in several conventions and synods to review, and if necessary revise, the requirements for Church membership and the standards of religious discipline. The result of these conferences was, in brief, an opening of the doors of most, if not all, of the New England churches to those who would "do all in their power to lead a religious life and seek a Christian hope," [13] while not requiring them to give public testimony as to their actual transformation by saving grace.

This return to the sanctity of the inner life, immune from the probings of others, gave rise to a genuine sense of spiritual release. What is more, it allowed for a freedom of religious thought hitherto unknown in New England.[14]

Anne Bradstreet seems to exemplify, in her own inner life of faith, this mid-century change from the earlier rigid Puritan ethos

12. *The Heart Prepared: Grace and Conversion in Puritan Spiritual Life,* New Haven, 1966, p. 190.
13. *Ibid.* p. 198.
14. *Ibid.* p. 205.

to the more liberal search for the truth and for constant re-conversion to the "way." Although she grew up among the tensions in England that created the Great Migration, was closely associated with the founders, and received her religious education from one of the most inflexibly orthodox among them, her father, she belonged to the younger generation of the settlers. She had her family's adventurousness of mind, an unusually generous education in the humanities, and an unbigoted husband: Simon Bradstreet supported the broadening of ecclesiastical standards,[15] was a moderate in politics,[16] and, in his old age, was courageous in his refusal to co-operate with the hysterical fanaticism of the witchcraft trials.[17]

So it would appear that time and circumstances were, in a religious sense, on the side of Anne Bradstreet. The conflicts that are recorded in her private journal, and echoed from time to time, as Ann Stanford notes, in her public writings, were nowhere nearly as alarming to her children's generation as they would have been to that of her father. While the orthodox Puritan dogma was an inherent force in her life, her independent and inquiring mind found it necessary to examine critically a number of its tenets; that she could do so, however unobtrusively, was partly due to the beginnings of freer thought among her contemporaries, but more particularly because "the sanctity of the inner life," her own faith in a just and benevolent God, was ultimately inviolable.

On the 14th June, 1654, the first marriage in the Bradstreet family took place. Dorothy, the eldest daughter, then about eighteen years old, became the bride of the Reverend Seaborn Cotton, eldest son of the great Boston minister John Cotton, who

15. *Ibid.* p. 207.
16. Perry Miller, *The New England Mind: From Colony to Province,* p. 137.
17. J. G. Palfrey, *History of New England,* Vol. IV, p. 121.

was born in 1633 on board the ship *Griffin* while his father was escaping to New England from the officers of the Court of High Commission.[18] About two years later the second daughter, Sarah, also in her late teens, was married to Richard Hubbard of Ipswich, whose brother William was to become one of the historians of the colony. Apparently this marriage was not solemnized in Andover, as it is not entered in the Vital Records of the town. In this year, 1656, Anne Bradstreet had two serious attacks of illness, which she dated in her private journal "July 8th" (when her husband was away from home) and "August 28th"; perhaps for this reason she was not well enough to attend to the arrangements for a daughter's wedding, and Sarah may have been married in Ipswich, or in Wethersfield, Connecticut, where Dorothy and Seaborn Cotton were living at that time.

Also, on "June 25th, 1656," Simon Bradstreet, Junior, recorded in his diary, "I was admitted into the university, Mr Charles Chauncy being President." So three of the young Bradstreets, in fairly rapid succession, took their different ways from home, and the next year, during which Anne had several onsets of ill-health, brought the most drastic and alarming departure up to this time, when Samuel, the eldest of the flock, left on the 6th November, 1657, for four years' study of medicine in England. He was a passenger on the smaller of two ships that sailed together from Boston; the voyage, in that stormy season, probably took eight weeks or somewhat longer, but his family may have had to wait as long as eight months for news of his arrival. A contemporary diarist, John Hull, noted in June 1658, that a ship from England brought word that of the two that had sailed from Boston in the previous November, the larger one, with about fifty passengers

18. *Vital Records of Andover, Mass.*, Topsfield (Mass.), 1912, Vol. II, p. 62; also John Winthrop, *History of New England*, ed. Savage, Vol. I, pp. 128, 129, 131.

and a valuable cargo, had never been heard from and was presumed lost with all the souls on board.[19]

Anne Bradstreet's anxiety for the safety of her eldest, "The child I stay'd for many yeares," is expressed in a short poem, "Upon my Son Samuel his goeing for England," with which she resumed the recording of her personal memoirs in the manuscript book bequeathed to her children. The urgent verse-prayer contains a hint of the struggle between her human emotions and her religious faith, as well as, in the final line, one of the curious made-up words that she occasionally used.

> Preserve O Lord from stormes and wrack
> Protect him there and bring him back.
> And if thou shalt spare me a space
> That I again may see his face,
> Then shall I celebrate thy Praise
> And Blesse thee for't even all my Dayes.
> If otherwise I goe to Rest
> Thy Will be done, for that is best.
> Perswade my heart I shall him see
> Forever happefy'd with Thee.

In spite of her concern for her son, and her other family responsibilities, Anne's health improved again towards the end of 1657, and continued to be reasonably good until the beginning of 1661. "It hath pleased God to give me a Long Time of respite for these 4 years that I have had no great fitt of sicknes, but this year, from the middle of January 'till May, I have been by fitts very ill and weak," she wrote on the 11th May, 1661.

The next of the young Bradstreets to leave home was Dudley, who, aged about ten in 1658, probably went to Ezekiel Cheever's school in Ipswich in that year. Also in 1658 Anne Bradstreet began

19. *Works of Anne Bradstreet*, ed. J. H. Ellis, pp. 29–30 (note).

to write the poem called "In reference to her Children," which is the longest and one of the pleasantest of the thirteen pieces of personal verse included in the second edition of her work.

As she watched her older children growing into maturity and finding their way into adult life, Anne Bradstreet must have realized that she had become, in her mid-forties, a member of the older generation, with the most creative of her years behind her. And the recurrent attacks of illness gave her reason to believe that her life might be nearing its end. Yet verse was still her natural medium of expression; though she could not know it, there were fourteen more years in store for her, during which she was to write two formal poems of outstanding merit and several memorable personal ones.

The narrator image that she chose for her ninety-four lines, in four-stressed iambic couplets, about and to her children, was that of a mother-bird, anxious for the welfare of her young ones as they grew up and began to leave the nest. Although the symbolism is sometimes quaintly absurd, in general it is carried off with ingenuity and charm, and the tenderness and concern that animate the whole poem make one feel that Anne Bradstreet must have been a delightful parent (as well as a conscientious disciplinarian), sympathetic and understanding, humorous and sometimes even gay, a sharer of learning and a teacher of wisdom, whose unfailing love for her children was reflected in the love and respect that they felt for her and in the good and fruitful lives that all of them seem to have led. The poem begins:

> I had eight birds hatcht in one nest,
> Four Cocks there were, and Hens the rest,
> I nurst them up with pain and care,
> Nor cost, nor labour did I spare,
> Till at the last they felt their wing,
> Mounted the Trees, and learn'd to sing;

Chief of the Brood then took his flight,
To Regions far, and left me quite:
My mournful chirps I after send,
Till he return, or I do end,
Leave not thy nest, thy Dam and Sire,
Fly back and sing amidst this Quire.
My second bird did take her flight,
And with her mate flew out of sight;
Southward they both their course did bend,
And Seasons twain they there did spend:
Till after blown by *Southern* gales,
They *Norward* steer'd with filled sayles.
A prettier bird was no where seen,
Along the Beach among the treen.
I have a third of colour white,
On whom I plac'd no small delight;
Coupled with mate loving and true,
Hath also bid her Dam adieu:
And where *Aurora* first appears,
She now hath percht, to spend her years;
One to the Academy flew
To chat among that learned crew:
Ambition moves still in his breast
That he might chant above the rest,
Striving for more then to do well,
That nightingales he might excell.
My fifth, whose down is yet scarce gone
Is 'mongst the shrubs and Bushes flown,
And as his wings increase in strength,
On higher boughs he'l pearch at length.
My other three, still with me nest,
Untill they'r grown, then as the rest,
Or here or there, they'l take their flight,
As is ordain'd, so shall they light.

The reader will have recognized the venturing birds as Samuel in England, Dorothy, with her husband Seaborn Cotton in

Wethersfield, Connecticut—where he preached for two years—then flying northward with him to the coastal settlement of Hampton, New Hampshire, the second minister of which he became; Sarah, married to Richard Hubbard and living in Ipswich, about fifteen miles directly east of Andover; Simon Junior at Harvard, and Dudley, who was the fifth to leave the nest although he was the seventh child, at school in Ipswich. Remaining at home were Hannah, shortly to be married, Mercy who was about twelve years old, and the youngster John.

There is a puzzle about the dating of this poem: in most of the copies of *Several Poems*, 1678, and in Ellis's edition of the *Works*, 1867, the title reads "In reference to her Children, 23. June, 1656." This is surely an error, since Samuel did not go to England until the end of 1657, and Dudley was probably not sent to school in Ipswich until early in 1658. Ellis noted the discrepancy and suggested that the correct date was 1658; what he did not know, a fact that has only recently been observed, is that in a few copies of *Several Poems*, for example, those in the British Museum and the Massachusetts Historical Society, the date has been altered, probably by an editor who proofread the sheets as they came off the press, to "1659." [20] One might assume that the printer read the date correctly in the manuscript, but carelessly inverted the 9, thus changing it to a 6 when he set the type, except for one detail. Hannah Bradstreet, one of the children referred to in the line "My other three, still with me nest" was married, to Andrew Wiggin of Exeter, New Hampshire, on the 3rd June, 1659.[21] So obviously she was not still nesting at home on the 23rd June of that year. There are two possible explanations:

20. I am indebted for this information to Jeannine Hensley, who came upon it, and generously shared it with me, while she was collating the surviving copies of *Several Poems* for her edition of *The Works of Anne Bradstreet*, Cambridge (Mass.), 1967.

21. *Vital Records of Andover, Mass.*, Vol. II, p. 62.

one, that Anne Bradstreet dated the poem "23 June, 1658" and the year was completely mis-read by the printer; the other, and I think preferable, solution is that Anne began the poem in 1658, put it aside for some reason, then completed and dated it towards the end of June 1659, without troubling to alter the reference to Hannah's being at home with the younger children.

To return to the poem itself: after giving the nestlings their individual identities, their "Dam" warns of the many dangers that threaten young birds, from fowlers' nets and lime-twigs, hawks, and stone-throwing boys, and stresses her anxiety for them.

> O to your safety have an eye,
> So happy may you live and die:
> Mean while my dayes in tunes Ile spend,
> Till my weak layes with me shall end.
>
>   * * *
>
> My age I will not once lament,
> But sing, my time so near is spent.
> And from the top bough take my flight,
> Into a country beyond sight,
> Where old ones, instantly grow young,
> And there with Seraphims set song:
>
>   * * *
>
> When each of you shall in your nest
> Among your young ones take your rest,
> In chirping language, oft them tell,
> You had a Dam that lov'd you well,
> That did what could be done for young,
> And nurst you up till you were strong,
> And 'fore she once would let you fly,
> She shew'd you joy and misery;
> Taught what was good, and what was ill,
> What would save life, and what would kill.

Thus gone, amongst you I may live,
And dead, yet speak, and council give:
Farewel my birds, farewel adieu,
I happy am, if well with you.

Over and over again Anne Bradstreet revealed clearly her love of life, of its warm relationships, its treasures of the mind, and even its good and enjoyable material things. Behind the transparently simple, at times almost jocular, language of the poem, deep feeling can be sensed, and, as in the serious and poignant lyric, "Before the Birth of one of her Children," sadness at the thought of leaving, in death, all that she cherished on earth, even though she believed, and reminded herself repeatedly, that a felicitous immortality was in store for her. The poem tells us that she hoped for another kind of immortality as well, survival in the hearts and memories of those who had been nearest to her in the world, and in their progeny. It would seem that her wish was granted in this respect. More than fifty children were born to the eight young ones whom she had "nurst . . . up with pain and care"; not all of these grandchildren of Simon and Anne Bradstreet lived to maturity, but the many who did, and who established families of their own, handed on to succeeding generations an enduring reverence for the memory of those two pioneer ancestors.

In November 1659 Anne lost the first family member of her own generation, when her sister Sarah Pacey died at the age of thirty-nine. Since the scandal of her divorce, excommunication, and questionable remarriage, this unfortunate and probably unbalanced woman had been living obscurely, apparently in near poverty. Her father had left her a small annual stipend, and charged in his will that she should be given food and lodging when necessary; undoubtedly her relatives did, with conscientious kindness, what they could for her, but her death must have been as much of a relief as a sorrow for all of them.

Simon Bradstreet, Junior, whose filial devotion and whose abilities of mind and spirit without doubt brought much happiness to his parents, graduated from Harvard in 1660, and probably spent the next few years at home while completing his studies for the ministry. Early in 1666 he was called to preach in New London, Connecticut, and became pastor of the church there in 1670. He married his first cousin, Lucy, daughter of the Reverend John and Mercy Woodbridge, in 1667; they had five children, one of whom, another Simon, also became a minister. Simon Junior died in 1683, leaving, as well as the copy of his mother's autobiographical legacy to her children, his own manuscript diary that—fortunately transcribed and printed before it disappeared from view—contained much valuable information about his own and his family's lives.

The first half of 1661 brought bad health to several of the Bradstreets. Anne's prose entry in her journal, dated "May 11, 1661," notes that at the beginning of the month, when the weather was very hot, she had had a high fever for four days, and that from the middle of January on she had been "by fitts very ill and weak." Then follow three short poems of thanksgiving to God, the first for her own improvement, next "For the restoration of my dear Husband from a burning Ague, June, 1661," and finally "Upon my Daughter Hannah Wiggin her recovery from a dangerous feaver." After these mementoes of anxiety and relief comes a truly joyful paean of nine stanzas, "On my Sons Return out of England, July 17, 1661."

Samuel had come home from almost four years of absence; his mother's poem recounts the perils that he survived:

All praise to him who hath now turn'd
My feares to Joyes, my sighes to song,
My Teares to smiles, my sad to glad,
He's come for whom I waited long.

Thou did'st preserve him as he went,
In raging stormes did'st safely keep,
Did'st that ship bring to quiet Port,
The other sank low in the Deep.

From Dangers great thou did'st him free
Of Pyrates, who were near at hand,
And order'st so the adverse Wind
That he before them gott to Land.

In country strange thou did'st provide
And freinds rais'd him in every Place,
And courtesies of sundry sorts
From such as 'fore nere saw his face.

In sicknes when he lay full sore
His help and his Physitian wer't,
When royall ones that Time did dye,
Thou heal'dst his flesh and cheer'd his heart.

The smallpox was rife in London in 1660, the year of the restoration of King Charles II to the throne. In that autumn the cruel disease, from which Anne Bradstreet's son was fortunate enough to recover, took the lives of two members of the royal family. The king's brother the Duke of Gloucester died in September, and was followed, shortly before Christmas, by their sister Mary, the Princess of Orange, who had come from Holland to join in celebrating the return of the monarchy.

Samuel practised medicine in Boston, where he married Mercy, the daughter of William Tyng; of their five children only one survived infancy. In May of 1670 Samuel was listed as a deputy from Andover to the General Court, so he must have kept in close touch, during these years, with his parents and their community. But he was by nature a traveler; in the autumn of 1670 he sailed for Jamaica, and there he remained for the rest of his life.

Only a few months after her son's return from England Anne Bradstreet had to face the prospect of an absence that must have been particularly frightening for her: her husband was required to go on a difficult mission across the forbidding Atlantic Ocean. Having successfully weathered the Civil War and the period of Cromwell's Commonwealth, the New England colonies found themselves in a rather awkward position when the monarchy was restored in the mother-country. Charles II was naturally suspicious of all his subjects who were professed Puritans and who appeared to have an attitude of independence towards the Crown. Ships arriving at Boston brought the disturbing news that enemies at court were making slanderous statements which, if brought to the attention of the king, might result in serious curtailment of the political privileges of the colonists.

The governor of Massachusetts Bay, John Endecott, called a special session of the General Court, on the 7th August, 1661, for the public proclamation of the accession of King Charles II on the following day,

> Which was performed by the secretary, God save the king, at the time, in presence of ye Governor, Colonell Temple, Deputy Governor, Magistrates, Deputies, elders, & multitudes of people, ffower ffoote companies, one troope of horse, & masters of shipps in harbor attending.[22]

In England, the aged Lord Saye and Sele, Thomas Dudley's patron in earlier days, had been rewarded for his part in the

22. *Massachusetts Colony Records*, Vol. IV, Part II, p. 31.

restoration by appointment as Lord Privy Seal, one of the king's nearest officers. He remained a staunch friend to New England, and it was hoped that his good counsel would be beneficial. During the autumn, however, there came more rumors of complaints against the colonies, also an order from the Crown itself that emissaries should be dispatched to England to answer these complaints. Accordingly the governor called another special session, on the last day of the year, at which it was recorded that the General Court

> . . . judge meete to order, that Mr Symon Bradstreete & Mr John Norton be sent to England from this Court, to present this Courts addresse to our soveraigne lord, King Charles the Second, & negotiate our affaires with his majesty & his privy councill according to instruccions agreed upon by this Court.[23]

Their instructions were, as summed up by the historian Thomas Hutchinson, "to represent the colony as his Majesty's loyal and obedient subjects, to endeavour to take off all scandal and objections, and to understand his Majesty's apprehensions concerning them, to do nothing which might be prejudicial to the charter, and to keep the court advised of these transactions and all occurrences." [24]

Simon Bradstreet and his colleague, the Reverend John Norton, a celebrated Latin scholar and minister of the First Church in Boston, undertook their commission with great reluctance, but accepted it as their duty, and, after some delay, sailed for England on the 11th February, 1662. Anne Bradstreet's private poem of twelve stanzas, "Upon my dear and loving husband his goeing into England," directly follows the joyful lines on her son's return, and conveys the heartache and anxiety of this separation.

23. *Ibid.* p. 37.
24. *History of Massachusetts-Bay*, Vol. I, p. 188.

O thou most high who rulest All,
And hear'st the Prayers of Thine,
O hearken Lord unto my suit
And my Petition signe.

Into thy Everlasting Armes
Of mercy I commend
Thy servant Lord. Keep and preserve
My husband, my dear friend.

*   *   *

Lord bee thou Pilott to the Ship
And send them prosperous gailes,
In stormes and sicknes Lord preserve.
Thy Goodnes never failes.

Unto thy Work he hath in hand
Lord grant Thou good Successe,
And favour in their eyes to whom
He shall make his Addresse.

Remember Lord thy folk whom thou
To Wildernesse ha'st brought,
Let not thine own Inheritance
Bee sold away for Nought.

But Tokens of thy favour Give,
With Joy send back my Dear,
That I and all thy servants may
Rejoice with heavenly chear.

Lord let my eyes see once Again
Him whom thou gavest me,
That wee together may sing Praise
For ever unto Thee.

The ambassadors endured the long winter voyage, landed in
April, and soon presented themselves and their testimonials to
the king. Meanwhile in New England great concern was felt,

not only for the success of their mission but for their personal safety as well, for rumors had come that they had been arrested and thrown into prison. They did not, however, suffer any such ill-treatment, but were received graciously by King Charles, who confirmed the royal charter and granted pardon for all past errors, provided that the colonies would accept certain changes in the direction of religious toleration, increased control by the Crown, and less influence of the Church in civil government.

There is an interesting comment on the theological readjustments of this time, and how they struck the visitors from Massachusetts, in the autobiography of the presbyterian clergyman Richard Baxter.

> . . . the great Reason why my self, and some of my Brethren were made the King's Chaplains (in Title) was, that the People might think . . . that all that were like us should be favoured, and so might think their condition happy. And though we ourselves made no doubt but that this was to be the use that was to be made of us, and that afterward we should be silenced with the rest in time, yet we thought that it was not meet to deny their Offer. The People at London . . . were not much deceived: But those in the Country that were further off . . . especially those . . . in New-England who were yet more remote, were far more deceived by these Appearances. . . .
>
> Insomuch that there grew on a sudden in New-England a great Inclination to Episcopal Government; for many of them saw the Inconveniencies of Separation, . . . and they thought that the Church-Government here would have been such as we were pleased with: So that these and many other Motives made them begin to think of a Conformity: Till at last Mr. Norton, with one Mr. Broadstreet, a Magistrate, came over and saw how things went, and those in New-England heard at last how we were all silenced and cast out: And then they began to remember

again, that there is something beside Schism to be feared, and
that there lyeth as perilous an Extreme on the other side.[25]

Anne Bradstreet wrote three verse-prayers as the spring and
summer moved along; one asks for support "In my Solitary houres
in my dear husband his Absence," another is in gratitude for his
letters received from England. The last is an almost inarticulate
exclamation of thanks and praise, dated "Sept. 3, 1662," on
which day the ship *Society* brought Simon Bradstreet and John
Norton safely home from their journey.

It was not, in its public aspect, an entirely happy homecoming,
although the Court appointed a day of solemn thanksgiving for
the return of the messengers and the accomplishment of their
mission. For much resentment was soon expressed at the terms
of the king's pronouncement to his colonial subjects, particularly
those concerning toleration of other forms of worship and the
selection of political officers without regard to their church
affiliations. Thomas Hutchinson describes the situation:

> However reasonable the several things required by the King
> appear to us at this day, yet many of them were grievous to our
> ancestors. The agents met with the fate of most agents ever since.
> The favours they had obtained, were supposed to be no more
> than might well have been expected, and their merits were soon
> forgot; the evils which they had it not in their power to prevent,
> were attributed to their neglect or unnecessary concessions. Mr.
> Bradstreet was a man of more phlegm, and not so sensibly
> touched; but Mr. Norton was so affected that he grew melan-
> choly. He died suddenly, very soon after his return, (April 5,
> 1663).[26]

25. *Reliquiae Baxterianae, or Mr. Richard Baxter's Narrative . . . of his
Life & Times*, edited by Matthew Sylvester, 1696, Lib. I, Part II, pp. 297–98.
26. *History of Massachusetts-Bay*, Vol. I, pp. 190–91.

Such an ungrateful reception, of the results of so arduous an undertaking, undoubtedly brought sorrow and chagrin to the Bradstreet family. But it was no more than a temporary rebuff for the man who was later to serve as governor, from 1679 to 1686, again from 1689 to 1692, and to be revered as the "Nestor of New England" when he died, at the age of ninety-four, on the 27th of March, 1697.

There was an occurrence in the year 1662 that must have been of enough interest to Anne Bradstreet to distract her mind, temporarily at least, from the anxiety and loneliness that she felt during her husband's absence. This was the publication, in Cambridge, of *The Day of Doom: or A Poetical Description of the Great and Last Judgement,* by the Reverend Michael Wigglesworth, of Malden, Massachusetts. The author was younger than the Tenth Muse; born in England, he was brought to the colony in 1638 at the age of six, and became a graduate of Harvard and one of its teachers, a physician as well as a minister, an invalid for much of his life, and an introspective and often tormented Calvinist. His description of the Last Judgment is written in the old internal-rhyming "fourteeners" of ballad-verse; its beginning is ironically suggestive of that jolly nursery favorite "The Night before Christmas":

> Still was the night, Serene and Bright,
>   when all Men sleeping lay;
> Calm was the season, and carnal reason
>   thought so 'twould last for ay.
> Soul, take thine ease, let sorrow cease,
>   much good thou hast in store:
> This was their Song, their Cups among,
>   the Evening before.

*   *   *

They put away the evil day,
And drown'd their care and fears,
Till drown'd were they, and swept away
by vengeance unawares:
So at the last, whilst Men sleep fast
in their security,
Surpriz'd they are in such a snare
as cometh suddenly.

For at midnight brake forth a Light
which turn'd the night to day,
And speedily an hideous cry
did all the world dismay.
Sinners awake, their hearts do ake,
trembling their loynes surprizeth;
Amaz'd with fear, by what they hear,
each one of them ariseth.

They rush from Beds with giddy heads,
and to their windows run,
Viewing this light, which shines more bright
then doth the Noon-day Sun.
Straightway appears (they see't with tears)
the Son of God most dread;
Who with his Train comes on amain
To Judge both Quick and Dead.

And so on for two hundred and twenty-four stanzas, which become more and more horrific as the punishments of the damned are depicted. Moses Coit Tyler called the work "that blazing and sulphurous poem . . . which, with entire unconsciousness, attributes to the Divine Being a character the most execrable and loathsome to be met with, perhaps, in any literature, Christian or pagan." [27] It was, however, an immediate popular success; of

27. *History of American Literature, 1607–1765* (1878), Ithaca (New York), 1949, pp. 280, 287.

the eighteen hundred copies printed only a few were unsold by the end of the year; it was New England's "best seller" of all time, and continued to be in demand through edition after edition, in England as well as in America. Kenneth Murdock, editing a modern reprint of *The Day of Doom*, says that it was written for the edification and instruction of the pious and "relatively unlettered New Englander," who was "not offended by having the speeches of Christ and of human souls before the throne uttered in the jog-trot measure of *The Nut-Brown Maid*."[28] That the book's admirers literally read it to death is shown by the fact that the earliest surviving complete copy of any American edition is that of 1701, probably the fifth; it is in the Harvard Library and was used by Professor Murdock for this reprint.

Anne Bradstreet's opinion of this newcomer, to the field where previously she had stood alone, must have been somewhat mixed, in both a critical and a theological sense. The God whom she worshipped with devotion, trust, and a constant awareness of the blessings and mercies He had vouchsafed to her, who was her "shelter from the storm" and "shadow from the fainting heat," was a far different Being from the vengeful and relentless Judge of Wigglesworth's poem. Also, her literary tradition was essentially an aristocratic one; the poems that she allowed to circulate were written for an educated and fairly sophisticated audience, and within the bounds of her talent and personality, she strove for elegance of expression and urbanity of persuasion. The didactic ferocity and stylistic uncouthness of *The Day of Doom* may have repelled her; on the other hand, she was a strict enough Puritan to realize the value of Dr. Wigglesworth's strong medicine for those who could swallow it, she had a sufficient taste for both drama and violence to respond, perhaps, to their exploitation in

28. *The Day of Doom . . . with other poems by Michael Wigglesworth*, ed. with an Introduction by Kenneth B. Murdock, New York, 1929, p. vii.

this spectacle of Doomsday, and, as a published poet, she may well have felt the stirrings of envy at the success of the horrendous work.

Whatever Anne Bradstreet really thought about *The Day of Doom*, it is possible that the challenge of its appearance, and of its spectacular popularity, made her mindful again of her vocation as a poet. Since the publication of *The Tenth Muse* she had not, so far as her surviving work from those twelve years indicates, written any separate piece of formal verse except the elegy for Thomas Dudley, although her own lines tell us that she continued to work away at "The Four Monarchies," and that she also did much careful editing of the contents of *The Tenth Muse*, in preparation for its eventual reprinting. Within the next decade, however, which was the final period of her writing, she produced work, in both prose and verse, which may be considered to mark the high point of her literary achievement.

CHAPTER TEN

The Final Years

"... *in the Autumnal Tide.*"
(ANNE BRADSTREET—*Contemplations*)

Andover in 1662 was still very much a frontier village, with probably not more than five hundred inhabitants of all ages. Although only twenty-five miles from Boston by modern roads, it was far more remote in the mid-seventeenth century, as the wilderness trails zigzagged from one settlement to another and, before bridges were built, to the least dangerous places for fording the streams and rivers. The farmers carted their produce to the nearest market town, Salem, and other neighboring places; those who had business further afield, like Simon Bradstreet, journeyed on horseback, and the less prosperous travelers found their way on foot.

The houses of Andover were built fairly close together, both for safety and for convenience of communication, around the central point of the village, the small, square, unadorned but sturdy meetinghouse, used for public gatherings and the business of the community on weekdays and for divine worship on Sundays. Each householder had his home lot of from four to twenty acres, with a proportionate amount of meadow or farm land on the outskirts of the village.

Cattle were herded to the common pastures by day, but all domestic animals had to be penned or stabled, for security, on the house lots at night, and this was the cause of a good deal of trouble between neighbors. Simon Bradstreet was involved in at least two lawsuits concerning damage done by or to animals; once when Daniel Gage's swine broke through a fence and uprooted a field, and again, more seriously, when a mare belonging to Mr. Bradstreet was set upon by dogs, and killed, while she was eating the hay in Richard Sutton's yard.[1]

Beyond the cleared land around the village the forest stretched on every side, full of wild life, human as well as animal. The local Indians, though always somewhat unpredictable, were on peaceful terms with the settlers for more than thirty years after the founding of Andover (until the Sachem Metacomet, who came to be known as "King Philip," united the Massachusetts tribes in a general war against the English colonists that broke out in 1675). Bears, deer, and smaller game were hunted for food, and alewives and other kinds of fish were taken from the nearby rivers. Foxes and wolves were a constant annoyance to this and all the other isolated settlements; the traveler John Josselyn described the shooting, for sport as well as necessity, of foxes that had been lured by heaps of codfish-heads on moonlit winter nights. In Simon Bradstreet's accounts there is an order for "25 Wolf-hooks"; these were large fishhooks wrapped in wool and coated with tallow, then, according to Josselyn, "laid by some dead carcase which toles the wolves. It is swallowed by them and is the means of their being taken." [2]

1. Sarah Loring Bailey, *Historical Sketches of Andover*, Boston, 1880, pp. 33–34.
2. *Ibid.* p. 37.

Anne Bradstreet has been reproached by some of her most understanding critics, as has already been noted in this study, for taking her descriptions of nature, when they occurred in her earlier formal poems, not from the almost virgin countryside around her but rather from the established patterns of English pastoral verse. But perhaps these critics overlooked the fact that from the beginning of the New England experience, that first fearful winter when almost half of the colonists died and starvation faced the survivors until the ship *Lyon* came with life-saving provisions, the landscape of their new world was unmapped, untamed, and filled with terrors of many kinds. It was small wonder that, among the many diseases that beset these pioneers, homesickness for the orderly and unthreatening landscape of old England was one of the most prevalent.

Anne Bradstreet had known the English country at its gentlest, in the soft fens and fertile farm lands of Lincolnshire; she also had seen the pastures of antiquity, and the woods and fields of her native land, through the transfiguring eyes of the poets whose works she had read. So it is not really surprising that "The Four Seasons," the last and lamest section of her elemental quaternion, carries no echoes of the rough majesty of nature in New England, its timbered hills and rocky valleys, its violent winters and obstinate springs and the long rich summers turning to autumn's glory of harvest and color. Instead the poem is almost entirely a re-working of long-established conventional imagery—that has little or no relation to the realities of nature anywhere in the world—with here and there a pleasant nostalgic glimpse of some aspect of the English countryside, remembered as sheltering and benevolent in contrast to the fierce new land with which the colonists had to wrestle, every day of their lives, for sustenance and for survival.

It is remarkable, therefore, that almost twenty years after she wrote "The Four Seasons," when she was about fifty years old and conscious of the diminishing of both physical strength and intellectual ambition, Anne Bradstreet became intensely aware of the beauty of the landscape around her. "Contemplations," the most spontaneous, philosophical, and technically well-wrought of her formal poems, was inspired, as she tells us, by a late afternoon walk in the autumn, through the woods to a riverside, where she sat and thought of many things, while letting her eyes dwell on the running stream, the tall trees, and the sky and sun above them all.

There are three rivers near the Bradstreet homesite; the broad Merrimack about two miles to the northwest, the Shawshin, its tributary, one mile westward, and the little Cochichewick, connecting two sizable ponds, only half a mile away. Yet it would not have been seemly or safe for Mistress Bradstreet to walk alone, late in the day, so far from her dwelling as to the bank of any one of these water-courses. It is most likely that she went with her grown son Simon, and the younger children, on an outing to pick wild grapes or gather mushrooms or nuts, and that, feeling secure in their company, she wandered off a little way by herself, and let the rhythms of nature and her own meditations quicken the poem that was in her.

"Contemplations" is composed in thirty-two numbered, seven-line stanzas, rhyming *ababccc*, of iambic pentameter except for the last line which is an Alexandrine, and a final stanza of four heroic couplets. This graceful variation of rhyme-royal was probably suggested to Anne Bradstreet by a re-reading of Phineas Fletcher's *The Purple Island*, of 1633, which I have already mentioned as a possible inspiration for "The Four Elements" and "Of the four Humours in Mans Constitution." The thought-sequence in "Contemplations" is digressive but purposeful; the mind of the wanderer dwells at first on the beauty of the scene dominated by the sun's glory, then passes to the memory of man's beginning, in Eden, and the turbulence of his earthly destiny. As the argument of the poem unfolds, contrasting the orderly perfection of the Creator's natural world with the restlessness and ambition of His greatest creature, man with his double composition, of flesh and spirit, is shown as the link between Heaven and Earth, made to be immortal but beguiled and tormented by material things until at last he realizes that only by overcoming the world can he approach the peace and joy of eternity.

The poem begins with a clear and charming picture of New England on an October day:

> Some time now past in the Autumnal Tide,
> When *Phoebus* wanted but one hour to bed,
> The trees all richly clad, yet void of pride,
> Where gilded o're by his rich golden head.
> Their leaves and fruits seem'd painted, but was true
> Of green, of red, of yellow, mixed hew,
> Rapt were my sences at this delectable view.

> 2

> I wist not what to wish, yet sure thought I,
> If so much excellence abide below;
> How excellent is he that dwells on high?
> Whose power and beauty by his works we know.
> Sure he is goodness, wisdome, glory, light,
> That hath this under world so richly dight:
> More Heaven then Earth was here, no winter & no night.

> 3

> Then on a stately Oak I cast mine Eye,
> Whose ruffling top the Clouds seem'd to aspire;
> How long since thou wast in thine Infancy?
> Thy strength, and stature, more thy years admire,

Hath hundred winters past since thou wast born?
Or thousand since thou brakest thy shell of horn,
If so, all these as nought, Eternity doth scorn.

4

Then higher on the glistering Sun I gaz'd,
Whose beams was shaded by the leavie Tree,
The more I look'd, the more I grew amaz'd,
And softly said, what glory's like to thee?
Soul of this world, this Universes Eye,
No wonder, some made thee a Deity:
Had I not better known, (alas) the same had I.

The next three stanzas salute the sun as the "Bridegroom" of the earth, bringing life to all of its inhabitants and, in the language of the old cosmology, creating the seasons by its "swift Annual, and diurnal Course." If the sun is so dazzling in its glory that no human eye can endure its direct rays, and so far away that no "earthly mould" can approach it,

How full of glory then must thy Creator be?
Who gave this bright light luster unto thee:
Admir'd, ador'd for ever, be that Majesty.

Then the author takes a solitary walk, and listens to some of the smallest music of nature.

8

Silent alone, where none or saw, or heard,
In pathless paths I lead my wandring feet,
My humble Eyes to lofty Skyes I rear'd
To sing some Song, my mazed Muse thought meet.
My great Creator I would magnifie,
That nature had, thus decked liberally:
But Ah, and Ah, again, my imbecility!

9

I heard the merry grashopper then sing,
The black clad Cricket, bear a second part,
They kept one tune, and plaid on the same string,
Seeming to glory in their little Art.
Shall Creatures abject, thus their voices raise?
And in their kind resound their makers praise:
Whilst I as mute, can warble forth no higher layes.

The pleasant imagery of this stanza may have influenced a more gifted poet than Anne Bradstreet, her younger contemporary Edward Taylor, who spent his adult life as both minister and physician to the frontier village of Westfield in Massachusetts. Taylor's remarkable devotional poetry, passionately personal and elaborately, sometimes naïvely, metaphysical, was apparently never circulated in his lifetime and remained unknown until well into this century, when it was discovered in manuscript and printed.[3] Although Taylor was a man of great learning and familiar with all the serious poets of his time, only one book of English verse, "Mrs bradstreets poems" (probably the Boston, 1678, edition), was listed in his extensive library when he died in 1729.[4] The third stanza of the twenty-second of Taylor's "Preparatory Meditations before my Approach to the Lords Supper" seems to echo the lines above; certainly the little homily from nature is the same, although there is characteristic contrast

3. First in book form in a selection included by William Rose Benét and Norman Holmes Pearson in their *Oxford Anthology of American Literature,* New York, 1938, pp. 60–63; then as *The Poetical Works of Edward Taylor,* ed. Thomas H. Johnson, New York, 1939, and in a more comprehensive collection as *The Poems of Edward Taylor,* ed. Donald E. Stanford, New Haven, 1960.
4. *The Poetical Works of Edward Taylor,* ed. Johnson, pp. 202 and 212.

between the classical serenity of Anne Bradstreet's stanza and the emotional urgency and baroque vocabulary of Taylor's style.

> But shall the Bird sing forth thy Praise, and shall
> The little Bee present her thankfull Hum?
> But I who see thy shining Glory fall
> Before mine Eyes, stand Blockish, Dull, and Dumb?
> Whether I speake, or speechless stand, I spy,
> I faile thy Glory: therefore pardon Cry.[5]

Stanzas 10 to 16 of "Contemplations" are a meditation on the beginnings of the human race, as Anne Bradstreet's orthodox faith interpreted the creation in the Garden of Eden. She sees Adam in disgrace, "turn'd . . . to a naked thral," and Eve sitting in sorrow, with "in her lap, her bloody *Cain* new born." The description of Abel's murder and of his brother's subsequent outlawry and despair recalls the preoccupation with violent crime that is often apparent in "The Four Monarchies." Anne's treatment of the episode also suggests that these two sons of the first parents were symbolical to her of the dual nature of mankind: the bestial Cain, dominated by his passions and forever damned, and Abel the innocent sacrifice, whose blameless life assured him the reward of heaven. The meditation develops a soliloquy on time, based on the long ages of the scriptural "Fathers."

17

> Our Life compare we with their length of dayes
> Who to the tenth of theirs doth now arrive?
> And though thus short, we shorten many wayes,
> Living so little while we are alive;
> In eating, drinking, sleeping, vain delight
> So unawares comes on perpetual night,
> And puts all pleasures vain unto eternal flight.

5. *The Poems of Edward Taylor*, ed. Stanford, p. 37.

18

When I behold the heavens as in their prime,
And then the earth (though old) stil clad in green,
The stones and trees, insensible of time,
Nor age nor wrinkle on their front are seen;
If winter come, and greeness then do fade,
A Spring returns, and they more youthfull made;
But Man grows old, lies down, remains where once he's laid.

20

Shall I then praise the heavens, the trees, the earth
Because their beauty and their strength last longer
Shall I wish there, or never to had birth,
Because they're bigger, & their bodyes stronger?
Nay, they shall darken, perish, fade and dye,
And when unmade, so ever shall they lye,
But man was made for endless immortality.

The author then moves to another part of the landscape, and sits down to let her thoughts go on again.

21

Under the cooling shadow of a stately Elm
Close sate I by a goodly Rivers side,
Where gliding streams the Rocks did overwhelm;
A lonely place, with pleasures dignifi'd.
I once that lov'd the shady woods so well,
Now thought the rivers did the trees excel,
And if the sun would ever shine, there would I dwell.

For seven peaceful stanzas she muses on the "happy Flood . . . / Thou Emblem true, of what I count the best" that without hindrance pursues its course to the longed-for sea, on the fish that live out their ordered lives in "this liquid Region . . . / You watry folk that know not your felicity," and, when "The sweet-tongu'd Philomel percht ore my head,/ And chanted forth a most melodious strain," on the carefree existence of the birds, never at a loss for food or drink or shelter, and passing, when their singing season is done, into a place "Where winter's never felt by that sweet airy legion."

After these observations on the tranquil progresses of lower nature the poem turns, almost abruptly, to "Man at the best a creature frail and vain,/ In knowledg ignorant, in strength but weak," who is constantly exposed to "Troubles from foes, from friends, from dearest, near'st Relation." And yet, the author says, "This weather-beaten vessel wrackt with pain,/ Joyes not in hope of an eternal morrow," but voyages on through life's temptations "As if he had command of wind and tide,/ And now become great Master of the seas." The two final stanzas firmly state the Puritan way of thought, and end with a symbol that held deep meaning for Anne Bradstreet: the white stone of Revelation, II, 17, in which was "a new name written, which no man knoweth saving he that receiveth it," with its gloss in the Geneva Bible: "Such a stone signifieth here a token of Gods favour & grace; also it was a signe that one was cleared in judgement."

32

So he that saileth in this world of pleasure,
Feeding on sweets, that never bit of th' sowre,
That's full of friends, of honour and of treasure,
Fond fool, he takes this earth ev'n for heav'ns bower.
But sad affliction comes & makes him see
Here's neither honour, wealth, nor safety;
Only above is found all with security.

33

O Time the fatal wrack of mortal things,
That draws oblivions curtains over kings,
Their sumptuous monuments, men know them not,
Their names without a Record are forgot,
Their parts, their ports, their pomp's all laid in th' dust
Nor wit nor gold, nor buildings scape times rust;
But he whose name is grav'd in the white stone
Shall last and shine when all of these are gone.

This deeply felt avowal of admiration for the beauty of the natural world, of compassion for mankind's bewilderments and trials, and of trust in the promise of the mystic talisman of Revelation, is still a homespun poem by an unpretentious poet. It is occasionally flawed by repetition and false rhyme, a few lines are metrically unbalanced, and there are instances of wrongly conjugated verbs so glaring as to seem deliberate. Yet the effect of the whole is that of a symphonic meditation attuned to nature's music: the wind in the tree-tops, the songs of grasshopper and bird, and the rippling melody of the river. Anne Bradstreet chose an attractive, and rather difficult, stanza-form for her long poem, and on the whole she handled it with ingenuity and eloquence. A modern critic comments on the "good craftsmanship" shown in the extended final lines of her stanzas, and adds: "The author of the ninth and eighteenth stanzas of 'Contemplations' was a genuine lyrist." [6]

It is not surprising, because of the kind of poem it is, that "Contemplations" here and there recalls to us the words and thoughts of other poets. There are echoes of Catullus, of the makers of the Bible, of Sidney and Raleigh, an anticipation of Shelley, and a reminder of another dreamer beside a river:

6. Scully Bradley, in *The American Tradition in Literature*, ed. S. Bradley, R. C. Beatty & E. H. Long, New York, 1962, Vol. I, p. 34.

I was wery forwandred and went me to reste
Under a brode banke bi a bornes side,
And as I lay and lened and loked on the wateres,
I slombred in a sleping, it sweyued so merye.[7]

This is not so far-fetched a comparison as it may seem, for
Thomas Dudley's library contained the only recorded copy in
early America of *Piers Plowman*, and his daughter would surely
have been familiar with that fourteenth-century religious fable.

A recent critical study of Anne Bradstreet's work finds some
similarities of feeling and expression between "Contemplations"
and the writings of the Romantic poets, and goes so far as to
wonder if Wordsworth and Coleridge might have read Anne's
poems and been influenced by them! [8] Another commentator, in a
perceptive examination of "Contemplations," suggests that Stanza
18 is reminiscent, in style and theme, of Shakespeare, and that
Anne's train of thought, in the stanzas describing the happy
life of the birds, "is oddly similar to the one Keats was to follow
a hundred and forty years later in his "Ode to a Nightingale."
The same writer concludes that:

> The poetic level to which "Contemplations" rises in stanzas
> nine, eighteen, twenty-one and twenty-eight is one kind of testi-
> mony to the fact that in this poem Anne Bradstreet has reached
> that ideal but rare state of Puritan consciousness, a carefully
> reasoned and emotionally convincing resolution of the problem
> of how to live in the world without being of it. "Contempla-
> tions" spans both worlds. It accepts both worlds, perceives their
> connection, and acquiesces in that connection.[9]

7. [William Langland?], *Piers Plowman*, ed. W. W. Skeat (Early English
Text Society), 1950, p. 1.
8. Josephine K. Piercy, *Anne Bradstreet* (Twayne's U.S. Authors Series),
New York, 1965, pp. 99, 101.
9. Robert D. Richardson, "The Puritan Poetry of Anne Bradstreet," in
Texas Studies in Literature and Language, IX (Autumn 1967), pp. 329, 331.

In the 1678 edition of Anne Bradstreet's poems "Contemplations" is followed by "The Flesh and the Spirit," a dialogue in
one hundred and eight lines of four-stressed iambic couplets. This,
the most tense and self-analytical of her longer poems, and probably the last written of the three in which she gave considered
expression to the orthodox values of her own religious faith,
begins:

> In secret place where once I stood
> Close by the banks of *Lacrim* flood
> I heard two sisters reason on
> Things that are past, and things to come;
> One Flesh was call'd, who had her eye
> On worldly wealth and vanity;
> The other Spirit, who did rear
> Her thoughts unto a higher sphere:
> Sister, quoth Flesh, what liv'st thou on
> Nothing but Meditation?
> Doth Contemplation feed thee so
> Regardlessly to let earth goe?
> Can Speculation satisfy
> Notion without Reality?

"Flesh" continues her scornful speech, in language that suggests
a satiric use of the scholastic vocabulary, then she offers the
solid inducements of the world as preferable to the "things unknown" that seem to occupy her sister's mind.

> Dost honour like? acquire the same,
> As some to their immortal fame:
> And trophyes to thy name erect
> Which wearing time shall ne're deject.
> For riches dost thou long full sore?
> Behold enough of precious store:
> Earth hath more silver, pearls and gold,

Then eyes can see, or hands can hold.
Affect's thou pleasure? take thy fill,
Earth hath enough of what you will.
Then let not goe, what thou maist find,
For things unknown, only in mind.

"Spirit" replies vigorously, yet with a hint that she is not entirely immune to the temptations that her fleshly twin has profferred:

Be still thou unregenerate part,
Disturb no more my setled heart,
For I have vow'd (and so will doe)
Thee as a foe, still to pursue.
And combate with thee will and must,
Until I see thee laid in th' dust.
Sisters we are, yea twins we be,
Yet deadly feud 'twixt thee and me;

*　　*　　*

How oft thy slave, hast thou me made,
When I believ'd, what thou hast said,
And never had more cause of woe
Then when I did what thou bad'st doe.
Ile stop mine ears at these thy charms,
And count them for my deadly harms.
Thy sinfull pleasures I doe hate,
Thy riches are to me no bait,
Thine honours doe, nor will I love;
For my ambition lyes above.
My greatest honour it shall be
When I am victor over thee,
And triumph shall, with laurel head,
When thou my Captive shalt be led.

About a decade earlier, in England, Andrew Marvell had written "A Dialogue between the Resolved Soul and Created

Pleasure"; it is a more youthful and masculine poem than this, with greater beauties of imagery and music, yet its first Chorus is an interesting parallel to the lines above:

> Earth cannot shew so brave a Sight
> As when a single Soul does fence
> The Batteries of alluring Sense,
> And Heaven views it with delight.
>   Then persevere: for still new Charges sound:
>   And if thou overcom'st thou shalt be crown'd.

From what we know of her life it does not appear that Anne Bradstreet was ever exposed to any of the more luxurious and corrupting of earthly enticements. Certainly her pleasures were not "sinfull," and her riches, though adequate, were modest in degree; her genuine response to these would seem to be only a just appreciation of the blessings bestowed upon her. Perhaps "honour" was more threatening as a pitfall; she knew herself to be unusually gifted for a woman of her time, and the object of widespread praise for the writings that she had offered to her world. The sins of ambition and pride may have troubled her conscience, and in her moments of self-analysis she must have been aware of the flashes of anger and ferocity that found their way into her poems, the doubts and despondencies that sometimes assailed her, and even the too much love of living, among the good and pleasant aspects of her earthly lot, that the austerity of her creed condemned. Behind the outward grace and dignity that would seem to have characterized her conduct towards those around her, the inner tensions, with their resultant feelings of guilt, existed. She fought against these manifestations of her "unregenerate part" with the weapon of her faith; her determination to prevail and her trust that a glorious reward awaited her are expressed in the words with which "Spirit" continues to admonish and subdue her sister "Flesh":

> How I do live, thou need'st not scoff,
> For I have meat thou know'st not off;
> The hidden Manna I doe eat,
> The word of life it is my meat.
> My thoughts do yield me more content
> Then can thy hours in pleasure spent.
>
> *   *   *
>
> Mine Eye doth pierce the heavens, and see
> What is invisible to thee.
> My garments are not silk nor gold,
> Nor such like trash which Earth doth hold,
> But Royal Robes I shall have on,
> More glorious then the glistering Sun.

There follows a paraphase, in sixteen lines, of the description of the city of God from the book of Revelation, that great poetic document which held continual fascination for Anne Bradstreet. The poems ends with the assurance of everlasting happiness for those who have overcome the world:

> No Candle there, nor yet Torch light,
> For there shall be no darksome night.
> From sickness and infirmity,
> For evermore they shall be free,
> Nor withering age shall e're come there,
> But beauty shall be bright and clear;
> This City pure is not for thee,
> For things unclean there shall not be:
> If I of Heaven may have my fill,
> Take thou the world, and all that will.

Samuel Eliot Morison has commented that this "mature poem . . . is one of the best expressions in English literature of the conflict described by St. Paul in the eighth chapter of his Epistle to the Romans," and he finds in it "a dramatic quality which can only have come of personal experience." [10] Actually this debate between two personified antagonists is not as dramatic or as lively in style as the panoramic arguments of the allegorical females representing the four elements and the four humors. The two sisters of "The Flesh and the Spirit" are shadowy, faceless forms, glimpsed in the obscurity and gloom of a "secret place" beside a symbolical river of tears, and what they say to one another is couched in simple language of direct meaning. Such drama as the poem has exists in the contrast between the wraith-like character of the two speakers and the realistic intensity of their dispute, led off by the persuasive logic of "Flesh" and fought to a draw (not to be settled, it seems, until the end "When I am victor over thee") by "Spirit's" indomitable hope and determination.

In the early spring of 1664/65 Anne Bradstreet wrote a letter to her son Simon, who was about to take up his duties as a minister at the church of New London in Connecticut. This letter, surviving in her own hand, in the small manuscript book from which numerous quotations have already been taken, introduces her legacy to her son as follows:

FOR MY DEARE SONNE SIMON BRADSTREET

Parents perpetuate their Lives in their posterity, and their manners, in their imitation. Children do naturally, rather follow the failings then the vertues of their predecessors, but I am perswaded better things of you. You once desired me to leave something for you in writeing that you might look upon, when you should see me no more. I could think of nothing more fit

10. S. E. Morison, *Builders of the Bay Colony*, p. 323.

for you, nor of more ease to my self then these short meditations following. Such as they are I bequeath to you, small legacys
are accepted by true friends much more, by duty full children.
I have avoyded incroaching upon others conceptions because
I would leave you nothing but myne owne, though in value
they fall short of all in this kinde yet I presume they will be
better prised by you, for the Authors Sake. The Lord blesse you
with grace heer and Crown you with glory heerafter, that I may
meet you with rejoyceing at that great day of appearing, which
is the continuall prayer, of

March 20, 1664.   your affectionate mother A.B.

After this, also in Anne Bradstreet's clear and rather forceful
handwriting, under the title "Meditations Divine and morall,"
there are seventy-seven aphorisms in prose, varying in length from
three to twenty-seven lines. While these belong to a tradition as
old as English literature itself, they are, as their author stoutly
maintains, not imitative, but rather the fruit of the lessons she
had learned, the conclusions she had drawn, from her own
experience of a thoughtful and eventful life.

In a commentary on the prose writers of early New England,
Josephine Piercy concludes, after discussing the "didactic essays"
of such distinguished clergymen as Cotton Mather, Samuel Wil-
lard, Thomas Shepard, and John Rogers, that

> The best examples of the meditative paragraph are those of
> Anne Bradstreet's "Meditations Divine and Moral." They are
> more compact, more unified, more impersonal, more epigram-
> matic, more like the Baconian or didactic essay than any of those
> just quoted.[11]

And George Frisbie Whicher makes the interesting suggestion
that in

11. Piercy, *Studies in Literary Types in Seventeenth-Century America*,
New Haven, 1939, p. 152.

. . . the juxtaposition of profoundly serious thought and homely household metaphor . . . one may find in her prose "Meditations" more than one passage that might be described as inchoate Emily Dickinson. . . . The woman who could speak of herself as "rather preserved with sugar then brine" was akin to her who wrote of "muslin souls." The first step on the way to Emily Dickinson was to turn away from large impersonal subjects and to find poetry in personal and domestic matters. That step Mrs. Bradstreet took.[12]

No doubt Anne felt that these expressions of her deepest spiritual convictions would have more immediate appeal for her son, and for his descendants also, if they were set forth in the familiar imagery and language of their own household and its surroundings. But the "Meditations" are well worth reading today. They reflect a keen, occasionally even ironic, sense of values, and also give some direct glimpses of a way of life that was spare, sturdy, and always, of necessity, practical.

8

Downny beds make drosey persons but hard lodging, keeps the eyes open[;] a prosperous state makes a secure Christian, but adversity makes him Consider.

15

A low man, can goe upright, under that door, wher a taller is glad to stoop; so a man of weak faith and mean abilities, may undergo a Crosse more patiently then he that excells him, both in gifts & graces.

Might she not have been thinking of her father when she made this observation? That Thomas Dudley was a "tall" man in many

12. Whicher, *Alas, All's Vanity*, New York, 1942, pp. 27 and 28.

ways is undeniable, but among his virtues as a Christian that of humility does seem to have been markedly lacking.

19

Corne till it have past through the Mill and been ground to powder, is not fit for bread, God so deales with his Servants, he grinds them with greif and pain till they turn to dust, and then are they fitte manchet [13] for his Mansion.

39

A prudent mother will not cloth her little childe with a long and cumbersome garment, she easily foresees what events it is like to produce, at the best butt falls and bruises, or perhaps somewhat worse, much more will the alwise God proportion his dispensations according to the stature and strengh of the person he bestows them on; larg indowments of honour, wealth, or a helthfull body would quite overthrow some weak christian, therefore God cuts their garments short, to keep them in such a trim that they might run the wayes of his Commandment.

53

He that is to saile into a farre country, although the ship, cabin and provision, be all convenient and comfortable for him yet he hath no desire to make it his place of residence, but longs to put in at that port where his bussines lyes; a christian is sailing through this world unto his heavenly country, and heere he hath many conveniences and comforts but he must beware of desireing to make this the place of his abode, lest he meet with such tossings that may cause him to long for shore, before he sees land—We must therefore be heer as strangers and pilgrims, that we may plainly declare that we seek a citty above and wait all the dayes of our appointed time till our chang shall come.

This Meditation would seem to be an echo of Anne Bradstreet's unforgettable experience of sailing to a far country from her

13. "Manchet" is "a small loaf or roll of the finest wheaten bread." O.E.D.

native land, although on that voyage the arrangements of cabin and provisions must have been greatly lacking in either convenience or comfort.

64

We see in orchards; some trees soe fruitfull, that the waight of their Burden is the breaking of their limbes, some again, are but meanly loaden, and some have nothing to shew but leaves only, and some among them are dry stocks [;] so it is in the church which is Gods orchard, there are some eminent Christians, that are soe frequent in good dutys, that many times, the waight therof impares both their bodys and estates, and there are some (and they sincere ones too) who have not attained to that fruitfullnes, altho they aime at perfection. And again there are those that have nothing to commend them, but only a gay proffession, and these are but leavie Christians, which are in as much danger of being cut down, as the dry stocks, for both cumber the ground.

70

All men are truly sayd to be tenants at will, and it may as truly be sayd that All have a lease of their lives, some longer some shorter, as it pleases our great landlord to let; All have their bounds set, over which they cannot passe, and till the expiration of that time, no dangers no sicknes no paines nor troubles, shall put a period to our dayes, the certainty that that time will come, together with the uncertainty, how, where, and when, should make us so to number our dayes as to apply our hearts to wisedome, so that when wee are put out of these houses of clay, we may be sure of an everlasting habitation that fades not away.

Probably not more than two years after Anne Bradstreet wrote this Meditation, about the human tenants at will in their houses of clay, the house of oak and pine in Andover, that had sheltered the Bradstreets for about two decades, burned to the ground.

Their son Simon, the young minister in Connecticut, recorded this disaster, which took place a few months before the Great Fire of London, in his diary:

> July 12. 1666. Whilst I was at N. London my fathers house at Andover was burnt, where I lost my Books, and many of my clothes, to the valeiu of 50 or 60 lb at least; . . . Tho: my own losse of books (and papers espec.) was great and my fathers far more being about 800, yet yᵉ Lord was pleased gratiously many wayes to make up yᵉ same to us. It is therefore good to trust in the Lord.

Another dwelling-place was immediately provided for the family,[14] but it must have been very hard for Anne to begin again, as it were, in her middle fifties and in failing health, with only the barest household necessities and bereft of so many cherished possessions, particularly the books that were an essential part of her life. The lament that she wrote for these earthly treasures has an immediate poignancy that has caused it to be reprinted in many anthologies. Simon Junior preserved the poem in the manuscript book that his mother left to him:

Here followes some verses upon yᵉ burning of our house, July 10th, 1666. Copyed out of a loose Paper.

> In silent night when rest I took
> For sorrow neer I did not look,

14. Dr. Abbott Lowell Cummings has kindly informed me that private records, in the possession of the present owners of the original Bradstreet property, show that an "old house" was standing on that land, and was occupied, until 1751, and that parts of this old building were used in the construction of a new house on the lot in this same year. Dr. Cummings believes that a large, handsomely chamfered summer-beam, now installed in the woodshed of the present house, "is from a high-style mid-seventeenth-century house," very possibly that which Simon Bradstreet built to replace the one that burned in 1666. So one fragment, at any rate, may have survived from Anne Bradstreet's home for the last six years of her life.

I waken'd was with thundring nois
And piteous shreiks of dreadfull voice.
That fearfull sound of fire and fire,
Let no man know is my Desire.
I starting up ye light did spye,
And to my God my heart did cry
To Strengthen me in my Distresse
And not to leave me succourlesse.
Then coming out beheld a space
The flame consume my dwelling place,
And when I could no longer look,
I blest his Name y^t gave and took,
That layd my goods now in ye dust
Yea so it was, and so 'twas just
It was his own it was not mine
Far be it y^t I should repine,
He might of All justly bereft
But yet sufficient for us left.
When by the Ruines oft I past
My sorrowing eyes aside did cast
And here and there ye places spye
Where oft I sate and long did lye,
Here stood that Trunk, and there y^t chest
There lay that store I counted best
My pleasant things in ashes lye
And them behold no more shall I.
Under thy roof no guest shall sitt,
Nor at thy Table eat a bitt.
No pleasant tale shall 'ere be told
Nor things recounted done of old.
No Candle 'ere shall shine in Thee
Nor bridegroom's voice ere heard shall bee.
In silence ever shalt thou lye
Adeiu, Adeiu, All's Vanity.
Then straight I 'gin my heart to chide,
And did thy wealth on earth abide,
Didst fix thy hope on mouldring dust,

The arm of flesh didst make thy trust?
Raise up thy thoughts above the skye
That dunghill mists away may flie.
Thou hast an house on high erect
Fram'd by that mighty Architect,
With glory richly furnished,
Stands permanent tho: this bee fled.
'Tis purchased & paid for too
By him who hath Enough to doe.
A Price so vast as is unknown
Yet by his Gift is made thine own
Ther's wealth enough I need no more,
Farewell my Pelf, farewell my Store.
The World no longer let me Love
My hope, and Treasure lyes Above.

Anne's old battle between the flesh and the spirit was never more sharply joined than in her experience of this catastrophe, nor was a more touching epitaph ever made for the vanished *persona* of a beloved house. In August 1951 the poem was read, in a selection to mark the publication of *The Oxford Book of American Verse*, to the audience of the British Broadcasting Company; it must then have found an affecting echo, after so many years, in the hearts of many women who had only recently seen their belongings go down in rubble or up in flames.

Other losses came to Anne Bradstreet in these years, of human rather than material possessions. Her son Samuel's wife Mercy, whom he had married in about 1662, bore him five children, all but one of which died in infancy. Although Samuel was practising medicine in Boston, at this time, it seems probable that he was frequently at his parents' house in Andover and that his wife, who was apparently in very delicate health, was permanently living there. For the series of short elegies that Anne Bradstreet wrote for their children, which were printed with the other personal poems in the second edition of her work, show clearly that she knew these children intimately through their brief lives, when her own state of health would have made it all but impossible for her to undertake the difficult journeys to Boston, in order to see them often.

The first, and most lyrical, of these elegies is composed in the same stanza as "Contemplations," with the added refinement that the three final lines of each stanza have the same syllabic ending; the firm, rather sombre, Latin-derived "-ate."

IN MEMORY OF MY DEAR GRAND-CHILD ELIZABETH
BRADSTREET, WHO DECEASED AUGUST, 1665.
BEING A YEAR AND HALF OLD

Farewel dear babe, my hearts too much content,
Farewel sweet babe, the pleasure of mine eye,
Farewel fair flower that for a space was lent,
Then ta'en away unto Eternity.
Blest babe why should I once bewail thy fate,
Or sigh thy dayes so soon were terminate;
Sith thou art setled in an Everlasting state.

2

By nature Trees do rot when they are grown,
And Plumbs and Apples throughly ripe do fall,
And Corn and grass are in their season mown,
And time brings down what is both strong and tall.
But plants new set to be eradicate,
And buds new blown, to have so short a date,
Is by his hand alone that guides nature and fate.

This gentle and moving poem contains, in its penultimate line, the most significant suggestion among all her writings that Anne had read Shakespeare's works, or that at least she was familiar with his Sonnet 18: "Shall I compare thee to a summer's day?"

Hans Galinsky's examination of all the Shakespearian hints in Anne's poetry has already been mentioned; [15] he recognizes the elegy as the most convincing of these but acknowledges that the theme and spirit of the "transplanted sonnet" are very different from those of the elegy: Shakespeare was writing about an imaginative immortality, Anne Bradstreet about a real death.

No printed copy of any part of Shakespeare's works is known to have existed in New England during the seventeenth century. But two common-place books from around the 1650's survive, into which their owners, while students at Harvard, copied excerpts from Shakespeare's poetry. One of these books belonged to Elnathan Chauncy, the son of Harvard's president, and into it he put some lines from *Venus and Adonis;* the other was the youthful property (the blank pages of which were later thriftily used for church records!) of Anne Bradstreet's son-in-law the Reverend Seaborn Cotton, who included in two hundred pages of mixed verse and prose, some of it extremely bawdy, the song "Take, O, take those lips away," from *Measure for Measure.*[16] Both of these selections could have been taken from contemporary anthologies, but it would not have been strange if Shakespeare's works, particularly his separately published poems, had come to New England during the latter half of the seventeenth century and subsequently been read to pieces, destroyed, as in the fire that consumed the Bradstreets' library, or simply not recorded in the inventories of books that have come down to us.

So it is possible that Anne Bradstreet had an opportunity to read the *Sonnets,* during the later years of her life, and some of their incomparable music may have lingered in her mind. Yet

15. See pp. 65–66 above; also see Josephine K. Piercy, *Anne Bradstreet,* pp. 59–61, 95, 98.

16. Esther C. Dunn, *Shakespeare in America,* New York, 1939, pp. 19–21; S. E. Morison, *The Intellectual Life of Colonial New England,* New York, 1956, pp. 49–56.

surely the substance of the lament for Elizabeth cannot be directly traced to any source in Shakespeare or any one of the elegiac lyrics with which Elizabethan poetry abounds. The pioneers of Massachusetts had, from the start, all too many incentives for the writing of elegies, and Anne's earlier and more ambitious uses of that form of verse made her well able to handle it. This woman who had spent almost all of her life with countryside around her did not have to be told by Shakespeare that early buds can be blasted by bitter winds, or that seedling plants, hopefully set out, can be blackened and shriveled overnight by a late frost. When her infant granddaughter died, she was not far from the end of her own days, mature and experienced both emotionally and in the practice of her literary craft. The heart and hand that mourned for Elizabeth were indivisible, the grief and trust are clothed in words as old and simple as those that lament the early dead in the *Greek Anthology,* and the poem, a small but faultless work of art, is entirely its author's own.

After the fire of 1666, a family of three generations would seem to have been living in the house in Andover that had replaced the Bradstreets' former home. It was a rather restless household; Simon the patriarch, in his early sixties, was required to accept increasing political responsibility and was often absent for long periods attending to the business of the General Court, as well as to the management of his own widespread properties. Samuel, the Boston doctor, would have been back and forth on visits if, as seems probable, his wife was spending her difficult childbearing years with his family in Andover. Three of the Bradstreet children were still at home: Mercy, in her early twenties, beyond the age at which her sisters had married and doubtless concerned about that, but staying at her post to run the house as her mother became less and less able to do so; Dudley, aged about eighteen in 1666, who did not go to Harvard but was probably learning about politics and estate-management from his father, and John who was still, at fourteen, being educated by Andover's schoolmaster, the Reverend Francis Dane.

The only survivor of the third generation was Samuel's daughter Mercy, born in November 1667, who lived to grow up and marry a Boston physician, Dr. James Oliver, and among whose descendants were the more famous doctor, Oliver Wendell Holmes, and the orator Wendell Phillips. As we have seen, her eldest sister Elizabeth died in infancy in 1665; another sister, named Anne, was born in December 1665, but stayed for only three and a half years, dying in the summer of 1669 and causing her grandmother to write these bitter lines as part of the short poem in her memory:

> With troubled heart & trembling hand I write,
> The Heavens have chang'd to sorrow my delight.
> How oft with disappointment have I met,
> When I on fading things my hopes have set?
>
> *   *   *
>
> More fool then I to look on that was lent,
> As if mine own, when thus impermanent.

Birth and death came hand in hand to the family in that year, for in October Samuel's unfortunate wife bore another child, this time a son named Simon, who lived for only a month and a day and was mourned for in the last but one of Anne's elegies for the members of her family who had gone before her.

In this sad summer of 1669 Anne Bradstreet wrote her own farewell to the world, although she was to live for three years longer. The only one of her poems that survives in her handwriting, it is written on the last leaf of the little book into

which she put her "Meditations Divine and morall" for her son
Simon, and it remained in manuscript until the mid-nineteenth
century, to be first printed, with the entire contents of that
book, in 1867 in J. H. Ellis's edition of *The Works of Anne
Bradstreet.* Like the elegies, this poem of valediction seems to go
far back in time for its spiritual origins and for the stark sim-
plicity of the imagery with which the author expresses her acceptance of the end of life's laborious journey and her expectation
of immortality.

> As weary pilgrim, now at rest,
>   Hugs wth delight his silent nest
> His wasted limbes, now lye full soft
>   That myrie steps, have troden oft
> Blesses himself, to think upon
>   his dangers past, and travailes done
> The burning Sun no more shall heat
>   Nor stormy raines, on him shall beat
> The bryars and thornes no more shall scratch
>   nor hungry wolves at him shall catch
> He erring pathes no more shall tread
>   Nor wild fruits eate, instead of bread
> for waters cold he doth not long
>   for thirst no more shall parch his tongue
> No rugged stones his feet shall gaule
>   nor stumps nor rocks cause him to fall
> All cares and feares, he bids farewell
>   and meanes in safity now to dwell
> A pilgrim I, on earth, perplext
>   wth sinns wth cares and sorrows vext
> By age and paines brought to decay
>   [an]d my Clay house mouldring away
> [Oh] how I long to be at rest
>   [and] soare on high among the blest
> This body shall in silence sleep
>   Mine eyes no more shall ever weep

No fainting fits shall me assaile
   nor grinding paines my body fraile
Wth cares and feares ner' cumbred be
   Nor losses know, nor sorrowes see
What tho my flesh shall there consume
   it is the bed Christ did perfume
And when a few yeares shall be gone
   this mortall shall be cloth'd upon
A Corrupte Carcasse downe it lyes
   a glorious body it shall rise
In weaknes and dishonour sowne
   in power 'tis rais'd by Christ alone
Then soule and body shall unite
   and of their maker have the sight
Such lasting ioyes, shall there behold
   as eare ner' heard nor tongue e'er told
Lord make me ready for that day
   then Come deare bridgrome Come away

Aug 31 69

The lack of line-end punctuation may be due to the frail and worn condition of the manuscript leaf, as is the loss of the three line-beginnings that are bracketed. It may also be explained, along with the unpunctuated date, by the probability that it was written with intense feeling and in haste, at a time when its author was more than usually ill and weak, and did not therefore take the trouble to indicate stops and pauses with her customary care.

Another, and a complex, sorrow visited the family a year later. Samuel Bradstreet decided to emigrate to Jamaica, but left his wife with his parents, expecting that she would join him when she had recovered from her fifth pregnancy. Anne must have felt her eldest son's departure very keenly, knowing that she would not see him again. While he was on the ship that was taking

him to the island, his delicate wife Mercy gave birth to another
girl, also named Anne, on the 3rd September, 1670, and a few
days later both she and her little daughter died. Anne Bradstreet's
last poem, which either she or her printer dated wrongly by a
year, is *"To the memory of my dear Daughter in Law, Mrs.
Mercy Bradstreet, who deceased* Sept. 6. 1669. *in the* 28. *year of
her Age."*

> And live I still to see Relations gone,
> And yet survive to sound this wailing tone;
> Ah, woe is me, to write thy Funeral Song,
> Who might in reason yet have lived long,
> I saw the branches lopt the Tree now fall,
> I stood so nigh, it crusht me down withal;
> My bruised heart lies sobbing at the Root,
> That thou dear Son hath lost both Tree and fruit:
> Thou then on Seas sailing to forreign Coast;
> Was ignorant what riches thou hadst lost.
> But ah too soon those heavy tydings fly,
> To strike thee with amazing misery;
>
>   *   *   *
>
> I lost a daughter dear, but thou a wife,
> Who lov'd thee more (it seem'd) then her own life.
> Thou being gone, she longer could not be,
> Because her Soul she'd sent along with thee.
>
>   *   *   *
>
> So with her Children four, she's now at rest,
> All freed from grief (I trust) among the blest;
> She one hath left, a joy to thee and me,
> The Heavens vouchsafe she may so ever be.
> Chear up (dear Son) thy fainting bleeding heart,
> In him alone, that caused all this smart;
> What though thy strokes full sad & grievous be,
> He knows it is the best for thee and me.

Short-lived and unfruitful as she was, Mercy Bradstreet received a full measure of love from her husband's family. The Reverend Simon wrote in his diary: "Sept. 1670. My B^r Samuel Bradstreet his wife dyed, which was a soar affliction to him, and all his friends." Samuel married again, in Jamaica, and when he died there in 1682, his three orphaned children were sent to Massachusetts to be cared for by their grandfather, then governor, Simon Bradstreet.

In February of 1672, Dorothy, the wife of the Reverend Seaborn Cotton and the mother of nine children, died in Hampton, New Hampshire. She was the only one of Anne Bradstreet's children who did not survive her, and since no elegiac poem for Dorothy has come down to us, it seems probable that her mother was too ill at that time to compose a tribute, or even perhaps to know of the death of her eldest daughter.

There is documentary evidence concerning a few of the family problems that came to Simon Bradstreet in this year, while he grieved over his daughter's death and the rapidly declining health of his wife. His two younger sons were hailed before the county court on the 1st of May, John accused of creating a disturbance by "smoking late at night" with some cronies (not a very serious offense for a young man in his twentieth year) and Dudley "with Nathaniel Wade and others," of "shooting pistols and drinking in the Quartermaster's house."[17] These misdemeanors were clearly only the results of youthful high spirits and restlessness, for both of these men proceeded to lead orderly and useful lives, John as a farmer in nearby Topsfield, where he died in 1718, and Dudley as a leading citizen of Andover, serving as town clerk, selectman, magistrate, and deputy to the General Court, and holding the rank of colonel of militia at his death in 1702.

17. *Records and Files of Quarterly Courts of Essex County,* Vol. V, Salem (Mass.), 1916, p. 31.

Dudley's drinking companion Nathaniel Wade was courting his sister Mercy at this time, and, as was customary, their two fathers met to discuss a marriage settlement. Simon Bradstreet recorded, in a court deposition of 1683, that there had been a fairly serious financial disagreement between Jonathan Wade, Nathaniel's father, and himself, but that this was finally amicably settled and it was "soe agreed that the young persons might procede in marriage, with both our consents, which they accordingly did." [18] The wedding ceremony took place in Andover, as noted in the town records, on the 31st of October, 1672, and Mercy went with her husband to Medford, Massachusetts, where he became a major in the militia and died in 1707. Mercy, who was the mother of eight children, lived until 1715, dying, according to her gravestone in Medford, in her sixty-eighth year.

Beginnings, rather than endings, had been the significant factors in Anne Bradstreet's life. As a child she had traveled, mentally, as far and fast as she could in the world of knowledge, and as a very young woman she had traveled physically to a strange new world, and helped to create another England there. Her body gave eight strong and effectual men and women to the first generation of native-born Anglo-Americans, and her mind and hand together laid the cornerstone of literary America. In her sixtieth year she was ready, with steadfastness of spirit, for what must have seemed to her the most important of all beginnings. As the Massachusetts summer moved into early autumn, the Reverend Simon Bradstreet, in New London, wrote in his diary:

> September 16. 1672. My ever honoured & most dear Mother was translated to Heaven. Her death was occasioned by a consumption being wasted to skin & bone & She had an issue made in her arm bee: she was much troubled with rheum, & one of ye women y^t tended herr dressing her arm, s[ai]d shee never saw

18. *Essex County Court Papers*, Vol. XLIII, p. 66.

such an arm in her Life, I, s[ai]d my most dear Mother, but yᵗ arm shall bee a Glorious Arm.

I being absent fro[m] her lost the opportunity of comitting to memory her pious & memorable xpressions uttered in her sicknesse. O yᵗ the good Lord would give unto me and mine a heart to walk in her steps, considering what the end of her Conversation was, yᵗ so wee might one day have a happy & glorious greeting.

The entry in Andover's manuscript book of Vital Records, 1651–1700 (possibly written by Dudley Bradstreet as town clerk), reads:

1672.

Mʳˢ An Bradstreet: wife of Mʳ Simon Bradstreet dyed 16 Septembʳ and was buried the Wednesday after.

No stone marks her probable resting place, under the pine trees in the ancient burial ground a short distance from where her home once stood. But a fitting memorial to her life exists, in these prophetic words from Michael Drayton's ode "To the Virginian Voyage":

> And in regions far,
>   Such heroes bring ye forth
>   As those from whom we came;
>   And plant our name
>   Under that star
>   Not known unto our North.
>
> And as there plenty grows
>   Of laurel everywhere—
>   Apollo's sacred tree—
>   You it may see
>   A poet's brows
>   To crown, that may sing there.

Epilogue

"In Criticks hands, beware thou dost not come."
(ANNE BRADSTREET—*The Author to her Book*)

Almost four years after Anne Bradstreet's death, on the 6th of June, 1676, her husband married again; his new wife was another Anne, the daughter of Emanuel Downing and widow of Captain Joseph Gardner, of Salem, who was killed in King Philip's War in 1675. Simon Bradstreet went to live in Salem; he was made deputy-governor of Massachusetts in 1678, then served as governor from 1679 to 1686, and again from 1689 to 1692. He died on the 27th of March, 1697, at the age of ninety-four, and was buried in a handsome table-tomb in the Charter Street burying-ground in Salem.

The second edition of Anne Bradstreet's poems was printed in Boston, in 1678, by John Foster (1648–81), a New England-born Harvard graduate who was a schoolmaster, engraver, and astronomer, as well as the printer of about fifty publications, ranging from broadsides to substantial books, during his short life. The title-page of this new edition reads:

SEVERAL POEMS Compiled with great variety of Wit and Learning, full of Delight; Wherein especially is contained a compleat Discourse, and Description of The Four ELEMENTS, CONSTITUTIONS, AGES of Man, SEASONS of the Year. Together with an exact Epitome of the three first *Monarchyes Viz.* The *ASSYRIAN, PERSIAN, GRECIAN. And beginning of the* Romane Common-wealth *to the end of their last King:* With diverse other pleasant & serious *Poems,* By a Gentlewoman in *New-England. The second Edition, Corrected by the Author, and enlarged by an Addition of several other Poems found amongst her Papers after her Death. Boston,* Printed by *John Foster,* 1678.[1]

All the formal poems of *The Tenth Muse* are here, with the addition of "To the Memory of my dear and ever honoured Father Thomas Dudley, Esq.," "An Epitaph on my dear and ever honoured Mother Mrs. Dorothy Dudley," "Contemplations," "The Flesh and the Spirit," and "The Author to her Book." Then follows the group of thirteen personal lyrics, which we have examined in previous chapters, under the heading, "Several other Poems made by the Author upon Diverse Occasions, were found among her Papers after her Death, which she never meant should come to publick view, amongst which, these following (at the desire of some friends that knew her well) are here inserted."

The prefatory material is the same, through the fourth of the commendatory verses, but the fifth of these, signed "R.Q." and beginning "Arme, arme, Soldado's arme," is deleted. The other three verses, and the anagrams, are retained, and after them comes a new tribute, an elaborate poem of nine stanzas and a couplet, in the same verse-form as "Contemplations," entitled: "Upon

1. See *The Works of Anne Bradstreet,* ed. Jeannine Hensley, Cambridge (Mass.), 1967, pp. 309–12 (Appendix), for the location of extant copies of, and examination of textual variants in, both *The Tenth Muse* and *Several Poems.*

Mrs. Anne Bradstreet Her Poems, &c." and signed "J. Rogers."
John Rogers (1630–84) was born in England and emigrated
to Massachusetts with his family in 1636. He was educated at
Harvard, in both divinity and medicine, for a time assisted his
father, the Reverend Nathaniel Rogers, at the church in Ipswich,
and then devoted himself to medical practice. He married Anne
Bradstreet's niece, Elizabeth, the daughter of Major-General
Daniel Denison and his wife Patience Dudley, and in 1682 he
became the president of Harvard College. Cotton Mather wrote
of him, in the *Magnalia:*

> He was One of so sweet a Temper, that the Title of *Deliciae
> humani Generis* might have on that Score been given him; and
> his Real *Piety* set off with the Accomplishments of a *Gentleman,*
> as a *Gem* set in *Gold.*

The compliment that Rogers offered to his aunt-by-marriage
is composed in flowery classical language, and may have been
written soon after the publication of *The Tenth Muse,* for presentation to the author. "Madame, twice through the Muses
Grove I walkt, / Under your blissfull bowres . . . ," he exclaimed,
and again, "Twice have I drunk the Nectar of your lines," which
suggests that he had read Anne's poems first in manuscript and
later in their printed form. The last three stanzas have an extremely youthful tone, along with an attractive touch of personal
communication.

7

Thus weltring in delight, my virgin mind
Admits a rape; truth still lyes undiscri'd,
Its singular, that plural seem'd, I find,
'Twas Fancies glass alone that multipli'd;
Nature with Art so closely did combine,

I thought I saw the Muses trebble trine,
Which prov'd your lonely Muse, superiour to the nine.

8

Your only hand those Poesies did compose,
Your head the source, whence all those springs did flow,
Your voice, whence changes sweetest notes arose,
Your feet that kept the dance alone, I trow:
Then vail your bonnets, Poetasters all,
Strike, lower amain, and at these humbly fall,
And deem your selves advanc'd to be her Pedestal.

9

Should all with lowly Congies Laurels bring,
Waste *Floraes* Magazine to find a wreathe;
Or *Pineus* Banks 'twere too mean offering,
Your Muse a fairer Garland doth bequeath
To guard your fairer front; here 'tis your name
Shall stand immarbled; this your little frame
Shall great *Colossus* be, to your eternal fame.

The final couplet, which stands by itself at the end of the poem, carries a definite statement and brings up an interesting point:

I'le please my self, though I my self disgrace,
What errors here be found, are in *Errataes* place.

Jeannine Hensley has made the convincing suggestion that John Rogers had accepted the responsibility of seeing the book through the press as its final editor. During the years between 1650 and her death Anne Bradstreet had, as her own lines tell us, made many corrections and revisions, in expectation of a second edition, to the text of *The Tenth Muse.* In 1678, therefore, a capable co-ordinator would have been required, to present these improved versions of the original poems, along with the additional material, to the printer. "Reason tells us," Jeannine Hensley observes, "that her family provided the printed poems, the corrections, and those poems not yet printed, but neither the title-page nor tradition reveals an editor's name."[2] She points out that Rogers was an accomplished scholar, a member of the Dudley family circle, and an outspoken admirer of Anne's work, but her most telling argument for his editorship is based on the couplet quoted above. For an actual page of *errata* exists, in the "Prince" copy at the Boston Public Library, the only one of the seventeen known examples of *Several Poems* in which this added final leaf, without signature or pagination, survives. Thirty-three corrections of printer's errors are listed, with page and line guides, on one side of the leaf, and it seems therefore as though John Rogers were telling us, in the couplet at the end of his poem, that he had carefully proofread the text, in his capacity as editor, and insisted on the inclusion of an *errata*-leaf before the book was bound.

Jeannine Hensley suggests that Rogers refers to the first and second editions of Anne's poems in writing that he has walked "twice through the Muses Grove" and "Twice . . . drunk the Nectar of your lines." But it seems more probable that he had encountered the poems first in manuscript, while he was a student at Harvard, then read them again soon after their appearance in *The Tenth Muse* and was consequently inspired to compose his poetic eulogy to their author. Rogers was forty-eight years old in 1678, so it would be rather absurd for him to speak, as he does in Stanza 7, of his "virgin mind," also his contrived image, in the same stanza, of "your lonely Muse, superiour to the nine," would be out of place in a poem written after it had apparently been decided, either by Anne Bradstreet herself or by her family, to drop "The Tenth Muse" as the title of her book. My own con-

2. *Works of Anne Bradstreet*, ed. J. Hensley, pp. xxvii–viii (note).

clusion is that Rogers wrote his poem in the early 1650's (and it must have given Anne great pleasure to receive this tribute from an accomplished young man who was to become, in 1660, her niece's husband), decided to include it among the commendatory verses in the second edition of Anne's poems, and added a footnote, as it were, of two lines in which he somewhat obliquely revealed himself as the editor.

In marked contrast to the lively, almost intimate tone of John Rogers's offering is a lugubrious composition of ninety-six lines, in rhymed couplets, that appears at the end of *Several Poems*. It is "A Funeral Elogy, *Upon that Pattern and Patron of Virtue, the truely pious, peerless & matchless Gentlewoman Mrs. Anne Bradstreet, right* Panaretes, *Mirror of Her Age, Glory of her Sex, whose Heaven-born-Soul leaving its earthly Shrine, chose its native home, and was taken to its Rest, upon* 16th Sept. 1672." The final flourish is almost as grandiloquent as the title: "*Finis & non.* John Norton. *Omnia* Romanae *sileant Miracula Gentis.*" The Reverend John Norton (1651–1716) was the pastor of Hingham, Massachusetts, and the nephew of the elder John Norton who was Simon Bradstreet's companion on the mission to England in 1662. His memorial tribute to Anne Bradstreet is a late and hollow-sounding imitation of the extravagant early seventeenth-century elegies, outstanding among which are John Donne's *Anatomie of the World* and *Second Anniversary*, of 1611 and 1612. Among Norton's most ridiculous lines are:

> Could *Maro's* Muse but hear her lively strain,
> He would condemn his works to fire again,

which would surely have gone against the grain of Anne's respect for Virgil and the other great classical writers. Only the inevitable pun brings a touch of life to the heavy testimonial.

> Her breast was a brave Pallace, a *Broad-street*,
> Where all heroick ample thoughts did meet,
> Where nature such a Tenement had tane,
> That others souls, to hers, dwelt in a lane.

John Harvard Ellis, who was unaware of the existence of the one surviving *errata*-leaf, mentioned the possibility that Norton was the editor of *Several Poems*.[3] But it does not seem likely that a man so much younger than John Rogers, and who probably knew Anne Bradstreet only slightly if at all, would have been chosen by her family to carry out this task or even to collaborate with Rogers. The fact that Norton was a relative of Simon Bradstreet's second wife suggests a reason for the inclusion of his elegy in *Several Poems*.[4] Otherwise his contribution is only a conventional encomium to a deceased public personage, without the slightest hint that he had anything to do with the preparation of the volume.

George Frisbie Whicher writes, of the appearance of *Several Poems*, that "the production of a volume of secular verse, the earliest indubitable piece of *belles lettres* printed in the English colonies, is an event of luminous import."[5] Certainly Anne Bradstreet's work had had no significant rival, since the beginning of the century, among the verse efforts engendered by the English-speaking settlements in North America. Probably the first of these was Richard Rich's *Newes from Virginia* (London, 1610), a ballad-form account of the Jamestown colony, with a description of a shipwreck on the Bermudas which may have contributed some local color to Shakespeare's *The Tempest*. In 1625 a Cambridge graduate named William Morrell, after spending a year in Massachusetts, published *New England, or a Briefe Ennarration of the*

---

3. *Works of Anne Bradstreet*, ed. J. H. Ellis, p. 413 (note).
4. *Works of Anne Bradstreet*, ed. J. Hensley, p. xxvii (note).
5. Whicher, *Alas, All's Vanity*, New York, 1942, p. 7.

Ayre, Earth, Water, Fish and Fowles of that Country. With a Description of the Natives, in Latin and English verse. Next, in 1626, came a more literary product of the New World, the translation by George Sandys of Ovid's *Metamorphoses,* much of it done during the four years that he spent in Virginia, as an official of the colony. The far north of the continent was the origin of *Quodlibets, Lately Come over from New Britaniola, Old Newfoundland. Epigrams and other small parcels, both Morall and Divine.* This book, of original verse and translations, was printed in 1628 and survives in only sixteen copies; it was the work of Robert Hayman, a citizen of Bristol who spent some years in Newfoundland and claimed that he was "Sometimes Governour of the Plantation there." [6]

The Whole Booke of Psalmes Faithfully Translated into English Metre (Cambridge, Mass., 1640) was the first book printed in English-speaking America; it is now one of the rarest, represented by only eleven copies, and, bibliographically speaking, the most important. As a work of art it leaves much to be desired, both in its physical appearance, which is rough and unadorned, and in the uncompromising literalness with which its translators rendered the original Hebrew into what they considered the most edifying language for their congregations to use. Three scholarly clergymen, Thomas Welde, John Eliot, and Richard Mather, were the authors of *The Bay Psalm Book,* as it is generally called, and in spite of its unmusical wording it was literally sung to death, through edition after edition, in the churches of New England.

After the appearance of *The Tenth Muse* in London, but before that of *Several Poems* in Boston, came Michael Wiggles-

6. See David Galloway, "Robert Hayman (1575–1629): Some Materials for the Life of a Colonial Governor and First 'Canadian' Author," *William and Mary Quarterly,* 3rd Series, Vol. XXIV, No. 1 (January 1967), pp. 75–87.

worth's *succès fou*, *The Day of Doom*, in its first printing, of 1662, at Cambridge, Massachusetts. Another collection of Wigglesworth's verse, *Meat out of the Eater, or Meditations Concerning the Necessity, End and Usefulness of Affliction unto Gods Children*, was published in Boston in 1670. A little book of only twenty-two pages, *Daily Meditations: or, Quotidian Preparations for, and Considerations of Death and Eternity*, appeared in Cambridge in 1668. The title-page identifies the author as "Philip Pain: Who lately suffering Shipwrack, was drowned"; no more is known about him except that, as revealed by his pious verses, he was a very young man when he died, and that his poetic remains were popular enough to warrant a second edition in 1670.[7] The first identifiable native-born poet to publish a book of verse was Benjamin Tompson (1642–1714), a Massachusetts schoolmaster and physician. His metrical narrative of King Philip's War, appropriately entitled *New England's Crisis*, issued from the press in both Boston and London in 1676; it is written in lively and skilful rhymed couplets, with a satiric wit that seems inherited from the old serio-comic pioneer Nathaniel Ward.

These three last-named men were contemporaries of Anne Bradstreet, and two of them gained high repute as poets in their time. But Wigglesworth's writings were entirely pietistic, in matter and intent, as was Philip Pain's small legacy, while Tompson dealt with local history and, in his numerous tributes to New England personages, with elegiac biography. None of these works can seriously compete with Anne Bradstreet's. Their subject matter is restricted and they show no comparable sense of vocation.

Another woman won great recognition as a poet of the New

7. The unique copy of the edition of 1668, in the Henry E. Huntington Library, has been reproduced in facsimile, with an introduction by Leon Howard, as a Huntington Library Publication, San Marino, California, 1936.

World, before the end of the seventeenth century, though it is doubtful if she had ever been heard of in New England. This was Sor Juana Inés de la Cruz (1651–1695), born the daughter of a prosperous Hispano-Mexican *haciendado*, educated in Mexico City and at the court of the Spanish Viceroy, and at the age of seventeen so celebrated for her learning that she was challenged to an academic debate with a large team of Mexico's most erudite men. After this ordeal, in which she carried the day, she retired into a convent for the rest of her life, but continued her studies in all branches of learning, and wrote a substantial amount of graceful and accomplished verse, both secular and devotional. Her poems were published, during her lifetime, in several printings, and are still available in scholarly modern editions. The American poet Muna Lee, who translated a number of Sor Juana's finest sonnets, chose this Mexican nun and our New England Anne Bradstreet as the subjects of a university lecture on "Two Seventeenth-century Women," and made the interesting comment that "in greatness of spirit, generosity of outlook, love for learning as a path toward truth; in their quick responsive delight in the everyday wonder of the world and their devout faith in the greatness and the goodness of God, Anne Bradstreet and Juana Inés de la Cruz —the one a Puritan, the other a Roman Catholic—were very close akin." [8]

We have seen that Anne's work was noticed with some respect, in England in her own century, by the bookseller William London, the educator Mrs. Bathsua Makin, and the literary chronicler Edward Phillips. But her greatest tribute, before the century was out, came from another New Englander, the scholarly churchman Cotton Mather. In his account of Thomas Dudley, in the

8. From the Steinman Poetry Lecture at Tufts University, given on the 13th April, 1960. Quoted by permission of the author.

encyclopaedic *Magnalia Christi Americana,* after quoting the lines of verse found in the old governor's pocket after his death,[9] he continued:

> But when I mention the *Poetry* of this Gentleman as one of his Accomplishments, I must not leave unmentioned the Fame with which the *Poems* of one descended from him have been Celebrated in both *Englands.* If the rare Learning of a *Daughter,* was not the least of those bright things that adorn'd no less a Judge of *England* than Sir *Thomas More;* it must now be said, that a Judge of *New-England,* namely, *Thomas Dudley,* Esq; had a *Daughter* (besides other Children) to be a *Crown* unto him.
>
> Reader, *America* justly admires the Learned Women of the other *Hemisphere.* She has heard of those that were *Tutoresses* to the Old Professors of all Philosophy: She hath heard of *Hippatia,* who formerly taught the Liberal Arts;

and, he goes on, of such female prodigies of early times as the Empress Eudocia, the learned nun Roswitha, and the historian Pamphilia, then

> The Writings of the most Renowned *Anna Maria Schurnian,* have come over unto her. But she now prays, that into such Catalogues of *Authoresses,* as *Beverovicius, Hottinger,* and *Voetius,* have given unto the World, there may be a room now given unto Madam ANN BRADSTREET, the Daughter of our Governour *Dudley,* and the Consort of our Governour *Bradstreet,* whose *Poems,* divers times Printed, have afforded a grateful Entertainment unto the Ingenious, and a Monument for her Memory beyond the Stateliest *Marbles.*[10]

9. See p. 296–97 above.

10. C. Mather, *Magnalia,* Book II, p. 17. Mather's comment on Anne Bradstreet in the MS. *Life of Dudley* (Adlard, *Sutton-Dudleys and Dudleys,* p. 36) is less flamboyant; he notes that she was "endowed with so many excellencies, as not only made her known in the gates of her own city, but in the

Although Mather's comparative citations reflect the scholastic curriculum of a Puritan parson's studies, it is notable that he mentions only Margaret Roper, Sir Thomas More's daughter, of all the learned ladies of old England. He may have felt, indeed, that the more up-to-date authoresses, like Katherine Philips and the Duchess of Newcastle, were too worldly and frivolous to be placed alongside the high-minded daughter of Governor Dudley. Yet there is perhaps a suggestion here that an independent culture was beginning to develop in New England, placing more emphasis on the emerging character of the colony itself, and marking the end of the primarily Anglo-centric period in thought and letters.

Possibly this change would have been more gradual if the Civil War had not occurred in England. The Puritans who left the mother-country to colonize northeastern America never questioned the fact that King Charles I was their sovereign, in spite of their dislike of many of his policies. When the war came they shared the distress of many Parliamentary supporters in England at the conflict between the king and his people. And during the Protectorate their attitude towards Cromwell, who looked on New England, they felt, "only with an eye of pity, as poor, cold, and useless," [11] was respectful but without enthusiasm.

The restoration of the monarchy caused recurring periods of anxiety as to the preservation of the civil and religious rights of the colonial settlements, and the New Englanders did not find their hearts drawn homeward by very much in the character or way of life of King Charles II or his successor King James II. So

high places of the world, by some choice pieces of poetry, published with great acceptation (as may be seen by the testimony of sundry gentlemen well skilled in that art, prefixed thereunto); of her may Solomon's words be really verified,—'though many other daughters had done wonderfully, yet she excelled them all.' "

11. C. M. Andrews, *The Colonial Period of American History*, Vol. I, pp. 498–99.

the parent and child began to move apart, and from 1700 onward the rapid development of the colonies, and the increase of a vigorous native-born population, encouraged the growth of nationalism and a social pattern which, though modeled on that of old England, soon acquired an individuality of its own.

Although Mather's *Magnalia* was published in 1702, it was written during the last quarter of the seventeenth century. No critical comment about Anne Bradstreet seems to have found its way into print during the whole of the eighteenth century; at any rate I have not been able to locate one. But she was not without honor in her own country, for a third edition of her poems appeared in Boston in 1758. It was the work of an unknown printer and reproduced the text of *Several Poems,* with occasional alterations in spelling and some new typographical errors of its own. The title-page follows that of 1678 as far as the imprint, which is somewhat misleadingly changed to read:

> The THIRD EDITION, corrected by the Author, and enlarged by an Addition of several other POEMS found amongst her Papers after her Death. Re-printed from the second Edition, in the Year M.DCC.LVIII.

Colonial New England was approaching its drastic ordeal of separation, by war, from the mother-country when this book was issued. No doubt the anonymous publisher felt that the patriotic fervor of many Bostonians would lead them to purchase these first fruits of verse from the Massachusetts Bay colony.

Two early nineteenth-century anthologies gave modest recognition to the Tenth Muse on both sides of the Atlantic. The first is an attractively printed and bound little book: *Specimens of British Poetesses,* collected as he says by a "tedious chase through the jungles of forgotten literature," by the Reverend Alexander Dyce of Oxford and published in London in 1827. Anne Bradstreet is represented in it by the major part of the speech of "Spring" from "The Four Seasons" and the first of the two epitaphs from "In Honour of Queen Elizabeth." Next there appeared in Boston, in 1829, Samuel Kettell's *Specimens of American Poetry*. This three-volume work is, according to the compiler, the first attempt at a representative collection of the new nation's verse; it contains samples from the writings of more than two hundred authors, many of them with good reason forgotten now. Kettell deals with the "rude and feeble attempts" of the founders in his Introduction, where he says:

> The earliest poet of New England, however, was ANNE BRADSTREET. . . . We must come down to a late period in the literary annals of the country before we find her equal, although her productions are not without the marks of the barbarous taste of the age.

All thirty-three stanzas of "Contemplations" are presented, to show that their author "possessed genuine poetical feeling." [12]

As the century progressed those who read Anne's poems, with however critical an eye, were apparently impressed by the warmth and integrity of her personality. One of these was the poet John Greenleaf Whittier; a Quaker, a humanitarian, and a lover of justice, he was also, like Nathaniel Hawthorne, a student of the social and psychological aspects of his ancestral New England. His one published novel, *Leaves from Margaret Smith's Journal*

12. S. Kettell, *Specimens*, Vol. I, pp. xvii, xx–xxii. Kettell also says (pp. xxvii–xxviii): "The sister of Mrs. Bradstreet, Mrs. [Mercy Dudley] Woodbridge, . . . was likewise an adventurer in verse. An epistle which she addressed to her sister upon the subject of her volume, is still extant. The poetry is respectable, but has no striking passages." According to H. S. Jantz, *First Century of New England Verse*, p. 284, Kettell's was the "last direct reference" to the existence of this poem.

in the Province of Massachusetts Bay, 1678–9 (Boston, 1849), is much concerned with the witchcraft trials, the troubled relations with the Indians, and the persecutions for religious unorthodoxy, that were plaguing the colony. In a dramatic passage one of his characters, "an ancient Woman," reminiscently describes Anne Bradstreet's anguish on the day when a young Quaker mother was put to death (this is based on the hanging of Mary Dyer on the 1st June, 1660), and the reproachful sorrow with which she received her husband, the magistrate, and the minister John Norton when they returned from the execution. Although it might well have happened, there is no historical evidence that such a scene took place, and Whittier made no pretense, in this book, of treating history in other than a fictional way. But it is interesting that he chose Anne Bradstreet, among all the founders of New England, as the one most likely to feel compassion and moral indignation on behalf of the persecuted Quakers.

Soon after the appearance, in 1867, of John Harvard Ellis's complete and carefully documented edition of *The Works of Anne Bradstreet*, their author was criticized in a book that has become a classic of its period. Moses Coit Tyler's *A History of American Literature during the Colonial Period, 1607–1765* was published in New York in 1878; his remarks about Anne Bradstreet are interesting as a reflection of the current literary taste that rejected all but the very greatest of the English seventeenth-century poets. Discussing the verse of the Puritans in America, Tyler says: "There was . . . belonging to this primal literary period, one poet who, in some worthy sense, found in poetry a vocation. The first professional poet of New England was a woman." He goes on to describe the dire influences on Anne's writing:

. . . she was taught to seek for the very essence of poetry in the quirks, the puns, the contorted images, the painful ingenuities of George Wither and Francis Quarles, and especially of "The Divine Weeks and Works" of the French poet Du Bartas, done into English by Joshua Sylvester. . . . It is easy enough to find in the writings of Anne Bradstreet grotesque passages, preposterous stuff, jingling abominations;

but, he says, neither she, nor other American verse-writers of her time, can be blamed for this. They were the victims of a serious literary disease that, originating in Italy in the sixteenth century, "swept westward and northward like the plague" and had a desolating effect on the literatures of Spain, France, and England.

The worst lines of Anne Bradstreet . . . can be readily matched for fantastic perversion, and for the total absence of beauty, by passages from the poems of John Donne, George Herbert, Crashaw, Cleveland, Wither, Quarles, Thomas Coryat, John Taylor, and even of Herrick, Cowley and Dryden.

So Tyler, who presumably taught his students at the universities of Michigan and Cornell unequivocally to despise the metaphysical poets and their contemporaries, states that Anne Bradstreet's literary sins were modeled on those of what now seems a very respectable company indeed! His final conclusion, after a close look at some of Anne's writings, with particular attention to "Contemplations," is a moderately kindly one:

Upon the whole, it is impossible to deny that Anne Bradstreet was sadly misguided by the poetic standards of her religious sect and of her literary period, and that the vast bulk of her writings consists not of poetry, but of metrical theology and chronology and politics and physics. Yet, amid all this lamentable rubbish, there is often to be found such an ingot of genuine poetry, as proves her to have had, indeed, the poetic endowment. . . . In the Prologue to her volume, she speaks of her writings in diffident lines, whose merit alone would prompt us to grant to her a higher poetic rank than she herself asks for.[13]

Half a century later an American poet had the courage, and the good sense, to present a group of Anne's poems to the public on their own merits alone. Conrad Aiken's anthology, *American Poetry, 1671–1928* (New York, 1929), opens, without any notice on the author or even the dates of her life, with four poems: "The Flesh and the Spirit," "Contemplations," "A Letter to her Husband [absent upon Publick employment]," and "As weary pilgrim, now at rest," which is entitled "Longing for Heaven." This presentation marks the beginning of the recognition of Anne Bradstreet as a competent poet; Jeannine Hensley comments on it that Aiken's "printing several of her poems . . . on aesthetic grounds alone, with no apologies for filial piety or anti-chauvinistic protestations, was reconsideration enough . . . it is no longer necessary to treat Anne Bradstreet with condescension." [14]

The discovery and publication of Edward Taylor's remarkable poems was a great event in the realm of seventeenth-century letters. A multiplying number of criticisms and studies of New England colonial verse has appeared since these intensely subjective and brilliantly inventive devotional lyrics came to light in the 1930's; all of these take into account the major status of the newly emerged poet, and place his immediate predecessor Anne Bradstreet beside him as the only other significant poet of the period.[15]

13. M. C. Tyler, *History of American Literature* . . . *1607–1765* (1878), Ithaca (New York), 1949, pp. 239, 243, 252–53.

14. *Works of Anne Bradstreet*, ed. J. Hensley, pp. xxxiii–xxxiv.

15. Ann Stanford has contributed "An Annotated Check-list of Works by and about Anne Bradstreet" to *Early American Literature*, Vol. 3, No. 3 (Winter 1968–69), pp. 217–28. This list is particularly useful as regards

This new interest in the early American writers is not limited to the English-speaking world. In addition to the work of Hans Galinsky of Mainz,[16] an Italian scholar has recently shown perceptive appreciation of the ways of thought and life in pioneer New England. Biancamaria Tedeschini Lalli, in her anthology *I Puritani*, presents an interpretation of the colonial writers from William Bradford to Jonathan Edwards. Her selection from Anne Bradstreet includes the whole of "Contemplations," "Upon the Burning of our House," and excerpts in prose and verse from the spiritual memoir that Anne bequeathed to her children. A brief biographical introduction shows that this editor from the Latin world is aware of the perils, both physical and mental, that contronted Anne Bradstreet as one of the earliest *"gentildonne inglesi trasferitesi in America,"* and she comments with understanding on an important psychological point:

> If in a literary sense she is in fact a child of the renaissance, and her religious sentiments, expressed in classical terms, do not present much of Puritan spirituality, biographically that spirituality, particularly in the diurnal, sometimes painful, personal colloquies with God, comes to the surface incontestably. The figure that emerges, with its consternations, its dejections and its pure will to have faith, illustrates in terms that are not heroic, and yet are so much the more humanly persuasive, the moral and spiritual problems of her time.[17]

nineteenth- and twentieth-century commentaries on Anne Bradstreet in American books and periodical publications.

16. See pp. 65–66, 271, and 351 above.

17. *I Puritani*, ed. B. Tedeschini Lalli, Biblioteca di Testi Americani I, Bari (Italy), 1966, pp. 327, 328–29. See also the same author's "Anne Bradstreet," in *Studi Americani*, Vol. 3, Rome, 1957, pp. 9–27. Other European commentaries are in: Nilo Peltola, "The Compound Epithet . . . in American Poetry from Bradstreet through Whitman," *Annales Academiae Scientarium Fennicae*, Ser. B., Bd. 105, Helsinki, 1956, pp. 39–42, and Zdeněk Vančura, "Baroque Prose in America," *Studies in English*, Vol. IV, Charles University, Prague, 1933, pp. 52–53, where Anne Bradstreet's "Meditations" are called "This modest American counterpart of Pascal's 'Pensées'."

The most unusual tribute that Anne Bradstreet has ever received is contained in the fifty-seven stanzas of the modern poet John Berryman's *Homage to Mistress Bradstreet*. This complex, erotic, and strangely moving poem tells of an encounter beyond time and space between the spirit of the Puritan woman and the tormented, world-stricken mind of the twentieth-century man.

> . . . We are on each other's hands
> who care. Both of our worlds unhanded us. Lie stark,
>
> thy eyes look to me mild. Out of maize & air
> your body's made, and moves. I summon, see,
> from the centuries it.[18]

Although Berryman dismisses Anne's verse as "bald abstract didactic rime" and "proportioned, spiritless poems," his own stanzas show that his romantic image of the poet herself grew from a thorough reading of her work. And his familiarity with such related material as Winthrop's journal and other contemporary histories, and with Helen Campbell's semi-fictional biography of Anne Bradstreet, give depth to his portrait. A few of his lines already quoted [19] seem to depict Anne's experience of the harshness of winter in a strange northern land, and the chaotic building of the first rough dwellings, more graphically than many pages of prose, however eloquent, could do.

The reading of Berryman's poem, as an introduction to the work of Anne Bradstreet herself, is recommended by Hyatt H.

18. J. Berryman, *Homage to Mistress Bradstreet*, New York, 1956, Stanzas 2 and 3. Copyright © 1956 by John Berryman. Reprinted by permission of Farrar, Straus & Giroux, Inc., and Faber and Faber Ltd., London. See Carol Johnson, "John Berryman and Mistress Bradstreet: A Relation of Reason," in *Essays in Criticism*, Vol. XIV, No. 4, Oxford, 1964, pp. 388–96, for an arresting critical analysis of the poem; also my review in *The New England Quarterly*, Vol. XXIX, No. 4, 1956, pp. 545–48.

19. See p. 233 above.

Waggoner in his recently published critical study, *American Poets from the Puritans to the Present*. In his appraisal of Anne's writings he says of "Contemplations" that "parts of the poem introduce themes and images that have contributed to engage our poets through several centuries. Attachment to 'the things of this world' and detachment, *contemptus mundi*, are explored here with sensitivity and intelligence." [20]

This relates to what may be called the main intention of Waggoner's book, that is, "to throw more light on the question of what's *American* about American poetry." He enlarges on this:

> . . . it appears that Anne Bradstreet in her "Contemplations" and, much more clearly, Edward Taylor in such lines as his "Oh! What a thing is Man? Lord, Who am I?" begin to sound the notes that have characterized American poetry for more than three centuries now. Our poetry has been, and continues to be, more concerned with nature than with society or culture, and more concerned with the eternal than with the temporal. . . .
>
> Most of our chief poets have been religiously unorthodox, to be sure, with a strong tendency among them toward antinomianism; but very few if any of them have been religiously indifferent or unconcerned, or properly to be described as "secular." [21]

If this be accepted, it follows that the Puritan verse-writers may be related to America's most important woman poet, Emily Dickinson. I would suggest, however, that she seems to have much in common with the idiosyncratic Edward Taylor, and it is two more modern poets, Elinor Wylie and Marianne Moore who, because of their essential intellectuality and philosophical integrity, might be considered as spiritual descendants of Anne Bradstreet.

In Anne's own day, in a century that delighted in using the language of symbol and analogy, a great deal was said about

20. *American Poets*, Boston, 1968, p. 8.
21. *Ibid.* p. xv (Preface).

crowning the poet's brows with the evergreen leaves of *Laurus nobilis*, the true Laurel, or Bay. In her lifetime, and soon after her death, Anne Bradstreet was offered garlands from Apollo's sacred tree by her young admirers John Rogers and John Norton. But her own lines tell us that she did not ask for a poet's bays; for her writings she wished only a "Thyme or Parsley wreath," and for her pilgrimage through life she sought the reward of final conquest, by her Puritan spirit, over the too-much-cherished things of the world.

> Be still thou unregenerate part,
>
> *   *   *
>
> My greatest honour it shall be
> When I am victor over thee,
> And triumph shall, with laurel head,
> When thou my Captive shalt be led.

It is as a human being, however, that she can still appeal to us over the centuries. She had a firm and lively character, avid for knowledge, generous in affection and admiration, with a quiet but perceptive humor and a philosophy that was able to transcend, in its humanistic tolerance and wisdom, the rigid conformity of the Calvinistic thought-patterns of her community. She possessed objectivity and humility, yet her expression is sometimes forceful to the point of violence, and her deepest convictions are stated with passion. These are the qualities that give to the best of her writing its perennial freshness and charm; if her verse is not incandescent with the flame of genius, it is warmed by genuine poetic sensibility; if it does not rise to high-flown heights of eloquence, it is capable of conveying deep feeling in direct and telling idiom. Her work is, moreover, an interesting product of a fascinating period of transition. She was born while the age of Queen

Elizabeth I still lingered in mens' minds; the currents of that era's classicism and conquest, of the Jacobean theological controveries, and of the Carolinian political and religious strife, with its resulting colonial expansion, met and crossed through the first half of the seventeenth century, and left their mark on all who lived and thought in that time.

Anne Bradstreet was one of these, and in this study I have tried to point out the ways in which the varied influences and experiences of her life affected the form and content of her writing, from its tentative and awkward beginnings, through the productions of a conscientious but somewhat derivative apprenticeship to the achievement of full command of an individual talent. She herself kept a clear sense of proportion about her literary vocation, never allowing herself to become unduly discouraged by failure, or to set too much value on success, or to be carried away by ambition or the sheer delight of self-expression. She wrote seriously and purposefully, and always for a higher audience than herself or any other human being. If any "Critick" should ask if Anne Bradstreet really believed that the Lord Himself would take the trouble to read what she had written, the answer is indubitably yes. The whole of this woman's life bears witness to her deep personal relationship with the God who had chosen her as an elected Christian, to her trust in His constant care for her welfare and the perfecting of her soul, and to her anxiety that her every act, particularly the rendering of her thoughts into words for the world around her to read, should be acceptable in His sight.

Anne Bradstreet as a writer has experienced neglect and condescension, but not the oblivion that has largely overtaken the other female versifiers of her century, some of whom were greatly acclaimed in their own day. The natural vitality that animates most of her lines, and the lyric felicity of the best of them, have given her writings the power to survive the battering of time and the changing moods of critical opinion, and have earned them an appreciation that has increased markedly over the last half-century. An excellent example of this is in Perry Miller's paperback anthology *The American Puritans*, where that wise interpreter of early New England's life and thought presents eight of Anne's shorter poems and all seventy-seven of the "Meditations," with this graceful character-sketch (following a description of her longer poems):

> If these show that a Puritan could combine deep piety with a genial culture, more importantly Anne Bradstreet's occasional lyrics, inspired by the native setting or the homely incidents of her daily life, show that a Puritan could further combine piety with sexual passion, love of children and good furniture, humor —that the female Puritan, in short, could be both a Puritan and a woman of great charm.[22]

As Anne Bradstreet was an Englishwoman born, and a life-long student of history, it seems suitable that the last words of this study should be contributed by an English scholar who, commenting on the first writers of New England, says:

> Their early literature shows best in the writings of their historians—the sincerity and truthfulness, prime qualities for an historian, of Bradford and Winthrop. But what a story they had on hand to write! Then shortly, after the winter, they would be putting forth shoots of poetry, naive, musical, delightful as a bird's song with Anne Bradstreet.[23]

22. *The American Puritans: Their Prose and Poetry*, ed. P. Miller (Double-day Anchor A 80), New York, 1956, p. 266.
23. A. L. Rowse, *The Elizabethans and America*, New York, 1959, pp. 157–58.

Thomas Dudley's Books

When Thomas Dudley died in 1653 the inventory of his estate included a list of forty-four titled books and a miscellaneous group of unnamed items, those for which titles are given being valued at £4. 14s. 1d. This small collection was probably only the remnant of the library that Dudley had assembled during his life and had distributed largely to his family and friends before his death. But it is of considerable interest, even so, because of the variety of subjects, and the dates and types of publications, represented, and also because all of these books were presumably accessible to Anne Bradstreet while they belonged to her father.

The list has, to my knowledge, been only twice printed: in *The New England Historical and Genealogical Register,* Vol. XII, pp. 335–36 (October 1858), and in Dean Dudley's *History of the Dudley Family,* Vol. I, pp. 84–85, with, in each case, only a few of the titles identified, and there is a passing mention of it in Thomas Goddard Wright's *Literary Culture in Early New England.* I have been able to identify, at least approximately, all but two of the abbreviated titles listed, and I have been greatly helped in doing so by John E. Alden, Curator of Rare Books at the Boston Public

Library, and by D. G. Neill and Miss Mitchell of the Bodleian Library.

Quite a few of these books have been mentioned in the foregoing pages, in connection with Anne Bradstreet's education and the source-material of her longer poems; some remarks about the collection as a whole may be made here. Ten or possibly twelve of the books were in Latin, which shows that Cotton Mather did not greatly exaggerate when he wrote that Dudley could "understand any Latin author as well as the best clerk in the country." A third of the titles represent publications of the sixteenth century; their subjects are largely religious or historical and three law-works are included. It seems likely that Dudley received these books, by gift or bequest, from the eminent judge Sir Augustine Nicolls, by whom he was employed as a "clerk" or secretary from about 1594 to 1616, and that he brought them to Massachusetts and kept them through his whole life.

Just over half of the collection consists of books on religion; the earliest of these is the *Confessio Christianae* of 1575, by the celebrated Calvinist theologian Théodore de Bèze, and the latest is John Clarke's *Ill Newes from New England*; this account of the arrest and trial of Clarke, a Baptist clergyman of Rhode Island, for holding a private service in Massachusetts, was published in 1652, only a year before Dudley's death. History accounts for ten of the titles; most of these are standard works, with an interesting exception: *The Swedish Intelligencer*, by the Anglican divine William Watts, who traveled extensively on the Continent, wrote this description of the campaign of Gustavus Adolphus in Germany (published 1632–33), and later served as chaplain to the king's nephew, Prince Rupert, during the Civil War. The remaining ten named books are divided among the law, literature, and medicine, with a Latin dictionary and one unidentified work, No. 24, possibly a grammar or spelling-book.

It is a pity that "M^r. Jn° Johnson," who inventoried this collection, thought so little of the "8 french bookes Several pamplets new bookes & Smale writings" that he did not even give them a nominal value; there may have been a manuscript or two by Anne Bradstreet among them. At any rate this list, brief as it is, reveals some of the lifetime reading of a man of action who was also a thinker and a faithful Christian.

KEY TO REFERENCES

BODLEY—The Bodleian Library, Oxford.

BPL—The Boston Public Library, Boston, Massachusetts.

BRINSLEY—John Brinsley, *Ludus Literarius*, edited, with Bibliographical Notes, by E. T. Campagnac, 1917.

BM—*The British Museum Catalogue of Printed Books*.

PRINCE—*Catalogue of the Prince Collection in the Boston Public Library*.

STC—A. W. Pollard and G. R. Redgrave, A *Short-title Catalogue of Books Printed in England, Scotland & Ireland, & of English Books Printed Abroad, 1475–1640. 1926.*

TAYLOR—"Taylor's Library," in *Poetical Works of Edward Taylor*, edited by Thomas H. Johnson. New York, 1939.

WATT—Robert Watt, *Bibliotheca Britannica*. Edinburgh, 1824.

WING—Donald Wing, A *Short-title Catalogue of Books Printed in England, Scotland, Ireland, Wales & British America, 1641–1700.* New York, 1945–51.

YUL—Yale University Library.

All books printed in London unless otherwise noted.

BOOK-LIST FROM THE INVENTORY OF THE ESTATE
OF THOMAS DUDLEY, ESQ., TAKEN 8TH AUGUST, 1653.

(Suffolk County, Massachusetts, Probate Court Records,
Vol. 2, p. 131).

1. Steph Szegedini Cõmunes Loci—Stephan de Kis, called Szege-
   din, *Theologiae sincerae loci communes de Deo et homine,*
   Editio quinta cum vita auctoris. Basle, 1608. (Brinsley, pp.
   358–59)
2. yᵉ generall History of Netherlands—Grimestone, Edward, *A*
   generall historie of the Netherlands. Fol., 1608, 1609 &
   1627. (STC 12374–76)
3. yᵉ Turkish History—Knolles, Richard, *The generall historie*
   of the Turkes. Fol., 5 editions, 1603–38. (STC 15051–55)
4. Junii Tremelii Trans Bibl Sacr—*Testamenti veteris biblia*
   sacra, quibus etiam adiunximus noui testamenti libros, Tr.
   ab I. Tremellio et F. Junio. 1580 & other eds. to 1597.
   (STC 2055–62)
5. Livius—Livius, Titus, *Romanae historiae principis libri omnes,*
   1589; or *The Romane historie . . . ,* trans. Philemon Holland, 1600. (STC 16612 or 16613)
6. Canderi Annale Regnante Eliza—Camden, William, *Annales*
   Rerum Anglicarum et Hibernicarum Regnante Elizabetha,
   ad annum salutis MDLXXXIX. Fol., 1615. (STC 4496)
7. Diction Lat—? *A Dictionarie English and Latin.* 1623. (STC
   6831)
8. Commentaryes of yᵉ warrs in france—Serres, Jean de, *The*
   three parts of Commentaries of the Ciuill Warres of
   France, trans. Thomas Timms, 1574, and *The fourth*
   parte . . . , trans. T. Tymme, 1576. (STC 22242–43)

9. Buchanany Scot Hystory—Buchanan, George, *Rerum Scoti-carum Historia.* Fol., Edinburgh, 1582. (STC 3991)

10. an abstract of Pennall Statutes—*An Abstract of all Penall Statutes which be generall.* 1577 & other eds. to 1600. (STC 9527–32)

11. yᵉ vision of Pierce Plowman—[? Langland, William], *The Vision of Pierce Plowman, now fyrste imprynted.* 1550 & other eds., to 1561. (STC 19906–08)

12. Apology of yᵉ Prince of Orange—Languet, Hubert, *The Apologie or Defence of the most noble Prince William.* Delft, 1581 & 1582. (STC 15209–10)

13. Cottons bloody Tenet washed—Cotton, John, *The Bloudy Tenent Washed, and made white in the bloud of the Lamb.* 1647. (Prince, p. 17)

14. Cottons Holynes of Ch-members—Cotton, John, *Of the Holinesse of Church-Members.* 1650. (Prince, p. 17)

15. a Cõment on yᵉ Cõmandemᵗˢ—? Dod, John & Robert Cleaver, *A Treatise or Exposition upon the Ten Commandements.* 1603 & other eds. to 1635. (STC 6967–79)

16. Rogers Sermons—Rogers, Richard, *Certaine Sermons.* 1612. (STC 21203)

17. an Exposition of yᵉ 9th & 10th of Pverbs—Dod, John, & Robert Cleaver, *A Plaine and Familiar Exposition of the Ninth and Tenth Chapters of the Proverbs of Salomon.* 1606, 1608 & 1612. (STC 6954–56)

18. Byfield doct of Xᵗ—Byfield, Nicholas, *The Beginning of the Doctrine of Christ.* 1630. (STC 4210)

19. Caluine on yᵉ Cõmandemᵗˢ—Calvin, Jean, *Sermons upon the X. Commandementes,* Trans. J. H[armer]. 1579–1581. (STC 4452–56)

20. another Cõment on yᵉ Cõmandemᵗˢ.

21. Baynes Letters—Baynes, Paul, *Christian Letters*. 1620 & other eds. to 1637. (STC 1629–33)

22. yᵉ Swedish intelligencer—[Watts, William], *The Swedish Intelligencer*. 1632 & other eds. to 1633. (STC 23521–25)

23. Mantuani Buiclica—Spagnuoli, Baptista, *B. Mantuani adolescentia seu Bucolica*. London and Cambridge, 1532 & other eds. to 1638. (STC 22978–89)

24. Alpha Tagle (or ? Table).

25. Jacob of yᵉ Church—Jacob, Henry, *The Divine Beginning of Christ's Church*. Leyden, 1610. (STC 14336)

26. yᵉ Regiment of health—*Regimen Sanitatis Salerni, or the Schoole of Salernes Regiment of Health, Reviewed, Corrected & Enlarged with a Commentary*, trans. T. Paynell; commentary trans. Philemon Holland. 1634. (YUL)

27. a Reply to defeñcdona—? [Ames, William], *A Reply to Dr. Morton's general defence of three nocent ceremonies*. 1623. (STC 14336; YUL)

28. Survey of booke of Coḿon prayer—? *A Survey of the Booke of Common Prayer, by way of 197 queres*. 1606 & 1610. (STC 16450–51)

29. Clarkes ill newes—Clarke, John, *Ill Newes from New England*. 1652. (Wing C4471)

30. Mʳ Deerings workes—Dering, Edward, *Maister Derings Workes*. 1590, 1597 & 1614. (STC 6676–78)

31. yᵉ booke of Lawes—? *Institutions; or Principle Grounds of the Lawes and Statutes of England*. 1546. (Watt, I, p. 532)

32. Demonstr Causarū belli in Germania—? Julius, Benignus, *De Bello Germanico ejusque causis, inter Divum Matthiam Divum Ferdinandum II*. Fol., Frankfort, 1638. (Watt, II, p. 559)

33. Corderius—Cordier, Mathurin, *Colloquiarum Scholasticorum*

libri quatuor ad pueros in sermone Latino paulatim exercendos. Geneva, 1563. (Brinsley, p. 347)

34. Nortoni Respad Apoll—Norton, John, *Responsio ad totam quaestionum syllogen a clarissimo viro Domino Guilielmo Apollonio, ecclesiae Middleburgensis pastore, propositam . . . Per Iohannem Nortonum ministrum ecclesiae quae est Ipsuici in Nova Anglia.* 1648. (BPL; Taylor 19)

35. Mercurius Gallobelg—A *Relation of all matters passed, especially in the Low-countries, according to Mercurius Gallo-Belgicus,* [Trans. by R. Boothe]. 1614. (STC 20862)

36. Amesy Cas: Consc—Ames, William, *De Conscientia et ejus jure vel casibus, libri quinque.* Amsterdam, 1630. (Taylor, 87). Or the trans.: *Conscience with the power and cases thereof.* 1639. (STC 552)

37. & 38. Cottons Keyes & vyalls—Cotton, John, *The Keyes of the Kingdom of Heaven, according to the Word of God.* 1644. (Watt, I, p. 262; Prince, p. 17). And *Treatise on the Pouring out of the Seven Vials, Rev. xvi.* 1641. (Watt, I, p. 262)

39. de Jure magistr in subdites—Bèze, Théodore de, *De Jure Magistratuum in Subdites . . . in Lat. conversus* [from *Du Droit des Magistrats sur leurs subiets*]. Lyons, 1576 & 1580; Frankfurt, 1608. (Bodley)

40. Matheros Reply to Rotherford—Mather, Richard, *A Reply to Mr. Rutherford.* 1647. (Wing M1275) (Samuel Rutherford wrote *Lex, Rex; the Law and the Prince.* 1644)

41. Hildershams humiliation for Sinne—Hildersam, Arthur, *The Doctrine of Fasting & Praier, & Humiliation for Sinne, Delivered in sundry sermons at the Fast appointed by publique authority, in the yeere 1625.* 1633, (BM 4452 d. 11) & 1636. (STC 13459–60)

42. of Baptisme—? Rogers, Daniel, *Treatise of Baptism and the Lords Supper.* 1636. (Watt, II, p. 812)

43. ye doctr of Superiority—Pricke, Robert, *The Doctrine of Superiority and of Subjection, contained in the 5th Commandment of the Holy Law of Almighty God.* 1609. (STC 20337)

44. Bezd Confess Xtiana—Bèze, Théodore de, *Confessio Christianae fidei et eiusdem collatio cum papisticis haeresibus.* 1575. (STC 2006)

8 french bookes Severall pamplets new bookes & smale writings.

BIBLIOGRAPHY

A Selected List of Manuscript and Printed Sources Used in the Preparation of This Study

MANUSCRIPTS

The Royal Library, Valletta, Malta. *Archives of the Order of St. John in Malta*, 1543–1560.

The British Museum, London. Harleian MS. 1189: *Herald's Visitation of Leicestershire*: Pedigrees of Purefoy and Thorne.

———. Additional MSS. 24487–24492: Hunter, Joseph, *Chorus Vatum Anglicanorum*. 5 vols.

The Public Record Office, London. *State Papers Domestic*: S.P. 12, Vols. 40, 213; S.P. 16, Vols. 40–41, 49, 57–58, 72–74, 139; *State Papers Foreign*: S.P. 70, Vols. 49, 57–58, 61; S.P. 78, Vols. 38–40.

———. *Exchequer Accounts*: E 101, Bundle 66, No. 5: Northants. Musters 33–44 Eliz.

———. *Inquisitiones post mortem* (1558–1642) of Dudleys of London and Northants.

Somerset House, London. Commissary Court of London: Reg. Storey, p. 166: Will of John Dudley, 1545; Reg. Clyff, p. 30: Will of Thomas Dudley, 1549.

——. Prerogative Court of Canterbury: 22 Bakon, Will of John Purefoy, 1579; 83 Cope, Will of Sir Augustine Nicolls, 1616; 77 Seager, Will of Frances, Dowager Countess of Warwick, 1634.

The Guildhall Library, London. Parish Registers of London Churches: St. John, Hackney; St. Batholomew the Great and St. Andrew, Holborn.

The Drapers' Hall, London. Original membership records of Thomas Dudley and his grandson Roger Dudley, 1487–1614.

The Northamptonshire Record Society, Lamport Hall, Lamport (now at Delapré Abbey, Northampton). MSS. concerning Dudley, Nicolls and Purefoy families.

The Lincolnshire Archives Committee, Lincoln. MSS. concerning St. Paul and Rich (Earls of Warwick) families.

The Town Hall, Boston, Lincs. *Minute Book of Corporation Records*: entries (1621–1630) concerning financial transactions of the Earl of Lincoln.

Broughton Castle, Banbury, Oxon. (by courtesy of Lord Saye and Sele). Family and estate papers of the sixteenth and seventeenth centuries.

Longleat, Warminster, Wilts. (by courtesy of the Marquess of Bath and his librarian, Miss Dorothy Coates). *Pedigree of Dudley*, executed on vellum, on 57 pages, by Robert Cooke, Clarencieux King of Arms, *c.* 1583 (Longleat MS. 249B).

Stradishall Manor, Stradishall, Suffolk. Family papers owned by the late Hugh Dudley Waddell Dudley, Esq.

Parish Registers of churches outside of London. Essex: Holy Cross, Felstead.

————. Northants.: Canons Ashby House, Canons Ashby; St. Mary, Fawsley; St. Edmund, Hardingstone; St. Andrew, Yardley Hastings.

————. Lincs.: St. Botolph, Boston; St. Andrew, Horbling; St. Andrew, Sempringham; Holy Trinity, Tattershall; St. Lawrence, Snarford.

Suffolk County Probate Court, Boston, Massachusetts. Case 129: Will of Thomas Dudley, 1653; *Transcript Records*: Inventory of Estate of Thomas Dudley, 1653; Will of Simon Bradstreet, 1697.

Massachusetts Historical Society, Boston. *Transcript of the original records of the First Church in Boston, 1630–1687*; Unpublished papers of the Winthrop family.

The Town Hall, Andover, Massachusetts. *Book of Land Records and Town Meetings*; *Town of Andover: A Record of Births, Deaths and Marriages, begun 1651, ended 1700.*

The Stevens Memorial Library, Andover. MS. book of 49 leaves, containing Anne Bradstreet's "Meditations Divine and morall" in her own hand, followed by her son Simon's copy of the spiritual legacy, in prose and verse, which she had written for her children, also his copy of "some verses upon the burning of our house, July 10th, 1666," a translation into Latin of four of the "Meditations" and their dedication, by Anne Bradstreet's great-grandson the Rev. Simon Bradstreet, and on the last leaf, the poem beginning "As weary pilgrim, now at rest," also in Anne Bradstreet's own hand.

The Essex Institute, Salem, Massachusetts. Seventeenth-century letters and documents in various collections of family papers.

PRINTED SOURCES

(Only principally used books and periodicals are listed here; many other sources are referred to in footnotes. All books for which no place of printing is given were published in London.)

Abbot, Abiel. *History of Andover.* Andover (Mass.), 1829.

Adlard, George. *The Sutton-Dudleys of England and the Dudleys of Massachusetts in New England.* New York, 1862.

Aiken, Conrad, ed. *American Poetry 1671–1928.* New York, 1929.

Andrews, Charles M. *The Colonial Period of American History.* Vol. I, *The Settlements.* New Haven, 1935.

Babb, Lawrence. *The Elizabethan Malady.* East Lansing (Mich.), 1951.

Bamborough, J. B. *The Little World of Man.* 1952.

Banks, Charles E. *The Planters of the Commonwealth.* Boston, 1930.

———. *The Winthrop Fleet of 1630.* Boston, 1930.

Battis, Emery. *Saints and Sectaries: Anne Hutchinson and the Antinomian Controversy.* Chapel Hill (N. C.), 1962.

Baxter, Richard. *Reliquiae Baxterianae, or . . . Narrative . . . of his life and Times.* Ed. Matthew Sylvester. 1696.

Behn, Aphra. *Selected Writings.* Ed. R. Phelps. New York, 1950.

Berryman, John. *Homage to Mistress Bradstreet.* New York, 1956.

The Bible. (Geneva, 1560), "Imprinted at London by Robert Barker," 1610.

Birch, Thomas. *The Court and Times of Charles the First.* Ed. R. F. Williams, 1848.

Bradstreet, Anne. *The Tenth Muse.* 1650.

———. *Several Poems.* Boston, 1678.

———. *Several Poems.* Boston, 1758.

———. *The Works of Anne Bradstreet in Prose and Verse.* Ed. J. H. Ellis. Charlestown (Mass.), 1867. Facsimile reprints: New York, 1932, and Gloucester (Mass.), 1962.

———. *The Poems of Mrs. Anne Bradstreet, together with her Prose Remains.* Ed. F. E. Hopkins. New York, 1897.

———.*The Tenth Muse (1650) and, from the manuscripts, Meditations Divine and Morall together with Letters and Occasional Pieces.* Facsimiles with Introduction by Josephine K. Piercy. Gainesville (Florida), 1965.

———.*The Works of Anne Bradstreet.* Ed. Jeannine Hensley. Cambridge (Mass.), 1967.

———. *Poems of Anne Bradstreet.* Ed. Robert Hutchinson. New York, 1969.

Bridenbaugh, Carl. *Vexed and Troubled Englishmen.* New York, 1968.

Bridges, John. *The History and Antiquities of Northamptonshire.* Ed. P. Whalley. 1791.

Bush, Douglas. *English Literature in the Earlier Seventeenth Century.* Oxford, 1945.

———. *Science and English Poetry.* New York, 1950.

Buxton, John. *Sir Philip Sidney and the English Renaissance.* 1954.

Caldwell, Luther. *An Account of Anne Bradstreet the Puritan Poetess.* Boston, 1898.

Camden, William. *Britain, or a Chorographicall Description . . . of England, Scotland and Ireland.* Trans. from Latin by Philemon Holland. 1610.

Campbell, Helen. *Anne Bradstreet and Her Time.* Boston, 1891.

[Cary, Elizabeth, Viscountess Falkland]. *The Tragedie of Mariam, the Faire Queene of Jewry.* 1613.

Cavendish, Margaret, Duchess of Newscastle. *Poems and Fancies.* 1653.

Chamberlain, John. *The Letters of.* Ed. N. E. McClure. Philadelphia, 1939.

Clinton, Elizabeth, Dowager Countess of Lincoln. *The Countesse of Lincolnes Nurserie.* Oxford, 1622.

Coffin, R. P. T. and A. M. Witherspoon, eds. *A Book of Seventeenth-Century Prose.* New York, 1929.

C[okayne], G. E. *Complete Peerage.* Vol. VII, ed. H. A. Doubleday and Lord Howard de Walden. 1929.

Collins, Arthur. *Letters and Memorials of State.* 1746.

Compton, William Bingham, Marquess of Northampton. *History of the Comptons of Compton Wynyates.* (Privately printed), 1930.

Cook, Canon A. M. *Boston Goes to Massachusetts.* Boston, (Lincs.), 1945.

Cotton, John. *The Keyes of the Kingdom of Heaven* (1644). Boston, 1843.

Craig, Hardin. *The Enchanted Glass.* Oxford, 1950.

Crooke, Helkiah, M.D. *MICROCOSMOGRAPHIA or a Description of the Body of Man.* 1618.

de la Cruz, Sor Juana Inés. *Obras Escogidas.* Mexico City, 1928.

Davis, Richard Beale. *George Sandys, Poet Adventurer.* 1955.

Donne, John. *Complete Poetry and Selected Prose.* Ed. J. Hayward. 1929.

Dow, George F. *Everyday Life in the Massachusettts Bay Colony.* Boston, 1935.

Du Bartas, Guillaume de Salluste, Sieur. *The Works of.* Ed. U. T. Holmes, Jr., J. C. Lyons and R. W. Linker. Chapel Hill (N. C.), 1940.

————. *Du Bartas His Divine Weekes and Workes with . . . other . . . Workes Translated and written by . . . Joshua Sylvester.* 1641.

Dudley, Dean. *History of the Dudley Family.* Wakefield (Mass.), 1886–98.

Dudley, Thomas. "Letter to the Countess of Lincoln," in *Chronicles of the First Planters of Massachusetts Bay, 1623–1636*. Ed. Alexander Young. Boston, 1846.

Dugdale, Sir William. *The Baronage of England*. 1675.

Dunn, Esther C. *Shakespeare in America*. New York, 1939.

Dyce, Alexander, ed. *Specimens of British Poetesses*. 1827.

Finch, Anne, Countess of Winchelsea. *Miscellany Poems*. 1713.

Firth, Sir Charles. *Essays Historical and Literary*. Oxford, 1938.

Fiske, John. *The Beginnings of New England*. Boston, 1898.

Fletcher, Phineas. *The Purple Island*. Ed. H. Headley. 1816.

Fuess, Claude M. *Andover, Symbol of New England*. Andover (Mass.), 1959.

Fuller, Thomas. *History of the Worthies of England*. 1662.

Galinsky, Hans. "Anne Bradstreet, Du Bartas und Shakespeare im Zusammenhang kolonialer Verpfanzung und Umformung Europäischer Literatur," in *Festschrift für Walther Fischer*. Heidelberg, 1959.

Gardiner, Dorothy. *English Girlhood at School*. 1929.

Gardiner, Samuel R. *History of England, 1603–1642*. 1883–84.

———. *History of the Great Civil War, 1642–1649*. 1894.

Gardner, Helen, ed. *The Metaphysical Poets*. 1957.

Grant, Douglas. *Margaret the First: A Biography of Margaret Cavendish, Duchess of Newcastle*. 1957.

Grazebrook, H. S. "The Barons of Dudley," in *Collections for a History of Staffordshire* (Wm. Salt Archaeological Soc.), Vol. IX. 1888.

———. "Junior Branches of the Family of Sutton, alias Dudley," *ibid.*, Vol. X. 1889.

Grierson, Sir Herbert. *Cross-currents in English Literature of the Seventeenth Century*. 1929.

Haller, William. *The Rise of Puritanism*. New York, 1938.

Hole, Christina. *The English Housewife in the Seventeenth Century*. 1953.

Hotten, John Camden. *Original Lists of Persons who went from Great Britain to the American Plantations.* 1874.

Hudson, Hoyt H. "Penelope Devereux as Sidney's Stella," in *Huntington Library Bulletin,* No. 7, San Marino (Calif.), 1935.

The Humble Request of His Majesties Loyall Subjects . . . late gone for New England (1630). New York (New England Soc.), 1912.

Hutchinson, Lucy. *Memoirs of Colonel Hutchinson.* Ed. Rhys. 1936.

Hutchinson, Thomas. *History of Massachusetts-Bay* (1764). Ed. L. S. Mayo. Cambridge (Mass.), 1936.

Hyde, Edward, Earl of Clarendon. *History of the Rebellion and Civil War in England.* Ed. W. D. Macray. Oxford, 1888.

Jantz, Harold S. *The First Century of New England Verse.* Worcester (Mass.), 1944.

Johnson, Captain Edward. *Wonder-Working Providence of Sions Saviour in New England* (1654). Ed. W. F. Poole. Andover (Mass.), 1867.

Jones, Augustine. *Thomas Dudley, Second Governor of Massachusetts.* Boston, 1899.

Josselyn, John. *New England's Rarities Discovered* (1672). Ed. E. Tuckerman. Boston, 1865.

Kettell, Samuel. *Specimens of American Poetry.* Boston, 1829.

King, Sir Edwin. *The Knights of St. John in the British Realm.* Revised by Sir Harry Luke. 1967.

Lewis, C. S. *English Literature in the Sixteenth Century, excluding Drama.* Oxford, 1954.

Lovejoy, Arthur O. *The Great Chain of Being.* Cambridge (Mass.), 1953.

[Makin, Mrs. Bathsua]. *An Essay to Revive the Antient Education of Gentlewomen.* 1673.

Martz, Louis L. *The Poetry of Meditation.* New Haven, 1954.

Mather, Cotton. *Magnalia Christi Americana, or the Ecclesiastical History of New-England.* 1702.

Mathew, David. *The Age of Charles I.* 1951.

Meserole, Harrison T., ed. *Seventeenth-century American Poetry.* New York, 1968.

Miller, Perry. *The New England Mind.* Vol. I: *The Seventeenth Century.* New York, 1939. Vol. II: *From Colony to Province.* Cambridge (Mass.), 1953.

———. *The Puritans.* Ed. P. Miller and Thomas H. Johnson. New York, 1938.

———. *The American Puritans.* Ed. P. Miller. New York, 1956.

Morgan, Edmund S. *The Puritan Family.* Boston, 1956.

Morgan. Irvonwy. *Prince Charles's Puritan Chaplain.* 1957.

Morison, Samuel Eliot. *Builders of the Bay Colony.* Boston, 1930.

———. *The Founding of Harvard College.* Cambridge (Mass.), 1935.

———. *The Intellectual Life of Colonial New England.* New York, 1956.

Mulcaster, Richard. *Positions.* 1581.

Murdock, Kenneth B. *Handkerchiefs from Paul: Pious and Consolatory Verse of Puritan Massachusetts.* Cambridge (Mass.), 1927.

———. *The Sun at Noon.* New York, 1939.

———. *Literature and Theology in Colonial New England.* Cambridge (Mass.), 1949.

Nichols, John. *The History and Antiquities of Leicestershire.* 1795–1815.

Notestein, Wallace. *The English People on the Eve of Colonization, 1603–1630.* New York, 1954.

Osborne, Dorothy. *Letters to Sir William Temple.* Ed. E. A. Parry. New York, 1888.

Pain, Philip. *Daily Meditations* (1668). San Marino (Calif.), 1936.

Palfrey, John Gorham. *History of New England.* Boston, 1859–90.

Pettit, Norman. *The Heart Prepared: Grace and Conversion in Puritan Spiritual Life.* New Haven, 1966.

Philips, Katherine. *Poems by . . . the Matchless Orinda.* 1669.

Phillips, Edward. *Theatrum Poetarum, or a Complete Collection of the Poets.* 1675.

Piercy, Josephine K. *Studies in Literary Types in Seventeenth-century America.* New Haven, 1939.

———. *Anne Bradstreet.* New York, 1965.

Porter, Whitworth. *History of the Knights of Malta.* Vol. II. 1858.

Privy Council, Acts of the, (1623–1628). Ed. J. V. Lyle. 1933–40.

Raleigh, Sir Walter. *History of the World.* 1614.

Records of the Governor and Company of Massachusetts Bay in New England. Ed. Nathaniel B. Shurtleff. Boston, 1853–54.

Reynolds, Myra. *The Learned Lady in England.* Boston, 1920.

Richardson, Robert D. "The Puritan Poetry of Anne Bradstreet," in *Texas Studies in Literature and Language,* IX (Autumn 1967).

Rowse, A. L. *The Elizabethans and America.* New York, 1959.

Savage, James. *A Genealogical Dictionary of the First Settlers of New England.* Boston, 1860–62.

Scholes, Percy. *The Puritans and Music in England and New England.* 1934.

Shakespeare's England. Ed. Sir Walter Raleigh, Sir Sidney Lee, *et al.* Oxford, 1916.

Sidney, Sir Philip. *Works.* Ed. A. Feuillerat. Cambridge, 1922.

Silverman, Kenneth, ed. *Colonial American Poetry.* New York, 1968.

Sisson, C. J. *Thomas Lodge and Other Elizabethans.* 1933.

Souers, Philip W. *The Matchless Orinda.* Cambridge (Mass.), 1931.

Speght, Rachel. *Mortalitie's Memorandum, with a Dreame Prefixed.* 1621.

Spenser, Edmund. *Poetical Works.* Ed. J. C. Smith and E. De Selincourt. Oxford, 1912.

Stanford, Anne. "Anne Bradstreet, Dogmatist and Rebel," in *The New England Quarterly,* Vol. XXXIX, No. 3 (Sept. 1966).

State Papers: Domestic, Colonial, and Foreign, Calendars of. Reigns of Elizabeth I, James I, and Charles I.

———. *Letters and Papers Foreign and Domestic, Henry VIII.* Vols. 13 (1538) and 18 (1543).

Svendsen, J. Kester. "Anne Bradstreet in England: A Bibliographical Note," in *American Literature,* XIII (March 1941).

Taylor, Edward. *The Poems of.* Ed. Donald E. Stanford. New York, 1960.

Tedeschini Lalli, Biancamaria. "Anne Bradstreet," in *Studi Americani,* Vol. 3. Rome, 1957.

———. *I Puritani.* Bari, 1966.

Tillyard, E. M. W. *The Elizabethan World Picture.* 1948.

Trevelyan, G. M. *History of England.* 1927.

Trevor-Roper, H. R. *The Gentry 1540–1640.* Cambridge, 1953.

Tyler, Moses Coit. *History of American Literature, 1607–1765* (1878). Ithaca (New York), 1949.

Waggoner, Hyatt H. *American Poetry from the Puritans to the Present.* Boston, 1968.

[Ward, Nathaniel]. *The Simple Cobler of Aggawam . . . by Theodore de la Guard* (1647). Ed. D. Pulsifer. Boston, 1843.

Warren, Austin. *Rage for Order.* Chicago, 1948.

———. *New England Saints*. Ann Arbor (Mich.), 1956.

Waters, Thomas F. *Ipswich in the Massachusetts Bay Colony*. Ipswich (Mass.), 1905.

Wedgwood, C. V. *The Great Rebellion*. Vol. I, *The King's Peace*. 1955; Vol. II, *The King's War*. 1958.

———. *Poetry and Politics under the Stuarts*. Cambridge, 1960.

———. *The Trial of Charles I*. 1964.

Whicher, George Frisbie. *Alas, All's Vanity, or a Leaf from . . . Several Poems by Anne Bradstreet*. New York, 1942.

White, E. W. "*The Tenth Muse*—A Tercentenary Appraisal of Anne Bradstreet," in *The William and Mary Quarterly*, 3rd Series, Vol. VIII, No. 3 (July 1951).

W[hitney], Is[abella]. *A Sweet Nosgay, or Pleasant Posye*. 1573?.

Whittier, John Greenleaf. *Leaves from Margaret Smith's Journal in the Province of Massachusetts Bay, 1678–9*. Boston, 1849.

Wigglesworth, Michael. *The Day of Doom . . . with Other Poems*. Ed. Kenneth B. Murdock. New York, 1929.

Willey, Basil. *The Seventeenth-century Background*. 1934.

Wilson, F. P. *Elizabethan and Jacobean*. Oxford, 1945.

Winsor, Justin. *Narrative and Critical History of America*. Boston, 1884–89.

Winthrop, John. *History of New England, 1630–1649*. Ed. James Savage. Boston, 1853.

Winthrop Papers (Mass. Historical Society). Boston, 1929–47.

Winthrop, R. C. *Life and Letters of John Winthrop*. Boston, 1869.

Wood, Anthony. *Athenae Oxonienses*. 1691–92.

Wood, William. *New England's Prospect* (1634). Ed. E. M. Boynton. Boston, 1898.

Woolf, Virginia. *A Room of One's Own*. London and New York, 1929.

Wright, Louis B. *Middle-class Culture in Elizabethan England.* Chapel Hill (N. C.), 1935.

Wright, Thomas G. *Literary Culture in Early New England, 1620–1730.* New Haven, 1920.

Yonge, Walter. *Diary of, 1604–1628.* Ed. Roberts. (Camden Society, No. XLI). 1848.

Young, Alexander. *Chronicles of the First Planters of Massachusetts Bay, 1623–1636.* Boston, 1846.

Index